# JOURNALISM AFTER

"The best critique yet of how the media responded to September 11, 2001. It offers real insight into the challenges, compromises, successes and failures of the coverage that flowed from the attack on the Twin Towers in New York."

Jon Snow, Channel 4 News

"This is not a book just for journalists but for everyone concerned about democracy, freedom of speech and our future. The book tackles the crucial question: what did the media's reaction to September 11 tell us about modern media itself? All the ideological assumptions—voluntary censorship, market logic, journalistic patriotism, big corporation dominance—are dissected and those that do not stand up are ruthlessly buried."

Phillip Knightley, author of *The First Casualty*

The events of September 11 continue to resonate in powerful, yet sometimes unexpected ways. For many journalists, the crisis has decisively recast their sense of the world around them. Familiar notions of what it means to be a journalist, how best to practice journalism, and what the public can reasonably expect of journalists in the name of democracy, have been shaken to their foundations.

*Journalism after September 11* examines how the traumatic attacks of that day continue to transform the nature of journalism, particularly in the United States and Britain. It brings together an internationally respected group of scholars and media commentators to explore journalism's present and future by engaging with such pressing issues as trauma, free speech, censorship, patriotism, impartiality, and celebrity.

**Contributors:** Stuart Allan, S. Elizabeth Bird, Michael Bromley, James W. Carey, Simon Cottle, Stephen Cushion, Karim H. Karim, Robert W. McChesney, Victor Navasky, Jay Rosen, Michael Schudson, Annabelle Sreberny, Howard Tumber, Ingrid Volkmer, Silvio Waisbord, Barbie Zelizer.

**Editors: Barbie Zelizer** is the Raymond Williams Professor of Communication at the Annenberg School for Communication, University of Pennsylvania.
**Stuart Allan** teaches at the School of Cultural Studies, University of the West of England, Bristol.

# COMMUNICATION AND SOCIETY
## Series Editor: James Curran

# JOURNALISM AFTER SEPTEMBER 11

*Edited by Barbie Zelizer and Stuart Allan*

*With a Foreword by Victor Navasky*

London and New York

First published 2002
by Routledge
11 New Fetter Lane, London EC4P 4EE

Simultaneously published in the USA and Canada
by Routledge
29 West 35th Street, New York, NY 10001

*Routledge is an imprint of the Taylor & Francis Group*

Typeset in Goudy by The Running Head Limited, Cambridge
Printed and bound in Great Britain by MPG Books Ltd, Bodmin

*British Library Cataloguing in Publication Data*
A catalogue record for this book is available from the British Library

*Library of Congress Cataloging in Publication Data*
A catalogue record for this book has been requested

ISBN 0–415–28799–5 (hbk)
ISBN 0–415–28800–2 (pbk)

Distributed exclusively in India and Sri Lanka
by Roli Books, New Delhi

"The subtlest change in New York is something people don't speak much about but that is in everyone's mind. The city, for the first time in its long history, is destructible. A single flight of planes no bigger than a wedge of geese can quickly end this island fantasy, burn the towers, crumble the bridges, turn the underground passages into lethal chambers, cremate the millions. The intimation of mortality is part of New York now: in the sounds of jets overhead, in the black headlines of the latest edition."

*E. B. White, 1949*

This book is dedicated to the memory of all those lost in the events of September 11, 2001

# CONTENTS

CONTENTS

# CONTRIBUTORS

**Stuart Allan** teaches at the School of Cultural Studies, University of the West of England, Bristol. He is the author of *News Culture* (Open University Press, 1999) and *Media, Risk and Science* (Open University Press, 2002). His previous co-edited collections include *News, Gender and Power* (Routledge, 1998) and *Environmental Risks and the Media* (Routledge, 2000).

**S. Elizabeth Bird** is Professor of Anthropology at the University of South Florida, USA. She is the author of *For Enquiring Minds: A Cultural Study of Supermarket Tabloids* (University of Tennessee Press, 1992) and has published widely in media studies, with an emphasis on the cultural analysis of news, and audience reception of popular culture.

**Michael Bromley** is Professor and Head of Journalism at Queensland University of Technology, Brisbane, Australia. A former daily newspaper journalist, he has worked in a number of universities in the UK and USA. He has published widely on journalism and the media. Most recently he edited *No News is Bad News: Radio, Television and the Public* (Longman, 2001), and he is a founder and co-editor of the journal *Journalism: Theory, Practice and Criticism*.

**James W. Carey** is CBS Professor of International Journalism at Columbia University, USA. He previously was Dean of the College of Communications at the University of Illinois. Among his books are *Communication as Culture* (Unwin Hyman, 1989) and *Media, Myths, and Narrative* (Sage, 1988). His essays were collected as a reader in *James Carey: A Critical Reader* (E. S. Munson and C. A. Warren (eds), University of Minnesota Press, 1997). He is finishing an intellectual biography of Harold Innis and Marshall McLuhan.

**Simon Cottle** is Professor and Director, Media and Communications Program at the University of Melbourne, Australia. His books include: *TV News, Urban Conflict and the Inner City* (University of Leicester Press, 1993), *Television and Ethnic Minorities: Producers' Perspectives* (Avebury, 1997), as co-author *Mass Communication Research Methods* (Macmillan, 1998) and as editor *Ethnic Minorities and the Media: Changing Cultural Boundaries* (Open University Press, 2000).

**Stephen Cushion** is a postgraduate student in the School of Journalism, Media and Cultural Studies at Cardiff University, Wales. He is a graduate of the University of East Anglia. His research interests include the British press, as well as the role of information and communication technologies in national politics.

**Karim H. Karim** is Associate Professor at the School of Journalism and Communication, Carleton University, Ottawa, Canada. He is author of *Islamic Peril: Media and Global Violence* (Black Rose Books, 2000), which won the 2001 Robinson Prize. He has published widely on a variety of media issues, and is presently editing an anthology on the media of diaspora, to be published by Routledge.

**Robert W. McChesney** is Professor of Communication at the University of Illinois at Urbana-Champaign, USA. He is the author of seven books and some 120 journal articles and book chapters. His newest books are, with John Nichols, *Our Media, Not Theirs: The Democratic Struggle Against Corporate Media* (Seven Stories Press, 2002) and, with John Bellamy Foster, *The Big Picture: Understanding Media and Society through Political Economy* (Monthly Review Press, 2003). McChesney hosts a weekly radio program on WILL-AM in Urbana and is co-editor of *Monthly Review*.

**Victor Navasky** is the Publisher and Editorial Director of *The Nation* magazine. He is also Delacorte Professor of Magazine Journalism at Columbia University where he directs the George T. Delacorte Center for Magazine Journalism. He is on the board of the Committee to Protect Journalists. He has taught at a number of universities and was Visiting Ferris Professor of Journalism at Princeton. A widely published writer, he was recently the recipient of the American Political Science Association's Carey McWilliams award.

**Jay Rosen** is Associate Professor of Journalism at New York University, where he is also Chair of the Department. He is also the author of *What Are Journalists For?* (Yale University Press, 1999). In October 2001, he helped edit the first book published on the attacks in New York and Washington: *09/11/01 8:48 am: Documenting America's Greatest Tragedy* (Booksurge.com, 2001).

**Michael Schudson** is Professor of Communication and Adjunct Professor of Sociology at the University of California, San Diego, USA. He is the author of books on the history and sociology of the news media, advertising, popular culture, and collective memory. His most recent works are *The Good Citizen: A History of American Civic Life* (Martin Kessler Books, 1998) and *The Sociology of News* (W. W. Norton, 2002).

**Annabelle Sreberny** is Professor at the Centre for Mass Communication Research, University of Leicester; she directed the Centre from 1992–9. She has written on globalization, the media and democratization in the Middle East, and diasporic movements. She recently trained as a psychodynamic counsellor and is now especially interested in the nexus between macro-processes and micro-structures in the process of identity-formation.

**Howard Tumber** is Professor of Sociology and Dean of the School of Social Sciences, City University, London. He is the editor of *Media Power, Policies and Professionals* (Routledge, 2000); *News: A Reader* (OUP, 1999); joint author of *Reporting Crime: The Media Politics of Criminal Justice* (Clarendon, 1994) and *Journalists at War* (Sage, 1988) and author of *Television and the Riots* (BFI, 1982). He is a founder and co-editor of *Journalism: Theory, Practice and Criticism.*

**Ingrid Volkmer** is Fellow at The Joan Shorenstein Center on the Press, Politics, and Public Policy, John F. Kennedy School of Government, Harvard University. She teaches at the New School for Social Research, and directs the international research project "Global Media Generations." Among her publications is *News in the Global Sphere: A Study of CNN and Its Impact on Global Communication* (University of Luton Press, 1999).

**Silvio Waisbord** is Associate Professor in the Department of Journalism and Media Studies and Director of the Journalism Resources Institute at Rutgers University, USA. His most recent book is *Watchdog Journalism in South America: News, Accountability, and Democracy* (Columbia University Press, 2000). He is the co-editor of *Media and Globalization: Why the State Matters* (Rowan and Littlefield, 2001) and *Latin Politics, Global Media* (University of Texas Press, 2002).

**Barbie Zelizer** is the Raymond Williams Professor of Communication at the Annenberg School for Communication, University of Pennsylvania, USA. She is the author of the award-winning *Remembering to Forget: Holocaust Memory Through the Camera's Eye* (University of Chicago Press, 1998) and *Covering the Body: The Kennedy Assassination, the Media and the Shaping of Collective Memory* (University of Chicago Press, 1992) and editor of *Visual Culture and the Holocaust* (Rutgers University Press, 2001). A former journalist and media critic, she is a founder and co-editor of the Sage journal *Journalism: Theory, Practice, and Criticism.*

# FOREWORD

*Victor Navasky*

We know what the journalism we witnessed in the aftermath of the event of September 11 had to tell us about terrorism and terrorists, Osama Bin Laden and the al-Qaeda, the Mayor of New York City, Islamic fundamentalism, the architecture of the World Trade Center, airport security, the condition of intelligence agencies, President Bush's so-called war on terrorism, striking the balance between the constitutional guarantees of civil liberty and the imperatives of national safety, the impact of trauma on civil society, Americans' amazing capacity to make a buck off tragedy, the pros and cons of military justice and secret tribunals, and a host of other issues and matters of community, local, state, national, and global concern. But what did it have to tell us about journalism itself? That, as much as *Journalism after September 11*, is the real subject of this book. The subject is an important one because journalism, the flow of news, information, and ideas, is the circulation system of our democracy, the way we find out what's what. It is based largely on journalism that we make up our national mind.

It would be a mistake to minimize the difficulties the media faced covering the uniquely traumatic and unprecedented events of September 11 and their aftermath. And it would be a mistake not to recognize, as James Carey and other contributors to this volume do, some of the signal journalistic achievements of the *New York Times* and others in crisis mode.

Nevertheless, the post-September 11 journalism to be found in most mainstream media including both reportage and analysis reflected a number of ideological assumptions: That this was a time for rallying around the flag and that those who questioned national policy were giving aid and comfort to the enemy; that any attempt to link the events of September 11 to America's previous role in the Middle East or elsewhere was unworthy of serious coverage or consideration and somehow smacked of apologetics; that (despite much rhetoric about all Muslims being entitled to the presumption of innocence) the demonization of the Muslim world indulged in by the American press over recent decades had been vindicated (see especially Karim H. Karim on the centuries old Western geneology of the Muslim Other, and Annabelle Sreberny on the "manufacture of the collective we").

Now of course it can be argued that the journalism incited by the events of September 11 was the exception and hence it would be a mistake to attempt any generalization based on it; or that this journalism in the penumbra of trauma— journalism in an emergency, "America under Attack" 24-hours-a-day journalism with its full-court press and wall-to-wall coverage—revealed the underlying values and assumptions of journalism as it is routinely practiced in the United States.

I would contend that the journalism practiced in the aftermath of September 11 was a little bit of both. And I would argue that while Ingrid Volkmer may indeed be right and a new global public sphere will make possible "a new world order," and while Barbie Zelizer makes an effective case for her contention that pictures played a crucial role in enabling the public to bear witness, some of the particular assumptions underlying September 11 coverage are peculiar to the episode. There are a number of longer-range extra-curricular factors which help define the cultural context within which the traumatic events of September 11 played out and which may have imposed invisible constraints on the journalists and journalistic organizations doing their best to report on the world around them. (I refer here to the "straight" media and not the tabs, which S. Elizabeth Bird notes routinely tackle questions that respectable journalists omit but discuss over lunch, such as did sexual rejection lead Bin Laden to hate America?)

First, there is media concentration, the new consolidation. For some years now scholars like Ben Bagdikian and Robert McChesney have been tracking how fewer and fewer corporations dominate more and more of the media landscape.

When Bagdikian first started keeping track in 1983 he counted something like 50 corporations which controlled more than half of all of the information, knowledge, and entertainment companies in the USA. He republished his book in 1987 and the number was down to 27. Now it is under ten. Usually people who cite these figures do so to lament that so much power is in the hands of so few. But my point here has less to do with power than with homogenization, the promulgation and recycling of the same, corporate and government-dominated messages. It becomes more and more difficult to hear minority voices in this majority thunder, Bagdikian said.

According to McChesney—and one needn't agree with his political analysis of the media system (he sees reporters as stenographers to power) to recognize the accuracy of his observation—"What is most striking in the US news coverage following the September 11 attacks is how that very debate over whether to go to war, or how best to respond, did not even exist." The picture conveyed by big media across the board was as follows: "A benevolent, democratic, and peace loving nation was brutally attacked by insane evil terrorists who hate the United States for its freedoms and affluent way of life. The United States must immediately increase its military and covert forces, locate the surviving culprits and exterminate them; then prepare for a long-term war to root out the global terrorist cancer and destroy it."

Stuart Allan adds that on the Web, one of the reasons the "diversity of viewpoints has been steadily diminishing in the aftermath of the crisis" has to do with the constraints imposed by the increasingly consolidated Internet Service Providers or ISPs.

A number of contributors to this volume add that in recent years network and newspaper overseas budgets have been slashed and correspondents reduced. Thus a corollary consequence of the new concentration and consolidation, i.e. the "market logic," is a new ignorance on the part of the US citizenry of the realities of other peoples, and countries, their politics, cultures, and beliefs.

A second factor has to do with the myth of objectivity. No sophisticated student of the press believes that objective journalism is possible. The best one can hope for is fairness, balance, neutrality, detachment. Nevertheless, opinion journalists like myself are thought to be ideological and as such, second-class citizens in the republic of journalism. (See also the interesting discussion by Howard Tumber on such matters as can the war correspondent ever be a disinterested observer?)

My own belief is that yes, a magazine like *The Nation* has the ideology of the left and yes, a magazine like Bill Buckley's *National Review* has the ideology of the right. But that mainstream institutions like the *New York Times*, the television networks, the news weeklies are no less ideological. They have the ideology of the center and it is part of the ideology of the center to deny that it has an ideology.

But when a traumatic event like what happened on September 11 occurs, the mainstream media show their colors. Consider Dan Rather, among the most ethical of anchors, on the David Letterman show: "George Bush is the President, he makes the decisions, and, you know, as just one American, he wants me to line up, just tell me where. And he'll make the call." Rather also explained to Letterman that the terrorists attacked us "because they're evil, and because they're jealous of us."

Thus in times of trauma not only are the mainstream media not in fact as objective as they claim to be, but also they tend to internalize the official line. Michael Schudson has noted that there are three conditions under which dissent and the ideal of objectivity are suspended: Tragedy, danger, and a threat to national security. September 11 represented all three.

Perhaps it is natural to rally round the flag in times of trouble. My problem is not with patriotism per se, but with the jingoistic brand of patriotism promulgated by the media, patriotism which says "my country right or wrong." Thus when National Security Adviser Condoleezza Rice famously got the heads of all the network news divisions on the line and asked that they think twice before running any more Bin Laden tapes, instead of objecting to this blatant and unprecedented government intrusion or reciting the press' traditional mantra about fairness and the obligation to present both sides, they all caved in to her request.

Jay Rosen reminds us of what happened when the head of ABC News spoke at the Columbia Journalism School not long after September 11. ABC News president David Westin was asked whether he considered the Pentagon to be a legitimate target for attack by America's enemies. His response was "I actually don't have an opinion on that . . . as a journalist I feel strongly that is something I should not be taking a position on."

The next day the right-wing attack machine, Rupert Murdoch's Fox network, the Scaife-funded Media Research Center, the *New York Post*, Matt Drudge and Rush Limbaugh all piled on, and Westin capitulated. "I was wrong," he said. "Under any interpretation the attack on the Pentagon was criminal and entirely without justification." Thus he dropped the façade of objectivity when his patriotism was questioned.

Jay Rosen suggests that Westin changed his mind because his consciousness was raised.

> As a journalist, or a boss of journalists, he was speaking favorably of objectivity, which is a little like a Republican Party official speaking favorably of the free enterprise system. What Westin did not appreciate is how completely the events of September 11 wiped out the normal boundaries separating the professional position of the journalist from the personal (indeed emotional) position of an American citizen. Speaking as a journalist, someone entitled to stand outside the political community, had become a morally hazardous act, whereas before it had been one of the safer places from which to answer a question about news. News from nowhere was not a very thinkable thing after September 11; and this had a disorienting effect.

Perhaps, although I would argue that any meaningful notion of patriotism ought to incorporate the right to dissent as a core value, that the First Amendment's protection of dissent and dissenters is what defines and distinguishes the United States as a nation. (See Silvio Waisbord's interesting chapter on the social climate in which mainstream journalism "opted to ignore dissent" and avoided questioning the dangers of exuberant patriotism.)

But in the aftermath of September 11 the national media have confused the questioning of official policy with disloyalty. For example one finds former *New Republic* editor Andrew Sullivan attacking *Nation* columnist Katha Pollitt because she wrote that war is the wrong way to solve the problem. But instead of dealing with her argument, he denounces her as a part of a "decadent left [which] may well mount a fifth column" and accuses her of supporting the Taliban.

This articulation of the Bush ethic—you are either for us or against us, "watch what you say" as his press secretary ominously put it—raises a fourth extra-curricular factor: The press' internalization of the Bush administration's ethic of secrecy. I don't mean to make a political argument here. Increased security may indeed require increased secrecy. But whether it does or not, the Bush administration has given us a cult of secrecy as the environment within which post-September 11 journalism has been operating. Its hallmark has been anti-openness, systematic unwillingness to trust the people with what has hitherto been public information.

The administration has issued an executive order blocking the routine release of previous Presidents' papers. Vice President Cheney refused so many requests from Congress's general accounting office for information about his secret meetings with energy executives that for the first time in history the agency sued the administration. Attorney General John Ashcroft reversed the Freedom of Information Act presumption that documents would be withheld only where harm would come from their disclosure. For the first time in history the Secretary of Health, Education, and Welfare was given the power to classify meetings. The *New York Times* has reported that the media was being frozen out of military operations far more than in any recent conflict. There are the secret military tribunals, the nameless prisoners being held in Guantanamo, and the so-called shadow government, a cadre of 200 senior officials said to be working outside the nation's capital in two secret locations. There is the aborted "Office of Strategic Influence," a plan to have the Pentagon join the CIA in putting out disinformation against foreign governments and the press. (You may say, well, at least we blocked that one. I would say that we think we blocked it. Since we now know that they are committed to lying as a matter of official policy why should we believe them when they tell us they have dropped the plan? Get with the program!)

There is the round-up and detention of foreign nationals held incommunicado, which has promoted a new alliance between the civil libertarian left and the libertarian right. Rumsfeld told reporters recently that he understands "the need to provide the press and through you, the American people" with the fullest possible information. Defending the American way is what the war in Afghanistan is all about, he said, "and that certainly includes freedom of the press." As Neal Hickey wrote in the *Columbia Journalism Review*, "it depends on what the meaning of the word 'freedom' is."

Conglomeration, the myth of objectivity, the misunderstanding of patriotism and the Bush administration's ethic of secrecy. Collectively, the convergence of these four factors has compromised the free flow of information, and the ability of journalism to do its job. Having said that, I should add that the situation would be less problematic were it not for a fifth factor or perhaps I should say the absence of a fifth factor: The loyal opposition. In the face of massive intrusions on the public's right to know, the Democratic Party and its principal leaders have been acquiescent and silent. It is true that the intervention of Senator Leahy and others has rendered the so-called USA Patriot Act of 2001 somewhat less draconian than it might otherwise have been. But after Attorney General Ashcroft warned that additional terrorist acts were imminent and Congress would be to blame if the bill were not passed immediately, the Democrats went along. So a piece of deeply troubling legislation was enacted with no public hearings, no mark up by the Senate, no meaningful floor debate, no committee reports that explain the bill and no real conference between the two houses.

In a system where the press reports the activities and assertions of those in power, there was nothing to report and so the press, like the (non-existent) overly "loyal" opposition, was silent.

If, indeed, national security, national safety or even the right to privacy means a cut-back in the traditional interpretation of Bill of Rights guarantees, one would hope that on such occasions the press, through exuberant exercise of its watch-dog franchise, would by its reportage protect the public from official abuse of its prerogatives.

These, then, are only some of the assumptions and factors, ideological and sociological, which seem to me to infect and affect journalists and journalism in the aftermath of September 11. My ruminations on them, like the chapters which follow, are intended to be the beginning rather than the end of the story. Although many of the examples here are site specific, the issues raised cross geographic, cultural, and political boundaries. How much for example do different approaches to news reflect "market requirements"? (See Michael Bromley and Stephen Cushion's comparison of the difference between the approach of Britain's "heretical" *Mirror* and its "unreformed" *Sun*.) How do television formats determine content and thereby shape public discourse? Simon Cottle offers an important analysis.

Given the complexity of the issues under inspection and the diversity of the subjects covered in what follows, it is a tribute to the editors of this volume that they seem to have encouraged its contributors to raise questions even where there are no answers. That way lies not only better journalism but the possibility of an expanded moral imagination.

# INTRODUCTION
## When trauma shapes the news

*Barbie Zelizer and Stuart Allan*

It was once said that journalism takes on its true colors when the world outside darkens, when prospects turn bleak and hope shrinks. It is no surprise, then, that the events of September 11 have already begun to recast expectations of journalism in the Western world. Shaken to their foundation have been familiar notions of what it means to be a journalist, how best to practice journalism, and what different publics can reasonably expect of journalists in the name of democracy.

September 11 has decisively transformed the everyday contexts within which many journalists routinely operate. Evidence of this transformation is everywhere, not least with regard to the struggle to negotiate the complexities of the crisis in a suitably fair or balanced manner. News organizations—together with their sources—lacked a readymade "script" to tell their stories, a frame to help them and their audiences comprehend the seemingly incomprehensible. From the perspective of today, of course, it is easier to discern the emergence and embodiment of the responses they crafted and the interests they sought to advance. Far less clear, however, is what their lasting impact will be for journalism in a post-September 11 world.

*Journalism after September 11* addresses these and related questions. It explores not only the subjunctive dimensions of journalistic form, content, and practice—how journalism *should* look in its new environment—but indicative ones as well—how it *does* look—and in so doing tackles a range of pressing issues. In pondering journalism's imperatives following the events that rattled the world, the book's contributors consider the emergent capacity of those invested with helping to give the events voice. At the heart of this discussion is a notion not previously addressed in scholarship on journalism, namely that of trauma. Frequently invoked as a label for a wide range of cognitive-emotional states caused by suffering and existential pain, it is our belief that journalists and news organizations covering the events of September 11 were wounded too. There were no detached vantage-points situated "outside" the crisis from which they could objectively observe. And indeed, as we have seen in the months that have since passed, trauma does not disappear lightly. It lingers, seems to fade, and then

1

re-emerges when least expected. To consider its impact on the news media, as engendered by the events of September 11, is tantamount to glimpsing into journalism's future. For it may be that we have entered a new period in which journalism in its recognizable form has changed, a period in which trauma and its aftermath will continue to constitute a key factor in shaping the news.

## Working through trauma

Investigations of trauma typically connect its emergence to large-scale cataclysmic events that shatter a prior sense of what it means, in moral terms, to remain part of a collective. "Trauma," Maclear writes, "cannot be resolved through the gathering of chronological facts and information because it produces effects that—belated and recurring—elude historical closure." Not only does it permeate the actual sites where communities have been violated, she argues, but it "strays into the moments when experience and comprehension become irreconcilable and communication breaks down" (Maclear 1999: 10). In this way trauma becomes an "open gash in the past," one which resists healing or absorption into the present. And yet the process of recovery commences nonetheless; the silences in trauma's wake begin to find a means of expression.

For journalists, the need to work through trauma has not only individual but collective repercussions, most of which are connected with the maintenance and consolidation of identity. Invested in the best of cases with a social mission to clarify the undecipherable to distant publics, journalism plays a key role in moving whole populations from trauma to recovery precisely through questions related to identity. The three stages of such a process—establishing safety, engaging in remembrance and mourning, and reconnecting with ordinary life (Herman 1992: 15)—are implicated in what Leys (2000: 33) has called the attempt to offset the dislocation of the "subject." In her view, the event that introduced the trauma becomes important primarily insofar as it is able to reflect upon the situation of identification that was thrown into disarray. Although Caruth (1996) carries the focus on the collective one step further, arguing that trauma cannot be located in a particular individual but only across individuals, the repercussions for journalists remain uppermost. Their negotiation of contending definitions of reality impacts upon the primary identification processes that equally involve the individual, the social group, and society more widely. For each, journalism needs to serve simultaneously as conveyor, translator, mediator, and meaning-maker (see also Zelizer 1998).

Evidently, then, the movement to a post-traumatic time and space involves a delicate path, in which priorities, goals, and interests are continuously being re-evaluated. For those who look to journalists to help chart this path and map its broad contours, significant responsibilities are distinguished. These responsibilities involve more than the much-touted journalistic function of information relay. Rather, journalists are called upon to assume a far broader range of tasks, none more important than contributing to the reconfiguration of identities, both individual and collective, that have been temporarily shattered. Given these considerations, it was not surprising that so much of the coverage of September 11 focused on the key question of trauma and its aftermath. Both the popular and trade presses (those publications written by journalists for journalists) ran stories detailing symptoms of stress, with reporters on the scene regarded as being particularly at risk (Kluger 2001; Ricchiardi 2001). Questions arose not only concerning the ways in which trauma altered ongoing journalistic roles, but about whether journalists themselves were capable of accomplishing what the broader collective expected of them during a crisis.

Against this backdrop, the news media faced two separate but interrelated tasks: how to report the events of September 11 as they unfolded, and how to fulfil the larger public responsibilities thrust upon them by traumatic events. Arising from both tasks was yet a third, and it too is addressed in the pages of this book: how best to reinvigorate the form, content, and practices of journalism so as to meet the new challenges posed by a post-September 11 reporting environment.

## Making the extraordinary routine

"Beginning at 8:48 am on September 11," Cynthia Cotts (2001) wrote in the *Village Voice*, "the newspapers and the networks stopped behaving like competing profit machines and strove to be instruments of democracy, producing a high volume of useful news and inspiring a nation under siege." Confronted with the atrocities of September 11, journalists crafted responses which involved excavating the far reaches of their reportorial resourcefulness, innovativeness, and raw energy. Through it all, they scrambled to provide breaking information, offset panic, and make sense of events that had devastated most existing interpretive schema. As one newspaper columnist put it:

> I needed facts in the confusion following the attacks, but even more I needed stories, narratives that ordered experience and instructed me on how to behave in the face of tragedy. I found myself reading editorials and op-ed opinions, background and interpretive articles, poems and letters to the editor as much as hard news. I needed to know what others thought and felt. I needed to be made part of the human community.
>
> (Murray 2001: ii)

Some members of the public turned away from the news coverage, unable to cope with the trauma engendered by the events. Others sought to protect their children from the haunting power of such devastating images, and so turned off their television sets. However, a far greater number of people scrutinized the coverage intensely, to the point of suspending everyday routines so as to follow every nuance of the unfolding crisis. Television on September 11, in the opinion of Peter Jennings of ABC News, became the broad "equivalent to a campfire in the days as the wagon trains were making their way westward and there was a catastrophe on the trail. Some people pulled the wagons around, and sat down and discussed what was going on and tried to understand it" (cited in Cohen 2001). If the coverage, especially the repetition of images showing the towers being hit, was too much to handle for some viewers, for others it somehow authenticated their experience.

"I think at first our audience and all the television news were like moths to the flame," stated John Stack, Fox News' vice president for news gathering. "We were addicted to the video of the horrific event" (cited in Gay 2001). The events exploded in a manner reflective of most major breaking news stories, providing little warning, few precedents, and insufficient time or resources in which to organize a coherent response. Journalists and news organizations turned to the story with a resolve to help it unfold as quickly, broadly, and clearly as possible, a task usually achieved by making the extraordinary routine (Tuchman 1978). By borrowing from routines implicitly set in place for covering a wide range of earlier breaking news stories, journalists pieced together their coverage. Some news reports likened the unfolding tragedy to a Hollywood disaster epic—"It looks like a movie," said NBC's Katie Couric—although as time moved on comparisons with real events in history came to the fore. "For those of certain generations," wrote Tom Shales in the *Washington Post*, "it was the most harrowing day of television since the assassination of President Kennedy in 1963" (cited in Heidkamp 2001). Other commentators pointed to more recent stories of similarly monumental breaking news—the 1972 Munich Olympics hostage crisis, the *Challenger* explosion, the Persian Gulf War, the death of Princess Diana, or the Columbine high school shootings—but the point remained the same. That is to say, many journalists found themselves looking backwards to figure out how to shape their coverage of September 11. Some recognized the crucial role they had to play not only in framing the story but in helping move whole populations from crisis into continuity. "We want to hold our breaths for a moment," advised ABC's Peter Jennings, "and not get in a mode that the country is under attack" (cited in Bianco 2001). CBS News anchor Dan Rather told viewers: "There is much that is not known. The word for the day is steady, steady" (cited in Geisler 2001).

The priorities of news organizations were rapidly rewritten so as to accommodate the trauma and crisis situation created by the events. Media resources were pooled, stories reassigned, and beats realigned. Competitive priorities—such as commercial profits, sponsorship, or broadcast ratings—were temporarily set aside. Differences that usually separated local news from national and global news collapsed, as coverage was shared across media and news organizations. The unfolding coverage was described by one news executive as "a convergence story," by which reporters and editors were assumed to be working together across media lines (Phillips 2001: 13).

In each of the different news media, the realignment of priorities took shape in different ways. In the early hours after the attacks, the four major US television networks agreed to share video and satellite footage. Suspending their programming schedules, they moved to continuous coverage of the catastrophe. Cable and satellite stations otherwise devoted to entertainment formats revolving around music videos, sport, or films began broadcasting news feeds instead. Commercials largely disappeared from the air for September 11 and most of September 12, costing the country's media outlets hundreds of millions of dollars in advertising revenue.

At first the story appeared to be almost made for television. In one *New York Times* reporter's words

> the images were terrifying to watch, yet the coverage was strangely reassuring because it existed with such immediacy, even when detailed information was scarce. Imagine how much worse the nightmare would have been if broadcasting had been destroyed. On a day of death, television was a lifeline to what was happening.
>
> (James 2001a: A25)

Broadcast and cable news organizations went into overtime as they attempted to ascertain the extent to which they could cover the events within the confines of recognizable routine. As if to signal the wide range of events it was responsible for covering, CNN ran multiple text lines across the screen's margin so as to accommodate the multiple story lines. The pressures placed on the shoulders of broadcast journalists were extreme, the extent of which was displayed during CBS anchor Dan Rather's guest appearance on *The Late Show with David Letterman* on September 17. Apparently overcome with emotion, Rather held Letterman's hand and wept as he described the tragic events in New York City. At one point the anchorperson stated: "George Bush is the President, he makes the decisions, and, you know, as just one American, he wants me to line up, just tell me where. And he'll make the call." For some, this emotional vow of support from a seasoned journalist was heartening, and as such to be welcomed. In Letterman's view, Rather's actions simply showed that he was a "human being." Jason Gay (2001), writing in the weekly *New York Observer*, argued that the news anchor's appearance made clear that the "television news business—so recently a fading, marginal sideshow of personalities, cheese, and manufactured hype—had been suddenly, gravely transformed. Mr Rather—as well as his counterparts on the other broadcast and cable networks—had renewed weight, gravitas." Or at least for now, he added. Other commentators, not surprisingly, were angered by Rather's appearance, suggesting that he had gone too far. The Letterman show reportedly received angry telephone calls from outraged viewers. In either case, Pat Aufderheide (2001) pointed out, it "was a moment when the training of professional journalists to use skepticism in the service of accuracy clashed with the role of the only national mass media—the television networks—to provide emotional reassurance."

Television news coverage of September 11 was clearly a time of breaking precedent. In the words of CBS News president Andrew Heyward, "this story, with all of its tragic dimensions, does illustrate the important role that network journalism still plays in the lives of Americans in times of crisis, and there is nothing like the networks for knitting the country together" (cited in Gay 2001). This was not to deny, of course, that serious lapses in judgment, as well as honest mistakes, occurred as well. ABC found itself criticized for broadcasting a report that an explosion had taken place at the Capitol, an error which CNN turned into a "Breaking News" headline: "Explosion on Capitol Hill." A report appeared on CBS News that a second plane was being aimed at the Pentagon. Fox News announced to its viewers that it had received a report that a hijacked airliner was on its way to the US Capitol. More than one network reported that a car bomb had exploded at the State Department, that staffers were fleeing the White House, and that five people had been pulled from the World Trade Center rubble. Other reports stated that Kabul, Afghanistan, was under retaliatory attack by the US military forces using cruise missiles. Another insisted that two armed hijackers had been arrested, while a report that the Democratic Front for the Liberation of Palestine had claimed responsibility for the attacks received wide coverage. Regarding the latter report, Geov Parrish (2001) wrote that it "turned out to be based upon one anonymous phone call to Abu Dhabi television, but it lasted for hours [on NBC News], until a DFLP spokesman could call and explicitly disavow it" (see also Barringer and Fabrikant 2001; Bianco 2001; Vejnoska 2001). Speculation was rampant across the airwaves. Points of conjecture threatened to turn into received truths in the telling, thereby adding to a collective sense of panic. "News divisions excuse such mistakes by saying they were just passing along reports as they were received," observed Robert Bianco (2001). Given that in this situation "reality was frightening enough," he added, more care should have been taken to ensure that television did not compound the problem.

Looking beyond the television coverage, the importance of the other news media comes to the fore. Several radio stations began broadcasting live television news feeds. Others produced their own reports direct from the different scenes, bringing to mind, for some listeners, Edward R. Murrow's wartime broadcasts from London. Indications of the latter style of reporting were evident in this letter by a listener of National Public Radio (NPR) regarding its coverage:

> The narrative of a walk in the disaster area—discovering life left in scraps of paper—a legal document, a resumé—will remain with me, etched in memory, forever . . .You provide us with the who, what, where, when and why as we seek answers, assign meaning to acts of madness, and imagine the menacing face of our response . . .Thank you for outstanding, responsible and responsive journalism. You provide us with depth, breadth and participation. Your very human judgment. You see for us, with us, through the tears . . . and thank you for—to quote Dylan—"bringing it all back home."
>
> (cited in Dvorkin 2001)

The letter was one of several cited by NPR's ombudsperson, Jeffrey A. Dvorkin, to characterize listener responses to the network's reporting. NPR had moved into full news special mode on September 11, which meant that it began broadcasting live 24 hours a day, keeping taped reports to a minimum. Some commercial radio stations had been just as quick to offer extensive coverage. "We received a news tip at our New York headquarters that a fire was burning at the World Trade Center at about 8:50 am," recalled ABC News Radio's vice president Chris Berry. "We aired our first special report at 8:52 am and began continuous anchored coverage at 9:00 am" (cited in Geisler 2001). According to a report issued by the Pew Research Center's Internet and American Life Project (2001), about 11 percent of people in the US used radio as their primary source of information in the first days after the attacks. Television, of course, was far and away the most widely used source during this time.

The print medium took on its traditional role as a provider of analysis and extended information, a role which was further consolidated in the days following the attacks. On September 11, however, it stepped into its capacity as an immediate conveyor of information. Newspapers filed special late editions—with the *Chicago Tribune* filing two late editions in a single day—while some news magazines printed special mid-week vignettes that featured more images than words. Bi-weekly newspapers turned into weeklies. The story's presentation in each case underscored its sheer intensity: editions grew in size, headlines were bigger and bolder, typeset was larger, pictures were more prevalent. Precedents were broken: for the first time in its 19-year history *USA Today* dropped its traditional front-page ears, the *Atlanta Constitution* ran a front page with only one story, and the *New York Times* ran more pictures and in more prominent places. Every available resource was used to capture and convey the enormous scale of what was transpiring. In some cases headlines were reduced to simple one-word phrases, like "Attack!," "Outrage," or "Infamy." *San Francisco Examiner* editor-in-chief David Burgin gave his choice of headline considerable thought. "I knew everybody was gonna do 'Terror' and 'Horror' and all that stuff," he said. "But I thought it had to have more vitriol, more bite to it, a little more fist shaking. I tried to imagine what they said at Pearl Harbor and 'Those bastards' is what I kept thinking" (cited in Johnson, S. 2001). As a result, he elected to remove the "Those" and ran "BASTARDS!" in large letters across the front page. "It fit the rage," the editor insisted, although not everyone agreed. Roy Peter Clark of the Poynter Institute for Media Studies, for example, commented: "At least it's original. But as you move from 'terror' to 'attack' you make a very, very important step. To 'bastards' is one step further. You move powerfully into the rhetoric of war" (cited in S. Johnson 2001). Of particular concern, he added, was a fear that the enemy—as well as "people who look and dress like the enemy"—would undergo a process of "demonization" as a result (see also Allan 1999).

For journalists at the *Wall Street Journal*, the logistics of covering the crisis were particularly formidable. The *Journal's* offices, located at the World Financial Center on Liberty Street, were directly across from the World Trade Center. At the time of the building's evacuation, the newspaper's staff members were "scattered amid the rubble and dust of the twin towers' collapse," wrote Felicity Barringer (2001), "and its editors had to pick their way through streets filled with debris and body parts before they could get back to work." And back to work they went, regrouping miles from the scene at two "emergency" newsrooms, complete with 55 workstations, at the South Brunswick offices in New Jersey. There they pulled together to produce that day's edition. Reporters filed their notes and stories, some working from home, others from their cars or telephone booths. Still, as a spokesperson for the newspaper acknowledged, the emotional toll was high. "We were eyewitnesses to the accident," he stated, "and our reporters and editors and all the Dow Jones [the *Journal*'s parent company] employees saw many people jumping [from the building] and the plane crash, and have had to suppress that emotion to get the paper out" (cited in Roh 2001). For Paul Steiger, the managing editor, images of people jumping from the burning towers continued to disturb him. "To realize those were not things falling, but human beings . . .," he said. "I'm sure others have similar things branded on their conscious and sub-conscious that will be with them for a long, long time" (cited in Baker 2001). Due to everyone's efforts, a streamlined edition of the newspaper appeared on September 12, headlined: "Terrorists destroy World Trade Center, hit Pentagon in raid with hijacked jets." Its mere presence was a reassurance for some readers. "One thing we have been astonished by," Steiger commented, "was how much people around the country were comforted by the fact the *Journal* was in their driveway the next day."

Stories of the missing and deceased from the various communities became a hallmark of the September 11 coverage, as staffers at numerous newspapers, including editors, helped write obituaries. One of the more unusual responses appeared on the pages of the *New York Times*. "It began as an imperfect answer to a journalistic problem, the absence of a definitive list of the dead in the days after the World Trade Center was attacked," wrote the newspaper's Janny Scott (2001). "But it evolved improbably in the weeks and months after September 11 into a sort of national shrine." The "shrine" in question was a poignant memorial section called "Portraits of Grief." There, the newspaper offered touching vignettes about people who had perished during the attacks, focusing not on their major accomplishments but on some mundane but humanistic area of inter-est. Examples drawn from one day's listing included:

> Keith J. Burns (practical joker with heart) bought his future wife, Jen-nifer, an engagement ring with a diamond the size of a baseball. And it was worth about as much: the ring was plastic. [. . .]
>
> Lourdes Galletti (grateful for a chance) liked to send words of encouragement or spiritual poetry by e-mail to her friends. [. . .]
>
> Edward DeSimone III (provider of amusement) always gave people a sore belly—either from laughing too hard or from eating too much of his calorie-celebrating cooking. [. . .]

Kathleen and Michael Shearer (together all the way): Their dream was a house with a view. It happened by accident. Kathleen Shearer was buying a chair in Dover, NH, while her husband, Michael Shearer, waited outside the store.

(*New York Times*, March 31, 2002)

In this way, the newspaper elevated these brief portraits, or sketches, of "ordinary people" into public commemorations, which became, in turn, a source of consolation for many readers. Each account was about 200 words, typically accompanied by a small photograph; those of executives appeared alongside those of window cleaners. More than 1,800 of them have been published to date, with reporters attempting to contact relatives or friends of nearly every victim they are able to locate. Many have been reprinted by other newspapers nationwide. The response, in the words of Jonathan Landman, the *Times*' Metro editor, has "been staggering, really. I've never really seen anything like it. People mostly write and say 'Thank you'" (cited in Campbell 2001). Innovations like this one proved to be important extensions of the journalistic voice in ways that could help the public move to a post-traumatic space.

As time moved on, the altered and refined practices set in place in the immediate days after the attacks received continued attention. By the end of September, the *New York Times* recognized that it needed both to address the ongoing events related to September 11 as well as deal with other ongoing news stories. The result was its creation of "A Nation Challenged," a section that offered a dedicated place for responding to the events of September 11 that was separated from the rest of the newspaper. The section continued until year's end.

News coverage of the events of September 11 was regarded by many as "an almost superhuman challenge" (Hazlett 2001: 2). Professional and trade forums began immediately after the events to generate evaluative statements of what had gone right and wrong: the American Press Institute published a 75-odd page booklet for crisis reporting "because the kind of advice we offer . . . will be of value if we ever have to do this again" (Watson 2001: iii), public forums ran symposia on the role of the press in wartime, and trade journals—like *Editor and Publisher* and the *American Journalism Review*—ran overviews of coverage. The *Columbia Journalism Review* pushed aside its own anniversary issue to accommodate the story (*Columbia Journalism Review* 2001). In both popular and trade forums, those invested with telling the story made their work seem non-heroic, a simple implementation of journalism as usual. "People just did their craft," said one managing editor in recalling how New York City journalists had gone about doing their business (Charlotte Hall cited in Hazlett 2001: 2). Yet endless stories of narrowly-missed brushes with the margins of fate filled the pages of the popular and trade press, suggesting that the heroic was constituted for many journalists in the very adherence to the routine and mundane. Journalists worked 12- to 18-hour days in shifts that were coordinated across large teams of reporters. Paradoxically, many journalists consolidated their investment in the event by just being there, not doing anything out of the ordinary. Although initial reportage was peppered with confusing claims or unsubstantiated rumor-turned-headline, the capacity to be ordinary under extraordinary circumstances was itself seen by most journalists as a feat of unusual proportion.

Not surprisingly, by the time the various awards ceremonies rolled around in mid-2002, the coverage of September 11 topped the list of the performances given recognition. In broadcast journalism, the Peabody Awards went to ABC and NPR for their news coverage of events, while other areas of broadcast presentation related to the topic—musical tributes, documentary films—also garnered awards. The Pulitzer Prizes delivered a round of tributes to the coverage of September 11, with the *New York Times* winning a record six prizes connected to its events, one for "A nation challenged," one for the *Times'* website, and two for photography. More broadly, the attacks and the war on terrorism received eight of the 14 awards given for journalism during the year. While awardees also included the *Wall Street Journal* and the *Washington Post*, what was unusual was that in each case the Pulitzers recognized journalistic teamwork, rewarding the staff efforts at each newspaper as public service.

## Evaluating journalism's role

Beyond the immediate reportage of September 11, however, were a slew of questions regarding journalism's broader role as interpreter and provider of context. "Even before the twin towers had fallen on Tuesday," wrote Arianna Huffington (2001) for Salon.com News, "the media hunt for the villains had begun." In the course of discussing several of the factors underlying what was being widely described as a "massive failure of intelligence," she pointed to a federal commission report that had predicted this kind of tragedy months earlier. The report, prepared by the US Commission on National Security headed by former Senators Gary Hart and Warren Rudman, identified several new dangers confronting the US in a post-Cold War era. It had been virtually ignored by the country's news organizations, Huffington argues, which at the time were "too busy ferreting out the latest info on the supposed defacing of the White House by Gore loyalists and, later, on Gary Condit, over-age Little Leaguers and shark attacks." Now, in the aftermath of September 11, the significance of this report looked very different. Huffington quoted Hart as stating:

> What happened ought to call into question what is important in our society and how the media cover it. But no one is asking this on TV, and I'd be amazed if there was a single discussion on the board of any newspaper asking: Did we do our job? There seems to be no self-reflection, no understanding by the media that they have a job under the direction of the Constitution to inform, not just entertain, the American people.
>
> (cited in Huffington 2001)

In wondering if the World Trade Center would still be standing if the report had been given the news coverage she believes it deserved, Huffington argued that US journalism's "penchant for rigorous—even merely diligent—reporting is rapidly disappearing, a victim of corporate pressure to build the bottom line and not rock the highly profitable status quo." It is therefore not surprising, given this commercial logic, that the Commission's findings received so little play either in print or on television. "[W]e are faced," she wrote, "with a media that gives us bread, circuses and people being forced to confront their darkest fears—while shying away from issues of vital importance out of fear of scaring viewers away."

Precisely how many news organizations have conducted the kind of self-reflective evaluation encouraged by Hart above will become more apparent in the months to come. At this point in time, with the images of September 11 so fresh in people's minds, there appears to be something of a reluctance to engage in this type of critique. Moreover, efforts to raise these questions are frequently met with derision by those who fear it will weaken the resolve of journalists to "support the war effort." As a result of these kinds of tensions the role of journalists as "patriotic citizens" has surfaced as the subject of intense debate in some quarters, not least in newsrooms across the US. Several networks carried on-air banners, logos, or graphics with US flags flying, while some journalists and news anchors began wearing red, white, and blue ribbons or flag pins on their lapels. CBS anchor Dan Rather believed the practice was understandable, commenting: "I've always felt I've had a flag in my heart every day, and that I don't need to wear one on my sleeve. But I have no argument with anyone who does" (cited in P. Johnson 2001). In the eyes of some critics, however, such attempts to play to the public mood blurred what should otherwise have been a clear distinction between editorializing and reporting. "At a time when many see the media as beating the drums for war, imposing the US flag over what should be balanced reporting doesn't help," stated an analyst with the Fairness and Accuracy in Reporting (FAIR) advocacy group. "It reinforces the view that the media are not independent" (cited in Bauder 2001). Several news directors, including Pat Dolan of News 12 in New York, responded to the dispute by banning the appearance of flag pins on screen. Public opposition to the decision was so strong, however, that Dolan went on the air to apologize and reaffirm that News 12 employees "are proud to be Americans." *Time* magazine's Matthew Cooper (2001), commenting on the dispute, shared the view that such displays were inappropriate. "There's plenty of flag waving going on but our job isn't to join in," he wrote. "Our job is to report what's happened and to ask questions. It's to explore the war effort, not to be a cheerleader for it; it's to explain the new national solidarity, not to help forge it. Others can do that."

One such question which appeared to be particularly awkward, and hence was only rarely asked, was "why?" Members of the public making their way through the September 11 coverage could learn much from what reporters told them about the "who," "what," "where," "when," and "how" of the attacks. The matter of "why," however, remained elusive. Any attempt to formulate a response, it follows from the discussion above, must begin with the recognition that news coverage of international affairs has been increasingly neglected in recent years. This decline was especially marked in US network television, the principal news source for people in that country, but critics are pointing out that it was apparent in mainstream journalism throughout the Western world. Absent from so much of the coverage has been a substantive treatment of historical context in news accounts, leaving audiences to make sense of events without the benefit of reporting concerned with the cultural, economic, and political factors under-pinning them. Investigative inquiries into the verity of official truth-claims have been few and far between, just as have been perspectives from outside a narrow range of "expert" (almost exclusively elite, white, and male) sources. In the current climate, those journalists committed to pushing beyond such platitudes were more than likely to have their "loyalty" called into question, their motives challenged. By this rationale, the task of reproducing Pentagon propaganda became a patriotic duty, at least in the eyes of those fearful that critical reporting would undermine the public interest.

The British Broadcasting Corporation's (BBC) World News, in the eyes of some US journalists, provided a much more in-depth approach to reporting the "war on terror." In her examination of its coverage, Caryn James (2001b) of the *New York Times* observed that it helps to know, "without sugar-coating," how people in other countries regard the US. She pointed to the BBC's wider scope, along with its "blunter attitude," as being particularly significant. The result, in her view, was coverage where the "range of issues and less defensive tone are wildly different from what American viewers get on network or cable news pro-grams, which share a myopic view and a tone that says, 'They'd love us if only they understood us.'" James saw in the enhanced ratings for foreign-based news since September 11 a "hunger for what is not being offered by American report-ing," and pointed out that alternatives like BBC World News were becoming easier to access as growing numbers of cable stations picked up the program. Britain's ITN *World News for Public Television* similarly attracted greater interest, with ratings up over 50 percent in the US. This turn to foreign news was not sur-prising, James argued, given the main networks' tendency over recent years to pay insufficient attention to international affairs. "After the terror attacks," she wrote, "stunned and baffled 'Why do they hate us?' articles flooded the news media, addressing a public that had been blinkered to what other parts of the world were thinking."

Nevertheless, James added, this "homebound point of view" persisted. In her opinion it was evidenced not only by news anchors wearing flag lapel pins, as noted above, but frequently in more subtle ways. Journalistic concerns about "patriotism" were such, she feared, that they interfered with the ability of reporters to do their job properly. In her words:

> Some of the American skittishness and us-against-them attitude is under-standable. The attacks did happen here and created a war mentality.

But after two months, American television's cautious approach has turned into knee-jerk pandering to the public, reflecting a mood of patriotism rather than informing viewers of the complex, sometimes harsh realities they need to know. Even as American reporters are expressing frustration at how fiercely the Pentagon is controlling information, the emphasis is not on getting better answers but on covering "the propaganda war" in the shallow, horse-race way elections usually are—who's winning?

(James 2001b)

It was in seeking out alternatives to this "tunnel vision," James argued, that the importance of the BBC World News and other foreign-based programs became evermore apparent. Mark Jurkowitz (2001), reporting for the *Boston Globe*, agreed. The BBC, he observed, "is known for crisp on-scene reporting, a tendency to determinedly grill a subject until a question is answered, and in this war, a view of the American-led military campaign that BBC fans find refreshingly objective, and that foes consider downright anti-American." One telling aspect of this approach, in Jurkowitz's view, was the BBC's reluctance to use the word "terrorist" to describe the individuals behind the September 11 attacks. Here he quoted Rachel Attwell, the Corporation's deputy head of television news, as stating that the decision was upheld on "the old basis that one man's terrorist is another man's freedom fighter. So we do say that an act of terrorism has been committed, but on the whole, will not say they have been committed by a terrorist" (cited in Jurkowitz 2001). Elsewhere, Mark Damazer, deputy director of news at the BBC World Service, similarly defended the policy, insisting: "However appalling and disgusting it [the attack] was, there will nevertheless be a constituency of your listeners who don't regard it as terrorism. Describing it as such could downgrade your status as an impartial and independent broadcaster" (cited in Wells 2001).

As might have been expected, stances such as this one sparked heated debates over whether "patriotism" can co-exist with "impartiality." Not surprisingly, certain critics from the political right made familiar allegations that journalists typically exhibit "liberal" tendencies, while critics from the political left responded by alleging the opposite. Several media monitoring groups waded into the fray as well. Examples included the Media Research Center (www.mrc.org), a self-described educational foundation, whose members regularly condemn the US media for a perceived "liberal bias" or other forms of "political skewed reporting." The Center took on a "new and vital mission" in the aftermath of September 11. "We are training our guns on any media outlet or any reporter interfering with America's war on terrorism or trying to undermine the authority of President Bush," wrote its founder in a fundraising letter (cited in Scherer 2002). Reports issued by the Center claiming to document evidence of liberal bias featured prominently in different news reports, especially where one news organization sought to distance itself from rivals on the basis of its appeal to

patriotism. Meanwhile the media watchdog group FAIR, a "liberal" organization
in the eyes of critics, found much of the ensuing war coverage wanting because of
this proclaimed support for the military. Once again, the BBC's coverage was
found to compare favorably against that provided by US newscasts. "Not only is
there a broader range of opinion," argued a senior analyst, "but the BBC 'presenters' and reporters are often more professional, ask tougher questions, and seem
to have a greater level of knowledge about news subjects than their US counterparts" (cited in Jurkowitz 2001; see also Higham 2002).

Certain journalists and commentators similarly took it upon themselves to critique the news coverage. In the US, for example, Wes Vernon (2001), writing on
NewsMax.com ("America's News Page") on September 13, accused "liberal
media outlets" of launching "a full-scale spin war against President Bush." The
next day Phil Brennan, also writing for the online site, went even further:

> While Washington scurries about looking for appropriate targets for
> retaliation against America's enemies, I have a few suggestions for
> Mr Bush about who he ought to put in the nation's cross hairs: Peter
> Jennings, Dan Rather, Andrea Mitchell, the *New York Times*, Mary
> McGrory, the *Washington Post* and all the other Benedict Arnolds in the
> anti-American media rat pack mindlessly attacking President Bush . . .
> Given the fact that untold thousands of our fellow Americans have
> been slain, and we are at war and must rally behind our commander in
> chief at such a perilous time, any media attempts to undermine public
> confidence in our President and thus hamper his ability to lead a united
> nation in combat against the monsters behind the assault on the World
> Trade Center and the Pentagon can be viewed as an outright betrayal of
> America and its people.
>
> (Brennan 2001)

Evidently shocked by these "anti-American elitists," Brennan proceeded to
encourage his readers to join him in applying pressure on the sponsors and advertisers associated with the respective news organizations. Let them know, he
declared, that "we will not spend one red cent more on their products as long as
they continue to subsidize these dangerous saboteurs of public faith in the President." For Dan Frisa (2001), the "leftist media" were undermining the President
"with relish." "The despicable traitors have made it their mission to undercut the
authority of President Bush during America's darkest hour," he wrote, "proving
themselves even more cowardly than the terrorist murderers who are the only
beneficiaries of such contemptible conduct." In addition to editorial writers at
the *New York Times*, other "leftist media egotists" singing this "same treasonous
song," according to Frisa, included: "Canadian Peter Jennings, democrat Dan
Rather, society boy Tom Brokaw, snivelling Howard Fineman of *Newsweek*,
pedantic Brian Williams of MSNBC and too-cute by half Katie Couric, among
dozens of others" (Frisa 2001).

It is typically the case that the allegations made about the "traitorous behavior" by "disloyal" journalists guilty of exhibiting "liberal bias" sought to align certain preferred discourses of "patriotism" with "professionalism." To the extent that this convergence of patriotism and professionalism was sustained, spaces for voices of criticism, let alone dissent, were decisively curtailed. "Most viewers," argued Alessandra Stanley (2001) in the *New York Times*, "are in no mood to listen to views they dismiss as either loopy or treasonous." To provide evidence for her characterization of the "national mood," she turned to a statement made by Walter Isaacson, president of CNN. "In this environment it feels slightly different," he commented. "If you get on the wrong side of public opinion, you are going to get into trouble." Criticisms of the US government's response to the crisis did emerge in some newscasts, but they were the exceptions that proved the general rule. "[M]ainstream news programs," Stanley argued, are "squeamish about broadcasting the dissenting views of Americans who are admittedly on the margins of mainstream opinion." Such an assertion, needless to say, helped to reinforce the perception that to be critical is to be marginal. Hence it is interesting to note in this context, once again, the improved ratings for foreign-based newscasts in the US. Reporting from news organizations like the BBC "may not be pleasant to hear," observed James (2001b), "but it does something American television usually does not: it assumes that the public is smart and grown-up enough to handle what the rest of the world thinks."

Such criticisms of the US media, which strike a familiar chord every time a national crisis takes over its front pages and television screens, need to be understood against the broader cultural—let alone spatial—distance from the events being reported. Indeed, it may be just that much easier to report some of the complexities of another's culture than it is to report on one's own. Such a point hardly excuses the narrow ideological parameters within which the US mainstream media tend to operate. Still, it may nonetheless explain in part why the media of other nations, such as Britain, emerge as more critical and nuanced in their reportage of events occurring within the US.

## Making sense of journalism in a post-September 11 world

While views differ with regard to how journalism has been changed by September 11, there appears to be something of a consensus that we are in a new era of reporting, a "new normal" to use a phrase frequently heard these days. Important questions about the direction this reshaping of journalism will assume continue to resist easy answers, in part because reporters are understandably more concerned with its here-and-now than with its future. Moreover, numerous uncertainties still remain regarding the capacity of journalism, as an institution, to learn from both the high points and failings that emerged from efforts to cover September 11 with integrity.

The chapters gathered here address such uncertainties. By engaging with the intertwining of issues like trauma, censorship, impartiality, patriotism, free speech, and celebrity, they segue across the horizon of journalistic form and practice. Each of the chapters raises vitally significant issues regarding what journalism can and should now look like in a post-September world.

Calling upon the expertise of a range of scholars from numerous places around the globe, each interested in the present and future shape of journalism, the book is divided into four sections that deal progressively with how trauma impacts upon the concentric circles in which journalism operates.

## Part I—the trauma of September 11

This section begins with a tracking of the immediate coverage of September 11. In "September 11 in the mind of American journalism," Jay Rosen examines how the terrorist attacks on New York City collapsed the "thought world" of American journalism. They exposed the thin roots of professional thinking, some previously hidden contradictions in journalism's self-image, and certain challenges for the press that could not be met by the common sense established in American newsrooms. Key here, among other developments, was the death of detachment as a guiding ethic for the press after September 11, 2001.

Michael Schudson, in "What's unusual about covering politics as usual," argues that journalism after September 11 shifted almost instantly and unconsciously from what Daniel Hallin has called the "sphere of legitimate controversy" to the "sphere of consensus." A prose of information became a prose of solidarity, and journalists delighted to find themselves embraced by, rather than alienated from, their audiences. Yet at least some news institutions returned within a couple of weeks to covering politics as usual. Schudson's close look at the New York Times' coverage of September 11 shows that Mayor Giuliani was again subject to harsh criticism before the end of September, with other evidence of division, contention, and critique much in evidence by that time in the news columns. Schudson sees this return to covering politics as usual positively. While media observers have in recent years criticized political reporting for being too critical and too cynical, Schudson argues that in the wake of the post-September 11 journalism of solidarity, the return to covering "politics as usual" offered a breath of fresh, divisive, contentious air.

Barbie Zelizer looks at photography on September 11 in her chapter, "Photography, journalism, and trauma." She argues that in times of trauma photography assists collectives in working through to a post-traumatic space, with the act of "seeing" helping traumatized individuals and groups move on. Yet the need to accommodate that very act of seeing forces a more central space for photographic documentation than in other periods of journalistic documentation. Zelizer demonstrates that a key attribute of trauma's photographic coverage is an alteration of editorial and reportorial decisions in the direction of what is presumed to be more frequent, more varied, and more sophisticated still visuals. In that regard, photographic coverage of September 11 repeated a template set in place for bearing witness that followed the liberation of the concentration camps of World War

II. Yet repetition of that template, when applied to the fundamentally dissimilar event of September 11, raises questions about the function of photography in trauma, for photography in both events was used to mobilize public support for military and political actions yet to come. At its core, the chapter considers how photography functions simultaneously as an integral part of journalism, a tool for easing the dissonance caused by trauma, and a means of generating support for governmental action. Trauma's photographic coverage, then, raises fundamental questions about decision-making in extraordinary circumstances of newsmaking.

## Part 2—news and its contexts

Under consideration in this section are the links connecting journalism with its larger social, cultural, economic, and political worlds. In "American journalism on, before, and after September 11," James W. Carey offers an historical overview to explain journalism's coverage of that difficult event. He argues that in order to understand journalism on and after September 11, 2001 one must go back at least to two defining events in the life of the American press during the early 1970s—Watergate and the Pentagon Papers. These high points in the tradition of independent, adversarial journalism were also the moment that tradition began to unravel. The consequences of such an undoing were more or less hidden from view until the Cold War waned and the forces building up behind that master narrative became apparent. A new journalism—trivial, self-absorbed, contemptuous of citizens—dominated the press between 1988, the most monumentally smarmy and irrelevant political campaign in modern history, and September 11. Carey cautions that whatever optimism one might hold for the press in the aftermath of September 11 must be conditioned by the damage done to democratic political institutions during the 15-year vacation journalists took from politics, rationality, and the public sphere. He doubts that the necessary repairs in both the institutions and the press can be accomplished in the short run, but at the least a rude shock has been delivered to journalists, who just might have realized that democratic institutions are not guaranteed; rather, they are fragile and can be destroyed by journalists as well as by politicians.

Robert W. McChesney, in "September 11 and the structural limitations of US journalism," links journalism with its broader economic and political surround. He argues that the US news media coverage of the political crisis following the attacks of September 11 was exceptionally problematic from a democratic perspective. The coverage tended to parrot the White House line and give short shrift to stories that ran counter to the official story. McChesney contends that the basic cause for the poor coverage was the code of professional journalism, which gave "official sources" considerable influence over what was covered and how it was covered. Locating the origins of professional journalism in the Progressive Era, then a response to the concentration of the newspaper market into single market monopolies or duopolies, he argues that this anti-democratic journalism was also apparent in the coverage of the Bush "election" to the presidency in 2000 and the Enron crisis of 2002. McChesney also contends that the recent wave of corporate consolidation affected September 11's coverage as well, in that the coverage of international affairs became too costly to maintain. As a result, the US population remained woefully uninformed about the world, and ideally suited for elite manipulation. The very media firms that are in lockstep praising "America's New War" are going before the Bush administration's Federal Communications Commission seeking media ownership deregulation that will make them each potentially far more profitable. This, contends McChesney, is a serious, yet never noted, conflict of interest.

In "Making sense of the 'Islamic Peril': journalism as cultural practice," Karim H. Karim connects journalism to some of its contending cultural influences. He argues that even though the events of September 11, 2001 were extraordinary, their reporting was routinely placed within the cultural frames that have long been in place to cover violence, terrorism, and Islam. The focus was on the immediate reaction rather than the broader causes of the attacks or the existence of structural violence in global society. As the hunt began for the "Islamic terrorists," the media failed to provide a nuanced and contextual understanding of Muslims or the nature of the "Islamic peril." Journalists generally echoed the Bush administration's polarized narrative frame of good versus evil. A significant responsibility for the media's failure to provide informed coverage of Muslim societies rests with Muslims themselves. They often stand bewildered at the West's kaleidoscopically-shifting media images and are suspicious of the constant, intrusive gaze of transnational media. The few Western journalists who produce informed accounts about Muslims are usually overshadowed by many others who continually use stereotypical frames. The ideal of a "specular border journalism" has the potential for providing genuinely global narratives in which groups are not arranged hierarchically. Recognizing the fundamentally cultural nature of journalism enables journalists to uncover and utilize the cultural tools of understanding that make possible genuine insight into human nature. The rupture resulting from the events of September 11 presents a longer-term opportunity for turning towards more authentic coverage of the world.

## Part 3—the changing boundaries of journalism

The contributions to this section consider some of the forms and practices existing at the margins rather than the centers of journalism. Stuart Allan, in his chapter "Reweaving the Internet: online news of September 11," identifies several pressing issues concerning online reporting of that day's tragic events. In the course of assessing the form and content of the news coverage, he considers conflicting perceptions regarding its relative advantages and limitations, especially when compared with television news. Above dispute was the fact that extraordinarily difficult demands were placed on online journalists, not least because news sites were overwhelmed by Web user traffic to the point that many sites ceased to operate effectively. Different strategies were adopted so as to help facilitate access, while several non-news sites stepped in to play a crucial role. Even more strikingly, ordinary people transformed into "personal journalists," acting the part of instant reporters, photojournalists, and opinion columnists. Eyewitness accounts, personal photographs, video-footage and the like appeared on hundreds of refashioned websites over the course of the day. Taken together, Allan argues, these websites resembled something of a first-person news network, a collective form of collaborative newsgathering that was very much consistent with the animating ethos of the Internet.

S. Elizabeth Bird, in "Taking it personally: supermarket tabloids after September 11," builds on her research on US tabloids to examine the newfound relevance of tabloids in the post-September 11 journalism landscape. In this chapter she shows that supermarket tabloids, like their TV counterparts and celebrity-driven journalism of all kinds, have long tended to ignore larger political issues. Yet after September 11, the political became personal, as these publications joined mainstream journalism in covering the events to the exclusion of everything else. Her chapter examines the tabloid coverage of the September 11 aftermath, showing how it focused on the personalization of key players (the demonization of Bin Laden, the glorification of New York heroes, and so on), while also providing further demonstration of how tabloid and mainstream reporting continue to move closer together as we move into a new century.

Michael Bromley and Stephen Cushion extend the conversation about tabloids to its British context. In "Media fundamentalism: the immediate response of the UK national press to September 11," they contend that throughout the twentieth century the idea has prevailed that journalism in the United Kingdom has been inexorably drifting towards more tabloid forms. Attempts to quantify this shift have produced only inconclusive evidence, however. For the most part they have focused on measuring convergences of news values—the extent to which journalisms supposedly located in different social markets nevertheless share a single, tabloid-inflected sense of what is news. Differentiations among journalisms are crucially dependent on other factors, too, such as the presentational and rhetorical use of language and illustration. Confronted with September 11 as "the story of a lifetime" in which there was overwhelming consensus over its value as news, *how* the national daily press of the UK treated this news could be expected to demonstrate whether tabloid forms of address are evident in all journalisms. An analysis of the front-page headlines and pictures in the ten national daily newspapers on September 12 found that there were greater apparent congruences between the themes contained in headlines and the newspapers' socio-market positions within both the broadsheet and the red-top tabloid press. Faced with the "what-a-story" of September 11 the national daily press of the UK responded by reverting to type, offering distinctive "quality," "popular," and tabloid journalisms.

Simon Cottle, in "Television agora and agoraphobia post-September 11," examines the role of UK current affairs programs in facilitating and containing public debate and deliberation surrounding the events of September 11, 2001.

He examines a sub-genre of high-profile national programs—BBC 1 *Question Time Special* (September 13, 2001), BBC 1 *Panorama Special: Clash of Cultures* (October 21, 2001), Channel 4, *War on Trial* (October 27, 2001)—and considers how each sought to provide distinctive "agora" for public participation and dialogue. Analyzing each of these programs in terms of their actual and potential contribution to dialogic and deliberative democracy, Cottle shows that public speech in each case was subject to tight editorial controls and delegated by program presenters into a form of "professional agoraphobia." In practice this professional dread of "wide open spaces" militated against their undoubted democratic promise. Even so, he demonstrates how these and similar current affairs programs provide a vital, albeit increasingly marginalized, resource for processes of deliberative democracy. For too long the complexities of current affairs programs have been under-researched and theorized. Here their democratic value and potential is illuminated in respect to their contribution to processes of wider public deliberation following September 11.

## Part 4—reporting trauma tomorrow

In the final section, some of the current tensions and problems regarding the ongoing coverage of trauma are examined. The authors tackle the persistence of such issues out of a concern for better predicting, locating, and managing trauma's lingering presence into the future. In "Journalism, risk, and patriotism," Silvio Waisbord argues that coverage of September 11 demonstrated that US journalism is ill equipped to serve the needs of democracy in the global risk society. Journalism's penchant for sensationalism and spot news, inability to talk about structural risks without "news hooks," and obsequiousness to official sources are hardly helpful for citizens coping with the prospects of risks involving terrorist attacks, bio-terrorism, or nuclear and chemical weapons and their traumatic consequences. The classic tropes that define journalism's political mission say little, if anything, about its function in situations of crisis, anxiety, and grief. Waisbord critiques the presence of two countervailing tendencies in journalism: while recommendations made in the past about journalism's mission in a democracy (to be fair, ethical, social responsible) are too abstract to provide a working roadmap in a world at risk, journalism's cultural and professional imaginary continues to be anchored in times where neither risk nor trauma were prominent features of social life as they are today. He thus argues that risk and trauma throw into disarray journalism's ideals such as objectivity and detachment. Partly as a result of its own confusion, journalism reaches out to safe cultural and political narratives such as patriotism and heroism and continues to offer a limiting version of "the national community" as a secure shelter for coping with trauma and finding solace in an unstable world. The violence of our time and its resulting trauma are presented as "ours," in ways that render invisible the globality of ever-present risks. Journalism is much better at handling the materialization (rather than the prospect) of risk, and makes trauma intelligible in terms of "the nation at risk."

Annabelle Sreberny, in "Trauma talk: reconfiguring the inside and outside," examines a rather neglected area in scholarship on journalism, the Commentary pieces, which in the liberal British newspaper the *Guardian* became a significant venue for airing responses to September 11. Sreberny uses the notion of the "inside–outside," a construct to be found in psychotherapeutic, sociological, and international relations theory, to explore the internalized "we-formations" that appear in selected Commentary articles. In a close textual reading of articles by two British novelists, Martin Amis and Deborah Moggach, and one *Observer* editorial, she explores the shifting nature of these writers' sense of collectivity, as exemplified by the way they construct who "we" are and how "we" feel. If daily fact-based journalism regularly reconfigures our view of the world, these pieces written by novelists reveal how that world is indeed internalized, and provide a very frank portrait of who we think we are. Sreberny argues that an agonistic and open public sphere requires affective responses as well as rational responses to global events, but it is also necessary to critically examine those responses and the deep-seated skeins of affiliation—and dis-affiliation—that they reveal.

In "Journalism and political crises in the global network society," Ingrid Volkmer builds upon her work on CNN to argue that what became obvious in the aftermath of September 11 was that news media are playing a new role in a globally enlarged public sphere. In the age of internationalization of the news media, national broadcasters extended their national coverage "across borders" and reflected international events in the dimension of "parachute journalism." This role challenged "global" news channels, such as CNN, which developed a new "worldwide journalism," through new program formats and journalistic styles of reporting. Volkmer argues that since September 11 it has become obvious that the concept of the "national public sphere" has—again—changed. Given the global interconnectedness of media, the public sphere has become increasingly integrated into a global network society, with new sub-national and supra-national coordinates, and—in consequence—new players and alliances, such as al-Jazeera, the broadcasting station from Qatar. Given this new news infrastructure, conventional formats of "domestic" and "foreign" journalism have to be reviewed, in order to define the particular role and responsibility of journalism in a global public sphere.

Finally, Howard Tumber, in "Reporting under fire: the physical safety and emotional welfare of journalists," examines one of the longstanding problems facing journalism on trauma: the physical safety and emotional welfare of journalists. One question that emerges from the reporting of international conflicts in the last century is why journalists are willing to subject themselves to psychological and physical dangers, sometimes going even further than the minimum necessary risks, in order to get a story. Tumber considers both the journalistic practices and the motivations that lie behind the desire to report as well as the dangers that follow. He argues that the recent spate of attacks on journalists suggests that news organizations are now specific targets. This raises the question of how news organizations should respond. Tumber explores how they balance the understandable urge of journalists to get a story with the safety of those involved and the degree to which they provide or should provide proper emotional support for journalists operating in war zones and other areas of potential trauma. As the journalist's role as an active interpreter becomes more pronounced and recognized, the psychological dimension of war reporting is opening up a new debate. In this regard, Tumber argues that post-September 11 has brought about a decisive change in journalistic culture.

*Journalism after September 11* tracks the lingering effects of trauma on journalism and journalistic culture in the Western world. The magnitude of the events of September 11 pushed trauma's presence into the public's eye, forcing us, as journalism scholars, to take note. And so we have. The unfolding of events on September 11 and their aftermath raise fundamental questions about how journalism can and should work in the Western world. The scholarship gathered in this collection approaches the topic through a score of questions, both implicit and explicit, about how journalism changes and resists change when trauma resides at its core. Though this collection leaves its readers with perhaps as many questions as answers to the issues raised here, it dresses the mantle of public consciousness with an urgency to think more creatively, cogently, and critically about what journalism in this new century might look like. Only then can we begin to consider the steps necessary to ensure that trauma remains a contained rather than rampant influence on journalism, as it and the events it covers move toward new contexts, new cultures, and new understandings of how the world might look different than it does today.

# References

Allan, S. (1999) *News Culture*, Buckingham and Philadelphia: Open University Press.

Aufderheide, P. (2001) Therapeutic patriotism and beyond, *Television Archive*, tvnews3.televisionarchive.org.

Baker, R. (2001) The *Journal* on the run, *Columbia Journalism Review*, November/December, XL (4): 16–18.

Barringer, F. (2001) Wall Street Journal finds a way to print, *New York Times*, September 14.

Barringer, F. and Fabrikant, G. (2001) As an attack unfolds, a struggle to provide vivid images to homes, *New York Times*, September 12: A25.

Bauder, D. (2001) Flap over displaying US flag causes conflict for TV reporters, *Detroit News*, September 21.

Bianco, R. (2001) Attacks and chaos unfold on national TV, *USA Today*, September 12.

Brennan, P. (2001) A few suggested targets, www.newsmax.com, September 14.

Campbell, K. (2001) *New York Times* portraits resonate coast to coast, *Christian Science Monitor*, December 6.

Caruth, C. (1996) *Unclaimed Experience: Trauma, Narrative, and History*, Baltimore, MD: Johns Hopkins University Press.

Cohen, P. (2001) When repetition is helpful rather than annoying, *New York Times*, September 17.

*Columbia Journalism Review* (2001) Before and after, Special 40th anniversary issue, XL (4).

Cooper, M. (2001) Life during wartime, www.time.com/time, September 18.

Cotts, C. (2001) Test of the Fourth Estate, *Village Voice*, week of September 19–25.

Dvorkin, J. A. (2001) Live vs. Memorex II: covering terrorism, www.npr.org, September 25.

Frisa, D. (2001) Traitorous media works leftist agenda, www.newsmax.com, September 14.

Gay, J. (2001) Network lions and cable jackals find essence of TV news is news, *New York Observer*, September 24.

Geisler, J. (2001) Covering terror and tragedy, Radio-Television News Directors Association and Foundation, www.rtnda.org, October.

Hazlett, C. (2001) The report from Ground Zero, in *Crisis Journalism: A Handbook for Media Response*, Reston, VA: American Press Institute, October: 2–3.

Heidkamp, B. (2001) Now rolling . . ., www.poppolitics.com, September 12.

Herman, J. (1992) *Trauma and Recovery*, New York: Basic Books.

Higham, N. (2002) America keeps its blinkers on, *British Journalism Review*, 13 (1): 13–18.

Huffington, A. (2001) Blinded by scandal, www.salon.com, September 13.

James, C. (2001a) Live images make viewers witnesses to horror, *New York Times*, September 12: A25.

James, C. (2001b) British take blunter approach to war reporting, *New York Times*, November 9.

Johnson, P. (2001) Inside TV, *USA Today*, September 17.

Johnson, S. (2001) San Francisco paper puts visceral reaction on page 1, *Chicago Tribune*, September 13.

Jurkowitz, M. (2001) BBC an objective observer on the battlefield, *Boston Globe*, December 4.

Kluger, J. (2001) Attack on the spirit, *Time*, September 24: 94–5.

Leys, R. (2000) *Trauma*, Chicago, IL: University of Chicago Press.

Maclear, K. (1999) *Beclouded Visions: Hiroshima-Nagasaki and the Art of Witness*, Albany, NY: State University of New York Press.

Murray, D. (2001) Behaving in the face of tragedy, in *Crisis Journalism: A Handbook for Media Response*, American Press Institute, October: ii.

Parrish, G. (2001) A media day in infamy, www.alternet.org, September 11.

Pew Research Internet Center and American Life Project (2001), How Americans used the Internet after the terror attack, www.pewinternet.org, September 15.

Real, M. (2001) In times of tragedy we depend on the media, *Crisis Journalism: A Handbook for Media Response*, American Press Institute, October: 59–61.

Ricchiardi, S. (2001) After the adrenaline, *American Journalism Review*, November, 23 (9): 35–9.

Roh, J. (2001) The Street.com, WSJ carry on, www.SiliconAlleyDaily.com, September 14.

Scherer, M. (2002) Framing the flag, in *Columbia Journalism Review*, www.cjr.org.

Scott, J. (2001) Closing a scrapbook full of life and sorrow, *New York Times*, December 31.

Stanley, A. (2001) Opponents of war are scarce on television, *New York Times*, November 9.

Tuchman, G. (1978) *Making News: A Study in the Construction of Reality*, New York: The Free Press.

Vejnoska, J. (2001) News rivals CNN, Fox offer different styles on crisis, *Atlanta Journal-Constitution*, September 17.

Vernon, W. (2001) *Washington Post*, Jennings, ABC step up attack on President Bush, www.newsmax.com, September 13.

Watson, W. (2001) A publishing project to help the media, *Crisis Journalism*, Reston, VA: October: ii.

Wells, M. (2001) World Service will not call US attacks terrorism, *Guardian*, November 15.

Zelizer, B. (1998) *Remembering to Forget: Holocaust Memory through the Camera's Eye*, Chicago, IL: University of Chicago Press.

# Part 1

# THE TRAUMA OF SEPTEMBER 11

# 1

# SEPTEMBER 11 IN THE MIND OF AMERICAN JOURNALISM

## Jay Rosen

I live in New York. For me it is impossible to get outside this subject, since I was inside the event—speaking relatively, of course. The World Trade Center's towers fell about fifty blocks from my office and home. To stand in Washington Square Park that day and watch the towers burn was to feel yourself being changed by a public event. In that perverse way intellectuals have, I remember thinking about the later consequences for my own thinking. "If I see fighter planes overhead, I'll have to undo everything I know about." Twenty minutes later, the F-15s came.

Here, I write about the mind of American journalism after September 11, but not because I have any special confidence in my judgment, which does not benefit from critical distance. I have no critical distance. For one thing, September 11 was the day I lost my daughter to the news. I hadn't expected anything like it, but then that sentence, "I hadn't expected anything like it" was said by almost everyone about that day. She was four years old at the time. By the time I got home, she had absorbed from television news images of destruction beyond what I had seen in my entire life. And they were real, local, in her big backyard.

The same images that struck at her also traumatized her parents. But the TV stayed on. All routines—the stability of life—stopped. Sirens were there instead. The sheer genius of the terrorist strike as strike, its terrible efficiency and accuracy and reach—this is clearest to me when I think about my daughter. The twin towers were the first civic structure she adored, her first landmark. Growing up in lower Manhattan, she had a mental geography that depended on their luminous presence. The fact that they were "twin" towers, identical, turned them into playful objects in a child's imagination. Millions of moms and dads would say the same, which shows that al-Qaeda knew what it was doing. They got to her. Inside the reality-making machine of her developing imagination they dropped the Two Biggest Things in the World from the sky.

In his 1990 lecture upon winning the Nobel Prize, the poet Octavio Paz recalls the day he lost his childhood to the news. It happened when an older child gave Paz a photograph from a news magazine, showing soldiers marching along a broad

27

avenue, most likely in New York. "They've returned from the war," he remembers being told. This handful of words disturbed him, implanting the knowledge "that somewhere far away a war had ended," and "that the soldiers were marching to celebrate their victory." This war was strangely unavailable; it had taken place "in another place and in another time, not here and now." By upsetting the temporal and spatial dimensions of his childhood, the photograph, says Paz, refuted him. He felt "dislodged from the present," expelled from his childhood garden, which in his case was real and planted with fig trees behind a bourgeois home in Mexico City.

In this world, faraway was the next roof top. Pirates were ever present. Seeing the news photo, he knew instantly that his childhood realm did not obey the requirements of reality. It was a play world where everything could be adjusted. At the instant he was forced into historical imagination (where are those men marching off to war?) Paz felt his childhood ending. He lost it to the news, evidence of an elsewhere he could not refute. For my daughter the moment of her historical imagination began with the news on September 11, the force of which she could not refute. (But she could verify the towers' destruction just by looking up when we went for a walk, and this she did.) History dawned for her when she reached the point of asking: who sent those planes that crashed? From where did they come and why? Though she could never understand the story, she certainly had the facts. Her facts raised questions, unanswerable in the little world she thought she knew. And this is how I lost her, momentarily, but with unknown and unknowable effect.

The terror attacks, I think, "got to" American journalism too, with the same ruthless efficiency and effective targeting that made September 11 a mentally terrible day for my daughter (who was physically safe). Normally, journalists don't get struck by events. They report when events strike others. And it is this basic immunity from action that makes the whole regime of neutrality, objectivity, and detachment even thinkable, let alone practical for journalists. When Tom Brokaw of NBC News was sent an envelope of anthrax by Someone Out There, no one talked about his neutrality or observer status. That may be a good thing. When observer-hood becomes unthinkable, new things can be thought. It is reasonable to hope that September 11 eventually improves the mind of American journalism. If it does, it will be an instance of creative destruction.

I begin with the mind of a man representing not journalism but ownership. He is Mel Karmazin, president of CBS, speaking at the Plaza Hotel in New York some months after the attacks. "Over the past ten weeks, we've been reminded why we do what we do," he told an industry crowd. "We want it said of us that when it mattered most we measured up." Observing this scene, Ken Auletta of the *New Yorker* added: "His peers at NBC, ABC, Fox, and CNN in the audience rose and applauded—both for Karmazin and, it seemed, themselves" (Auletta 2001: 60).

A dance with symbols was going on in the Plaza that day, and Auletta was on to it. Here was the pride and glory of journalism (Karmazin spoke about the performance of his news people), shining from the crown of a man with little loyalty to journalism. After all, the success of the news division in generating a return on investment has to be compared, in Karmazin's mind, not only to other possible uses of the same broadcast hours, but to every other media-related opportunity in the vast domain of Viacom, which owns CBS and its news operation. Karmazin himself, an industry insider and heavyweight, was well known for his toughness and tenacity, not in chasing a big breaking story (about which he knew nothing special), but in cutting costs and extracting harder work from employees.

CBS News in particular, with its rich history of public service at the dawn of the Television Age, was frequently said to be the most depleted of all the big American networks by the downsizing and withdrawal of investment, along with the lowering of broadcast standards, developments so insulting to serious journalists and so regularly in the news, that the veteran anchorman and public face of CBS, Dan Rather, had frequent cause to speak out publicly in op-ed forums and elsewhere against his own network's doings, charging the business of broadcasting with stupidly destroying what it had earlier created: a national treasure (that was how deep the mythology ran at CBS). It had precious value to the company because it demonstrated to all what a powerful public service the network really was. News was once the jewel of the company, once called the Tiffany network. Karmazin not only represented the reversal of all that; he had done some of the latest reversing himself.

But on September 11 and in the dazed days after, the news divisions at all the networks *were* the network. They took over in an emergency and stayed on the air. So powerful were the explosions set off by the attacks that they instantly inverted what had become the "normal" relations between CBS News and the whale of an empire that swallowed it. News was in charge, temporarily. Not just the commercials, but commercialism itself was suspended for a while, as the hugeness of the story became known and the audience swelled to include just about everyone. Journalism reigned again as the only plausible use of the airwaves that is vital to the national well-being. News had entertainment apologizing for itself and its banalities, in those strange weeks after the attacks when Hollywood people were saying (it does not matter if they were totally sincere) how empty their art and industry felt after seeing the destruction in New York and Washington. Some even vowed to become more serious or find a different line of work.

But journalists in those initial weeks had the work of a lifetime to do, and there was no choice but to stay out of their way and let them do it. Besides the public outcry that would have occurred if the network did not revert to all news in an emergency, there was a very good business reason for temporarily enthroning journalism on American television after September 11. The bigger your canvas as a global media empire, the less reason the home government has for identifying you as an especially American broadcaster. On paper, which means still in American law, the public owns the airwaves that originally created the combination called a network. It is true that this fact has been ignored in practice and then eventually in principle during the Reagan years, when the very notion of the public interest as distinct from market outcomes went dead. But the basic principle is still there—sleeping, as it were—and so is the law that states it.

From a smart CEO's point of view, the political value of network news in keeping Viacom or Walt Disney or General Electric an identifiably American company is beyond measure, in the same way that the economic value of having the First Amendment is beyond measure. Dan Rather, Peter Jennings, and Tom Brokaw are *American* icons, even though one is Canadian. They identify a spreading empire with a home polity. They brand social duty as serious. In a national emergency as grave as any since the Cuban Missile Crisis, Dan Rather and company, to the degree that he still had a company of serious news people, were allowed to be the jewel again, or, as Karmazin seemed to say, the *raison d'être* of broadcasting. "We've been reminded why we do what we do." Here he seemed to be announcing that news and the public service it provides are the reason we at CBS exist. This was a cynical statement, of course, because it fabricated the "we." But more interesting was how easy the statement was to put over.

Mel Karmazin, never before mentioned as a champion of broadcast journalism and glancing backward at the performance of people who probably hated and feared him, had no trouble aligning himself with their professionalism and strong sense of public mission during a true national emergency, when broadcast news mattered as never before. Once again a great public service had been performed. Once again television news had proven its immense power to call the American nation into being. About a moment that would last in cultural memory infinitely longer than the profit statements that normally consumed him and his executive corps, Karmazin was able to say: "We want it said of us that when it mattered most we measured up" (Auletta 2001: 60).

He did not get laughed off the stage. He did not have to endure trial by gaffe, which happens when someone makes a publicly unacceptable remark. Not only did he and his corporate parent, Viacom, have power *over* CBS News. They actually had on tap the residual power *of* CBS News, its not-quite-depleted store of cultural legitimacy, its remaining public service glow, its continued professionalism and seriousness. This was just in case someone like Mel Karmazin needed these things, or wanted them as his, during the days when people got down to thinking through what actually happened in New York and the nation's living rooms.

Karmazin's credit-claiming was particularly gross because by the time he spoke the main action had shifted from Ground Zero to the newly-opened war on terrorism. If there was such a war, it was happening in the far-flung international arena, from which CBS and other American networks had been steadily withdrawing correspondents, a conspicuous development that was often deplored by journalists and others concerned with the public's role in foreign policy. Always the answer was that American television viewers weren't very interested in foreign news, a "lucky" fact from a cost-cutter's perspective, since international coverage is the most expensive to produce. ·

The argument had market logic on its side. It also contradicted the logic of the news media as public service, which is the only non-market thing in Viacom's domain, and thus a unique source of national legitimacy, though easy to undervalue. In a universe where public service values hold sway, an inattentive or casually informed public only makes the watchful journalist's role more important. News people are supposed to pay attention for us when we can't or don't—and then sound the alarm when danger rises. Could CBS News have done that as the bitter current of anti-Americanism built around the world? Probably not. Did it have the people in place to sound the alarm? Definitely not. The priorities that created this retreat from the larger world had, as I said, a certain logic to them. And it was that logic that Mel Karmazin favored, imposed, enforced, represented.

"Why are we so hated in other countries?" A story that, miraculously, came into the center of public debate after September 11, was out there, gathering force in the international arena for several years before the crisis of 2001. It is hard to fault the press corps as a whole, including CBS, for failing to anticipate how big that story would become. The same could be said of the White House, the State Department, the FBI, the CIA, the Pentagon and most of the US foreign policy establishment. When the crisis hit, these agencies had to spring into action. It mattered a lot whether you had people there, whether they knew the territory and were plugged in. Those who report from overseas learn to rely on what are called "fixers" in the TV correspondent's trade. These are locals who know how to get around obstacles, as they help arrange for the correspondent's complicated passage through troubled country. If you're a competitive TV reporter, you want the best fixers in Islamabad when you suddenly have to report from Islamabad. Correspondents for the American networks have told me how the BBC's early coverage from Pakistan and Afghanistan put theirs to shame. "We got our butts kicked," they would say in their vernacular way. Part of the reason, they said, is that the BBC had never left some of the countries the Americans were being dropped into.

Just as the US government "pulled out of" various places around the world where there was deep misery but no American interest or will to act, so it could be said that network television in the United States pulled out of whole regions of the world where there was "deep news" going on but no audience interest or network act of will. So these places went dark in the newsroom's mattering map. CBS did not have the best fixers on the ground when it had to report from multiple fronts in Pakistan. Moreover, it had earlier decided that it would not, should not, and could not. "Viewers aren't interested, what can we do?" In this light, the network president's boast, "We measured up," is especially perverse, the applause from peers kind of sickening.

When you cannot stop—when no one can stop—the people who degrade and devalue and defund your accomplishments from grabbing credit for those accomplishments, you are in a culturally weak position. This is what media boss Mel Karmazin was cynically saying to the journalists in his employ, at a time when the importance of journalism—specifically journalism, not just television or "media"—was crystal clear to everyone. In the years leading up to September 11, it was made steadily more obvious that news and information were not especially included in the *raison d'être* of a global media company. The opposite was more true. CBS News was worth investment only if it improved, as well as other Viacom divisions improved, the current balance sheet of the company, which any college freshman knew was the relevant *raison d'être* for a network executive. The mind of American journalism had taken in this fact, old news by 2001, and was depressed by it.

A few months later, ABC almost did away with its late night news program, *Nightline*, hosted by Ted Koppel, in favor of comedy from David Letterman, whose contract was up at CBS. (Letterman ultimately declined to switch to ABC.) Koppel's program was one of the few on television known for its interest in foreign affairs. *Nightline* had reasonably strong ratings, often outpacing Letterman in raw numbers. It was not losing money; it actually made money. Because younger Americans preferred Dave to Ted, and advertisers paid more for younger eyeballs, and thus marginally more money could possibly be made by switching hosts, a solid news franchise that ABC had spent 23 years developing became expendable overnight. As soon as Letterman became a free agent, Disney executives said they were willing to trim *Nightline* from ABC. The clarity of these developments caused Mike Wallace of CBS News (who is, along with his 60 *Minutes* producer Don Hewitt, the senior broadcast journalist in America) to speculate on the air that Disney would, if it could, do away with news and be rid of such controversies.

This is what I mean by a depressed mind. Michael Eisner, CEO of Disney and occasionally described as a genius, artfully distanced himself from the public relations downer ABC suffered when Letterman declined to shift networks. He said he never thought it would happen—despite the hopes heard at his own unit, ABC—because a self-conscious broadcaster like Letterman would not want to be responsible for journalist Ted Koppel's demise. Press reports cited this as a factor in the comedian's decision. All of this confirms the residual cultural power of news, the legitimacy factor that somehow remains attached to it, even after suffering its downgrading and disinvestment and dilution. Mike Wallace might have felt less depressed if he saw that for the moment, doing away with news was still an unthinkable act for the likes of Disney. They would if they could . . . but why is it they cannot?

They cannot because the loss of legitimacy, the risk of uncoupling the empire from its base in the American polity, are simply not worth the cost savings and headache reduction. News, we were frequently told by realists, had become a minor part of a media empire like Viacom, Disney, and Time Warner. Serious news, we were told, was a minority taste in a culture of entertainment and its soapy narratives. But news becomes major when there is a decisive shift in public mood toward an interest in the world. Such events are more powerful than Disney. News is instantly cured of entertainment values when there is something extremely serious afoot. This is obvious, when you see it happen. True, it took a stunning, destructive, and historic event like 3,000 dead in terror attacks to show us that trends in the American media that might look permanent are interruptible. But they *are* interruptible. History is not over, and that includes media history.

Shift to David Westin, president of ABC News (but not of ABC itself), who actually did endure trial by gaffe a few weeks before Karmazin was strutting Dan Rather's stuff at the Plaza Hotel. It was an interesting gaffe for students of American journalism. Westin spoke at Columbia University's Graduate School of Journalism. He was asked whether some in the Muslim world might consider the Pentagon—as opposed to the World Trade Center—a legitimate target, which might in turn mean that it was not quite terrorism, from a certain point of view. Westin said the following (as imperfectly transcribed from a video tape):

> The Pentagon as a legitimate target? I actually don't have an opinion on that and it's important I not have an opinion on that as I sit here in my capacity right now. The way I conceive my job running a news organization, and the way I would like all the journalists at ABC News to perceive it, is there is a big difference between a normative position and a positive [ist?] position. Our job is to determine what is, not what ought to be and when we get into the job of what ought to be I think we're not doing a service to the American people. I can say the Pentagon got hit, I can say this is what their position is, this is what our position is, but for me to take a position this was right or wrong, I mean, that's perhaps for me in my private life, perhaps it's for me dealing with my loved ones, perhaps it's for my minister at church. But as a journalist I feel strongly that's something that I should not be taking a position on. I'm supposed to figure out what is and what is not, not what ought to be.
>
> (Cyber Alert Extra 2001)

The fact that Westin was a lawyer and corporate insider at ABC, not by training a journalist, made his answer a sharper glimpse into the standard mindset of the American press. For Westin was no fool, either. He had an intelligent grasp of the people who worked under him, and they praised his division leadership after the attacks in New York and Washington. In his earnest but ill-conceived way, he was trying to give the good journalist's proper answer, and thus stay within what he knew to be the thought world of the American press. True, he used elevated—or at least academic—language in talking about a "normative" decision. He wisely divided public realm from private. He spoke carefully, like a lawyer, but also passionately in speaking up for the moral code by which his troops in news lived. "As a journalist, I believe strongly . . ."

The next week, Westin was forced to issue a statement: "I was wrong . . . Under any interpretation, the attack on the Pentagon was criminal and entirely without justification. I apologize for any harm that my misstatement may have caused." In other words: "I must have been out of my mind." In a way he was.

Westin was trying to get inside the mind of mainstream American journalism, in order to speak from there to Columbia students. But the mind of journalism was somewhere else by then, because the events of September 11 had moved it. Westin's "I'm supposed to figure out what is and what is not, not what ought to be . . ." was a perfectly conventional notion in newsrooms on September 10, an answer that would have touched down safely on the wide, soft, mushy center of the average journalist's thinking, an ethic that could not easily be argued with before the attacks, and which even had a certain nobility to it despite many evasions and flaws. By October 2001, it was a hideous and embarrassing mistake, an unsustainable speech act, so publicly wrong-headed that one's only real choice was to reverse oneself and then stand outside one's just-reversed self to ask a weird and humiliating question: how dare I?

In other words, Westin's move was a gaffe. Well, how could he? Westin's mistake is not hard to track. As a journalist or boss of journalists, he was speaking favorably of objectivity, which is a little like a Republican Party official speaking favorably of the free enterprise system. This is the most common form of common sense about news—meaning "news" in the mind of the major news suppliers in the US. Stick to the facts. Don't make too many judgments. Leave opinions out of it. Separate your personal convictions from your professional duties. Remain neutral. Offer people good information; let them decide what it means. Treat both sides with respect, don't pick one over the other. Strive for the balanced view. Try to be as objective as possible, even though we are all human. Stay detached. Don't get sucked in by the emotions of the moment. I write redundantly because it is a redundant thought system that has many ways of arriving at the same idea.

Westin was preaching all that, and he reached a logical but ultimately depraved conclusion. His thinking went something like this: "I can see how some might define the Pentagon as a valid military target, if you look at it from their point of view. I'm not saying I share that perspective. I'm not saying I don't, either. In my role, it's important to look at these events from no one's point of view. That's how we can best serve the American people."

What Westin did not appreciate is how completely the events of September 11 wiped out the normal boundaries separating the professional position of the journalist from the personal (indeed emotional) position of an American citizen. "Speaking as a journalist," someone entitled to stand outside the political community, had become a morally hazardous act, whereas before it had been one of the safer places from which to answer a question about news. News from nowhere was not a very thinkable thing after September 11; and this had a disorienting effect.

If on September 10 someone had asked Frank Bruni, a correspondent for the *New York Times* who covered the rise of George W. Bush, whether he wanted Bush to succeed in office, Bruni would surely have given the Westin answer: "that is not for me to say. I stick to reporting the news." But by the following day, Bruni and his colleagues knew they were no different from other Americans in hoping that the President's leadership and decision-making were up to the historical task: the defeat of a worldwide terrorist threat. Interviewed on the public affairs network C-Span in March 2002 about his book on Bush, *Ambling into History*, Bruni said that we wanted George W. Bush to succeed, and that it was remarkable to see how he rose to the moment and became a leader.

This must have been a strange emotion, or at least strange to concede. "We were rooting for the President" is not normal talk from a reporter in the Washington bureau of the *New York Times*. If journalists like Bruni hoped the current President could succeed as a leader and decision-maker, that is odd enough. They also had to commit journalism aware of this rooting interest in a national leader, which is far odder, for it brings journalists face to face with ultimate questions about their political commitment. Westin mistakenly thought that the princi pled thing to do was profess none whatsoever. Later he realized he was utterly wrong under any interpretation sustainable in the "new" mind after September 11. Work as a journalist became a specific way of being a patriot: an American first, a professional after that. Just one of the new things we can observe about the press on the day its observer-hood gave way.

News pulls people, like my helpless and inquisitive daughter, into history. But history also pulls people into the news, and there is no telling when this factor—sleeping deeply under the visible trends—will suddenly explode, creating an instant and attentive public for the journalist's best work by enlarging people's everyday imagination. Well-paid executives who run the major commercial franchises in news sometimes act like they can dispose of news on a whim, or dilute it indefinitely. They want market logic to apply everywhere, but the smarter ones like Michael Eisner know it does not. Journalists in the United States are not so sure. They can see the day when they get replaced by David Letterman, and it is a depressing picture. Letterman—as big a star as there is in the entertainment sky—just didn't want to be blamed for the demise of news. Maybe he knows something that eludes Mike Wallace and the mind of American journalism.

Journalism is one of the ways we have of being serious and alive in our time. There is untold demand for that, so we need to keep journalism alive. The media, which sometimes seek to be the successor institution to journalism, are not necessarily willing to sustain serious news coverage as a kind of independent mattering map for the public at large. Yet it is stubbornly hard to get rid of news tellers because history—"the time of the real present," Octavio Paz put it—keeps happening. Will September 11 change anything in the ongoing battle to preserve journalism's cultural strength and reserve it for democracy? I hope so, but you see I lack distance. I live in New York.

# References

Auletta, Ken (2001) Battle stations, *The New Yorker*, December 10: 60–7.
Cyber Alert Extra (2001) www.mediaresearch.org/news/cyberalert/2001/-cyb20011031
_extra.asp, October 31.

# 2

# WHAT'S UNUSUAL ABOUT COVERING POLITICS AS USUAL

*Michael Schudson*

The September 28, 2001 issue of the *New York Times* marked the end of over-whelming consensus in post-September 11 journalism. Of course, even now, months later, some of the patriotic fervor and the sense of national unity that burst forth after September 11 survives in journalism as in American society gen-erally. But it endures as one element of national politics and national political reporting, not as the whole thing.

On September 28 the *Times* ran a front page story, "In Patriotic Time, Dissent is Muted" (Carter and Barringer 2001), that recounted the fate that had befallen Americans, both prominent and obscure, who had not toed the patriotic line. At least two small-town journalists had been fired for impolitic expression, and sev-eral corporations withdrew their sponsorship of Bill Maher's TV program, *Politically Incorrect*. In another front page story, Washington correspondent Robin Toner wrote of the decline of bipartisanship after its initial rush and of how the Congress was "taking a second look—and a third and a fourth—at the administration's proposals for new law enforcement powers to fight terrorism" (Toner 2001).

This was not the end of news of dissent and contention in the wake of the terrorist attack. A story from San Francisco reported how Japanese-Americans, remembering the internment camps of World War II, took it upon themselves to speak out against attacks on Arab-Americans (Nieves 2001). A local story reported that some Americans responded to September 11 with newly devised charity scams to exploit the generous spirit of their fellow citizens (Petersen 2001). Another local story reported that 8,000 frustrated residents were still displaced from their apartments near the World Trade Center. For some of them, "the mood has turned to anger." The residents were reported to be highly critical of the city administration (Lambert 2001).

These stories bring us to Mayor Rudolph Giuliani. In the first days of the crisis, Giuliani arose as a city and national hero. He acted with dignity, calm, tireless energy, and deep humanity. A news analysis in the *Times* on September 14 said as much, observing that Giuliani had taken charge of the city's response from the very first moments.

Acting at once as chief operating officer of the city—personally moni-toring, for instance, how many pounds of debris have been removed by the hour to securing low-interest loans to rebuild the city—to city psy-chologist, trying to assure a grief-stricken and terrified population that they are safe and that he knows they are hurting, the mayor has almost unilaterally managed to create the sense that the city and by its proxy, the nation, are scratching their way back to normalcy.

The ungainly length of that sentence accurately represented the breathless awe in which people who once criticized the mayor now regarded him (Steinhauer 2001).

On September 28, however, the newspaper was no longer in awe. The *Times'* man-about-town columnist, John Tierney, laid into Giuliani's plan to stay on as mayor for three months past the end of his term of office. Giuliani had proposed this to the three leading candidates seeking to replace him and, appallingly, two of them accepted it without worrying over the fact that they had no legal author-ity to do so. "You might think," Tierney wrote, "that it's delusional of him now to believe that the city can't get along without him next year. But don't under-estimate his sincerity. Mr. Giuliani is quite capable of believing himself indispensable" (Tierney 2001). Nor was this all. In a sharply worded lead editor-ial, the *Times* declared its views on the Mayor's extra-legal plan to remain in office: "This is a terrible idea" (*New York Times* 2001b).

The American news media did an extraordinary job in the wake of September 11. The work of the *New York Times* staff was little short of miraculous in cover-ing the terrorist attacks and their aftermath intensely, humanly, and in large measure fairly. I myself did not recognize this immediately. Although I normally read the *Times* along with my local newspaper daily, in the first few days after September 11, like most of my fellow citizens, I watched television obsessively. It took me a week to realize that the *Times* was up to something extraordinary. On Tuesday, September 18, the regular "Science Times" section ran stories on every conceivable scientific facet of the tragedy—the engineering task of clearing debris without risking the foundations of neighboring buildings (Overbye 2001); the engineering task of building skyscrapers in the future less vulnerable to air-planes (Chang 2001); the adaptive advantage of altruism in evolutionary perspective (Angier 2001); the question of whether barring asbestos from build-ings had reduced the Trade Center's capacity to withstand the fires that destroyed them (Glanz and Revkin 2001); the dangers of dust inhalation in lower Manhat-tan (Revkin 2001); how to make jet fuel safer (Broad 2001); two first-hand accounts by physicians who happened to be both regular contributors to the *Times'* science section and providers of emergency medicine at Bellevue Hospital and at Ground Zero on September 11 (Jauhar 2001; Zuger 2001); the problems for blood banks of maintaining a blood supply (Altman 2001); the ways individ-uals cope with trauma (Brody 2001)—all in separate, detailed stories that no one could have imagined when the section was originally planned.

37

This terrible tragedy for the world proved a great opportunity for journalism. People were willing to watch and read far beyond what they normally absorbed. Journalism is a curriculum, as James Carey has suggested (Carey 1986: 151–2), with breaking news only the intro course. After that comes the human interest side-bar, the biographical sketch of a person in the news, news analysis, the lengthy magazine piece, later the book. After September 11, many people were prepared to go well beyond the intro course. At the same time, journalists expanded the curriculum with the invention of new forms of reportage, notably the *New York Times'* poignant quasi-obituaries for the people killed in New York. Through December 31, 2001, these obits were printed as part of the *Times'* special news section devoted exclusively to news related to September 11 and terrorism, "A Nation Challenged."

It is surprising, in retrospect, how quickly this remarkable series of obituaries emerged. On Saturday, September 15, its first installment ran under the heading, "Among the Missing." The next day the heading was, "After the attack: portraits of grief," and "Portraits of Grief" would become the permanent head, still in use months later. Without directly referring to what was clearly becoming a series, the *Times* editorialized on Sunday, September 16: "The faces emerge." The editorial called attention to the fliers posted across New York seeking information on missing friends and relatives. It called attention to the obituaries beginning to appear in newspapers across the US. It observed the arbitrariness of who was caught in the World Trade Center that day and who was not, and it called for readers to pay attention to

> a remarkably precious opportunity to witness a portrait of this nation assembled out of memories and pictures, out of the efforts of everyday people to explain in everyday words who it is they lost on Tuesday. They hold out their photographs to strangers and television cameras. The faces looking out of those pictures could not have imagined knowing what we know now. You can tell it by the way they smile.
>
> (*New York Times* 2001a)

Each day "A Nation Challenged" featured an interpretive news summary at the bottom of the first page. This was another innovation, a fairly free-form structure, sometimes more essay than news, as on December 26 when Jane Gross wrote:

> Holidays have come and gone, none more poignant than this first Christmas in a changed world, a changed city, where no amount of tinsel can replace the sparkle of nearly 3,000 lost lives. But hesitantly, reluctantly, inevitably people are inching toward more normal lives, groping for wisdom and perspective.
>
> (Gross 2001)

Gross fell into an elegiac tone, worlds away from ordinary *Times* prose. The tone of the "Portraits of Grief" was even more unusual. These portraits were not the formal, heavy obits readers were used to but quick sketches, efforts not to list family and survivors but to suggest a spark of life that made each person special or different. Their stylistic heritage was more from the feature story than from obituary writing, but they represented a new hybrid, a kind of haiku obit. They were a form of journalism as tribute, journalism as homage, journalism as witness, journalism as solace, and journalism aspiring to art.

The "A Nation Challenged" section was discontinued at the end of the calendar year. The ushering in of 2002 seemed a fitting occasion to return to normal, with all the mixed feelings that "returning to normal" brings to a family, or nation, in mourning.

Despite the exceptional quality of the journalism that developed so quickly after September 11, I found that the *New York Times* edition of September 28 came as a great relief. For two very long weeks, journalists wrote in a way that emphasized not only factual accuracy and analytical power but human connection to their community. And still, a return to reporting a kind of politics in a style that was reporting as usual felt redemptive, as if a fever had just broken after a prolonged illness. Why? Where is the comfort in the normality of political reporting?

Syndicated columnist Ellen Goodman wrote on December 7, "When terrorists struck on September 11, there was only one side. No editor demanded a quote from someone saying why it was fine to fly airplanes into buildings. No one expected reporters to take an 'objective' view of the terrorists" (Goodman 2001). While criticizing the Fox News Channel for slanted, jingoistic coverage, Goodman found herself nonetheless ready to embrace the mantra of Fox news director Roger Ailes: "be accurate, be fair, be American."

The same day, broadcast anchorman Tom Brokaw wrote a newspaper column comparing September 11, 2001 and December 7, 1941. Among the similarities he noted was the centrality of the news media: "On that long ago Sunday and the more recent Tuesday, Americans were glued to news broadcasts, bringing this vast land to a standstill." In both cases, he observed, "the nation bonded electronically" (Brokaw 2001).

September 11 blew out the fuses of preconceived ideas about journalism and just about everything else. Journalists ran on instinct, on professionalism, and they did their best to get the story, to get to the scene, to cover the facts, to interview the President, the mayor, the police chief, the emergency-room physician, the wounded, the witness. They reported too many rumors but they made their corrections. They did not have a language for the terrorism at first. Tragedy. Atrocity. Yes. But is this war? Or is this criminal activity? Where is responsibility? Where is resolution? The President spoke angrily, perhaps even recklessly, but backed off. Republicans called for increased federal power in the economy, not hands off. Democrats supported greater police and military authority. The public, somewhat skeptical of President George W. Bush, rallied behind him. And then what? What happened to journalism?

Two things happened immediately and with some enduring effect. First, journalism moved quickly away from its standard handling of political events as part of what Daniel Hallin has termed the "sphere of legitimate controversy" (Hallin 1986: 116). Hallin's conceptualization is useful and clarifying. He argues in his influential study of the US media during the Vietnam War that journalism's commitment to objectivity has always been compartmentalized. That is, within a certain sphere—the sphere of legitimate controversy—journalists seek conscientiously to be balanced and objective. But there is also a "sphere of consensus" in which journalists feel free to invoke a generalized "we" and to take for granted shared values and shared assumptions (ibid.: 117). When President Kennedy was assassinated, no journalist felt obliged to seek out sources to praise the assassin as well as to condemn him. In fact, there were Americans who initially exulted in the assassination, but journalists did not feel any obligation to represent them as legitimate voices in news coverage. The assassination was treated as a national tragedy and the media audience addressed as part of a large national family that had suffered a grievous blow.

Hallin points also to a third sphere, a "sphere of deviance," where journalists also depart from standard norms of objective reporting and feel authorized to treat as marginal, laughable, dangerous, or ridiculous individuals and groups who fall far outside a range of variation taken as legitimate (ibid.: 117). Pre-teen girls swooning over adolescent rock stars can be presented in a mocking or condescending tone that would never be appropriate for covering members of Congress. A vegetarian or temperance candidate for President can be presented as a light side-note to the seriousness of the main arena of politics.

After September 11, journalists felt thrust into the sphere of consensus. Neither deferential objectivity nor tough, assertive professionalism, modes appropriate to covering legitimate controversies, seemed adequate to the moment. Journalism as an instrument of providing information and analysis of public affairs did not seem enough. And so journalists shifted modes as if changing to another musical key or switching to a different language. They moved toward the sphere of consensus. They moved into what might even be called a priestly or pastoral mode. The tone of detached neutrality was replaced by a quiet, solemn tone, as if speaking at a funeral. There is no doubt much ill that could be spoken of the dead. Certainly there is much ill that could be spoken of the President and the previous President and the Congress, all of whom largely ignored the reports on terrorism, conscientiously written and edited and published and then put on the back burner—as did most of the media, for that matter (Evans 2001). All of this unfolded while President Bush focused his energies in a crusade on behalf of $300 tax rebates. Criticism of the short-sightedness of national leadership was, at most, muted. Journalists were not out to find scapegoats. It was just not appropriate at a time of national mourning.

Instead, post-September 11 journalism sought to provide comfort or reassurance, not just information or analysis. One journalist at the *Times* explained that the point of the "Portraits of Grief" was to give solace to the families of the victims.

But, as journalist and media critic James Fallows observed, "the real significance of this series is clearly to give solace to a community—not simply the community of New York or those who knew the victims personally but the entire national community for which the remembrances have become a powerful sacrament." Fallows not only praised the *Times* for the "Portraits of Grief" but mischievously observed that this was exactly the sort of "public journalism" that *Times* editor Howell Raines had vigorously condemned. That is, it was a journalism that "stopped kidding itself about its ability to remain detached from and objective about public life. It is trying to help its city and its nation and it is succeeding" (Fallows 2002: 17).

There are three occasions when US journalists instinctively and willingly abandon the effort to report from a neutral stance. In moments of tragedy, journalists assume a pastoral role. On television, correspondents adopt quiet, even reverent tones, an air of solemnity. This is evident, for instance, in news coverage of assassinations of political leaders, in state funerals, and since September 11 in coverage of the mourning of the victims.

Second, in moments of public danger, journalists replace professional objectivity with neighborly reassurance, whether danger comes from terrorists or hurricanes. They seek to offer practical guidance and to communicate fellow feeling. They become part of a public health campaign, not just a public information system.

Third, journalists also reject neutrality during threats to national security. When they are convinced that national security is at risk, they willingly withhold or temper their reports. American journalists did so at the time of the Bay of Pigs invasion of Cuba in 1961, for example, and on other occasions where releasing information might put American military forces in harm's way.

September 11 combined all three moments into one: tragedy, public danger, and a grave threat to national security. Journalists did not have to be instructed to speak reverently of the victims of the terrorist attacks. They did not have to be directed to pronounce the firefighters and police officers at the World Trade Center heroes. They did not have to be commanded to reassure citizens when anthrax infection threatened public panic. In tragedy, public danger, and threats to national security, there are no "sides." We are all in it together. Much reporting after September 11 turned toward a prose of solidarity rather than a prose of information.

The second thing that happened to journalism happened to the journalists themselves and came perhaps as something of a revelation to them: they liked the new intimacy of the consensual "we." They felt connected and important to their audience. They felt appreciated as they rarely do. Many American journalists who reported about September 11 and later the war in Afghanistan felt good about their work. "At last!" they seemed to sigh. "This is what journalism is about! This is why I am a journalist!" Nick Spangler, on September 11 a journalism student at Columbia University on an election-day assignment for a reporting class (September 11 was to be the mayoral primary in New York), found himself near Ground Zero when the terrorists attacked. He took his camera and notepad and covered what he could. "I felt an intense passion in those hours, an exaltation," he later wrote. "I felt alone at the center of the world. All details became iconic and crucial. I tried to record everything" (Spangler 2001). *New York Times* reporter Katherine Finkelstein reached Ground Zero before the towers collapsed and stayed there for 40 hours. A police officer gave her his pen when she lost hers; she wrote down a list of what supplies the medics needed to help them. She was reporting, but not as an outsider. She was performing a community service, as many (but not all) around her recognized in befriending her; she represented an institution and a function that could help (Finkelstein 2001). Even the most professional, detached reporting could feel like a service to the country's highest ideals, as when reporters did stories on critics of American policy who had suffered intense criticism or on Muslim-Americans who were assaulted by stupid and vengeful fellow citizens.

Not incidentally, even print journalists found occasion to praise their broadcast colleagues. There was a "new, if fleeting, dignity" that September 11 conferred on broadcast journalism, wrote Orville Schell, Dean of the School of Journalism at the University of California, Berkeley. He observed that the broadcast media

> helped inform and calm us so that we could keep some part of our critical faculties in abeyance to think reasonably about what had befallen us. The result has been an unprecedented sense of togetherness and common purpose for which we owe a profound debt of thanks to television and radio.
>
> (Schell 2001)

"For one week there was no race, just the human race," said *New York Times* reporter Charlie LeDuff. He was obviously moved by covering the recovery efforts at Ground Zero as construction workers, medical personnel, migrant workers, hundreds of volunteers went to work. "You were surrounded by humanity down there," he told his journalism school alumni newsletter, "It was inspiring to watch" (Carvalho 2001: 3).

It was inspiring, even at a distance. And everyone seemed to be watching and, in whatever way they could, participating. I got a form letter from my brokerage, "Dear Valued Client: On Tuesday September 11, many of us who worked at The World Trade Center returned home to our loved ones. Sadly, all of us did not." I even received a holiday season form letter from my dentist, "Dear Friends, Many people have been affected by the terrible events of the recent past." It promoted a teeth whitening procedure, profits from which would be donated to the Red Cross. People in my office made sure that I, as a college administrator, wore an American flag on my lapel. I appreciated the gesture and I felt solidarity with the office staff as I wore it. I attended memorial services at the university and I sang "God Bless America" with the others. The media were, for a week or two, only the tip of the communicative iceberg. Everyone called friends and family in New

York. Everyone spoke to their children, or worked out for themselves why they would not speak to them; everyone shared the TV with the kids or shielded them from it self-consciously. My next door neighbor is a firefighter, and I looked at him with new regard.

But now, my dentist is again my dentist, not my comrade, and my neighbor is again my neighbor. Normality is in the United States the enemy of patriotism, not its underpinning. Pastoral journalism cannot be sustained. It seeks to offer reassurance, not information; it seeks to speak to and for a unified people rather than a people divided by conflict and interested in conflict; it seeks to build community rather than to inform it. This is not peculiar to the United States. Up to the day he was assassinated, Israel's Prime Minister Yitzhak Rabin was a politician. The next day he was a statesman, a martyr, and a saint. For a time after his death, it was not possible to criticize him in the press (Peri 1997). This was not because there was censorship from outside but because journalists knew, internally and intuitively, that criticism would be unseemly.

Journalism after September 11 showed that it could not only inform but console, not only make us think but make us cry. We learned deeper truths than journalism is ordinarily prepared to handle, and one of these truths was about journalism itself—that it never stands entirely outside the community it reports on.

But the moment passed. It passed before the media were prepared to let go of it. The result is that the neon banners on television like "America Under Siege" or "America Strikes Back" or the other slogans used by print and broadcast but most gratingly by television outlasted their usefulness. They fairly quickly felt like marketing, not journalism. They seemed forced, false, cloying, self-aggrandizing, jingoistic. Likewise, the labeling of anti-terrorist appropriations in the "USA Patriot Act" (a sophomorically clever acronym for legislation labeled "United and Strengthening America by Providing Appropriate Tools Required to Intercept and Obstruct Terrorism") seemed embarrassing. This was not so at first, not in the heat of the shattering moment, but it became so soon enough.

Somewhere in late September, even as preparations for the war in Afghanistan mounted, the unquestioning "we" began to dissolve. "I hate the first-person plural . . . I grew up with 'we' and 'us': in the kindergarten, at school, in the pioneer and youth organizations, in the community, at work," wrote Slavenka Drakulic of life in Yugoslavia. "I grew up listening to the speeches of politicians saying, 'Comrades, we must . . .' and with these comrades, we did what we were told, because we did not exist in any other grammatical form" (Drakulic 1996: 2). The "we" and the "us" turned up repeatedly in news accounts of September 11. That there was cause for this, one cannot doubt. The terrorist attack was a clear message that from the perspective of a disciplined, cruelly single-minded suicidal hijacker, the only good American was a dead one. The friends and admirers of these terrorists would shed no tears over those who died, rich and poor, American and foreigner, Christian, Jew, and Muslim. The victims included Americans of old stock and newly arrived immigrants. No terrorist could see inscribed in the

43

name of one of the most severely affected brokerage houses, Cantor and Fitzger-
ald, an extraordinary symbol of some of the best of the past century of American
history, the marriage of two ethnic groups, of two religious groups, Jew and
Catholic, both of them widely treated as dirt just a hundred years ago. The twin
towers were not only about world trade, that was only their business; they were
about the bargaining and contracts one human being makes with another, the
hopes and loves of individuals reaching from their parochial backgrounds
through commerce, desire, love, ambition, and comradeship to connect.

So it is easy to recognize the adoption of a "we" affirmed in post-September 11
journalism. It is easy to accept that American flags appeared on the lapels
of reporters and local TV anchors and flew over the headquarters of news
organizations.

At the same time, how can one be an American journalist and a patriot simultaneously? In World War II, this question did not arise. In that war, the US
government treated reporting as "essential service" and grounds for exemption
from the military draft, just like work in defense plants. Journalists and government officials alike took reporting to be a weapon in the war. In the Korean War,
reporters accompanying UN troops traded access to information for agreement
not to criticize the troops. Only in Vietnam, and then rather late in the war, did
"our war" became "the war" (Hallin 1986: 127). Journalists took up a professional
detachment rather than a patriotic deference to military authority. Ever since,
US journalists have sought maximum access to information during war and have
chafed at military information control and censorship.

Journalism under normal circumstances is something else again. Under normal
circumstances, American society operates with security taken for granted, with
public danger at bay, and with tragedy a matter of private circumstance rather
than public sharing. Under normal circumstances, our lives are both enriched
and complicated by dissent and conflict. Under normal circumstances, dissent
and conflict enhance and express the nation's democratic aspirations rather than
undermine their possibility. Under normal circumstances, citizens are both
drawn to and put off by the self-serving-ness and the arrogance and the guile of
political language. Under normal circumstances, journalists serve society by
adhering to their professional ideals and not by worrying too much over how
they might assuage the hurts of their communities.

Covering politics as usual means operating within a sense of assurances and
securities. It means learning to live with a relatively high level of noise, of raised
voices, of fists shaking in anger, of a rhetoric of outrage and of outrageous
rhetoric. It means learning to manage the histrionics of competition, rivalry, and
even a degree of skullduggery. This is not everybody's cup of tea. Politics *is* dirty.
That is something to work with, however, not to fear. It drives people to find
community and solidarity in other spheres, not in a national politics.

There is much to cherish in this. Politics should serve society, not command it.
It should enlarge and enrich and secure the space for human beings to prosper in
common. Part of what was striking about the patriotic outburst after September

11 is that it was so chastened. People spoke words they will (or should) regret, the Rev. Jerry Falwell's taking first prize. But there were not many, and remarkably few from the nation's elected leaders. There was reserve and resolve and a self-conscious awareness that patriotic fervor was appropriate and necessary but also dangerous. This was certainly true in the media where, within days, prominently placed news reports raised concerns about how national security could be enhanced without unduly damaging the civil liberties that are part of America's very definition of itself (Greenhouse 2001).

So, as much as I admire the coverage the *New York Times* provided in the days after September 11, there was something profoundly reassuring in that edition of September 28. It was reassuring that Democrats and Republicans were arguing with each other in Congress, that journalists were on Mayor Giuliani's back, that there was resistance when he tried to transform his demi-god status into a demagogue's, that downtown Manhattan residents were bitching at the city bureaucracy, that Japanese-Americans out of their own deep injury at the hands of the American government were looking out for Arab-Americans, that punitive responses to those who dissented from the consensus of the moment were being criticized.

It was wonderful to see all that messiness again, all that conflict, all that stuff that makes people turn in disgust from the back-biting, back-stabbing, power-grabbing low-down of politics. Media scholars have been apt in recent years to complain that standard political reporting in the American press is cynical, indicating between the lines that politicians are motivated invariably by the desire for office or re-election, not by actual conviction about anything beyond their own careers (Patterson 1993; Cappella and Jamieson 1997). I am among those who have complained (Schudson 2000). Well, the cynicism is surely there, but it represents more democratic virtue and vigor than critics have allowed.

## References

Altman, L. K. (2001) Donors flood blood banks, but a steady stream is what's needed, *New York Times*, September 18: D4.

Angier, N. (2001) Of altruism, heroism and evolution's gifts, *New York Times*, September 18: D1.

Broad, W. J. (2001) Making planes safer by making fuels safer, *New York Times*, September 18: D3.

Brody, J. E. (2001) During traumatic times, small acts can bring a measure of comfort, *New York Times*, September 18: D4.

Brokaw, T. (2001) Two dates which will live in infamy, *San Diego Union Tribune*, December 7: B13.

Cappella, J. N. and Jamieson, K. (1997) *Spiral of Cynicism*, New York: Oxford University Press.

Carey, J. W. (1986) Why and how?: The dark continent of American journalism, in R. Manoff and M. Schudson (eds) *Reading the News*, New York: Pantheon, 146–96.

Carter, B. and Barringer, F. (2001) In patriotic times, dissent is muted, *New York Times*, September 28: A1.

Carvalho, I. (2001) Alumnus LeDuff chronicles lives lost, *North Gate News*, newsletter of the Graduate School of Journalism, University of California, Berkeley, CA: 28 (8) Fall: 3.

Chang, K. (2001) Defending skyscrapers against terror, *New York Times*, September 18: D1.

Drakulic, S. (1996) *Café Europa: Life after Communism*, New York: W. W. Norton.

Evans, H. (2001) Warning given . . . story missed, *Columbia Journalism Review*, November/December: 12–14.

Fallows, J. (2002) The New York Times: a civic nomination, *Civic Catalyst*, Winter 2001: 17. Reprinted from *Slate*, December 3.

Finkelstein, K. E. (2001) 40 hours in hell, *American Journalism Review*, 23 (November): 28–33.

Glanz, J. and Revkin, A. C. (2001) Haunting question: did the ban on asbestos lead to loss of life? *New York Times*, September 18: D2.

Goodman, E. (2001) Post-September 11 dilemmas for journalists, *San Diego Union Tribune*, December 7: B12.

Greenhouse, L. (2001) The clamor of a free people, *New York Times*, September 16, section 4: 1.

Gross, J. (2001) A muted Christmas, corporate obligations, the anthrax mystery, *New York Times*, December 26: B1.

Hallin, D. C. (1986) *"The Uncensored War": The Media and Vietnam*, New York: Oxford University Press.

Jauhar, S. (2001) They had everything they needed, except survivors to treat, *New York Times*, September 18: D3.

Lambert, B. (2001) 8,000 residents, still displaced, grow frustrated and then angry, *New York Times*, September 28: A25.

*New York Times* (2001a) The faces emerge (editorial), September 16, section 4: 10.

*New York Times* (2001b) The mayor's dangerous idea (editorial), September 28: A30.

Nieves, E. (2001) Recalling internment and saying "never again," *New York Times*, September 28: A14.

Overbye, D. (2001) Engineers tackle havoc underground, *New York Times*, September 18: D1.

Patterson, T. E. (1993) *Out of Order*, New York: Alfred A. Knopf.

Peri, Y. (1997) The Rabin myth and the press: Reconstruction of the Israeli collective identity, *European Journal of Communication*, 12: 435–58.

Peterson, M. (2001) Reports of scams preying on donors are on rise, *New York Times*, September 28: A18.

Revkin, A. C. (2001) Dust is a problem, but the risk seems small, *New York Times*, September 18: D2.

Schell, O. (2001) The media clarified, *North Gate News*, newsletter of the Graduate School of Journalism, University of California, Berkeley, CA: 28 (8) Fall: 9.

Schudson, M. (2000) Is journalism hopelessly cynical?, in S. Kernell and S. S. Smith (eds) *Principles and Practices of American Politics*, Washington, DC: CQ Press: 742–51.

Spangler, N. (2001) Witness, *Columbia Journalism Review*, November/December: 6–9.

Steinhauer, J. (2001) Giuliani takes charge, and city sees him as the essential man, *New York Times*, September 14: A2.

Tierney, J. (2001) Most heroes would go, but Giuliani isn't most, *New York Times*, September 28: A26.

Toner, R. (2001) Bush law-enforcement plan troubles both right and left, *New York Times*, September 28, 2001: A1.

Zuger, A. (2001) They had everything they needed, except survivors to treat, *New York Times*, September 18: D3.

# 3

# PHOTOGRAPHY, JOURNALISM, AND TRAUMA[1]

*Barbie Zelizer*

Not long after the September 11 attacks on the World Trade Center and the Pentagon, a memo from the American Press Institute went out to US news editors and reporters, advising them on the "correct" way to utilize photographs in crisis reporting. In part the directive said, "our backs are to the podium and our cameras are focused on the faces of the crowd" (Lower 2001). This was curious, for among photojournalists the idea of using images to draw from and upon the public rather than to depict the events being witnessed was antithetical to what good journalism is supposed to do.

And yet, the role played by photography in response to the events of September 11 offered one of the seemingly more redemptive stories in the many tales circulating about the professional triumphs, tragedies, and conflicts confronting journalism in a post-September 11 world. Photography, it was widely claimed, rose to fill the space of chaos and confusion that journalism was expected to render orderly. Photographs in the popular press helped register—and counter—the disbelief in which people the world over found themselves lodged, and the frequent, systematic, and repetitive circulation of photographic images—in newspapers, news magazines, and eventually year-end reviews and commemorative volumes—created a place in which the public could see and continue to see the core visual representations of an event that seemed to buckle under existing interpretive schemes. The fact that they did so by deviating from normal journalistic routine seemed to be almost beside the point.

This is troubling, for the wide availability of the photographs related to the September 11 attacks obscured far-reaching questions concerning what was depicted and how. This chapter considers those questions, analyzing the visual template through which the events of September 11 were represented in the American popular press. It demonstrates that the photos facilitated public responsiveness and attentiveness, helping the public to bear witness and move from its initial state of disarray and shock toward a post-traumatic state, all the while securing public support for the political and military actions in Afghanistan that were to come.

Significantly, this use of photographs and its creation of a specific kind of public viewing position were not without historical precedent. Using photos to facilitate public responsiveness echoed an earlier historical moment—response to the liberation of the concentration camps of World War II in 1945. Then, too, photos were used to help people bear witness while reviving their support for the Allied campaign during the war. This chapter argues that the invocation of that earlier visual template raises issues that are crucial to understanding how photography functions simultaneously as an integral part of journalism, a tool for easing the dissonance caused by public trauma, and a facilitator for achieving certain strategic political and military aims.

## Photography, journalism, and trauma

The well-worn adage of "seeing is believing" seems to work particularly well in times of trauma. Public trauma occurs when actions—wars, major disasters, or other large-scale cataclysmic events—rattle default notions of what it means morally to remain members of a collective. Recovering from trauma entails travelling a delicate path from the trauma itself to some kind of post-traumatic space. While on such a path, people work through recovery's three stages—establishing safety, engaging in remembrance and mourning, and reconnecting with ordinary life (Herman 1992: 155). When trauma involves intentional assaults, such as the planned violence typical of terrorism and military action, recovery from trauma often involves mobilizing the collective to agree on a plan of compensatory action for the trauma experienced. Reconnecting with ordinary life, then, proceeds on the basis of an altered vision of what such a life can look like. Alliances are reordered, practices changed, actions ranked and treated differently, and beliefs about the broader system revisited and fine-tuned in accordance with the trauma endured.

Photography is well-suited to take individuals and collectives on the journey to a post-traumatic space. The frozen images of the still photographic visual record are a helpful way of mobilizing a collective's post-traumatic response. They help dislodge people from the initial shock of trauma and coax them into a post-traumatic space, offering a vehicle by which they can see and continue to see until the shock and trauma associated with disbelieving can be worked through. Not every person recovers from trauma at the same moment, and photographs allow people to continue looking until they can work through the dissonance caused by trauma. Unlike moving pictures, whose images disappear almost as quickly as their spectators encounter them, still photographs are, in Marianne Hirsch's words, "inherently elegiac." (Hirsch 2002). This suggests that the movement from trauma to a post-traumatic space may be facilitated at least in part by photography, not only in its strategic relay—the making of photographs—but also in the usage of photographs over time. In display, prominence, centrality, and sheer number, photographs create a space of contemplation in the documentary record, through which people move at varied paces on their way to

49

recovery. It is no wonder, then, that governments the world over have recognized the power of the image in helping them reach strategic aims. "Seeing," for many, has become the *acte imaginaire* of the contemporary era, and in campaigns as wide-ranging as the battle over Antietam during the US Civil War to the recent war crimes tribunals on Balkan atrocities, the still photo has been treated as a vehicle possessing tremendous potential influence over publics.

The events of September 11 were no exception. Unusual in that they unfolded in real time for a global public through the news media, the events of September 11 were shaped largely through their visual representation. Images were everywhere. As the planes hit the World Trade Center, people ran to their television sets and stayed there for hours on end, watching an endless loop of reruns of the actual attack whose ordering began to look more like still photographs than moving images.[2] When people began to dislodge themselves from their televisions over the following days, the popular press provided its own immediate and powerful visualization of what was happening.

Not only did newspapers print late editions that were bursting with photographs over the first few days, but newsmagazines put out mid-weekly photographic supplements structured primarily around images. The popular press was dominated by photographs for days—of the attacks themselves, shattered buildings and streets, people running or grieving, sites of mourning—and they appeared repeatedly on front pages, inside pages, supplementary photographic sections, and double-page pictorial spreads. They appeared in groups and alone, in color and black-and-white, and with bold captions, connected only in broad strokes like headings such as "Terror in America." The predominance of photographs persisted as the days of unfolding events turned into weeks. The *New York Times* continued to publish more photos, bigger photos, and more colour photos in the months following September 11 than in the preceding time period, with each edition typically offering twice as many photos as the editions from before September 11.[3] No wonder, then, that by the end of November one poll reported that the percentage of people watching network television had dropped dramatically, while those depending on the popular press for information had tripled from the first week after the attacks (Pew 2001). Not only was the longstanding distinction between television and the press invoked—with print newsrooms, in one news executive's words, providing "context and explanation" alongside the briefer news-breaks of television (Mike Phillips in *Crisis Journalism* 2001: 13)— but the visual dimension of the popular press offered an accessible and memorable way to retain shards of the horrific story as it unfolded. Within this template, pictures played a crucial role as tools of recovery.

This is key, for despite photography's role in alleviating trauma, in journalism photographs draw upon a troubled relationship with the words at their side. Even today, some 150 years after the birth of photography and over 70 years after the arrival of wire-photo, there are still no definitive guidelines for how to select and use photographs in news. Assumptions about accreditation, captioning, and the mere placement of images in the newspaper or news magazine—how to connect a text and a picture—are largely intuitive. While the reliance on intuitive cues for selecting and using photographic images is problematic in the normal ups and downs of news selection and presentation, it becomes particularly so during crisis or trauma, when the lead-time involved in responding to news events is substantially reduced and decision-making takes place under tension. In such circumstances how do photographers and their editors know how to respond? From where do they take their cues in the coverage of trauma?

It is here that historical precedent becomes relevant. In the best of cases, journalism involves the application of routine practices to unpredictable circumstances (Tuchman 1978). One place from which to gain directives about how to use photographs in covering trauma is from earlier events in other times and places. Sometimes, comparisons can be invoked between events not necessarily similar in content because the form of their visual representation is seen as similar. This means that events not necessarily alike might receive a similar visual treatment in the news because the events can invoke a similar spectator response.

Such was the case with the events of September 11. Although the photos of September 11 were likened to the depictions of diverse historical events— including Iwo Jima, Pearl Harbor, the Kennedy assassination, the *Challenger* explosion, and the airplane crash in which J. F. Kennedy Jr died—one historical precedent was particularly apt in positioning journalists and the public with regard to the events of September 11. This was journalism's photographic address to the liberation of the concentration camps of World War II, which was repeated almost in full following the events of September 11. Responses to both events were structured as instances of what the literature on trauma calls "bearing witness."

This is curious, for the Holocaust and September 11 were fundamentally dissimilar events. One occurred during a world war, the other the result of a terrorist attack. Unlike the Holocaust, an event intended not to be seen, the attacks of September 11 were meant to be witnessed, photographed, and filmed. While photographs of the Holocaust were taken against the will of the perpetrators, September 11 needed visualization to exert its enormous symbolic value, even beyond the number of actual casualties. Moreover, while the images from 1945 showed the damage inflicted on individual people, the images of September 11 showed a plane damaging a building, leaving spectators to imagine what it was like in the building for those trapped inside.

Journalism's response to September 11 was thus not a novel reaction to events even if it was based on a faulty parallel. Rather, historical record became its pedagogical template, an earlier precedent that had successfully employed photography to move collective sentiment from shock and horror into a post-traumatic space demanding responsiveness and action. In other words, US journalism— needing to respond yet having no obvious template through which to shape its response—went back in time to find a singular event that could provide such a template—and it found it in the liberation of the concentration camps in World

51

War II. The parallel response to the two events, however, obscures differences in the events themselves. This raises questions about the implications of and reasons for invoking a parallel that requires positioning basically dissimilar events as alike.

## Bearing witness and photography

It has long been argued that bearing witness offers one way of working through the difficulties that arise from traumatic experience. Bearing witness brings individuals together on their way to collective recovery. Defined as an act of witnessing that enables people to take responsibility for what they see (Zelizer 1998: 10), bearing witness moves individuals from the personal act of "seeing" to the adoption of a public stance by which they become part of a collective working through trauma together. In Shoshana Felman's words, bearing witness is "not merely to narrate, but to commit oneself and . . . the narrative to others: to take responsibility for history or for the truth of the occurrence . . . [it is] an appeal to community" (Felman 1992: 204). The act of bearing witness helps individuals cement their association with the collective as a post-hoc response to the trauma of public events that, however temporarily, shatter the collective. By assuming responsibility for the events that occurred and reinstating a shared post-hoc order, bearing witness thus becomes a mark of the collective's willingness to move toward recovery.

Bearing witness, as a collective response to events taking place across time and space, depends on mediated forms of representation, by which the media help people encounter the events as a prelude for taking responsibility for them. Still photographs have been a viable way of encountering events since photography's inception in the mid-1800s, particularly events requiring public response. From the US Civil War—when the popular press was not yet equipped to handle photographs, but sidewalk exhibits and the display of engravings of both the dead at Antietam and prisoners in Confederate prison camps prompted fierce public debate—to World War I—when extensive censorship regulations restricted images, prompting one photojournalist to say that "photographs seem to be the one thing that the War Office is really afraid of" (Jimmy Hare cited in Goldberg 1991: 195)—photographs were assumed to have influential power.

The photograph came of age, however, during the course of World War II. This coincided with wire-photo's introduction, where the ability to send and receive photos as quickly as words meant that photos could be accommodated from the onset in shaping public reaction to distant events. Photos were quickly recognized as tools of persuasion, with one such photo, of three dead American soldiers, helping to mobilize the purchase of war bonds (Goldberg 1981: 199). By the time the concentration camps of Nazi Europe were liberated in April and May of 1945, the recognition of photography was more solid. No surprise, then, that the record of the camps' liberation, possibly the signal event requiring a public response of bearing witness, was characterized by the wide-ranging and frequent display of still photographs. Seeing the photos helped turn lingering disbelief and skepticism about what had happened in Nazi Europe into a stunned recognition that the stories of Nazi atrocity were true.

## The original template

Journalism's response to the horrors of the concentration camps of World War II provided a way of bearing witness that allowed publics near and far to take responsibility for what was transpiring in the camps. Facing a diminishing level of American public support for the war, General Eisenhower recognized that the scenes of the camps were a powerful way of driving home what the Allies were doing in distant lands and why their presence was needed. He ordered photographers within a 100-mile radius to reach the camps and take images, arranged tours of the camps for parliamentarians and editors, and facilitated the display of atrocity images in sidewalk exhibits, theatres, and auditoriums.

The response to the call to bear witness was swift and wide-ranging. Complying with military and governmental imperatives, journalists and photographers toured the camps and recorded what they saw in full detail. Photographic spreads and detachable supplements were published daily in nearly every US newspaper and newsmagazine for over three weeks, showing scores of images in a way not yet imagined by the public. These images of atrocity—what I have called the photographic aesthetic of the Holocaust—offered the primary depictions of Nazi horror (Zelizer 1998).

The images were wide-ranging in their diversity yet systematic in their patterned depiction of what had transpired. Beyond the now-familiar images of scenes of human carnage and devastation, one primary visual focus was the act of bearing witness. The images emphasized in some fashion the capacity not only to see horror but the response that came with "looking" at horror. In this regard, the act of bearing witness provided the linchpin of the broader photographic response to atrocity. It was essential to establish that the photos were assisting people "to see" what had happened.

Around that linchpin, an elaborated aesthetic evolved that offered various extensions of the very act of bearing witness. Photos depicted different kinds of people in varying witnessing practices. Much attention was paid to groups of people, depicted as collectives to help offset the disbelief that still lingered around what had happened. Images showed people looking at stacks of bodies or open boxcars. Visiting delegations, soldiers, or German civilians brought into the camps under Eisenhower's denazification campaign were depicted in the act of looking. People were shown looking at atrocities that were not depicted, forcing spectators to fill in what they knew existed but was nowhere within the camera's frame. And images showed people looking at photographic exhibits of the atrocities. In short, "to see" what had happened was the ultimate public response, in that it signified a level of responsibility on the part of publics who had until then largely been unresponsive. Photography—with its still, frozen images that could be looked at again and again—helped shape that response, both in the pictures it produced and repeatedly displayed and in the uses of images that it facilitated (Zelizer 1998).

All of this suggests that the elaborated template for bearing witness in 1945 created a rich precedent for using photographic images to respond to horror, trauma, and the aftermath of other atrocious events. Although no other event in the following years came close to causing the devastation perpetrated by the Nazis, the precedent nonetheless established a standard of coverage of trauma for journalists. It signaled to journalists to highlight photographic images when traumatic events required extensive attention and responsiveness. Photographs, then, were woven into the record expected in the aftermath of traumatic public events.

## Repeating the template's form

Despite the availability since 1945 of this elaborated journalistic template, with its focus on photography as a key dimension of bearing witness, the events of September 11 were the first set of events to repeat it almost completely. For the first time since 1945, photographs appeared and reappeared after September 11 in large numbers and great frequency, in places of central prominence, and with memorable markers. Even when a short-lived ban prohibited photography of the site, the sheer willingness of the popular press to turn over its pages to accommodate pictures and continually show them was key in building an act of bearing witness parallel to that seen in 1945. Moreover, the focus on photographs continued beyond the event's expected closure—the three- or four-day period of photographic documentation that has tended to characterize other traumatic events[4]—and the rich template for bearing witness sustained the images' display into the days and weeks that followed. Photographs appeared in a more sustained fashion, more frequently and repeatedly, and in more parts of the journalistic record.

This near-full repeat of the Holocaust aesthetic was distinct from what had been portrayed during the 50-odd intervening years since the liberation of the Nazi concentration camps. During those years, no other event was accorded the same degree of photographic attention as that given Nazi atrocity. Traumatic events received targeted but limited photographic coverage, often reduced to the circulation of certain memorable images. Events echoing the horror of Nazi atrocity—barbarism toward civilians in Cambodia, Bosnia, or Rwanda, for example—called for a marked level of public visibility but received instead a narrowed visual photographic template. In these latter cases, photographs of bearing witness eschewed the varieties of depiction seen in 1945, featuring none of the shots of various kinds of people engaged in varying witnessing practices. Even the fundamental group shot of collectives bearing witness disappeared (Zelizer 1998).

Moreover, when photographs did appear they became quickly iconic, burdened with a representational force that was not supported by extensive depiction. To be sure, photography in certain events helped mould public response: for instance, the brutal shots of police racism in Birmingham, Alabama in 1963 created a public furore and spurred the government to take action over the violations of civil rights (Goldberg 1981). Yet they were few in number, narrowed in focus, and iconic or symbolic rather than referential in nature.

This changed with the events of September 11. Here, as in 1945, photographs took center stage, and they did so primarily by expanding upon presentational strategies used in 1945. As one editor saw it, the events of September 11 did not put "to use a 'new standard' [for photographs] at all. It is a tradition of American journalism that when the event or history is raised to a level of great importance, we use pictures to reflect that importance" (Bill Marinow cited in Nesbitt 2001a: 23). But the only precedent for the scope, scale, and magnitude of such photos dated to 1945. Thus, the *New York Times* featured over 50 photos in its front section the day after the attacks, a tendency echoed in other newspapers, compared with the 20 or so that were normally displayed. Even one month later, the use of photos remained proportionately high, when a full 52 photos graced the paper's front section and accompanying reportage on September 11 (*New York Times*, October 12, 2001). In *Times*' picture-editor Philip Gefter's words, September 11 "caused a sea change" in the then-current use of photographs (cited in Hirsch 2002).

In form, the sheer prominence, number, and centrality of the photos echoed that displayed more than 50 years earlier. Detachable photographic supplements, mid-week newsmagazine photographic editions, pictorial spreads, and photographic sections all hearkened back to the wide display of images made available during World War II. The display of photographs was ongoing. Not only did newsmagazines and daily newspapers utilize more photos than usual, but certain newspapers initiated new venues to accommodate the marked interest in the event's visual representation. Leading here was the *New York Times*, which initiated both "Portraits of Grief," a memorial tribute to those killed on September 11 that featured photographs and short vignettes about each person lost, and "A Nation Challenged," a special section on the events of September 11 that became a place for displaying relevant photographs alongside texts. In the latter case, high numbers of photos were prominently displayed, covered larger portions of the page than usual, were featured in color as well as black and white, and figured as central visual markers of a broader news story. One typical section alone ran over 35 photographs, including two full-page photographic spreads (*New York Times*, September 23, 2001). Other newspapers set off portions of their front sections by devoting them to September 11 with graphic logos and banner headlines; here too photos were prevalent.

The foregrounding of photography following September 11 had many aspects—in images' selection, presentation, design, and contextualization. Images were selected with great care and thoughtfulness because, in one editor's view, "the pictures meant everything" (Wenner 2001: 32). Debates in newsrooms tackled how many pictures to use, how to group them, and where to feature them. Pictures in newspapers covered full pages, half pages, and quarter pages; in newsmagazines, they appeared as double pages and in pull-outs three-pages wide, with simple broad captions, often shared across images, and little extraneous text. In its first full issue after the attacks, for instance, *Newsweek* featured ten separate double- and triple-page photographic spreads only four days after it had put out its own independent mid-week photographic supplement ("Special Report: God Bless America" 2001). Photos tended to be captioned broadly, as in "Bearing Witness" or "Icon of Evil." And in a manner reflective of photos from 1945, images documented the broad collective response to the tragedy as much as the contingent event at hand: One *New York Times* article on the state of air-line travel was accompanied by a photograph of the National Guard patrolling the World Trade Center site (McFadden 2001). The connection between image and text made sense only by invoking the larger sensibilities regarding terror that had been raised in the days after September 11, even if those sensibilities were not mentioned in the article adjoining the photograph. Thus, even if photos were not given specific captions and were not presented in direct link with the texts at their side, they documented the larger story of horror.

Additional practices helped underscore photography's centrality. For instance, the *New York Times* layered its presentation of images by highlighting and adding color to sets of photos on themed pages, such as "Waving flags and fists" or "A day of prayer" (*New York Times* 2001a; *New York Times* 2001c). Other practices had to do with visual layout. Newspapers on the days immediately following September 11 typically used front page design strategies that focused on photographs, including the "dominant art" page—which used 60 percent or more of the front page "to display the chilling images of the day"—and the "funeral front"—which used black ink "to make the images stand out and provide a visual sense of the tragedy" (Nesbitt 2001b: 19).

Two characteristics, both reflective of the template from 1945, were striking about this display of photos. First, the same images tended to be shown time and again, with no direct linkage to the time in which the event depicted had occurred. Thus, an image of the planes striking the towers was shown repeatedly—the next day, the following week, the next month, and at year's end. Such a display pattern itself suggested that the photographs served the aim of bearing witness more directly than that of establishing newsworthiness, which would have discredited a repeated display of the same image. Second, the images tended to repeat the depiction of other images in the same display set. For instance, in its issue following the events of September 11, one magazine published 18 separate images of people running from the World Trade Center (*People* 2001). In both cases, newsworthiness was pushed aside to accommodate the images' role in helping people bear witness.

Unlike the template of 1945, historical precedent was visually invoked here in helping journalists explain the event. Throughout the coverage, pictures of earlier events abounded alongside the photographs of September 11. For instance, the *Philadelphia Inquirer* featured photographs from the 1993 bombing of the World Trade Center and the bombed hull of the *USS Cole* (pictures appended to Goldstein 2001) and positioned two photos side by side—one of the 1941 assault on Pearl Harbor, the other of the collapsed World Trade Center towers (pictures appended to Infield 2001). In both cases, the willingness to lend valuable news-space to pictures from the past underscored the unusual value of both history and photography in shaping coverage of this event.

In sum, the act of seeing was a central part of shaping a public response to the events of September 11. To see also meant to start the road to recovery. As one front-page headline termed it, "Many Come to Bear Witness at Ground Zero" (Murphy 2001). It is no surprise, then, that journalism itself loosened its adherence to usual norms of newsgathering and presentation to frame the act of seeing as an integral part of coverage.

## Repeating the template's content

In content, the act of bearing witness was strikingly similar to that displayed in 1945. Pictures displayed a wide-ranging repetition of the various depictions of bearing witness that had appeared in earlier years. Repeating the Holocaust aesthetic helped establish the act of bearing witness as a prolonged moment of depiction within the broader coverage.

There was a certain mission driven into the display of photographs that went beyond the aims and goals of journalism. Although the still images after September 11 underscored a response to a surgical strike completed before cameras ever reached the site, the repetitive display of photos accompanied the onset of war that was a retaliation after the fact. Photos of ruin, victims, and memorialization were central to mobilizing support for the political and military response yet to come.

Thus, the display of the still photograph as a relay of memorialization and grieving, uppermost in the days after the attacks, went alongside the propaganda appeal of the same photos. Not only were numerous public grieving spots erected with pictures of the missing, but people posted family photos of individuals about whom they still hoped to gain information. The press followed with this impulse, perhaps best exemplified in the *New York Times*' section "Portraits of Grief," where the still photograph took on a central role in moving people through the grieving process.

Yet there were other dimensions of photography's display that catered directly to what had been seen in 1945. As then, again the photographic aesthetic had four main parts, each depicted repeatedly: the site of the attack—primarily the World Trade Center; people witnessing the site of the attack; people witnessing the site of the attack without depiction of the site itself; and people viewing depictions of the site of the attack (primarily photographs) or taking photographs themselves. Each category of depiction featured a return of the group shots seen predominantly in 1945. Together, these depictions—which, other than initial pictures of the attack site, were not particularly newsworthy—offered a way for publics to bear witness to the horror of what was transpiring. At the same time, they filled a broader mandate by allowing people "to see" as a way to signal their responsiveness to what had happened and to what would yet take place.

## The site of the attack

The majority of photographs in the first days after the events of September 11 featured the World Trade Center far more frequently than the Pentagon or the open field in western Pennsylvania. Newspapers and newsmagazines portrayed the burning or smoking World Trade Center towers as they progressed to smoking rubble. While smaller pictures offered depictions of people running from the attacked buildings, the images of the towers themselves functioned like "a kind of wallpaper" (Potter 2001).

The World Trade Center depictions offered a way of visually marking the journey from trauma to recovery. The first images showed the planes hitting the towers of the site, the towers on fire, and the towers imploding (see Figure 3.1).

Later pictures showed the towers being reduced to rubble. In one collection of front-page depictions the day after the attacks, 85 percent of the front pages displayed shots of the burning towers (Poynter Institute 2001). The front pages of some newspapers—the *Los Angeles Times*, the *Dallas Morning News*, and the *Tennessean*, among others—showed a series of shots of the building crumbling. After the pictures of the standing towers faded, they gave way to evolving depictions of the towers as they diminished in size. Images were also taken from alternative angles, such as sky views (picture appended to *Philadelphia Inquirer* 2001: A17). In magazines and journals, the towers appeared on covers and were shown repeatedly even within the same newspaper or journal. From *Newsweek* and *Time* to *In These Times*, *Business Week* and *TV Guide*, the towers were established very quickly as the predominant visual marker of the events of September 11.

The towers in their various forms were depicted in ways that extended the function of images in non-crisis journalism. The photograph of the burning towers was turned into a logo by the *Philadelphia Inquirer* during the first days after the attacks. An image of the rubble of the site became the focus of an advertisement, in which the United Way used it to justify giving money for relief (*New York Times*, September 16, 2001). Certain depictions displayed the towers in the pre-September 11 era: on September 13 the *New York Times* ran a pair of shots showing the same skyline before and after September 11 (pictures appended to Dunlap 2001). This kind of photograph was repeatedly displayed in newsmagazines and journals, despite its seeming lack of newsworthiness.

In that these pictures played such a central role in the broader act of bearing witness, it is no surprise that they continued to appear months after the September 11 attacks. Images of the towers appeared repeatedly over time, with the shot of the burning towers featured at year's end as *Newsweek*'s cover photo of its

*Figure 3.1* (Timepix)

special year-end double issue (*Newsweek* 2001–2). On December 31, 2001, the image topped a special *New York Times* section entitled, "The Year in Pictures." As late as January of 2002, visiting dignitaries from Korea were shown in the *New York Times* looking over the rubble of Ground Zero, while in late February photographs portrayed the last point of excavation in the site. In March, newspapers displayed repeated shots of the six-month memorial services at the site.

Newspapers and newsmagazines continued to document the site's evolving status, which became a visual corollary of the public's journey away from trauma. This suggests that in much the same way that the concentration camps liberated in 1945 became the insignia for Nazi horror, the World Trade Center became the visual signature of the events of September 11.

In this way, depictions of the towers became key to the act of bearing witness. As with the liberation of the concentration camps in 1945, the presumption here was that people needed to "see" what had happened so as to mobilize a public response to the events. Although "seeing" became possible via the numerous pilgrimages that people made to the site of the attack, initially the capacity to see was restricted to the depictions offered by the media. And while television offered its own version of what had happened, the still photograph's frozen ephemerality and materiality emerged as a powerful and effective way of visually encountering the horrific event.

## People witness the site of the attack

Photographs also appeared that showed people witnessing the site themselves. Portraying people posed alongside the rubble offered a basic depiction of bearing witness that was crucial for recovery. In a fashion directly reminiscent of the visits arranged by Eisenhower to the concentration camps, New York City Mayor Rudolph Giuliani "made a point of personally ferrying heads of state, United States senators and other lawmakers and leaders to the site." In the *New York Times*' view, he did so because "they need to see for themselves what happened," both "to get them angry" but also to "drum up financial support for the city and military support" (cited in Steinhauer 2001). People's ability to see what had happened was thus woven into the journey to a post-traumatic space.

Key here were the firefighters and emergency medical technicians who were involved in rescue and recovery efforts. In a sobering prediction of how little the rescue efforts would actually find, one of the first photos on September 12 focused on firefighters alongside the rubble, under a caption that told readers that they were looking at "firefighters peering at the ash and rubble" (picture appended to Schmemann 2001: A15). Already then, the firefighters' work was portrayed as an act of looking rather than doing, itself a grim indicator of how difficult their job would be.

Individuals were portrayed in the act of bearing witness, as in Figure 3.2 from the *Philadelphia Inquirer*. But far more prevalent were depictions of groups engaged in the act of collective looking. These witnesses included members of official delegations, including that of the mayor, the US President, humanitarian organizations such as the Red Cross, and foreign delegations. Group shots of such witnesses were portrayed almost daily over more than a month of coverage, with people positioned as an embodiment of the broader public response to the attack.

Other than identified public personalities, the majority of photos depicted

*Figure 3.2* (AP/Wide World Photos)

anonymous masses of people in proximity to the site. Usually unidentified crowds were shown visiting the impromptu memorial sites and information centers. Unnamed rescue workers were depicted as they began to work through debris. Central here were large-scale pilgrimages, trekking to the site after it was reopened and viewing platforms erected. Rarely were these people identified other than by group membership, such as "mourners" or "rescue workers." Some images showed people looking at the Pentagon (picture appended to Clines

2001), though as with pictures of the site itself these were markedly fewer than those of witnesses around the World Trade Center. The press also periodically ran photos of memorial services and relatives paying homage at the site (pictures appended to Merzer 2001; *New York Times* 2001e; *New York Times* 2001g; *New York Times* 2001h).

As in 1945, displaying the act of looking in the press was important not because of its newsworthiness but because it performed a therapeutic function. The photos reminded people of the importance of responding to the tragedy, even if that response was limited to the act of bearing witness. Keeping the site visible also made it easier to mobilize support for the US military and political response in Afghanistan.

## People witness an undepicted site of the attack

Photographs also portrayed people looking at the site without evidence of the site itself. This kind of photo is unusual in news, for it lacks newsworthiness and thereby departs most strongly from journalistic convention.

Yet this kind of shot, common in 1945, persisted here too for a fundamental reason, already hinted at in the earlier categories of depiction: The need "to see" outpaced the need to provide newsworthy documentation of what was happening. Thus, already on the day after the attack, two separate pictures in the *New York Times* depicted people staring at some horror not shown in the shot (pictures appended to Dwyer and Sachs 2001; Schmemann 2001: A14). Even amateurs

*Figure 3.3* (Angel Franco, *New York Times*)

reproduced this kind of photo, walking onto the streets of New York City in order to take pictures of "what they found" there (Witty 2002).

The depiction of spectators here was important, for connecting individuals to the collective helped support the aim of bearing witness. Thus, it continued to appear repeatedly: the *New York Times* reran the photo depicted in Figure 3.3 three separate times: first directly after September 11, then again on September 16 under the telling title "Bearing Witness" (*New York Times* 2001d), and then again eight days later in an article about the fear of New Yorkers (*New York Times* 2001b: B8). In neither of the later appearances was mention made that the photograph had been taken days earlier.

This kind of photo was crucial, for it forced spectators to fill in what was known but not pictured beyond the camera's frame. Understanding a photo of this sort required the spectator to call to mind the slew of other images already seen—of the towers, people grieving, or rubble and devastation—and thus helped connect each concrete depiction with the larger story about terrorism. That larger story, in turn, was necessary for mobilizing public support for the military actions in Afghanistan.

## People and photos of the site of the attack

The fourth kind of photo underscored the centrality of photos as documents in the collective act of bearing witness. This kind of photo had two main thematic focal points—looking at photos and taking photos. In each, the act of bearing witness was elaborated by including photographic shots as material evidence both in the documentary record and its ensuing historical record.

Pictures of people looking at photos of September 11 followed on the heels of the earliest images of people looking at television screens the day after the attack (pictures appended to Burringer and Fabrikant 2001). As the primary visuals of events gave way to still photos, the press began to run depictions of people looking at photographs of the site. Appearing in newspapers, journals, and newsmagazines, these shots stood in for a general inaccessibility to the site, particularly during the few weeks that it was closed to the public.

Dozens of photographic exhibits related to September 11 opened. One such exhibit, pictured in Figure 3.4 (see next page), was crowded with visitors from its opening in late September. Entitled "HereIsNewYork: A Democracy of Photographs," the exhibit displayed over 4,000 images taken by hundreds of professional and amateur photographers and strung on wires across the ceilings and walls (Zelizer 2002). In one organizer's words, "the photographs are the memorial to September 11" (Traub 2001).

A second impulse involved taking photos. Although the city imposed a ban on taking photographs of the site that stayed in effect until early October, once it was lifted the press ran shots of people crowding barricades to take photographs of the site. While the site itself tended not to be depicted in these shots, numerous images ran of people creating their own documentary record (picture

63

# Snapshots Of Sept. 11: A Gathering Of Witnesses

By ROBERTA SMITH

Nancy Siesel/The New York Times
Visitors to 116 Prince Street are surrounded by images of Sept. 11.

"We're making this up as we go along," said Charles Traub as he stood in a storefront at 116 Prince Street in SoHo, surrounded by a quiet swarm of people.

Some were hunched over computers and scanners or tending printers; others were busy with papers, cellphones and visitors at a table in the back. Most, however, were studying the photographs lining the walls floor to ceiling and strung overhead. All the images pertained to a subject most of the visitors knew by heart: the Sept. 11 attack on the World Trade Center and its aftermath.

The images are the core of "Here Is New York: A Democracy of Photographs," an unusual exhibition that is the latest form of grass-roots public mourning, like the shrines, sidewalk drawings and expanses of writ-ten messages that sprang up around New York in the days just after the attack. But the exhibition may also be a major archive in the making, one that reflects history in a new, egalitarian way, containing images by professionals and amateurs alike.

And like the big soup kitchens set up by TriBeCa restaurateurs to feed the rescue workers at ground zero, the exhibition is also another instance of New Yorkers trying to contribute to the physical or emotional mending of the city by pursuing their usual lines of work, only differently.

The show represents the photography world's attempt to reveal and enable people to experience one of many signal facts about the tragedy: that it was witnessed and photographed by more people than any event of a similar magnitude.

Some of the pictures on display were taken by professional photographers who rushed to the scene minutes after the attack began; they have appeared in magazines and newspapers. But just as many were

Continued on Page 4

*Figure 3.4* (N. Seisel, *New York Times*)

appended to "Photographs allowed" *New York Times* 2001f). The titles to these photos—such as "bearing witness" (Murphy 2001)—were telling for the directed interpretation the act of looking was given.

As with the other categories of depiction, these images helped prolong the act of witnessing. They were central to the larger aims of moving toward recovery and mobilizing support, though not particularly relevant to norms of journalistic newsgathering and presentation. Together, these categories of depiction created a space for shaping public response to the events of September 11 that had little to do with the aims and goals of journalism in non-crisis times. Photography thus helped extend journalism's function beyond that normally accorded it.

## What was not repeated

The template of 1945, however, was not repeated in its entirety. One type of depiction was missing altogether after September 11—that of bodies and human devastation. Images of corpses, body parts, and human gore were absent from the coverage following the events. Unlike the repeated display of stacks of corpses and open gaping pits of bodies seen in 1945, here the images of bodies were simply excised from view. "We chose not to show a lot," said one news executive

(Erik Sorensen cited in Rutenberg and Baringer 2001: A24). One picture of a perfectly formed and severed human hand appeared in the *New York Daily News'* evening edition the night of the attacks. But it disappeared by the following day.

The closest that the press came to showing human bodies in photographs was in the uneven depictions of people hanging out of upper-story windows or jumping to their deaths from the burning towers. Yet here too fierce discussions ensued, with the images' display "heavily debated" among picture assignment editors at the major newspapers (ibid.: A20). One editor justified the selection of a particularly difficult photograph—the Associated Press' picture of a man falling headfirst to his death from the World Trade Center towers—by comparing it with earlier difficult photos, such as the Eddie Adams shot of a Vietcong officer being shot or that of the napalmed girl running down a Vietnamese street (Bill Marinow in Nesbitt 2001a: 23). Yet when these images did appear—for instance, in the *Chicago Tribune, Washington Post, Philadelphia Inquirer,* and the *New York Times*—they were displayed discreetly, appearing generally on inside rather than front pages and in black-and-white rather than color. By the weekend, they basically disappeared from view, appearing in few newsmagazines, and remained out of view in much of the commemorative literature over the following months (Zelizer 2003, in press). What remained instead was the reigning image of the burning towers, where we were left to imagine—rather than see—the bodies dying inside. The towers, then, displaced the bodies that might have been visualized instead.

This means that the template of 1945 was fully repeated except for the core reason underlying the parallel between the two events—the devastating loss of innocent civilian human life. It may be that the close parallel between the photographic responses facilitated leaving the bodies unseen in the later event. In this respect, the lack of visualization repeats that accorded the images of just about every other event involving carnage seen in earlier years. Repeating other aspects of the earlier response made it possible to substitute the visualization of bodies from 1945 for the bodies not seen in 2001. There was, in effect, no need "to see" the bodies in the later event, for the structural similarities in presentation called to memory the corpses of earlier times.

## Conclusion: when the past stands in for the present

What does it mean to say that the popular press borrowed from a template set in place for a different kind of event that occurred more than 50 years earlier? Three separate answers can be offered to that question, each of which involves the distinct functions of photography in the events of September 11—photography as an integral part of journalism, as a tool for easing post-traumatic dissonance, and as a mobilizer of support for strategic action.

Photography's function as an integral part of journalism is what allowed the press to run the images in the first place. Yet while people applauded September 11 for "changing the meaning of photography" (Ferresto 2002), the lack of standards for incorporating images in journalism remains the same as it was in 1945. The only guideline existing now that did not exist then is precedent. But even the precedent for covering unusual events like September 11 is riddled with incomplete directives and insufficient standards. As in 1945, September 11 produced more pictures, bigger pictures, and more prominent pictures. But their precise relation to the texts around them or to the events they depict remains as amorphous as it was half a century ago. The willingness to lend increased space to press photos in times of crisis, without clarifying the guidelines for doing so, needs to be further examined.

The second function of photography provides an answer to that left unaddressed in the first. Although photos do not follow existing journalistic guidelines particularly well, they are powerful tools for easing the dissonance caused by public trauma. Just as a child reaches mastery over difficult tasks by repetition, so too does the repeated display of images work its way into acceptance or acquiescence. Yet because this function is not a part of journalism's official sense of itself, there are no guidelines for optimum journalistic performance. This means that in times of crisis, the press shifts to a mode of photographic relay that proceeds without any directive other than historical precedent. Bearing witness thus becomes instrumental because it offers a precedent for shaping photography even when it goes beyond journalism's normal mandate of providing news. In other words, bearing witness allows unusual news judgments to be made in a way that facilitates faulty comparisons across events.

All of this highlights photography's third function, by which it facilitates the accomplishment of certain military and political strategic ends. While the visuals of September 11 helped the public work through its trauma, they also made it easier to mobilize support for the war in Afghanistan. Significantly, that war has also not been seen. Thus, the extensive visualization of September 11 stands in here too for an undepicted continuation of those events. We are seeing many pictures, but what we see are not necessarily the most newsworthy images. This in turn raises questions about the ultimate value of the parallel that has been constructed, for whom and to what end.

On all three counts, we see here how the past works its way into the present. Yet the establishment and maintenance of a parallel between events with no seeming internal resemblance to each other raises questions about the workability of the parallel. It suggests that parallels can be struck by journalism not only when events are similar but also when the surrounding mandates for interpreting them resemble each other. This should give us pause. As informed publics, we need to be asking closer questions about the impact of such parallels on our capacity to produce critical readings of events in the public sphere. For their uncritical acceptance suggests not only that we are complacent about seeing less when we should be seeing more. But that in seeing what seems like more we in fact still see less. And in a post-September 11 era, that may no longer be sufficient.

# Notes

1  Thanks to Bethany Klein for research assistance and to Barbara Kirshenblatt-Gimblett and Marianne Hirsch for commenting on an earlier draft of the manuscript. Parts of this manuscript were presented to the Centre National de Recherch Social Scientifique (CNRS) in Paris, France, in February 2002; to "Voice/Over," a symposium in honor of Roger Abrahams at the University of Pennsylvania in March 2002; and to the Solomon Asch Center for the Study of Ethnopolitical Conflict in April 2002.

2  Indeed, these moving images on loops repeat themselves so often that they come to have the quality of photography. They also appear in the same spaces as photographs, as in the online version of the *New York Times* or CD-ROM documentary compilations. Thus, while the temporal quality of still images and the repetition of moving images differs, the ordering of still images and repetition of moving images make them more alike. Photographs, however, still possess material status, which digital or moving images do not. Thanks to Barbara Kirshenblatt-Gimblett for this point.

3  A comparison of the number of front section photos over the first six days of the crisis, compared with the same time period from the preceding year, went as follows: 12/9/02—17/9/02: 50, 49, 48, 61, 64, and 45 photos; 12/9/01–17/9/01: 22, 19, 21, 27, 24, and 19 photos.

4  The three- or four-day spate of photographs after major traumatic events has been the case in events as wide-ranging as the Kennedy assassination and the *Challenger* explosion. For instance, in the *New York Times* photos of the latter dropped from 30 photos the day after to only six photos within two days.

# References

Barringer, F. and Fabrikant, G. (2001) As an attack unfolds: a struggle to provide vivid images to homes, *New York Times*, September 12: A25.

Clines, F. K. (2001) Stunned tourists, gridlocked streets—fleeing and fear, *New York Times*, September 12: A24.

*Crisis Journalism: A Handbook for Media Response* (2001) Reston, VA: American Press Institute, October.

Dunlap, D. W. (2001) A birth of great praise, a death beyond words for a symbol of strength, *New York Times*, September 13: A14.

Dwyer, J. and Sachs, S. (2001) A tough city is swept by anger, despair, and hopelessness, *New York Times*, September 12: A6.

Felman, S. (1992) The return of the voice: Claude Lanzmann's *Shoah*, in Shoshana Felman and Dori Laub (eds) *Testimony: Crises of Witnessing in Literature, Psychoanalysis and History*, New York: Routledge.

Ferresto, M. (2002) Interview, National Public Radio, March 7.

Goldberg, V. (1991) *The Power of Photography*, New York: Abbeville Publishing.

Goldstein, S. (2001) Speculation on Bin Laden based on past, *Philadelphia Inquirer*, September 13: A9.

Herman, J. (1992) *Trauma and Recovery*, New York: Basic Books.

Hirsch, M. (2002) The day time stopped, *Chronicle of Higher Education*, January 25: B11.

Infield, T. (2001) Tuesday's terror evoked echoes of Pearl Harbor, *Philadelphia Inquirer*, September 13: A11.

Lower, J. (2001) Photos bring the story home, *Crisis Journalism: A Handbook for Media Response*, Reston, VA: American Press Institute, October, 28.

McFadden, R. D. (2001) Airplanes return to the skies, and investigators trace the outlines of a plot, *New York Times*, September 14: A3.

Merzer, M. (2001) US squads enter Afghanistan, *Philadelphia Inquirer*, September 29: A1.

Murphy, D. E. (2001) Many come to bear witness at Ground Zero, *New York Times*, September 18: A1.

Nesbitt, P. (2001a) Tragedy in photos, a new standard?, *Crisis Journalism: A Handbook for Media Response*, American Press Institute, October, 23–5.

Nesbitt, P. (2001b) Designing for a tragedy, *Crisis Journalism: A Handbook for Media Response*, American Press Institute, October, 19–22.

*New York Times* (2001a) After the attacks: waving flags and fists, September 14: A14–15.

*New York Times* (2001b) New York faces fear with prayer and parachutes, September 14: A1, B8.

*New York Times* (2001c) After the attacks: a day of prayer, September 15: A12–13.

*New York Times* (2001d) After the attacks: bearing witness, September 16: A3.

*New York Times* (2001e) A kind of farewell, September 28: B1.

*New York Times* (2001f) Photographs allowed, October 4: B10.

*New York Times* (2001g) A pause for remembrance, October 12: B1.

*New York Times* (2001h) Tokens of Loss, October 29: A1.

*Newsweek* (2001) Special Report: God bless America, September 24.

*Newsweek* (2001–2) September 11, December 31–January 7.

*People* (2001) September 11, 2001, September 24.

Pew Research Center for the People and the Press (2001) *Terror Coverage Boosts News Media's Influence*, November.

*Philadelphia Inquirer* (2001) Wider plot emerges in probe of hijackings, September 19: A1, A17.

Potter, D. (2001) It isn't over, *American Journalism Review*, 23 (9): 76.

Poynter Institute (2001) *September 11, 2001: A Collection of Front Page Newspapers Selected by the Poynter Institute*, Kansas City, MO: Andrews McMeel Publishing.

Rutenberg, J. and Barringer, F. (2001) The ethics: news media try to sort out policy on graphic images, *New York Times*, September 13: A20, A24.

Schmemann, S. (2001) Hijacked jets destroy twin towers and hit Pentagon in day of terror, September 12: A1, A14–15.

Steinhauer, J. (2001) Famous faces with pull get into disaster zone, *New York Times*, October 4: B10.

Traub, Charles (2001) Interview with author, November 13.

Tuchman, G. (1978) *Making News*, New York: Free Press.

Wenner, K. S. (2001) Getting the picture, *American Journalism Review*, 23 (8): 32–3.

Witty, P. (2002) Interview with author, January 28.

Zelizer, B. (1998) *Remembering to Forget: Holocaust Memory Through the Camera's Eye*, Chicago, IL: University of Chicago Press.

Zelizer, B. (2002) Finding aids to the past: bearing personal witness to traumatic public events, *Media, Culture, and Society*, August, 24 (5).

Zelizer, B. (2003) The voice of the visual in memory, in Kendall Phillips (ed.) *Framing Public Memory*, University of Alabama Press, in press.

# Part 2

# NEWS AND ITS CONTEXTS

# 4

# AMERICAN JOURNALISM ON, BEFORE, AND AFTER SEPTEMBER 11

*James W. Carey*

## Journalism on September 11

Before the events in New York and Washington could be grasped as history, they appeared only as chronology and narrative. At 8:50 am on that day, the morning news programs on the major American television networks were coming off a commercial break, ready for what was for most the last segment before switching to game shows, soap operas, and the light chatter that would normally dominate the remainder of the day. As the clock clicked to 8:51, Diane Sawyer, looking typically grave on ABC's *Good Morning America*, broke the flow of the show by saying: "we just got a report that some sort of explosion has occurred at the World Trade Center . . . that a plane may have hit one of the towers." This was six minutes after the crash had actually occurred. A camera aloft on a helicopter to give morning weather and traffic reports immediately went live with a shot of the North Tower, smoke billowing out of gaping holes on two sides of the upper floors.

For viewers of a certain age and those with a historical memory, the event was not without parallel and the immediate thought was of a repeat of the accidental crash of a light plane into the Empire State Building in 1944. Sawyer's tone was measured, even reassuring; we were at the scene of an accident. At 8:53 Sawyer's co-host, Charles Gibson, referred to the explosion at the base of the towers in 1993 and quickly added that he didn't mean to imply an act of terrorism: "We just don't know what has happened."

By 8:54 an ABC correspondent who happened to be in the area was on the phone and on the air to report that he had heard something like a missile overhead, a powerful whooshing sound, the instant before the explosion. He added that he didn't want to cause speculation but he thought, if not a missile, it had to be a large plane, though it sounded as if he favored the former. At 9:02 with the camera still live, another plane, apparently a commercial airliner, suddenly appeared on the right side of the screen and disappeared without a trace into one of the buildings, flames and smoke bursting forth from the left side of the tower.

The reporters were as startled as the viewers. The correspondent exclaimed "Oh my God," Gibson added "that looks like a second plane" and Sawyer asked to "see that scene again so we can be sure we saw what we think we saw." They believed at first that both planes had hit the same tower, the second tower was hidden from the camera behind the first. Moments later the on-the-spot correspondent confirmed that the South Tower, tower two, had been hit, "about half-way down," though "there doesn't seem to be as much damage as to the North Tower." At 9:03 Gibson declared that "this looks like some kind of concerted attack; it is terrifying, awful . . ." thus dropping the first hint that this was more than an accident. Still, both Sawyer and Gibson refrained from speculation as to the nature or source of the aircraft.

By 9:11 ABC, the network that provided the steadiest and most comprehensive coverage, had switched to full alert mode. Peter Jennings, the principal news anchor, took over in the main ABC studios and provided coverage that would continue without commercial break throughout the day. All the substantial resources of the network were immediately brought to bear. A correspondent was with the President on the peregrinations of Air Force One from Florida to Louisiana to Nebraska. Another correspondent was in the Pentagon, though in the early moments unavailable by phone. By 9:12 it was reported that air space over New York had been closed and the city was under lockdown. Information was still scanty so a slow-motion version of the second plane invading the South Tower was repeated every few minutes, as it would be throughout the week that followed. At 9:34 an ABC producer living in the neighborhood phoned in live reports of the sequence of events and the confusion and chaos of lower Manhattan. By 9:37 Jennings was sure the weapon had been a commercial airliner. At 9:44 it was reported that fire had broken out at the Pentagon in an interior courtyard, and that a plane had crashed nearby. It would take another 30 minutes to determine that the Pentagon had been hit by that plane and one wall of the building had collapsed.

At 9:58 the South Tower—the second tower hit—came down before a disbelieving Jennings. Question: "You mean a portion of the tower collapsed?" Answer: "No, the entire building went down, it's gone." A half-hour later, at 10:28, the North Tower imploded, televised in sunlit, theatrical brilliance. Jennings: "Good Lord, it just . . ." The sentence was never completed for at that moment the extraordinary extent of possible casualties became apparent to everyone.

Slowly the magnitude of the events dawned on the reporters. The towers were described as vertical cities fulfilling a dream of Frank Lloyd Wright and Mies van der Rohe. Fully occupied, more than 30,000 people—workers, tourists, travelers, and shoppers—would be inside. Had the planes hit an hour later, after the various exchanges had opened, the shopping plazas filled, subway and railway cars running under the buildings packed, the number of casualties would have been uncountable. As it was, months would pass before even an approximately correct estimate was available.

By 11:00 am the basic details were known and confirmed: the North Tower was struck by American Airlines Flight 11 at 8:45; at 9:03 the South Tower was struck by United Airlines Flight 175; the Pentagon was struck by American Airlines Flight 77. United Airlines Flight 93 had gone down in Shanksville PA, southeast of Pittsburgh. All of this was delivered in a tone of shock but without speculation or accusation. Lessons had been learned at the Oklahoma City bombing when premature speculation pinned it to terrorists from the Middle East.

The performance of ABC on September 11 was typical of the major American television outlets: calm, poised, systematic, without panic or speculation, thorough and factual. Television did what it does the best, covering breaking news, but it did so in a tone of calm assurance that checked any incipient panic. The fact that the disaster occurred in New York, where the resources of the nation's communication system are concentrated, contributed to the success of the coverage, as did the ubiquity of hand-held video cameras. Videotape was quickly available from freelance cameramen and boulevardiers who just happened to be in the area, and the full carnage and destruction were shown from every conceivable angle from the first attack forward. Advertising revenue was willingly sacrificed and enormous resources poured into non-stop coverage. The network was on the air, commercial-free, covering the story for 91 consecutive hours, through the weekend that followed. Throughout the city and nation people queued up before television sets, not only in private homes but in offices and lounges and most of all in pubs, taverns, and restaurants. By noon of September 11 the scene was reminiscent of the day of John Kennedy's assassination, with knots of people collected all over the city exchanging information and condolences and fears about friends who were missing or at least out of touch.

What is apparent on reviewing the videotape is that no one, not the reporters, not the military or intelligence service, grasped what was happening for about two hours following the initial explosion. While it was clear, following the second crash, that these were deliberate acts rather than a spectacular coincidence, no one was sure that the episodes in New York and Washington were not a prelude to an even wider attack on multiple sites across the country. There were fears that the political leadership of the country had been targeted for elimination, and reporters traveling with the President were instructed not to use cell phones lest they be tracked. It took time to determine, as Jennings said more than an hour into his broadcast, that "it was not bombs but passenger planes" that were the weapon of choice. It then took considerable time to account for all the aircraft, private and commercial, aloft in American air space. The television networks knew that President Bush had gone to the "safe place" designed for him in case of a thermonuclear exchange. In the words of one reporter, he "went down into the rabbit hole," into the underground headquarters of the Strategic Air Command in Nebraska, in part for protection (some believed he was the target of a hunt) but also to assemble, via teleconference, the National Security Council. Had these incidents occurred during the Cold War, the bombers would have been aloft, or so one must assume.

The calm and poise of the television networks during these fateful hours of ignorance represented an admirable professionalism. Perhaps it couldn't last. By the end of the day speculation was pouring forth from the political centers of the country. As the week progressed, television coverage degenerated. Banners were unfurled, inevitably in red, white, and blue, along the crawl space at the bottom of the television screen announcing "America at War," or "America under Attack" as if the story were about a basketball or football tournament. News anchors appeared, though not on the networks, with flags pinned to jackets, and patriotism, long banished from television, was unhappily rediscovered. Such journalistic failures were not fully the responsibility of the networks as little help and guidance was forthcoming from the White House. President Bush, finally back in Washington, appeared briefly on television on the evening of September 11 but he said little and did less to explain what happened or to calm frayed nerves. About all he did was register outrage and encourage people to go on with their lives, not to allow the terrorists a victory by altering routine. This was not what people wanted to hear. Following the address, he disappeared until Friday night when he came before Congress to galvanize the legislature and citizenry for a protracted struggle against terrorism. Behind the scenes he encouraged the stock markets to stay open (they did not) so as not to hand a victory to the terrorists.

In the absence of a declaration of a national period of mourning, similar to that following the Kennedy assassination, television and the celebrity community stitched together concerts and other events to raise money but more to provide an outlet for grief and condolence, complementing the spontaneous memorials, mock funerals, prayer meetings, and other acts of emotional identification that sprang up around the city and nation. An ad hoc media event, in the technical sense that Daniel Dayan and Elihu Katz (1992) gave that phrase, was implicitly organized by media and citizen groups to fill the void left by an inert administration. Normal life was suspended by and on television. But without a framework of coverage that could be supplied only by the state—this was a national emergency after all—the television networks and stations lost control, repeating endlessly, as time filler, the scenes of the plane striking tower two, the collapse of both buildings and the carnage and chaos on the ground: a national ceremony became a national nightmare. Endless interviews with the same cast of experts and commentators were repeated across the television dial, each adding little more than uninformed speculation, heightening national fears without providing a coherent account of the past, present, and future.

In the weeks that followed, to make matters worse, the Bush administration in an inept attempt to preempt coverage sent National Security Adviser Condoleezza Rice to hector network executives into self-restraint in re-broadcasting al-Jazeera interviews with Osama Bin Laden, lest they inadvertently transmit propaganda or carry coded instructions from the "terrorist-in-chief" to al-Qaeda operatives worldwide. As the networks were re-nationalized (on which more later), they struggled to find their feet, a position from which to report the news, sympathize with the victims, critique the administration, and skirt the charge of treason. When they erred, they did so on the side of patriotism but the choice is easier to condemn by hindsight than initial judgment. Perhaps one praises television rather too much, because the medium was so completely transformed, if only for a moment, on September 11. The news was rescued from its normal triviality and placed at the center of concerted attention. Gone was enslavement to ratings and advertisers. News was a cost center and a public service rather than a profit center of private pleasure.

It took a national tragedy of epic proportions, as Orville Shell put it, to shake the broadcast media loose from their market servitude and to again exercise leadership. Broadcast journalists were momentarily given the opportunity to pursue their calling as narrators of the central conversation of the culture and we were reminded in the midst of incomparable sadness of the potential of the medium. Again, Shell (2001):

> Given the magnitude of the national tragedy, it was perhaps not surprising that Americans experienced one of the most intense feelings of community within memory. While it is true that such tragedy can bring a nation together like nothing else, it is also true that such togetherness can only be cultured in some sort of commons . . . They helped inform and calm us so that we could keep some part of our critical faculties in abeyance to think reasonably about what had befallen us. The result has been an unprecedented sense of togetherness and common purpose for which we owe a profound debt of thanks to television . . . But above all, what has flickered forth from our screens has been a reminder of what the media can be and do if it is encouraged to keep an eye more on the public's need to know than on ratings.

Newspapers took journalistic leadership over from the television networks within the first week, closely followed by the newsweeklies and journals of opinion. The *New York Times* set the example that other papers, within the limits of resources, followed. The paper quickly established a special, advertising-free section, for once aptly named "A Nation Challenged," that would continue for more than three months. In the section, coverage of the attacks and their aftermath in Afghanistan and elsewhere were centralized. Stories appeared, for the most part thorough and reliable, on every conceivable aspect of the chronicle. The paper threw unimagined resources into the coverage, writing not only about the attacks themselves, the suspected perpetrators, the whereabouts of Osama Bin Laden, the nature of the threat from al-Qaeda, and the response of the Bush administration but the human drama within: "What Muslims think," "How American Muslims were coping," "How the skyscrapers were built," "How anthrax was spread," and dozens of tales of grief and suffering in the city. Best of all was the decision to expand obituaries beyond the famous and celebrated to include every person confirmed dead whose family wanted an obituary. The "Portraits of Grief" section detailed in unique and intelligent ways the lives of ordinary people and gave the suffering meaning in personal terms. This was no act of "do-good" journalism but a response to the actual life of the city, to the memorials (a picture of a firefighter with the note "Has anyone seen my daddy?" tacked to a wall) that spontaneously appeared outside fire stations, in subway stops, along buildings and fences on the perimeter of the World Trade Center site. All of this reflected and organized a useful sense of solidarity and a quickened recognition of the value of public workers. Talk of privatizing the police and firefighters ceased as it dawned on people that only public workers would willingly sacrifice their lives en masse for the welfare of others. Suddenly no one wanted to hear from corporate or entertainment personalities; Rudolph Giuliani so resurrected his career as spokesman for the public good that even his enemies praised him.

## Journalism at the interregnum

If the conduct of the press and television on September 11 and the days and weeks that followed was praiseworthy, that performance only underscored the massive failure of intelligence that lay behind the events. At the instant those three airliners, brimming with jet fuel, slammed into the twin towers and the Pentagon, Americans, and not only Americans, experienced in a moment of nonplussed apprehension a massive failure in intelligence. Military and security intelligence had broken down of course but, more significantly, Americans were face-to-face with an event that defied understanding and for which, despite Oklahoma City, the African embassies, the military compound in Beirut, they were unprepared. The news media, the political class, intellectuals—all the distant and early warning systems of the culture—had failed and Americans were left baffled, muttering questions like "What is going on in the world? Who were these people anyway? What went wrong?" Or, most plaintively, "Why don't they like us?" At the moment of crisis Americans were armed with only a historical analogue: "It's Pearl Harbor all over again." While the comparison lacked precision (this was not an attack of one nation on another), it did register the horror that more people had died on September 11 than on December 7, 1941.

Part of the reason Americans were bewildered was that for the decade following the end of the Cold War journalists along with the intellectual and political class had been on a vacation from reality, preoccupied with one media event after another: OJ, Tanya, Monica–Linda–Bill, Gary, to put handy names to them. The political class was turned into "Davos Man," focused on economic growth, the stock market, interest rates, social security and health insurance, affirmative action, the so-called "culture war." When the first of the reports from the United States Commission on National Security, co-chaired by former senators Warren Rudman and Gary Hart, was issued in September 1999 containing a devastating indictment of the fragmented and inadequate structures and strategies in place to prevent and respond to attacks on US cities, which the commission predicted, it was studiously ignored not only by leading news outlets but by their former colleagues in Congress as well. And the intellectual class, when it was not preoccupied by and writing about the events in the day's headlines, was busily extolling the power and principles (in both spellings and meanings of the word) that fueled economic growth and technological innovation. The words on everyone's lips and pens were globalization, privatization, deregulation, innovation, the Internet and World Wide Web. As far as Americans were concerned, the 1990s were a holiday from history.

All of that came to a temporary end on September 11 and Americans were thrust back into an uncertain world. All that can be said with assurance is that the heady atmosphere of the '90s, the vision of a world united in theory and practice—one market, one culture, one politics, one seamless global communications system—is over, just as assuredly as the guns of August 1914 brought to an end an earlier phase of globalization driven by the telegraph, railroad, underwater cable, the steamship and the gold standard. Whether the consequences will be as devastating—two world wars and a cold war; whether the interregnum will last as long—world trade recovered to 1914 levels only in 1970, capital flows in 1985—no one knows. But whatever happens, it will be on a model different than was planned during the '90s when predictions were based on the laws of economics and technology and when almost everyone took human nature, social relations and political structures as givens, exogenous to the real processes governing the world of affairs. History, politics, and human nature were back on the agenda of the press but the capacity of the media to deal with new realities that were in truth old stories is still in question. There was a failure of journalism on September 11, a failure deeper and more deadly than, say, missing the story of the collapse of the Savings and Loan system in the late '80s. The failure was a collapse of the elites of American journalism.

Recovery took a while and is far from complete. The use of file footage on Afghanistan, Pakistan, and Central Asia was evidence of how long it had been since television reporters had been in such places. Newspaper and broadcast journalists had to be re-stationed around the world because of the elimination of foreign bureaus in an age of "parachute" journalism, and the long, systematic retreat from coverage of the globe had to be reversed. The paradox of declining global media in a putative age of globalization was part of the background as journalists moved quickly to grasp unknown cultures in barely known places. Old lessons had to be relearned before reporting would become intelligible: global expansion does not guarantee peaceful international relations; the global village is an intrinsically fractious place; groups marginalized by history reappear as a militant opposition in the new order of things; globalization breeds both winners and losers and the latter were not likely to be good sports about the whole thing; the values of Davos Man were unlikely candidates for a universal culture.

## Journalism before September 11

To understand journalism's role in the events of September 11 and their aftermath requires, in short, a history of the American press over the last 100 years.

77

As that is impossible here, a brief account will have to suffice until the larger story can be written.

The modern era of journalism stretches from the 1890s to the 1970s. In the United States truly national media and a national audience displaced from a local public did not emerge until the 1890s with the creation of national magazines and a national network of newspapers interconnected via the wire services. These media cut across the structural divisions in society, drawing their audience irrespective of race, ethnicity, occupation, region, or social class. This was the first national audience and the first mass audience and, in principle, it was open to all. Modern communications media allowed individuals to be linked, for the first time, directly to the "imaginary community of the nation" without the mediating influence of regional and local political parties. Such national media laid the basis for a mass society, understood in its most technical and least ideological sense: the development of a form of social organization in which intermediate associations of community, occupation, and class did not inhibit direct linkage of the individual and primary groups to the state and other nationwide organizations through mass communications.

During this period one outlook on journalism dominated the American press. As everything has to have a name if only to have a stick with which to beat it, let us call it modern journalism, described by the terms journalists themselves would use: independent, neutral, adversarial, objective, non-partisan, a genuine Fourth Estate. Modern journalism emerged within the Progressive Movement as a declaration of the independence of journalism from political parties and partisan interests. This was not a declaration, initially at least, of independence from society or democracy nor was it a claim to be neutral about values and priorities. It was solely an insistence to be independent of parties and ideologies.

The progressive movement was a complex phenomenon. The movement contained separate wings, one populist in outlook and the other scientific. Together they sponsored reforms aimed at changing the economic and political system while laying the basis for a modern culture. What held the movement together was above all an attack upon the plutocracy, upon concentrated economic power, and upon the national social class that increasingly had a stranglehold over wealth and industry. The economic dimension of the movement, however, also included the struggle by middle-class, salaried professionals—scientists, intellectuals, lawyers, journalists, social workers, government bureaucrats, etc.—to become a national class, to find a place in the national occupational structure and the national system of class influence and power. The national class of progressive professionals was, in many ways, merely a less powerful imitation, the shadow movement, of the national class of plutocrats, the new titans who ran and controlled industrial America.

Journalists were central to this new progressive class of professionals. The contribution journalists made to the movement was to create a form of writing and reporting that was non-partisan, neutral, fair, objective, in a manner of speaking scientific and, as a crucial characteristic, independent. The needs of a press that was increasingly commercial and monopolistic merged with the Progressive Movement to create a reform-minded journalism that while non-partisan advanced a particular agenda: modernity, a scientific as opposed to an ideological approach to civic matters, opposition to concentrations of wealth and power, hostility to corruption and urban machines, support for civil service over patronage, advocacy of city manager forms of government along with the referendum and recall, everything implied by the phrase "good government." Paradoxically, independent journalism became a new ideology of the press, an ideology aligned with commercial interests as one needed financially strong, successful newspapers to carry out these goals but progressivism supported as well the independent voter over the party loyalist, the civil servant over the party employee, and a rational, scientific approach to public affairs over an ideological program. Journalists formed themselves into national groups and lobbied to professionalize their standing through news organizations such as the American Society of Newspaper Editors. They sponsored histories of their profession and a new reading of the First Amendment along with ethical codes of conduct to justify their newly found status in the middle-class, professional world. Newly emerging schools of journalism played a role as well. These somewhat marginal academic enterprises justified themselves by embracing progressive and modern norms of reporting and writing emphasizing factual accuracy, fairness, neutrality, and disdain for sectarian squabbling. This was a far step from being scientific but it was to cozy up to science and to get as close to that legitimating household of modern intelligence as was possible in a hit-or-miss craft where standards of evidence were weak and evanescent.

All the varied wings of progressivism were joined to one common desire: a desire to escape the merely local and contingent, an enthusiasm for everything that was distant and remote, a love of the national over the provincial. The national media of communication, particularly magazines and books but including as well newspaper journalists who found themselves pursuing a career that took them from city to city and paper to paper, assignment to assignment, were the arena where the progressive program was set out and the place where the struggle for its legitimation occurred.

It was in this situation that the traditions of modern journalism and the particular conceptions of media and democracy formed themselves in mutual relief. The press, in effect, broke away from politics. It established itself, at least in principle, as independent of all institutions: independent of the state, independent of political parties, independent of interest groups. It became the independent voter writ large; its only loyalty was to an abstract truth and an abstract public interest. This is the origins of objectivity in journalism, as Michael Schudson has shown (1978). Objectivity was a defensive measure, an attempt to secure, by quasi-scientific means, a method for recording the world independent of the political and social forces that were shaping it. In this rendition, a democratic press was the representative of the people, of people no longer represented by political parties and the state itself. It was the eyes and ears of a public that could not see and hear for themselves or indeed speak for themselves. It went where the public could not go, acquired information that the public could not amass on its own, tore away the veil of appearances that masked the play of power and privilege, set on a brightly lit stage what would otherwise be contained off stage, in the wings, where the real drama of social life was going on unobserved. The press seized hold of the First Amendment and exercised it in the name of a public that could no longer exercise it itself. The press became an independent profession and a collective institution: a true Fourth Estate that watched over the other lords of the realm in the name of those unequipped or unable to watch over it for themselves.

To carry out the progressive program, journalists invented two new forms of coverage: the beat system and muckraking which later became investigative reporting. The beat system was a "journalism of buildings" as it required posting journalists at the most important sites of government: city hall, the courts, police headquarters, the board of education or, in Washington at the White House, Capitol, Supreme Court and the major federal bureaucracies such as State and Treasury, creating in effect a journalistic shadow government. Muckraking was dedicated to uncovering abuses of power and wrongdoing, both public and private, and also engaging the form of unmasking that in Europe was known as *Ideologiekritik*.

Modern journalism sought and received protection from the courts; indeed the press was the most successful litigant before the Supreme Court during the era. In a series of cases, beginning in the 1920s, the ideology of independent journalism was inscribed into case law: the press was to serve the interests of citizens not of parties, to serve as a Fourth Estate and a check on government, to investigate and seek out the truth without "fear or favor." Supreme Court Justice Potter Stewart gave this outlook one kind of official expression when he wrote that the primary purpose of the constitutional guarantee of a free press was

> to create a fourth institution outside the government as an additional check on the three official branches . . . The relevant metaphor is of the Fourth Estate. The Free Press guarantee is, in essence, a *structural* provision of the Constitution. Most of the other provisions in the Bill of Rights protect specific liberties or specific rights of individuals . . . In contrast, the Free Press Clause extends protection to an institution. The publishing business is, in short, the only private business that is given explicit constitutional protection.
>
> (Stewart 1975: 633)

In furthering this view the courts and legislatures granted special rights to the press denied ordinary citizens: occasional immunity from giving testimony, the right to withhold sources, protection against many libel claims, access to government documents and information. All of those protections were designed to allow journalists to serve as agents of citizens in checking an inherently abusive government.

Modern journalism was never hostile to the state, however. Indeed, journalists looked to the state to engineer social reform and to the courts for protection of their rights. The press was simply hostile to partisan government and corrupt administration. At times of national emergency, such as World Wars I and II and during the periodic "red scares" and on issues of national security, it proved as dependent and subservient as any other patriotic institution. Nonetheless, modern journalism defined a new role for the reporter and editor as figures above and outside political parties and partisan politics.

When broadcasting came upon the scene as an essentially entertainment medium, it was saddled with the responsibility of serving the "public interest, convenience, and necessity." To meet that burden broadcasting stations and networks created news departments that adopted the ideology enshrined in newspapers and within the requirements of regulatory law strove, not always successfully, to perform as independent arbiters of truth and promoters of the values and norms of modernity.

Modern, independent American journalism was always compromised and subject to searching critique because it carried with it strong inclinations toward monopoly and concentrated economic power. This critique reached its zenith with the publication of the report of the Commission on Freedom of the Press in 1946 with its dire warnings of the antidemocratic tendencies of all media. Those warnings were disregarded and modern journalism both reached its apogee and registered its greatest achievements during the Civil Rights Movement and the Vietnam War. Courageous reporters were instrumental in breaking the back of resistance to the extension of equal rights to Black Americans, the ending of restrictions on voting and political participation by Blacks and in bringing the South closer to a national consensus, if not a national will, on race relations. During the Vietnam War, after initial hesitation, the press broke loose from the state even on matters of national security. Reporting from Vietnam turned steadily against the Johnson and Nixon administrations and journalists regularly questioned both the veracity and motives of the military on the ground. While the press generally takes too much credit for ending the war (who can take credit for ending the longest war in the nation's history?) it nonetheless reported the war in broadcasting, newspapers, and magazines with an unusual accuracy, an absence of partisanship and exemplary nerve and daring.

The shortcomings of modern journalism were many. As the old slogan has it, the watchdog may have as often been a lapdog. However, the notion of an independent press as the press which represents the public, a press which unmasks interest and privilege, a press which shines the hot glare of publicity into all the dark corners of the republic, a press which searches out expert knowledge among the welter of opinion, a press which seeks to inform the private citizen, these are ideas and roles which served the nation well through some dark times.

Despite those successes, modern journalism started to unravel in excess and to attract public hostility in the last third of the twentieth century. Nothing exhibits those contrary tendencies better than the two most honored and exemplary episodes of the period, the publication of the Pentagon Papers and the Watergate investigation, which brought down a President.

## The Pentagon Papers and Watergate

These stories are well known so they will only be sketched here. Robert McNamara, the Secretary of Defense during most of the Vietnam War, asked his staff to gather together government documents detailing the "slippery slope" of American engagement in Southeast Asia. He requested this be done as his own doubts about the efficacy of American policy and military engagement in the region became more pronounced. He wanted to leave behind a trail of warnings concerning an inadvertent war that finally entailed massive suffering and destruction, in his words, "to bequeath to scholars the raw material from which they could re-examine the events of the time." Daniel Ellsberg, a member of McNamara's staff, took a copy of these classified documents with him when he left government and later turned them over to a reporter, Neil Sheehan, of the *New York Times*. Sheehan xeroxed the 47 volumes in California and flew them back to New York to his paper. The *Times* rented a floor of a Manhattan hotel in which to study the papers in complete secrecy, a secrecy that extended to staff at the *Times* not directly involved in the project. After some internal debate it was decided not to publish the documents but to craft stories that used the papers as evidence not only of America's progressive involvement in the war but of systematic deception practiced against the citizenry by the state. To support that narrative the *Times* had to go outside the Pentagon Papers, as they were now called, for evidence from the papers alone would not justify such a view.

The *Times* published the first of what was intended as a long series on June 14, 1971. The story was insufferably dull and one assumes largely unread because a committee wrote it. Nonetheless, the Nixon administration sought and was granted a temporary injunction halting publication while the case was adjudicated. The *Times* complied, as the effect of violating the injunction would have made moot the basic issue: does the First Amendment protect the press from government control even in cases of national security. That was the issue and in the past the courts had supported the government in national security cases or implied at least that press freedom stopped at the door of national security. As the case made its way through the courts other papers, the *Washington Post* and *Boston Globe*, initiated publication of the documents.

The case quickly reached the Supreme Court where deeply divided jurists overturned the injunction. Hugo Black arguing for the majority in what was perhaps his finest, certainly his most noted, opinion concluded that:

> In the First Amendment the Founding Fathers gave the free press the protection it must have to fulfill its essential role in democracy. The Press was to serve the governed not the governor. The Government's

power to censor the press was abolished so that the press would remain forever free to censure the government. The press was protected so that it could bare the secrets of government and inform the people. Only a free and unrestrained press can effectively expose deception in government. And paramount among the responsibilities of a free press is the duty to prevent any part of the government from deceiving the people and sending them off to distant lands to die of foreign fevers and foreign shot and shell. In my view, far from deserving condemnation for their courageous reporting, the *New York Times*, the *Washington Post* and other newspapers should be commended for serving the purpose that the Founding Fathers saw so clearly. In revealing the working of government that led to the Vietnam War, the newspapers nobly did precisely that which the Founders hoped and trusted they would do.

(Black 1971)

Chief Justice Warren Burger, in a stinging dissent from Black's opinion, argued that the papers were stolen documents and that journalists, like all citizens, were expected to obey the law. More importantly, he wanted to know the status of "the public's right to know," which the *Times* used as a defense, during the three months the *Times*' staff was holed up in a hotel studying the documents. When did the public's right become effective? When the *Times* received the papers? When the Court received the papers? Moreover, by seeking immediate injunctive relief the *Times* arrogated unto itself a right it denied the Court: the time necessary to study the documents to see if their publication would actually constitute a threat to national security. He was asserting, I believe, that the *Times* was being disrespectful to the Court and arrogating unto itself the right to decide when it was proper to invoke national security. Burger's impatience with the *Times* mirrored a dramatic moment during the hearing when Justice Potter Stewart asked a question of the *Times*' attorney, Alexander Bickel of the Yale Law School, that went, roughly paraphrased, as follows: suppose upon retiring to chambers and reading the documents (which they clearly would not have an opportunity to do), we find that a number of soldiers will die as a result of their publication, How many have to die before we suppress the *Times*' right to publication? One, ten, one hundred? Bickel admitted that his humanitarian impulses trumped the First Amendment when he contemplated 100 deaths, though this was not the answer many at the *Times* and the "friends of the court" wanted. Stewart nonetheless voted with the majority in upholding the *Times*' right to publish.

The journalistic community took the *Times*' victory in the Pentagon Papers case as a collective triumph, as they also did when the reporting of Bob Woodward and Carl Bernstein led to the resignation of Richard Nixon in the Watergate affair. Thanks to a motion picture this episode in press history is even better known than the Pentagon Papers. All it is necessary to note here is one underemphasized moment in the investigation. As Woodward and Bernstein searched for the "smoking gun" that would link President Nixon to the Watergate break-in and subsequent cover-up, the story went cold. No one would talk to the reporters and the *Post*, having crawled out on a limb, felt dangerously exposed to the retaliation of the administration. Ben Bradlee, the editor of the paper, told an interviewer that he was "ready to hold Woodward's and Bernstein's heads in a pail of water until they came up with another story." In desperation Woodward, hearing that a grand jury in Virginia was looking into the Watergate case, visited the county court house and memorized the names of possible grand jurors. The reporters then started calling around and visiting potential jurors, trying to identify people actually sitting on the jury in order to get hold of the testimony that might provide further leads for their own investigation. One of the grand jurors reported the visit to a prosecutor who informed the judge presiding over the grand jury, John Sirica. Sirica reprimanded the reporters before a packed courtroom for a violation of the law, though he did not identify them by name. Woodward and Bernstein were relieved not to be held in contempt and pursued the story by other avenues. But the precedent and memory remained of what journalists were prepared to do to serve their own interests or, better, the extent to which they unquestioningly identified the interests of journalists with the interests of democracy.

The *New York Times* was right in publishing the Pentagon Papers and the *Washington Post* was right in vigorously pursuing the Watergate story. Both were triumphs for independent journalism and the First Amendment. But the reason for claiming that these two cases constitute both the apogee of independent journalism and its incipient unraveling is that in both cases the press engaged in and sanctioned anti-democratic practices and, in the long run, the new arrogance of the press, its self-declared dispensation from the norms of democracy, did not go unnoticed. The willingness to accept stolen documents and to tamper with grand juries in cases where the fate of the republic was not clearly at stake was a declaration that a free press was not only necessary to a democracy but that the press could disregard the welfare of other democratic institutions and go it alone. It was as if journalists decided that an independent judiciary, a strong executive, an active public, free universities and a deliberative legislature were mere ornaments to democracy as long as one had a free press.

That belief was certainly not lost on the American establishment which, as Bob Woodward has himself testified, opened its arms to embrace journalists and welcome them into the household of the privileged. Showered with honors, invited to the right parties, and consulted by the political and economic elite, journalists were no longer allowed to swing free of the centers of power but were incorporated into the Establishment. At that moment the vaunted progressivism of journalism was abandoned; or, better, journalists accepted the role of progressive intellectuals with a mission to participate in the management of society and simultaneously abandoned the populist wing of progressivism with its dictate to "afflict the powerful and comfort the afflicted."

Independent journalism could work only if a number of basic requirements were met: the public had to believe the press was authentically its representative and therefore in a responsible and fiduciary relation to it; the public had to believe that the press was not in cahoots with the state, with the most powerful of interest groups or both; and the public had to believe that the press was capable of representing the world, that is, of rendering a reasonable, unbiased, true, and factual account of it. The press has been found wanting on all these counts and in the wake of Watergate lost credibility and respect; it was no longer believed. As poll after poll showed, journalists had earned the distrust of the public and were increasingly seen as a hindrance to, rather than an avenue of, politics and political reform. Rather than supporting democracy, the press, in the eyes of many, was an impediment to the democratic process. While the press dismissed the rising tide of criticism as merely reactionary politics, the problem went deeper. In the public's eyes, the press had become the adversary of all institutions, including the public itself. Journalism was not only independent of partisan politics; it was independent of democracy itself. Some felt that the press had come to practice what was called Werner von Braun journalism: "we just send the rockets up; we don't know or care where they come down." As the press sought greater constitutional power for itself and greater independence from the state, as it sought to remove all restrictions on its activities and its newsgathering rights, it pressed the legal and ideological case that it was a special institution with special rights—rights that trumped the interests of ordinary men and women and other institutions necessary to democracy.

## Journalism in the 1980s

Growing distrust of journalists coincided with the break-up of the structural basis of an independent press during the 1980s. While the break-up began in the mid-'70s with the launching of broadcast satellites and the spread of cable television, technical change massively accelerated as personal computers came on line, the telephone industry was re-organized and broadcasting deregulated (and, elsewhere in the world, privatized) during the Reagan administration. The communication system, suffering from massive excess capacity, entered into a phase of merger and acquisition that absorbed once proud news organizations into larger entertainment enterprises that were increasingly global in reach. Traditional news media, such as newspapers and magazines, redefined themselves as part of the "information industry" in order to find a niche in which they might survive in the new order. As firms grew larger, news in the traditional sense became a smaller and increasingly insignificant part of total corporate enterprise. Freed from effective requirements to serve the "public interest, convenience, and necessity," broadcasting operations were subject to ruthless cost-cutting and paring in order to make an appropriate contribution to the bottom line of increasingly rationalized and bureaucratized corporations. Excess capacity created more intense competition for audiences, particularly as the Internet and World Wide Web absorbed major portions of leisure time from individuals, and newspaper readership and viewing of network news precipitously declined. News had been a profit center for years but increasingly it was seen only as a profit center. International coverage, always expensive and to some degree redundant given the presence of Reuters and the Associated Press, was cut back, foreign bureaus closed, and veteran reporters with international experience (and high salaries) cut adrift and, in most cases, not replaced. All these factors contributed to making the news system increasingly hit or miss and reduced staffs led to greater emphasis on more mechanical and cheaper forms of coverage. Cable news networks, cursed with small, marginal audiences, were particularly vulnerable to puffing up minor scandals and celebrity outcroppings into major media events. To meet this competition traditional media became awash in the thrilling, marvelous, breathtaking, and trivial. Journalists adopted the language of nomads, irony, ever more often as they gave in to the cosmopolitan desire to transcend the very society they were describing.

The parenthesis enclosing the 1988 and 1992 Presidential primaries and election turned out to be a watershed period in American politics and journalism. In the aftermath of the 1988 election there was widespread disgust with American politics and with the press itself. It was a monumentally smarmy campaign, reduced to a few slogans and brutal advertisements that produced yet another record low in voter turnout. Joan Didion caught the theatrical and hermetically sealed quality of the campaign:

> When we talk about the process, then, we are talking increasingly, not about "the democratic process," or the general mechanism affording citizens of a state a voice in its affairs, but the reverse: A mechanism seen as so specialized that access to it is correctly limited to its own professionals, to those who manage policy and those who report on it, to those who run the polls and those who quote them, to those who ask and those who answer the questions on the Sunday shows, to the media consultants, to the columnists . . . to the handful of insiders who invent, year in and year out, the narrative of public life . . . What strikes one most vividly about such a campaign is precisely its remoteness from the actual life of the country.
>
> (Didion 1992: 49–50)

The widespread disenchantment of the public with the spectacle of politics—with what Didion called "Insider Baseball," a game only for the players, not even the fans—was evident not only in low voter turnout but in the decline in the audience for political conventions. Following the 1988 election there were renewed calls for the press to reconstruct its approach to politics. Despite that, the 1992 primary season opened pretty much as a re-enactment of the worst of the lessons learned in 1988. At that point, political hope dissipated: the campaign re-entered the simulated world of journalism: Bill Clinton's character moved to the forefront, his dalliance with Gennifer Flowers became an obsession, his Vietnam draft status an easy and never-ending story. Feeding-frenzy journalism reigned and voter interest declined, such that primary voter turnout in some states was down by almost one-third over 1988. Everything journalists and politicians promised to avoid post-1988 was again the norm as the campaign swung into summer.

There was a moment of hope during the campaign when it was believed that the "new news," namely the World Wide Web, would rush in to rescue journalism from declining voter interest, stage managed politics and the delights of the sensational. The hope was misplaced. If, as Joan Didion put it, political campaigns "raise questions that go . . . vertiginously to the heart of the structure" (Didion 1992: 50) of the press and politics, then the campaigns of 1988 and 1992 sounded the requiem for independent journalism.

In the aftermath of those campaigns, movements grew to create under the banner of public journalism a basis to reform practice by placing respect for the public and attentiveness to public need at the center of reporting. While critical of the movement, journalists themselves initiated a variety of reforms designed to make the press more responsive and responsible, to preserve the best in the tradition of independent journalism while curbing its excess and adapting to the new realities of commerce and politics. Such efforts however had hardly made a dent in professional practice the day the twin towers collapsed and the cozy world of corporate journalism went down with them.

## Journalism since September 11

The first and most general effect of September 11 was to draw journalists back within the body politic. Cosmopolitanism and ironic distance from society along with independence from the institutions of democracy were exposed as an unsustainable fraud. Mutual dependence and solidarity, not altogether salutary, became the order of the day. The press was re-nationalized, global corporations found they needed the protection of democratic practice, and journalists experienced the vulnerability that is at the root of patriotism and nationalism.

Some of this was all to the good, for it exposed the myths of globalization and the enduring importance of nation states. Some of it was worrisome, as it fed into the jingoism that is the ugly backside of nationalism. The long-run consequences could work to the benefit of journalism but only if a number of reforms, some originating in the last two decades, are carried forward along with a bold rethinking of the First Amendment and a reorientation of broadcasting.

Some of the practices of public journalism, though without the name attached, found their way into the elite press. The *New York Times*, as previously noted, discovered a renewed connection with its readers. This was evident not only in the "Portraits of Grief" and other innovations necessary to cover the disaster but earlier on in at least three other episodes. The first was the admission of error, a confession really, that took the form of an editorial on the mishandling of the Ho Wen Lee case. Lee was falsely accused of breaching national security at the Los Alamos Laboratory and the *Times* had earlier relied on misleading FBI informants in reporting, indeed prosecuting his guilt. The *Times* also showed unusual enterprise in running a series on race relations in the United States that was pegged not to external events but to differences within its own newsroom that connected to the real state of racial conflict without in the society. Through a variety of "outreach" activities, many commercially but not inappropriately motivated, the paper attempted to intensify its contact to and awareness of the views of its readers. Finally, the *Times* became more than usually open to its readers in identifications, the admission of error and in providing access via e-mail to its reporters and writers. These are signs of hope given the position of leadership within the American press. That hope is augmented by an even higher quality of national and international reporting in the paper in the months after September 11.

Still, as Joan Konner (2002) put it in a courageous essay, there is a curtain of prescribed patriotism that has descended over the media, particularly television, and a tendency to turn the war on terrorism into yet another version of the O. J. Simpson trial. These developments signal the need to restore a democratically independent press, fully within the society it reports and represents, attentive to the needs of people everywhere affected by American commerce and politics.

The 1990s saw serious damage done to American political institutions, including the press. Part of that damage came about because journalists and other elites forgot part of the wisdom embedded in democratic and republican traditions. It was a central belief of the Founding Fathers, based on the experience of history, that republican institutions are fragile, the moments of their existence fleeting in historical time (a life expectancy they put at around 200 years), and citizens had to guard against lurching back into a life of domination. In recent decades Americans acted as if these valuable institutions were indestructible. Journalists seemed to believe that democratic politics, which alone underwrites their craft, is a self-perpetuating machine that would run of itself, that can withstand any amount of undermining. Nothing is further from the truth.

One of the beliefs central to the economics of globalization was that government and civil society should be disciplined by markets. The truth is that democratic practice disciplines markets in any successful and enduring economy. The First Amendment is not, in the first instance, designed to protect property rights but to grant a public trust to the press to be exercised in the name of a wider community. Freedom of the press came to mean, in the new economy, a mere property right establishing the ground rules for competition in an increasingly global economy. A political right was converted to an exclusively economic one and democracy came to mean solely economic democracy.

While the economic world prizes efficiency, it has less patience with political freedom and democracy. Whereas the triumph of democracy is everywhere heralded, the commitment to actual democracy everywhere has weakened or, more precisely, our imagination of democracy has shrunk. Instead, it is equated solely with a limited aspect of even economic democracy: the existence of free and open markets. This has been true not only among the public, whom it is rather too easy to blame, but even among privileged classes, including journalists.

But political democracy does not follow from the presence of effective market economy and a politically free press does not follow from an economically free one. Indeed, when economic values come to dominate politics, liberty is often at risk. One does not have to believe in conspiracies to observe that economic interests can profit from a weakened nation state. In the absence of global political institutions only nations are strong enough to contain economic forces. Modern economic developments seem to favor authoritarian rather than democratic regimes. Ralf Dahrendorf, from whom I take much of this, reminds us that "authoritarian does not mean totalitarian," for such regimes do not require a Great Leader nor an invasive ideology nor permanent mobilization. Nor do they require a self-perpetuating class unwilling to relinquish power. Authoritarian countries can be quite nice for the visitor as well as predictable and undemanding for the native. For the poet and journalist, and many others, they are unbearable.

The indifference to or tolerance of the erosion of democratic institutions including the press is predicated on the belief that times will always be good. They are not any longer, but when the going gets rough people begin to doubt the constitution of liberty and embrace illiberal projects. In such a crisis it is difficult to reinvent and repair institutions that have been carelessly damaged.

If during the past decade journalism had been sold off to the oil industry, we would all be alarmed at investing a democratic institution to the care of a private enterprise with global interests and virtually unlimited political power. In recent years journalism has been sold, to a significant degree, to the entertainment and information industries which market commodities globally that are central to the world economy of the twenty-first century. This condition cannot be allowed to persist.

The reform of journalism will only occur when news organizations are disengaged from the global entertainment and information industries that increasingly contain them. That is the only way of removing journalism from the profit expectations and opportunity costs that rationalize global enterprise. The creation of an independent press will require both judicial and legislative action so that journalism can earn enough profit to make it attractive but release it as well from slavish dependence on the laws of the market. One can hear the howls of protest: "You mean in the name of the First Amendment and the political rights therein embodied, Disney should not be allowed to own ABC, Time-Warner own CNN and Microsoft should be required to stick to software and leave broadcasting and publishing alone." That is exactly what I mean. Alas, the press may have to rely on a democratic state to create the conditions necessary for a democratic press to flourish and for journalists to be restored to their proper role as orchestrators of the conversation of a democratic culture.

## References

Black, H. (1971) Concurring opinion, *New York Times Co. vs. United States*, No. 1873, Before the Supreme Court of the United States, June 26: 714–72.

Dahrendorf, R. (1989) *After 1989: Morals, Revolution and Civil Society*, London: Macmillan.

Dayan, D. and Katz, E. (1992) *Media Events: The Live Broadcasting of History*, Cambridge, MA: Harvard University Press.

Didion, J. (1992) *After Henry*, New York: Vintage International.

Konnor, J. (2002) Media patriotism provides a shield for Bush, *Long Island Newsday*, January 9: A31.

Schell, O. (2001) The media clarified, *North Gate News*, newsletter of the Graduate School of Journalism, University of California, Berkeley, CA: (Fall): 9, 12.

Schudson, M. (1978) *Discovering the News*, New York: Basic Books.

Stewart, P. (1975) Or of the press, *Hastings Law Journal*, 26: 631–7.

# 5

# SEPTEMBER 11 AND THE STRUCTURAL LIMITATIONS OF US JOURNALISM[1]

*Robert W. McChesney*

The questions before us are elementary. What explains the nature of US news media coverage of the political response to the September 11, 2001 terrorist attacks in the United States? Is September 11 a defining event for US journalism? We have been roundly told that "September 11 changes everything," but does it change journalism? I argue that the US press coverage of the political response to the September 11 attacks was exactly what one would expect from looking at historical precedent. September 11 may be changing a lot of things about our world, but with regard to journalism it has merely highlighted the anti-democratic tendencies already in existence.

## The war against terrorism and the US press coverage

The September 11, 2001 attacks on the World Trade Center and the Pentagon, for most Americans, were similar in effect to having a massive attack from outer space. Almost entirely ignorant of global politics, devoid of any understanding of the Islamic world, educated primarily by Hollywood movies featuring Arnold Schwarzenegger, Bruce Willis, and Sylvester Stallone, Americans were ideally prepared for a paranoid and hysterical response. Mix in an opportunistic class of politicians and powerful special interests that benefit by militarism, and you have the recipe for much of what transpired thereafter. The immediate consequence of the September 11 attack was for Congress to pass, by a virtually unanimous vote, and with no substantive debate, an act granting President George W. Bush the power to engage in global war against enemies he is free to define with little accountability to Congress. At the same time Congress authorized a sharp increase in military, intelligence, and national security spending. Within a few weeks the United States began its aerial bombings of Afghanistan. In his public statements President Bush was emphatic that the United States was engaged in a global war on terrorism, and that those nations and peoples who did not support the US effort would be regarded as sympathetic to the enemy and dealt with accordingly. Insofar as this was a war without borders, that logic would apply domestically as well as abroad. Moreover, this was to be a war with no end in sight, for as long as terrorists lurked the prospect of another deadly attack loomed, and our forces needed to be on guard. Pre-emptive strikes were justified and necessary. The initial name the US government gave for the war, Operation Infinite Justice, captured the world-historical nature of the conflict. In short, we were in the early stages of World War III.

Central to this process were the news media, and the media system more broadly. Moments like these are the "moments of truth," so to speak, for establishing the commitment to democracy of a nation's media system. The decision to enter war, not to mention world war, is arguably the most important any society can make. Tens of thousands, perhaps millions, even tens of millions, of lives will be lost, and those that survive will be vastly less happy than they would have been otherwise. The political-economic cost of war is very high as well. Standards of living must be cut, government non-military services reduced, and civil liberties curtailed. In a free society, such a decision must be made with the informed consent of the governed. Otherwise, the claim to be a democratic nation is dubious, if not fraudulent.

Over the past century, as the United States has emerged as the dominant economic and military power in the world, it has engaged in hundreds of wars and invasions and bombing missions across the planet. According to a list compiled by the Congressional Research Service, the United States has employed its military forces in other countries over 70 times since 1945, not counting innumerable instances of counterinsurgency operations by the CIA. The American people were ignorant of most of these actions; they were made in our name but without our informed consent. Such is the price of being the dominant superpower in the world.

When the wars go from quickie carpet bombings or bankrolling mercenaries and death squads to full-scale hostilities, the citizenry cannot remain in the dark. Governments need active support for the war effort, both to pay for the cost of war, and to provide the soldiers willing to die for the war. It has proven to be a difficult job in the United States to enlist such popular support for war. Over the past century the US government has worked aggressively to convince the citizenry of the necessity of going to war in numerous instances. In cases like World War I, Korea, Vietnam, and the Gulf War, the government employed sophisticated propaganda campaigns to whip the population into a suitable fury. Candidates won the presidency in 1916 and 1964 on peace platforms when the record shows they were working diligently to go to war. It was well understood within the establishment at the time—and subsequently verified in historical examinations—that the government needed to lie in order to gain support for its war aims. The Pentagon Papers provided the most chilling documentation imaginable of this process.

And how have the media served us during these various war campaigns? Despite all the talk about being a feisty Fourth Estate, the media system in every one of those cases proved to be a superior propaganda organ for militarism and war. This is widely understood among US journalism educators, and when we teach of these historic episodes of journalism it tends to be addressed with remorse and concern. This is the context for understanding the media coverage since September 11. The historical record suggests that we should expect an avalanche of lies and half-truths in the service of power. Journalists, the news media, should be extremely skeptical, demanding evidence for claims, opening the door to other policy options, and asking the tough questions that nobody in power wants to address; the historical track record is emphatic in this regard. Such a free press would "serve the governed, not the governors," as Supreme Court Justice Hugo Black once put it.

What is most striking in the US news coverage following the September 11 attacks is how that very debate over whether to go to war, or how best to respond, did not even *exist*. It was presumed, almost from the moment the South Tower of the World Trade Center collapsed, that the United States was at war, world war. The picture conveyed by the media was as follows: a benevolent, democratic, and peace-loving nation was brutally attacked by insane evil terrorists who hated the United States for its freedoms and affluent way of life. The United States needed immediately to increase its military and covert forces, locate the surviving culprits and exterminate them; then prepare for a long-term war to root out the global terrorist cancer and destroy it.

In fact, the leap from the September 11 attacks to unchecked world war was hardly natural or a given. Extraordinarily logical questions, questions that would be posed by US journalists arguably to any other government in a similar situation, were ignored or marginalized. Why should we believe that a militarized approach would be effective? Moving beyond the September 11 attacks, why should the United States be entitled to determine—as judge, jury, and executioner—who is a terrorist or a terrorist sympathizer in this global war? What about international law? Why shouldn't this be regarded like most other terrorist acts, as crimes against humanity and not as formal acts of war? The list went on and on.

Most conspicuous was the complete absence of comment on one of the most striking features of the war campaign, something that any credible journalist would be quick to observe were the events taking place in Russia or China or Pakistan: there are very powerful interests in the United States who greatly benefit politically and economically by the establishment of an unchecked war on terrorism. This consortium of interests can be called, to use President Eisenhower's term, the military–industrial complex. It blossomed during the Cold War when the fear of Soviet imperialism—real or alleged—justified its creation and expansion. A nation with a historically small military now had a permanent war economy, and powerful special interests benefited by its existence.

Since the fall of the Soviet Union, the US military–industrial complex has thus been seeking a substitute for the Cold War with which to justify its massive budgets and privileges. Various alternatives have been offered: a war on terrorism, the struggle against "rogue states," a "clash of civilizations" (Islam and China versus the West, offered up as a proposal by Samuel Huntington), a war on the global drug trade, and humanitarian intervention—all of them up to now seen as unsatisfactory, but sufficient to keep the military budget from shrinking drastically after the Cold War. As General Colin Powell voiced the problem in 1991: "Think hard about it. I'm running out of demons. I'm running out of villains" (*Toronto Star*, April 9, 1991; see also Gibbs 2001). The military lobbyists so dominated Washington politics that both parties agreed to maintain high levels of military spending, even with no powerful adversary. In 2000 the United States accounted for around one-third of all military spending in the world.

The war on terrorism was a gift from heaven for the military–industrial complex. (Just like the military response to terrorism may well be a gift from heaven to the terrorists.) It justified vast increases in budgets and power, and less accountability to Congress. It was a war that was endless and could never be won. And it was a war that the public would never have any way of monitoring, since the terrorist enemy was by definition detached from governments that could be defeated. Moreover, the very nature of terrorism lent itself to a hysteria that was highly conducive to emotional support for war and discouraging to the possibility of rational inquiry.

For journalists to raise issues like these did not presuppose that they opposed government policies, merely that the policies needed to be justified and explained, so the support would be substantive, not ephemeral, the result of deliberation, not manipulation. Such has not been the case.

In sum, much of mainstream US journalism has been, to be frank, propagandistic. The propagandistic nature of the war coverage was made crystal clear by CNN a few weeks after the war began in Afghanistan. CNN was not only the leading US cable news network; it was the leading *global* cable and satellite news network. Yet the war has put CNN in a pickle. If it broadcast the pro-US coverage it generated in the United States to international audiences, audiences would react negatively. International audiences received a much more critical take on the war and the US role in their newspapers and other media, and they would not watch CNN if it were seen as a front for the Bush administration. On the other hand, if CNN presented such critical coverage to US audiences, it would outrage people in power here. CNN President Walter Isaacson solved this dilemma by authorizing CNN to provide two different versions of the war: a critical one for global audiences and a sugarcoated one for Americans. Indeed, Isaacson instructed the domestic CNN to be certain that any story that might undermine support for the US war needed to be balanced with a reminder that the war on terrorism was a good war.

In this climate it should be no surprise that most Americans supported the war, though they knew next to nothing about the region we were fighting in and its history, or the US role in the world.

## The structural limitations on US journalism

This distorted coverage reflects the weaknesses of professional journalism as it has been practiced in the United States, as well as the control of our major news media by a very small number of very large and powerful profit-seeking corporations. It does not reflect explicit state censorship. As George Orwell observed, the genius of censorship in free societies is that "unpopular ideas can be silenced, and inconvenient facts kept dark, without any need for an official ban" (cited in Pilger 1998: 486). As I will argue, the coverage following September 11 conformed to the main pattern of US news coverage on other important political stories in recent years.

Professional journalism emerged in the United States around 100 years ago for a handful of important reasons. One crucial factor was the need among monopoly newspaper owners to offer a credible "non-partisan" journalism so that their business enterprises would not be undermined. To avoid the taint of partisanship, professionalism makes official or credentialed sources the basis for news stories. Reporters report what people in power say, and what they debate. This tends to give the news an establishment bias. When a journalist reports what official sources are saying, or debating, she is professional. When she steps outside this range of official debate to provide alternative perspectives or to raise issues those in power prefer not to discuss, she is no longer being professional. Background stories and contextual pieces that contradict and compromise the range of debate among official sources may appear briefly in the news, but they die off quickly without official source amplification. Most journalists have so internalized this primary role as stenographers for official sources that they do not recognize it as a problem for democracy. The best professional journalism is when there are clear and distinct debates between official sources; this provides considerable room for journalists to roam as they prepare their stories.

In matters of international politics, "official sources" are almost interchangeable with the term "elites," as foreign policy is mostly a preserve of the wealthy and powerful few—C. Wright Mills' classic power elite. At its worst, in a case like the current war on terrorism, where the elites and official sources are unified on the core issues, the nature of our press coverage is uncomfortably close to that found in authoritarian societies with limited formal press freedom.

Many working journalists would recoil at that statement. Their response would be that professional reliance on official sources is justifiable as "democratic" because the official sources are elected or accountable to people who are elected by the citizenry. This is a crucial issue so permit me a bit of a digression from the discussion of September 11. The problem with this rationale for stenography is that it forgets a critical assumption of free press theory: even leaders determined by election need a rigorous monitoring, the range of which cannot be determined solely by their elected opposition. Otherwise the citizenry has no way out of the status quo, no capacity to criticize the political culture as a whole. If such a watchdog function grows lax, corruption invariably grows, and the electoral system decays. If journalism that goes outside the range of elite opinion is dismissed as unprofessional or partisan, and therefore justifiably ignored, the media merely locks in a corrupt status quo and can offer no way out. If journalists require having official sources on their side to pursue a story, it gives people in power a massive veto power over the exercise of democracy.

Consider the Enron scandal which unfolded in late 2001 and the early months of 2002. Although this was a stunning example of supreme political corruption—a story that could topple governments in many nations—the coverage increasingly concentrated upon the business collapse of Enron, rather than the sleazy way in which it worked, legally as well as illegally, using the political system to make billions of dollars ripping off consumers, taxpayers, and workers. Why will it not turn into a political crisis that will end careers and lead to major reform? Most likely this will not happen, because the opposition Democrats are in no hurry to push the story to its logical political conclusion, since so many of them will be implicated as well. So professional journalism is restricted to the range of what those in power pursue, and the balance of the population has no one representing *its* interests. What about those who simply want the whole truth to come out, and the system changed so this sort of corruption is less likely to ever occur in the future? They are out of luck.

Another telling example is the manner in which the press reported President Bush's "victory" in the 2000 election. It is now clear that the majority of the people in Florida who went to vote for President in November 2000 intended to vote for Al Gore (see Vidal 2001). The semi-official recount conducted by the major news media in 2001 showed that by every conceivable way the votes might be counted, Al Gore won Florida (see also Nichols 2001). But Al Gore isn't President. Why is that? Or, to put it another way, why didn't the press coverage assure that the true winner would assume office? After all, if the free press cannot guarantee the integrity of elections, what good is it? The primary reason is due to sourcing: throughout November and early December of 2000, the news media were being told by all Republicans that the Republicans had won the election and Al Gore was trying to steal it. The Democrats, on the other hand, were far less antagonistic and showed much less enthusiasm to fight for what they had won. Hence the news coverage, reflecting what their sources were telling them, tended to reflect the idea that the Republicans had won and the Democrats were grasping for straws. When Greg Palast broke the story in Britain in November 2000 that the Florida Republicans had systematically and illegally excluded thousands of poor Floridians from voting—in itself, almost certainly enough to cost Gore the state—no US mainstream news medium dared pick it up, though the story was true. Why? Most likely this was because journalists would have been out on their own, because the Democrats had elected not to fight on this issue (see Palast 2002). Once the Supreme Court made its final decision, the media were elated to announce that our national nightmare was over. The media had helped anoint a President. The only losers were the irrelevant and powerless souls who clung to the belief that whoever gets the most votes should win the election, and that the press should tell the whole truth and let the chips fall where they may.

The willingness of the mainstream US news media to suspend criticism of President Bush almost *in toto* after September 11 should be considered in this light. When the recount report indicating that Gore won Florida was released two months after September 11, what was striking was how almost all of the press reported that the results were mixed or that Bush had won. The reason for the press making this judgment was it only looked at the recount in the few counties where Al Gore had requested it; who actually won the actual election in Florida seemed not to interest the press one whit. In a manner of thinking, the press had no choice but to provide this interpretation. If the media conceded that Gore, in fact, had won the race in Florida, it would have made people logically ask, "why didn't the media determine this when it mattered?" Moreover, a concession that the United States had an unelected President would make the laudatory coverage of President Bush after September 11 look increasingly like the sort that paeans to "maximum leaders" expected from the news media in tinhorn dictatorships. As soon as the leaders are not the product of free and fair elections, the professional reliance on official sources—which is wobbly by democratic standards to begin with—collapses.

In addition to this reliance on official sources, experts are also crucial to explaining and debating policy, especially in complex stories like this one. As with sources, experts are drawn almost entirely from the establishment. Since September 11, the range of "expert" analysis has been limited mostly to the military and intelligence communities and their supporters, with their clear self-interest in the imposition of military solutions rarely acknowledged and almost never critically examined. Since there has been virtually no debate between the Democrats and Republicans over the proper response, the military approach has simply been offered as the only option. As National Public Radio's Cokie Roberts put it on October 8 when asked on air if there was any domestic opposition to the bombing of Afghanistan: "None that mattered."

The full-throttle jingoism of the press coverage was tempered by late September, as it became clear that a full-blown war might be counterproductive to US military and political aims. The range of debate has broadened somewhat in elite circles, with some assuming the more "internationalist" position that the United States needed to win the "hearts and minds" of potential adversaries through more sophisticated peaceful measures, as well as have an unmatched military. This expansion of elite debate will almost certainly lead to a broadening of journalism, but this should not be confused with a genuine democratic debate or democratic journalism. Fundamental issues will remain decidedly off-limits. The role of the military as the ultimate source of power will not be questioned. The notion that the United States is a uniquely benevolent force in the world will be undisputed. The premise that the United States and the United States alone—unless it deputizes a nation like Israel—has a right to invade any country it wants at any time if it so wishes will remain undebatable. And any concerns that US military actions will violate international law will be raised not on principle, but only because it might harm US interests to be perceived by other nations as a lawbreaker.

Here we should recall the media coverage of the US invasion of Vietnam in the 1960s and 1970s. From the time the United States launched its ground invasion in earnest, in 1965, until late 1967 or early 1968, the news coverage was a classic example of the "big lie" of all war propaganda. The war was good and necessary for freedom and democracy; those who opposed it were trivialized, marginalized, distorted, or ignored. By 1968 the coverage began to take a more charitable stance toward antiwar positions. But while it reflected growing public opposition to the war to a certain degree, this coverage was influenced much more by the break that emerged in US elite opinion by this time: some on Wall Street and in Washington realized that the cost of the war was far too high for any prospective benefits and favored getting out. The news coverage remained within the confines of elite opinion. The United States still had a "007" right to invade any nation it wished; the only debate was whether the invasion of Vietnam was a proper use of that power. The notion that the very idea of the United States invading nations like Vietnam was morally wrong was off-limits, although surveys revealed that such a view was not uncommon in the general population.

Another flaw of establishment journalism is that it tends to avoid contextualization like the plague. The reason for this is that providing meaningful context and background for stories, if done properly, tends to commit the journalist to a definite position and enmesh him in the controversy professionalism is determined to avoid. Coverage tends to be a barrage of facts and official statements. What little contextualization professional journalism does provide tends to conform to elite premises. So it is that on those stories that receive the most coverage, like the Middle East, Americans tend to be almost as ignorant as on those subjects that receive far less coverage. Such journalism is more likely to produce confusion, cynicism, and apathy than understanding and informed action. Hence one of the paradoxes of professional journalism: it is arguably better at generating ignorance and apathy than informed and passionately engaged citizens.

## Structural limitations and September 11

Considerable context and background have been generated in the US news media since September 11, but the context conforms to elite premises. So it is that there have been numerous detailed reports on Osama Bin Laden and his terrorist network, and related investigations of factors concerning the success or failure of prospective military actions in Afghanistan and elsewhere. Information about the fundamental context that falls outside the range of US elite interests may appear periodically, but it gets little follow-up and has negligible impact. This becomes abundantly clear when one peruses the Internet to see what is being reported in the international press or in the US independent and alternative media. Here, one often finds stories about US complicity and the complicity of US allies with terrorists and terrorism. Here, one is more likely to find a much more complex world where the US government's motives are held to the same standard as those of other governments. (See, for example, the superior US website, www.accuracy.org, which collects much of this material.) But these stories, often by world-renowned journalists like Robert Fisk, are all but unknown in the news consumed by the preponderance of the US population.

The weaknesses of the coverage are augmented by the structural context for US journalism. Over the past two decades the US news media have become consolidated into the hands of a very small number of enormous media conglomerates. For many of them, journalism accounts for a small percentage of their revenues and profit. These new owners have paid huge sums to acquire their media empires, and they expect to generate maximum returns from their assets. Accordingly, a baldly commercial logic has been applied to journalism in recent years. As a result, among other things, the number of overseas correspondents has been slashed, and international political coverage has plummeted, as that is expensive and generates little revenue. Whereas Americans once tended to be misinformed about world politics, now they are uninformed. The US citizenry is embarrassingly and appallingly ignorant of the most elementary political realities in other nations and regions. It is an unmitigated disaster for the development of a meaningful democratic debate over international policy, and highlights a deep contradiction between the legitimate informational needs of a democratic society and the need for profit of the corporate media.

The US media corporations also exist within an institutional context that makes support for US military seemingly natural. These giant firms are among the primary beneficiaries of both neoliberal globalization—their revenues outside the United States are increasing at a rapid pace—and the US role as the pre-eminent world power. Indeed, the US government is the primary advocate for the global media firms when trade deals and intellectual property agreements are being negotiated. Coincidentally, at the very moment that the corporate broadcasters are singing the praises of "America's New War," their lobbyists are appearing before the Federal Communications Commission seeking radical relaxation of ownership regulations for broadcasting, newspaper, and cable companies. Such deregulation will, by all accounts, lead to another massive wave of media consolidation. For these firms to provide an understanding of the world in which the US military and economic interests are not benevolent forces might be possible in some arcane twisted theory, but it is incongruous practically.

There is no simple or easy solution to the complex problem of how to best provide for a journalism that serves democracy, especially when powerful forces are pounding the drums of war. But it is a problem that must be addressed if we are to have any prospect of living in a humane and self-governing society. A viable solution ultimately will require reform of our media system, as well as broader reform of the US political economy. But this is not an issue to be decided here; it is an issue that deserves the attention and participation of all concerned with the future of democracy and peaceful international relations.

## Note

1  Parts of this essay appeared in an earlier form in McChesney, R. W. (2002) "The US news media and World War III," *Journalism: Theory, Practice, Criticism*, 3 (1): 14–21.

## References

Gibbs, D. N. (2001) Washington's new interventionism, *Monthly Review*, 53, September: 15–37.

Nichols, J. (2001) *Jews for Buchanan*, New York: The New Press.

Palast, G. (2002) *The Best Democracy Money Can Buy*, London: Pluto Press.

Pilger, J. (1998) *Hidden Agendas*, London: Vintage.

*Toronto Star* (1991) General advocates cuts to US military budget, April 9: A3.

Vidal, G. (2001) Times cries eke! Buries Al Gore, *The Nation*, December 17: 13–15.

# 6

# MAKING SENSE OF THE "ISLAMIC PERIL"

## Journalism as cultural practice

*Karim H. Karim*

The extraordinary nature of the terrorist attacks in the United States on September 11, 2001 produced a significant rupture in media reporting. Live pictures of an airplane crashing into a world famous skyscraper, which then crumbled to the ground, are not normal television fare. Scheduled live transmission of events tends to be well-planned and publicized, with events usually unfolding broadly within the parameters of a preconceived script. Rarely does the camera capture completely unforeseen incidents. Even in cases where television crews arrive moments after terrorist bomb explosions, the only "action" available for videotaping usually consists of emergency personnel's hurried movements, smoke billowing from damaged buildings, sirens wailing, and people weeping or shouting in anger.

But on September 11, TV viewers watched the United Airlines Boeing 767 approach the South Tower of the World Trade Center and ram into it at 9:03 am. Cameras had been set up around the site following the crash of an American Airlines plane into the North Tower some 15 minutes earlier. Perhaps the only earlier comparable live broadcasts had been the explosion of the space shuttle *Challenger* in 1986 on television, the on-camera shooting of accused presidential assassin Lee Harvey Oswald in 1963, and the explosion of the Hindenburg zeppelin in 1937 on radio. Journalists are completely taken aback by such traumatic incidents and scramble to provide coherent commentary as the disaster unfolds. In contrast to the well-rehearsed and controlled coverage of a scheduled live event, an unexpected disaster leaves the reporter disoriented. The completely unexpected action of an airliner being deliberately flown into one of the world's tallest and most symbolic buildings, followed by the massive loss of life, shook journalists' and viewers' cognitive foundations of reality. When faced with the unusual, journalists respond by falling back on set patterns of information gathering and reporting (Tuchman 1978). The resort to routine involves carrying out a prescribed series of actions for accomplishing coverage, such as contacting institutions to obtain access to relevant sites and persons, interviewing, attending press conferences, and using certain kinds of documentary sources. The contingencies of the news format—meeting deadlines and obtaining "facts," pictures, and quotations from specific categories of people (eyewitnesses, authority figures)—ensure that the routines are followed in a systematic manner.

At the same time, attempts are made to place even the most atypical occurrences within cognitive scripts and models of behavior shaped by the experience and the narration of previous events (van Dijk 1988). Dominant cultural and religious worldviews of society are critical in shaping these cognitive structures with which we make sense of ongoing events. Even though the events of September 11 were extraordinary, their reporting—following the initial period of disorientation—was shaped by frames that had been in place to cover such issues as violence, terrorism, and Islam.

There has emerged over the last three decades a set of journalistic narratives on "Muslim terrorism," whose construction is dependent on basic cultural perceptions about the global system of nation-states, violence, and the relationship between Western and Muslim societies. The dominant discourses[1] about these issues help shape the cognitive scripts for reporting the acts of terrorism carried out by people claiming to act in the name of Islam.

## Dominant discourses on violence

Media portrayals of "Islamic violence" are influenced by the dominant cultural meanings attached to both "Islam" and "violence." Societal consensus determines which actions are to be considered violent and which ones are not. Various discourses compete in the naming of violence, a phenomenon which is an integral, albeit enigmatic, feature of human history. Whereas force is often utilized to repress people, it is also a means to oppose and develop checks against excessive power. Since there is an integral link between power and violence, those who hold power have a vested interest in ensuring that their preferred meanings remain dominant.

Dominant discourses support the actions of hegemonic powers to preserve themselves from threats that they themselves name as violent and terroristic. The London-based *Independent*'s Middle East correspondent, Robert Fisk, whose reporting often provides alternative views on power and violence, writes that

> "terrorism" no longer means terrorism. It is not a definition; it is a political contrivance. "Terrorists" are those who use violence against the side that is using the word. The only terrorists whom Israel acknowledges are those who oppose Israel. The only terrorists the United States acknowledges are those who oppose the United States or their allies. The only terrorists Palestinians acknowledge—for they too use the word—are those opposed to the Palestinians.

> (Fisk 1990: 441)

102

In alternative discourses, such as those of Noam Chomsky (1991) and Edward Herman (1985), the violent world order also includes the support of powerful states for smaller "National Security States." The oppression of these states' populations (usually to ensure that supplies of raw materials and cheap labor keep flowing to Western corporations) and the arming of regional powers to destabilize neighboring countries is the "real terror network," according to Herman and Chomsky. They describe how the "Free Press" has in various periods overlooked US involvement in supplying and training the armies of repressive regimes. Dominant discourses on terrorism avert their eyes from what these authors call "wholesale violence," perpetrated by hegemonic states and their clients, and focus instead on the "retail violence" of non-compliant states and groups. Johan Galtung's (1981) concept of "structural violence" enables a broader understanding of the larger historical and social contexts of violence. "Structural violence" is manifested in the denial of basic material needs (poverty), human rights (repression) and "higher needs" (alienation) and is distinct from direct or "classical" violence. Consequences of systemic institutional behavior that does not involve direct, physical force but that, nevertheless, leads to alienation, deprivation, disability, or death, as under poor working conditions, is also not usually described as violent in dominant discourses. However, direct, forceful reactions to such structural violence are invariably called violent.

Few mass media organs addressed the existence of structural violence in relation to the death and destruction caused by terrorism on September 11. Some exceptions were found in periodicals. The British medical journal *The Lancet* published an editorial by Richard Horton, titled "Public Health: a neglected counterterrorist measure," in its October 6 issue:

> Medicine and public health have important if indirect parts to play in securing peace and stability for countries in collapse. Health could be the most valuable counterterrorist measure yet to be deployed. Attacking hunger, disease, poverty, and social exclusion might do more good than air marshals, asylum restrictions, and identity cards. Global security will be achieved only by building stable and strong societies. Health is an undervalued measure of our global security.
>
> (Horton 2001: 1,113)

Using the assumption that annual figures for deaths were evenly spread over the year, the November 2001 issue of the development-oriented periodical, the *New Internationalist*, provided the following information to contextualize the loss of life caused by the terrorist attacks:

- Number of people who died of hunger on September 11, 2001: 24,000
- Number of children killed by diarrhoea on September 11, 2001: 6,020
- Number of children killed by measles on September 11, 2001: 2,700.

(*New Internationalist* 2001: 19)[2]

Vincent Mosco notes that destruction on an enormous scale was conducted between 1959 and 1975 to make way for the redevelopment of lower Manhattan by government and corporate interests. This area had comprised adjoining neighborhoods that provided a thriving mixed economy and affordable housing. The project to extend New York's downtown, including the construction of the World Trade Center, required the razing of "over sixty acres of buildings, an area four times the site of the WTC attack . . . [and] eliminated 440,000 of 990,000 manufacturing jobs" (Mosco 2002). Historical assessment of the structural violence that went into building the towers was virtually absent in the dominant coverage of the September 11 attacks.

In a utopian state where absolute order is the norm, violence would be an anomaly. However, in practice, the state and the socio-economic elites continually use various kinds of structural and direct violence to exercise and maintain power, especially against those who challenge the status quo. Max Weber observed that "the right to use physical force is ascribed to other institutions or to individuals only to the extent to which the state permits it" (1946: 78). Those who carry out violence without authorization from the state are punished by the state's "bureaucracy of violence (police, army, jails)" (Kertzer 1988: 132). However, the contemporary state tends to downplay its own massive and systemic use of violence as it simultaneously emphasizes its opponents' violent acts.

The political violence of those who seek to upset the status quo is characterized as terrorism. "Experts" from government, the military, and academia emerge as the owners of dominant discourses on terrorism. They make themselves readily available through the mass media to the public, to define and describe the problem as well as respond to alternative discourses on the issue. This does not mean that they are engaged in a conscious, coordinated conspiracy to produce a monolithic view, but that they subscribe to a general common purpose and a common field of meanings (Hall 1979). These "authorized knowers" (Winter 1992: 40) have a privileged say in two additional aspects of assigning responsibility to terrorism: who and what causes it and who and what will deal with it. Issues involving political violence are generally shorn of their structural causes and placed under general rubrics such as "right-wing terrorism," "left-wing terrorism," "narcoterrorism," "nuclear terrorism," or "Islamic terrorism." A lack of security is often pinpointed as a key reason for the occurrence of terrorist incidents and the solutions are seen in technological and legislative improvements by the state to better detect, prevent, and punish terrorism. Persons who are not agents of the state and who use violence for political reasons are portrayed as criminals, to be dealt with within the juridical structures (including military tribunals). Public attention is thus kept focused on the *violence* rather than the *politics* of political violence.

Whereas mainstream journalists do not always subscribe overtly to official views on terrorism, the field of meanings in which they choose to operate inevitably leads them to produce only certain interpretations of political violence. Jacques Ellul (1969) maintains that integration propaganda in the technological state would not be possible without the elite-owned or controlled mass media, where it appears constantly and consistently. Unlike the overt tendencies of agitation propaganda, integration propaganda does not involve the aggressive presentation of specific views but a more subtle and ubiquitous mode which operates within dominant discourses. Although mainstream journalists in technological societies do challenge the day-to-day functioning of incumbent governments, they rarely bring into question the fundamental structures of thought or of power. Operating within a particular ideological system (be it free market, socialist, or Islamist), mass media workers consciously or unconsciously produce integration propaganda that serves the overall interests of elites. Although professional journalism in the liberal state is ostensibly autonomous of the political and economic elites, Stuart Hall (1979) describes how it operationally and structurally tends to reproduce dominant discourses and the perspectives of authorized knowers—which are generally presented as being rational and natural. Through the various mechanisms of censorship, licensing, access, and advertising, societal elites also ensure that the mass media primarily disseminate messages that promote the social and economic values helping to maintain the status quo.

On September 11, there was only one story and generally one perspective on the multiple TV networks of North America. Most experts interviewed responded to security matters and did not seem interested in the larger political, social, and economic causes of the attacks. The focus was primarily on the immediate reaction rather than on the larger issues. After some initial fumbling, the Bush administration was soon able to set the frames and the agendas for reporting the unfolding story. Indeed, most media—stunned by the events of the day—seemed all too willing to accept the government's lead. As the hunt began for the "Islamic terrorists," journalists' narratives failed to provide a nuanced and contextual understanding of Islam, Muslims, or the nature of the "Islamic peril."

However, the media should not be viewed as monolithic vehicles for only one type of discourse. Depending on the latitude allowed by owners, they do function as sites of contestation across various views. Oppositional, alternative, and populist perspectives may appear from time to time in media content, often on the back pages of a newspaper or near the end of a news broadcast. Occasionally, alternative views are even printed in high-profile parts of a newspaper, such as the editorial, opinion columns, and the front page. But often an alternative narrative in the text of a write-up is subverted by the adjacent placing of the dominant discourse in more prominent parts of the article format, such as the headline or an accompanying photograph (Karim 2000: 131–6). There were many voices that participated in the discussions that followed the terrorist attacks.[3] Karen Armstrong, who has written about religious militancy in Islam as well as in Christianity and Judaism, appeared on TV a number of times; however, her attempts at explaining the broader context of such conflicts were often brushed aside as interviewers sought confirmation for their perceptions about an endemically violent Islam. The dominant discourse's sheer ubiquity and maneuverability overshadow the presence of alternative perspectives.

The terrorist attacks of September 11, resulting in the deaths of some 3,000 people, revealed an overwhelming failure by the United States government to ensure the security of its citizens. However, relatively few questions were asked by journalists about the multiple lapses of security that had permitted the network of terrorists to plan, prepare, and execute the complex series of hijackings and attacks. The media spotlight was focused mainly on the incidents themselves rather than their broader causes. Instead of exploring how the American government's own activities abroad may have possibly laid the groundwork for the resentment leading to attacks against Americans, the media generally echoed the Bush administration's polarized narrative frame of good versus evil. The series of relationships between the US government and various Afghan groups, including the Taliban, over the preceding two decades also remained largely unprobed: for instance, Washington's support for the mujahideen forces fighting against the Soviet Union in the 1980s, followed by an almost complete withdrawal as the country faced social and economic chaos in the 1990s, was hardly ever mentioned in the media, which instead presented the US as a savior for the long-suffering Afghans. America's role as superpower and its involvement in and attacks on other countries were generally overshadowed. Instead, the righteous and moral stance of the US became a key component of the dominant journalistic script for reporting "the War against Terrorism"—a label produced by the administration and accepted uncritically as the rubric for the coverage of the US' military actions in Afghanistan.

## Demystifying Muslim societies

A significant responsibility for the failure of the Northern[4] mass media to provide informed coverage of Muslim societies rests with Muslims themselves. They have not explained sufficiently the ethical and humanistic content of Islam; by default, they also often allow militant Islamists to become the spokespersons for all Muslims. Underpinning the issue of miscommunication between Muslims and their Northern observers are a number of serious problems among the former. Most Muslim societies have had shortcomings in developing effective political leaderships, genuinely democratic and self-sufficient communities, dynamic civil societies, and workable mechanisms for conflict resolution among Muslims and with non-Muslims. They have also been slow to implement creative strategies for harnessing human and material resources, independent infrastructures for scientific research, or contemporary methodologies to study indigenous intellectual heritages. The results have been war, social instability, poverty, hopelessness, and a lack of confidence that makes individuals susceptible to the simplistic solutions offered by Islamists and political extremists. An overemphasis on material values by the dominant discourses of development, adopted by most governments of Muslim-majority countries, has also increased the appeal of solutions based on narrow interpretations of scripture.

Among the other key problems of Muslim societies is the failure to understand the North, and particularly the West. Muslim lands have been exposed to liberalism since the late nineteenth century, but an appreciation of related concepts such as freedom of expression seems frequently absent among governments. Even though the formal rights and freedoms of individuals in democratic societies are usually modulated by structures of power, they remain integral to the self-image of most Western societies. These contradictions appear confusing to many Muslims, who also find it hard to reconcile the West's secular ethos with its ethical and moral values. They often stand bewildered at the West's kaleidoscopically-shifting media images and plethora of consumer products, which they nonetheless consume without comprehending either their cultural origins or long-term effects. At the same time, Western support for Israeli governments which dispossess Palestinians of their property and dignity shed doubt on the Western commitment to universal justice. In a reversal of a long historical tradition of inter-communal tolerance, anti-Israeli feelings have mutated for a number of Muslims into anti-Jewish sentiments. This in turn has led transnational media discourses to view the religion of Islam as being anti-Judaic.

Whereas journalists need necessarily to continue reporting on corruption and human rights abuses wherever they exist, they also need to be more aware of the historical and socio-cultural backgrounds in societies they cover as well as the nature of their own relationships with them. The status of the Muslim female is a case in point. She remains under the constant threat of having her limited privileges revoked by conservative regimes. But Fatima Mernissi points out that, ironically, it is the unremitting panoptic gaze of the Northern powers that Muslim conservatives use as an argument against the establishment of greater freedoms for the individual, women, and minority groups: "when the enemy satellites are keeping watch, it is not the moment to wallow in one's individuality" (Mernissi 1992: 91). Intense feelings of vulnerability in the face of Northern cultural, economic, and military intrusions are factors in the unwillingness to address sufficiently issues of rights. The wagons also remain circled against the transnational media's relentless attacks; what is perceived as the latter's siege against Muslims gives conservative regimes the excuse to sustain and even strengthen societal restrictions. Northern observers are generally oblivious to, or perhaps choose to ignore, the consequences of their constant, collective gaze upon the Muslim object—a gaze which, despite its omnipresence, serves to mystify rather than enlighten.

The Northern mass media have the tendency to declare manifestations of Muslim belief such as wearing the *hijab* and performing the communal Muslim prayer as certain signs of "Islamic fundamentalism," whereas the wearing of Christian religious apparel or attending church in their own countries are not usually considered signs of fanaticism. The generalization and polarization of all Muslims as "fundamentalists" and "moderates," "traditionalists" and "modernists," "fanatics" and "secularists" serve to distort communication. They tend to make the Muslims who are interested in constructive dialogue with non-Muslims apologetic about their beliefs or, contrarily, disdainful about any interaction.

Such situations have been a recurring feature of crisis situations in the relation-ship between Northern and Muslim societies; for example, during the "Rushdie Affair" when Muslims who dared criticize any aspect of Salman Rushdie's controversial book, *The Satanic Verses*, risked being branded an "Islamic funda-mentalist" (Ahmed 1992: 261–2). Following September 11, many Muslims living in Western societies were fearful of wearing traditional clothing in public, let alone engaging in discussion with others.

One primary problem that underlies dominant constructions of Muslim societies is the failure to acknowledge their diversity. Whereas the followers of Islam adhere to a set of beliefs in common, a vast plurality exists not only in cul-tural but also religious behavior among the billion Muslims living around the world. In the absence of a singular authoritative "church," each Muslim group, insofar as it adheres to a particular school of law, can claim that its actions follow scriptural dictates. However, consensus does not exist even among radical Islamist groups on the legitimacy of issues such as using terrorism as a tactic. Nevertheless, the Northern-based transnational media tend uncritically to accept the "Islamicness" of these actions without putting them into the context of the rigorous debates among Muslims on such issues. On the other hand, they usually do not draw attention to the "Christianness" of extremist groups such as the White supremacists or cult members who use Christian symbols and offer religious rationalization for their actions.[5]

The simultaneous reporting of two events in the March 15, 1993 issues of *Time*, *Newsweek*, and *Maclean's* (Canada's largest newsweekly) illustrates this stark contrast in treatment. The stories were, respectively, the suspected involve-ment of Sheikh Omar Abdel-Rahman in the 1993 bombing of the World Trade Center and the deadly clash of the Branch Davidians with US federal agents in Waco, Texas. The articles about the former incident were punctuated with refer-ences such as "Muslim cleric," "Islamic holy war," "Sunni worshipers," "Muslim fundamentalist," "Islamic fundamentalist movements" in *Time*; "Islamic link," "Muslim sect," "Sunni sect," "Islamic community," "the Islamic movement," "Islamic populism," "Muslim fundamentalism," and "Islamic fundamentalist" in *Newsweek*; and "Muslim fundamentalist," "extremist Muslim terrorist groups," "Muslim militants" in *Maclean's*. However, the three North American magazines completely avoided using the adjective "Christian" to describe the Branch Davidians, even though they did report that their leader had claimed to be "Christ" and quoted from Christian scriptures. Whether conscious or uncon-scious, dominant journalistic discourses do tend to avoid describing as "Christian" the violent groups drawn from the Christian tradition. On the other hand, there almost seems to be a certain eagerness to pepper accounts about simi-lar groups from Muslim backgrounds with the appellations "Muslim" and "Islamic."

The particular global "problem" of the challenge that some Muslims present to the Northern-dominated global order is named "Islam," a term that is manipu-lated according to the needs of the particular source discussing it. Among other things, it has come variously to refer to a religion, a culture, a civilization, a community, a religious revival, a militant cult, an ideology, a geographical region, and an historical event. Whereas a number of Northern journalists, academics, and politicians have taken pains to state that Islam is not synonymous with violence or terrorism, their alternative discourses are usually overshadowed by many other opinion leaders who continue to frame information within dominant discourses (Karim 2000: 188–92). Consequently, "Islam," "Islamic," "Muslim," "Shi'ite," etc. have largely become what Gordon Allport called "labels of primary potency," that "act like shrieking sirens, deafening us to all finer discriminations that we might otherwise perceive" (Allport 1958: 175). Such a blurring of reality tends to place aspects of Muslims' lives in artificial categories that inhibit true understanding. Therefore, journalists who had made much of turbans and hijabs as being symbolic of "Islamic fundamentalism" were baffled that a number of the people whom the Taliban had oppressed chose to continue wearing these traditional garments even after the regime was deposed.

Due to the many disagreements about what is truly Islamic, it is necessary to separate between the two ways in which religion manifests. Mohammed Arkoun distinguishes the "metaphysical, religious, spiritual" dimension of Islam, representing the fundamental aspects of Muhammad's message as it appeared in the primary scriptural sources (the Koran and the Prophet's traditions), from "the second level of signification, [which] is the sociohistorical space in which human existence unfolds" (Arkoun 1980: 51). This difference between the theological ideals and the reality that Muslims encounter in pursuing such ideals points to the existence of diverse histories of respective Muslim peoples and governments of various Muslim countries, rather than a unitary "Islamic history," "Islamic people," or "Islamic government." Edward Said notes that "the word *Muslim* is less provocative and more habitual for most Arabs; the word *Islamic* has acquired an activist, even aggressive quality that belies the more ambiguous reality" (Said 1993: 64).

The acts of terrorism by individuals, groups, or governments professing Islam are seen here as belonging to "the sociohistorical space in which human existence unfolds." These actions are willy-nilly part of the history of certain Muslims who carry them out and, by extension, of the histories of their specific regional or national collectivities and even the global Muslim community, insofar as significant acts conducted by members of these groupings are part of these respective histories. However, the terrorist acts carried out by groups like al-Qaeda cannot be described as "Islamic," since these actions do not constitute part of the essential metaphysical, religious, or spiritual dimension of the faith. They cannot even be considered expressions of "*Muslim* terrorism" if this were to be posited as an essential feature of Islam. Nevertheless, the individuals who profess Islam and carry out terrorist acts could be viewed as "Muslim terrorists"—one would then similarly refer to "Christian terrorists," "Jewish terrorists," "Hindu terrorists," and "Buddhist terrorists." Distinguishing between the two dimensions helps to identify the ideological application of Islamic terminology in Northern and Muslim discourses. Sadly, the uninformed use of the terms related to Islam is endemic in the transnational media.

Jack Shaheen writes that television tends to perpetuate four primary stereo-types about Arabs: "they are all fabulously wealthy; they are barbaric and uncultured; they are sex maniacs with a penchant for white slavery; and they revel in acts of terrorism" (Shaheen 1984: 4). Such core images have been the bases for dominant Northern perceptions of Arabs/Muslims since the Middle Ages when they were viewed as being "war-mongers," "luxury lovers," and "sex-maniacs" (Kassis 1992: 261). Although these topoi may vary from time to time in emphasis and in relation to the particular Muslim groups to which they have been applied, they remain the most resilient of Northern images about Muslims. Variations of the four primary stereotypes of Muslims have not only been repro-duced in newspapers and television, but generally appear as the representations of the Muslim Other in popular culture, art, music, literature, school textbooks, public discourse, and computer-based media. Individual Muslims may indeed exhibit such characteristics, but it is grossly inaccurate to suggest that they are shared by significant proportions of Islam's adherents.

The legend of "the Assassins," first popularized in Europe by the Crusaders and by Marco Polo, has become a standard tale in Northern media discourses about "Islamic terrorism"; its attraction to Western journalists seems to be that it dra-matically reconfirms the well-established stereotypes about Muslims, namely those of violence, lust, and barbarism. This story, much embellished in the course of time, is about Nizari Ismailis who acquired a number of forts in northern Iran and Syria/Lebanon during the eleventh century. Under attack from the vastly superior military powers such as the Seljuk sultanate and the Crusaders, they sometimes used the method of assassinating the military and administrative lead-ers of their enemies rather than engage them on the battlefield. European writers imputed that the Nizari Ismaili guerrillas were convinced into risking their lives by being drugged with hashish and then led to a paradisiacal garden populated with enchanting damsels; eternal residence in this garden was promised to them upon their death. (The etymological origin of the word "assassin" in European languages is consequently attributed to "hashish.") Dominant media discourses regularly continue to reinscribe this lurid account even though it has been found to be lacking in historical evidence (Hodgson 1955; Daftary 1995). It is fre-quently used by journalists to present a genealogy of "Islamic terrorists" (Karim 2000: 75–7).

It is remarkable how widely the Assassins legend was used in post-September 11 coverage. Articles in the London-based *Financial Times* (Scott 2001) and the Toronto-based *Globe and Mail* (Mansur 2001) sought to link the terrorist attack to the historical group. A senior reporter with the Canadian Broadcasting Cor-poration, Joe Schlesinger, drew on the tale in the "Foreign Assignment" program on October 28, 2001. It also appeared in a news backgrounder by Emily Yoffe (2001) on MSN's online *Slate* magazine. Even a *New York Times* article that apparently sought to provide a positive historical understanding about medieval

Muslim science as a contrast to contemporary terrorism opened with the lead, "Nasir al-Din al-Tusi was still a young man when the Assassins made him an offer he couldn't refuse" (Overbye 2001). Nor was the script writer of the popular drama series *The West Wing* on the NBC network immune to the Assassins' bug: an episode titled "Isaac and Ishmael" aired on October 10, 2001 referred to the legend.

## Other ways of reporting

Stuart Adam, who proposes a greater emphasis on "the moral, the literary, and the philosophical faces of journalism education" (Adam 1988: 8), laments that the standard style manuals for journalists "rarely speak of the power of metaphor and other literary devices to convey meaning" (ibid.: 9). The focus on imparting professional skills in most journalism schools and the minimal exposure to the humanities or even the social sciences leave students with limited intellectual tools to understand the world. Future journalists also face the disadvantage that even as the presence of Muslims in current events grows, knowledge about their history and cultures is rarely imparted in Western educational systems.

But even if a journalist is well-informed about another culture how does she interpret events in it to produce a coherent account for the reader at home—without losing herself completely in the Other's discourse or conversely lapsing into an ethnocentric narrative? An answer may be found in Abdul JanMohamed's identification of "the specular border intellectual," who must disengage personally from allegiances to any one culture, nation, group, or institution "to the extent that these are defined in monologic, essentialist terms" (JanMohamed 1992: 117). The specular border intellectual/journalist "caught between two cultures . . . subjects the cultures to analytic scrutiny rather than combining them (97)." Instead of becoming disoriented and out of place, she uses the vantage point that she occupies to view horizons difficult for others to envision. The following by Robert Fisk seems to show that even though he was almost killed by Afghan refugees in December 2001, he nonetheless attempted to seek the causes of the incident from their perspective:

> And—I realized—there were all the Afghan men and boys who had attacked me who should never have done so but whose brutality was entirely the product of others, of us—of we who had armed their struggle against the Russians and ignored their pain and laughed at their civil war and then armed and paid them again for the "War for Civilization" just a few miles away and then bombed their homes and ripped up their families and called them "collateral damage."
>
> So I thought I should write about what happened to us in this fearful, silly, bloody, tiny incident. I feared other versions would produce a different narrative, of how a British journalist was "beaten up by a mob of Afghan refugees." And of course, that's the point. The people who were

assaulted were the Afghans, the scars inflicted by us—by B-52s, not by
them. And I'll say it again. If I was an Afghan refugee in Kila Abdullah,
I would have done just what they did. I would have attacked Robert
Fisk. Or any other Westerner I could find.

(Fisk 2001)

It appears that under such circumstances the forbearance required of the specular
border journalist is little short of heroic, but apparently not impossible. The foreign correspondent, by learning to question the essentialist bases of her own
socialization and placing herself in the Other's shoes, could genuinely begin to
understand the people she is covering. The ideal of a specular border journalism
has the potential for providing genuinely global narratives that are not monolithic but pluralist, in which cultures are not arranged hierarchically. Such
discourses become all the more crucial as people in different locations on the
planet seek to develop a worldwide civil society.

One significant barrier facing the development of informed reportage about
Islam is the lack of knowledge and unease among many Northern journalists
about religion in general. Henry A. Grunwald, a former editor-in-chief of *Time*,
arguing in 1993 for the need for a new journalism in the post-Cold War era,
noted:

> Crucial among the newer topics journalism must address are tribalism
> and ethnic self-assertion, phenomena about which social scientists, let
> alone reporters, know little; likewise with religion, a subject most jour-
> nalists have found unsettling ever since it wandered from the Sunday
> religion pages to the front page. Religious wars, large and small, seem
> increasingly likely in the decades ahead. *Time* magazine recently tied
> together in one cover package the bombing of the World Trade Center
> in New York City by Muslim fundamentalists, the siege in Texas of a
> group of cultists whose leader apparently thought he was a messiah, and
> the conflict between Muslims and Christians in Bosnia. This link was
> legitimate but frail, because these were very different manifestations of
> "religion." Not every Muslim fundamentalist wants to blow up New
> York City, and few Christian fundamentalists belong to cults ready for
> Armageddon. The press must discuss such distinctions knowledgeably
> and conscientiously.
>
> (Grunwald 1993: 14–15)

Unfortunately, such journalistic hindsight about "religious wars" seems to occur
usually after considerable damage has already been done by traditional media
discourses. Most Northern journalists covering Muslim societies are largely unfamiliar not only with the subtleties of the contemporary religious debates but also
with the primary beliefs and practices of their members. Deviant faith frequently
becomes the focus for reporters not familiar with issues of spirituality. The practice

112

of Sufism, popular in virtually all Muslim societies and which overtly emphasizes Islam's humanistic side in its aspirations for universal fellowship, has been almost unacknowledged in the news media.

Hamid Mowlana's study of the American mass media's coverage of the Iranian hostage situation (1979–81) considered alternative modes of reporting conflicts (Mowlana 1984: 94–5). He suggested that journalists should have attempted to assist in the resolution of the Iranian hostage crisis rather than inflame passions on both sides with their reporting. Mowlana proposed that, instead of contributing to a crisis mood, the Northern media could help create non-conflictual attitudes in periods of moderate stress. An exploration of "universal concepts of religious, ideological, or traditional values should be used to bridge the existing cultural communication gap. The common aspects of life that unite rather than divide could be emphasized" (94). However, these suggestions have gone largely unheeded following September 11 as the mass media adopted the Bush administration's "us versus them" frame.

Contemporary approaches of conflict resolution suggest the importance of understanding symbols and symbolic behavior (rituals) on the part of disputing parties. More than statistics or descriptions of events, the symbolic subtexts of human interactions should be among the primary foci of interest for journalists. Symbols and rituals help establish power and are key to interpreting gestures of peace-making, forgiveness, and harmonious co-existence (Cohen and Arnone 1988; Smith 1989). Underlying symbols and rituals is myth; it is vital for journalists as observers of the human condition to be cognizant of the place of myth and symbols. The mythical significance of Jerusalem, for example, is key to understanding the contemporary relations not only between Palestinians and Israelis but also among Muslims, Christians, and Jews. Media references to "the Temple Mount" rather than "Haram al-Shareef" privilege the Jewish perspective and history over the Muslim. Mohammed Arkoun has argued for a better appreciation of "the *radical imaginary*" (Arkoun 1994: 9) common to Jews, Christians, and Muslims. Viewed here as the singular Abrahamic root of these believers' respective sets of symbols, the "radical imaginary" could be tapped to understand the true universals shared by these communities for the development of dynamic national and transnational civil societies. Indeed, there is a larger need to extend understanding of human universals to engender a genuinely global civil society.

The dominant discourses of journalism are rationalistic. They tend to undervalue those actions and events that cannot be explained by "the logic of the concrete" (Tuchman 1981: 90), which derives from mainstream political or socio-economic theories. Media narratives therefore generally disregard the non-rationalist expressions of the human spirit. Quite apart from religious motivations, all human beings carry out actions whose causes have little to do with the rational faculty. Astute journalists have long recognized that compassion, love, devotion, faith, loyalty, honor, pride, ambition, guilt, jealousy, fear, anger, hate, and revenge are among the most powerful "positive" and "negative" impulses, driving people to behave in manners that rationalism fails to inspire.

Those who do not understand these fundamental workings of human communication fail to comprehend the non-rationalism of much of social, political, and economic behavior as well as the roots of truly universal values. As a result they tend to attribute the actions which they do not understand almost perfunctorily to "the bizarre," "the strange," "barbarism," "fanaticism," or "fundamentalism." They also fail to comprehend the direct, physical violence which is a reaction to the structural violence of the rationalist discourses that deny what Johann Galtung calls the "higher needs" of human beings. Understanding the dynamics of power and violence in the relationship between Northern and Muslim societies necessarily involves an appreciation of the continual assault by the dominant technological discourses on the spiritual as well as the rational sensibilities of people in these societies.

If Northern journalists wish to produce informed reporting on Muslims they will find it necessary to reorient their modes of operation. First of all, one has to understand the basis of one's own conceptualization about the Other. Collective cultural memories play a large part in our views about Islam, as do our society's fundamental myths. Recognizing the fundamentally cultural nature of journalism enables journalists to uncover and utilize the cultural tools of understanding that make possible genuine insights into human nature. Such cognition helps to comprehend the importance that religious beliefs hold for significant numbers of people. It helps to show that they cannot be dismissed as superstitious, bizarre, or quaint but need to be recognized for forming a vital part of many individuals' existence. The human spirit is the source of universal values; rather than dwell on superficial differences, the recognition of the truly universal can help the observer of foreign cultures to understand the basis of their members' actions. Symbols and rituals embedded in daily life constitute a language that is a truer guide to deeply-held attitudes than political and diplomatic discourses.

The journalists who realize the value of these fundamental forms of communication are able to decipher the reality that underlies words and gestures. Those who are mired in stereotypical images of groups and individuals produce hackneyed reports that do not go beyond conflictual scenarios. The institutional response of the mass media to a conflict situation is usually to react first, using clichés and stereotypes in almost unrestrained manners, and then to reflect upon the matter. Journalism as a craft has to explore seriously the ways of rising above those of its institutional structures that mould adherence to routinized forms of reporting and formulaic models inhibiting informed and conscientious reporting. The rupture resulting from the events of September 11 presents a longer-term opportunity for turning towards more authentic and insightful coverage of the world.

## Notes

1 For a discussion on the competition of dominant and other discourses in the media, see Karim 2000: 4–6.

2   When the US military went into Afghanistan to attack the Taliban regime and the al-Qaeda network, the limited coverage given to the air strikes' substantial damage to civilian property and the deaths of more than 3,000 Afghan civilians was in stark contrast to the extensive reporting of the handful of US casualties.

3   The presence of correspondents such as Robert Fisk in the *Independent* as well as the space given to guest writers like Karen Armstrong in *Time* magazine (October 1, 2001) and Mai Yamani in the *Sunday Times* (London) (October 7, 2001) provided for alternative discourses. Particularly significant was the growing number of senior journalists of Muslim backgrounds working for Western media, e.g. Yasmin Alibhai-Brown for the *Independent* and Haroon Siddiqui for the *Toronto Star*.

4   Given the growing alliance of interests of the West and Eastern Europe (since the collapse of the Soviet Union) and their generally similar historical and current stances towards Muslim societies, it is pertinent to use this broader geopolitical term. See Karim 2000: 7.

5   For a discussion of the Northern media's treatment of Christian Arabs, see Karim 2000: 99–101, 111–17.

# References

Adam, S. (1988) Thinking journalism, *Content*, July/August 4–11.

Ahmed, A. S. (1992) *Islam and Postmodernism: Predicament and Promise*, London: Routledge.

Allport, G. W. (1958) *The Nature of Prejudice*, Garden City, NY: Doubleday Anchor Books.

Arkoun, M. (1980) Islam, urbanism and human existence today, in The Aga Khan Award for Architecture, *Architecture as Symbol and Self-Identity*, Geneva: The Aga Khan Awards: 51–4.

Arkoun, M. (1994) *Rethinking Islam: Common Questions, Uncommon Answers*, translated by Robert D. Lee, Boulder, CO: Westview.

Chomsky, N. (1991) International terrorism: image and reality, in Alexander George (ed.) *Western State Terrorism*, New York: Routledge, pp. 39–75.

Cohen, S. P. and Arnone, H. C. (1988) Conflict resolution as the alternative to terrorism, *Journal of Social Issues*, 44 (2): 175–89.

Daftary, F. (1995) *The Assassin Legends: Myths of the Isma'ilis*, London: I. B. Tauris.

Ellul, J. (1969) *Propaganda: The Formation of Men's Attitudes*, translated by K. Kellen and J. Lerner, New York: Alfred A. Knopf.

Fisk, R. (1990) *Pity the Nation: Lebanon at War*, Oxford: Oxford University Press.

Fisk, R. (2001) My beating by refugees is a symbol of the hatred and fury of this filthy war, *Independent*, London, December 10.

Galtung, J. (1981) The specific contribution of peace studies to the study of violence, in UNESCO, *Violence and Its Causes*, Paris: UNESCO: 83–96.

Grunwald, H. A. (1993) The post-Cold War press: a new world needs a new journalism, *Foreign Affairs*, Summer: 12–16.

Hall, S. (1979) Culture, media and the "ideological effect," in James Curran, Michael Gurevitch, and Jane Woollacott (eds) *Mass Communication and Society*, Beverly Hills, CA: Sage: 315–48.

Herman, E. (1985) *The Real Terror Network: Terrorism in Fact and Propaganda*, Montreal: Black Rose.

Hodgson, M. G. S. (1955) *The Order of Assassins*, The Hague: Mouton.

Horton, R. (2001) Public health: a neglected counterterrorist measure, *The Lancet*, 358 (9288) October 6: 1,112–13.

JanMohamed, A. R. (1992) Worldliness-without-world, homelessness-as-home: toward a definition of a specular border intellectual, in Michael Sprinker (ed.) *Edward Said: A Critical Reader*, Oxford: Blackwell: 96–120.

Karim, K. H. (2000) *Islamic Peril: Media and Global Violence*, Montreal: Black Rose.

Kassis, H. E. (1992) Christian misconceptions of Islam, in Mordecai Briemberg (ed.) *It Was, It Was Not: Essays and Art on the War against Iraq*, Vancouver: New Star Books: 254–64.

Kertzer, D. I. (1988) *Ritual, Politics, and Power*, New Haven, CN: Yale University Press.

Mansur, S. (2001) The father of all assassins, *Globe and Mail*, Toronto, October 11.

Mernissi, F. (1992) *Islam and Democracy: Fear of the Modern World*, translated by Mary Jo Lakeland, New York: Addison Wesley.

Mosco, V. (2002) 9/11 for urban policy, paper presented at the Annual Meeting of the Urban Affairs Association, March, Boston, MA.

Mowlana, H. (1984) The role of the media in the US–Iranian conflict, in Andrew Arno and Wimal Dissanayake (eds) *The News Media in National and International Conflict*, Boulder, CO: Westview: 71–99.

*New Internationalist* (2001) Two terrors, November 18–19.

Overbye, D. (2001) How Islam won, and lost, the lead in science, *New York Times*, October 30.

Said, E. W. (1993) The phony Islamic threat, *New York Times Magazine*, November 21: 62–5.

Scott, T. (2001) Grim lessons from a legendary Muslim, *Financial Times Weekend*, London, October 6–7.

Shaheen, J. G. (1984) *The TV Arab*, Bowling Green, OH: Bowling Green State University Popular Press.

Smith, D. L. (1989) The rewards of Allah, *Journal of Peace Research*, 26 (4) 385–98.

Tuchman, G. (1978) *Making News: A Study in the Construction of Reality*, New York: The Free Press.

Tuchman, G. (1981) Myth and the consciousness industry: a new look at the effects of the mass media, in E. Katz and T. Szecskö (eds) *Mass Media and Social Change*, Beverley Hills, CA: Sage: 83–100.

van Dijk, T. (1988) *News Analysis: Case Studies of International and National News in the Press*, Hillsdale, NJ: Lawrence Erlbaum.

Weber, M. (1946) *From Max Weber: Essays in Sociology*, translated by H. H. Gerth and C. Wright Mills, New York: Oxford University Press.

Winter, J. (1992) *Common Cents: Media Portrayal of the Gulf War and Other Events*, Montreal: Black Rose.

Yoffe, E. (2001) Bernard Lewis: the Islam scholar US politicians listen to, posted Tuesday, November 13, 2001, slate.msn.com/?id=2058632.

Part 3

# THE CHANGING BOUNDARIES
# OF JOURNALISM

# 7

# REWEAVING THE INTERNET
## Online news of September 11[1]

*Stuart Allan*

"This unfathomable tragedy," online writer Rogers Cadenhead observed, "reminds me of the original reason the Internet was invented in 1969—to serve as a decentralized network that couldn't be brought down by a military attack." Cadenhead's comment was made to *New York Times* reporter Amy Harmon (2001a), who interviewed him on September 11 about the role his World Trade Center attack e-mail discussion list was playing that day in circulating news about what was happening. In the early hours after the attacks, most of the country's major news sites were so overburdened with "Web traffic" that they were unable to operate efficiently. "Amateur news reporters on weblogs are functioning as their own decentralized media today," Cadenhead added, "and it's one of the only heartening things about this stomach-turning day."

The development of the Internet as a news provider is often described as a series of formative moments, each of which highlights from a respective vantage point the evolving dynamics of online journalism. Such moments are typically said to include, for different reasons, the Oklahoma City bombing, the TWA 800 explosion, the Heaven's Gate mass suicide, Princess Diana's car crash, and the *Drudge Report's* posting of the initial revelations concerning former President Bill Clinton's relationship with White House intern Monica Lewinsky (see Borden and Harvey 1998; Davis 1999; Pavlik 2001). More recently, the conflict in Kosovo has been called the "first Internet war," namely due to the ways in which online spaces were created for alternative viewpoints, background materials, eyewitness accounts and interactivity with members of the public (see Taylor 2000; Hall 2001). In the aftermath of September 11, then, it is not surprising that several online news commentators have been quick to declare the attacks to be the biggest story to break in the Internet Age. Even for those who share this perspective, however, it does not necessarily follow that online reporters played a decisive role with regard to how it was covered. The precise nature of that role continues to be the subject of much discussion and debate. It is the aim of this chapter to contribute to this critical assessment.

STUART ALLAN

## Covering the crisis

Since the emergence of online news sites in the 1990s, a wide-ranging—and at times acrimonious—array of debates has transpired over their status as providers of quality reporting. To date there has yet to emerge anything resembling a consensus about the present, let alone potential, impact of new media technologies in shaping journalistic forms and practices. Some voices, frequently described as "members of the old guard," call for restraint to be exercised, while others, excited about new technological possibilities, herald their promise. Not surprisingly, individuals positioned on each side of these debates have found evidence in the September 11 tragedy to support their preferred stance. Above dispute, as noted, is the fact that many of the major online news sites in the US—such as CNN.com, MSNBC.com, ABCNews.com, CBS.com and FoxNews.com—were so besieged by user demand in the early hours of the attacks that they were largely inaccessible. Criticism leveled by some non-web journalists has been sharp and to the point. "At a time when information-starved Americans needed it as never before," *Detroit Free Press* newspaper columnist Mike Wendland (2001) declared, "the Internet failed miserably in the hours immediately following yesterday's terrorist attacks."

Before turning to the difficulties experienced by some Internet news sites struggling to cope with demand, it is important to note from the outset how this exigency was further compounded by problems arising from the destruction of the World Trade Center itself. Long distance telephone lines, numbering in the thousands, were severed when the North Tower collapsed. These lines formed a crucial component of the infrastructure connecting several major network sites to the Internet. At the same time, several radio and television stations lost their transmitter towers with the World Trade Center's collapse. Some stations were able to stay on the air, such as the local CBS affiliate once it switched to a backup antenna on the Empire State Building, while others were knocked off the airwaves completely. Included in the latter were the local affiliates of the ABC, NBC and Fox networks. An estimated 30 percent of households in the area relying on over-the-air antennas were unable to receive signals from them, although cable television subscribers were unaffected (Schiesel with Hansell 2001). Significantly, WNBC's Internet counterpart, The FeedRoom (www.FeedRoom.com), a streaming-news website, was able to provide live footage. Situated some ten blocks from the World Trade Center, the FeedRoom turned two of its digital cameras toward the towers following the first explosion (Hu 2001b).

Shortly after 9:00 am local time in New York, telephone communication came to a standstill in parts of the upper Eastern seaboard. As Nancy Weil (2001) reported, "it became impossible to get a phone call out of or into New York and other major East Coast cities, including Washington, DC, and Boston." Many people attempting to make telephone calls either to or from the affected cities heard only an "All circuits are busy" recording. Text messaging, via cell phones, proved to be effective for some, mainly because such messages were sent over different networks than those carrying voice calls. Hours would pass before telephone traffic could be re-routed, making the networks accessible again. In the meantime, for those New Yorkers unable to communicate via wireless and landline telephones, the Internet provided other ways of making contact with relatives, friends, and colleagues. Many went straight to e-mail and instant messaging, posted messages to their online communities and mailing lists, or logged on to instant IRC (Internet Relay Chat) services. Most e-mail services were largely unaffected by the sudden surges or "spikes" in Internet traffic and related technical breakdowns. E-mailed "I'm OK" messages were usually able to get through. One office worker in a building close to the World Trade Center said that he sent e-mails to "everyone I could think of" after the attacks. He sent the messages "as soon as things got really bad because I knew people would worry about me. After that, the e-mails I got were from people worried about other folks in Manhattan, and news updates" (cited in Olsen 2001).

The Internet's main "backbone" lines stayed functional, with the overall flow of data remaining stable. Nevertheless, the amount of network use was such that logjams formed at the hub, or server, computers responsible for routing traffic to and from websites (Glasner 2001; Schiesel with Hansell 2001). The websites of the airlines whose planes had crashed—American Airlines and United Airlines—were experiencing more traffic than they could manage. People looking for information about the tragedy, or seeking updates on transportation conditions, were likely to be frustrated in their efforts. Also experiencing difficulties were several of the law firms and small businesses located in and around the World Trade Center, who were looking to the Internet to post information about their status and what they were doing to cope with the situation. The website of one law firm, for example, posted the following message for employees' families and clients:

> Due to the tragic events that have occurred in New York and Washington this morning, we are closing all of our offices. We will keep you apprised of developments, as appropriate, via the Web site, voice mail and e-mails. Based on the information currently available to us, we understand that all of our personnel in the World Trade Center were evacuated safely.
>
> (cited in Olsen 2001)

Some companies, of course, were not so fortunate. Their websites were used to report the deaths of colleagues. Emergency numbers were also posted for staff members to contact in the event that they had survived. Relief organizations similarly moved quickly to establish a Web presence. The American Red Cross, for example, called upon technology companies to provide web space for public appeals for blood donations for those injured in the attacks. Moreover, the organization's Web team sent its own reporters to New York and the Pentagon so that they could post news updates at RedCross.org and DisasterRelief.org. The importance of keeping information continuously updated was emphasized by Phil Zepeda, the Red Cross' director of online media: "It's an immediate medium. People expect to go there and find out what's happening now, not what happened six hours ago" (cited in Walker 2001a). Still other Web users sought information from police and firefighter sites instead. It was possible to listen to dispatches between police officers on a NYPD scanner site (www.policescanner.com/policeNYPD.stm), for example, as well as other audio feeds from related sites for emergency workers. The unofficial site of the NY firefighters provided information updates, photographs, and archival links, such as to radio codes (Langfield 2001b). By mid-afternoon, however, most of these sites had also succumbed to Internet congestion (Wendland 2001).

Spurred into action to lend a hand, several members of the public rewrote their Web pages to create electronic spaces for dialogue. Science-fiction writer William Shunn, for example, opened up his site to create a shared list to circulate information amongst his family and friends. In a matter of hours, however, the site promptly burgeoned into the first online "survivor registry" for New Yorkers (www.shunn.net/okay/), affording everyone the space to post a brief note or contact details. As Shunn writes:

> Messages from across the country appeared in my inbox, some from users who had inadvertently posted the names of the missing as survivors. I worked as fast as I could to delete erroneous reports, to screen out profanity and hate speech, and to implement a much-requested search function.
>
> By midnight the URL had spread so far that high traffic rendered the board unusable. I had to close it down, freezing the list at 2,500 entries, and shift the burden of data collection to other unofficial registries.
>
> The next day, five hundred E-mails offered me thanks, blessed me, called me an American hero. A CNET reporter said my efforts were a mitzvah. Another hundred messages asked what I knew about missing loved ones, or begged me to reveal who had posted a son or daughter's name to the check-in list. Dozens more demonized me for the list's inaccuracies, or for the ugly jokes and racist diatribes that had sneaked on.
>
> I came to believe what I built on Tuesday, imperfect as it was, was right and necessary for that moment in time . . . Outbursts of terror and grief share the page with avowals of love, hope, and faith. Clots of insensitivity lodge among eloquent pleas for understanding, closed fists of hatred among prayers for surcease from pain. I find raw eruptions of anger and confusion cheek by jowl with moments of brilliant, shining joy.
>
> (www.shunn.net/okay/)

Shunn believed that the site received over a million hits that day and the next. Other survivor registries also emerged, as he noted, and like his site drew readers in such numbers that they too struggled to remain operational. Due to the kinds of problems Shunn identified, however, most began to direct visitors to official sites, such as the Hospital Patient Locator System (LiCalzi O'Connell 2001).

As for the major news sites, it is worth pointing out that to date no other news event had affected Internet performance to a greater extent than this crisis. While events such as the 2000 US election, or before it the release of the Starr Report in 1998, had a considerable impact, September 11 and its immediate aftermath produced the most dramatic decline in the availability of the major news sites yet witnessed. News sites, which the day before had been counting their "hits" in the hundreds of thousands per hour, suddenly experienced millions of such hits. Online news managers, like their mainstream news counterparts, were caught completely off-guard by breaking developments of this speed and magnitude. MSNBC.com, for example, reportedly registered as many as 400,000 people hitting its pages simultaneously. In the case of CNN.com, nine million page views were made per hour that morning. Where some 14 million page views would be ordinarily made over the course of an entire day, about 162 million views were made that day (Outing 2001b). Each of the other major news sites could be reached only sporadically as efforts mounted to ward off the danger of the Internet infrastructure undergoing a complete "congestion collapse."

Pertinent insights into these dynamics are provided in the accounts written both by Internet users, as well as by journalists, which will be discussed below. First, though, evidence provided in a report prepared by the Pew Internet and American Life Project helps to contextualize these accounts. The study's data were collected via a daily tracking survey of people's use of the Internet in the US. Specifically, telephone interviews were conducted among a random sample of 1,226 adults, aged 18 and older (some 663 of whom were Internet users), between September 12 and September 13. The results for such a limited study need to be treated with caution, not least due to the usual sorts of qualifications where opinion surveys are concerned (sampling error, interpretations of question wording, practical difficulties), yet may be broadly suggestive of certain types of patterns. The findings highlighted the difficulties Internet users experienced in reaching certain news sites on the day of the attacks:

> About 43% of them said they had problems getting to the sites they wanted to access. Of those who had trouble, 41% kept trying to get to the same site until they finally reached it; 38% went to other sites, 19% gave up their search . . . A high proportion of Internet users were actively surfing to get all the information they could about the crisis; 58% of those seeking news online were going to multiple Web sites in their hunt for information.
>
> (Pew Internet and American Life Project 2001: 4)

In general terms, however, the authors of the report stressed that "Internet users were just like everyone else in the population in their devotion to getting most of their news from television" (ibid.: 3). Consequently, these findings appear to confirm the assumption that for most Internet users online news provided a helpful supplement to television, by far their primary resource for news about the tragedy.

On this basis alone, some critics have been quite dismissive of the contribution made by the major online news sites to the coverage. "It's a bad day for Internet media," argues journalist Steve Outing (2001a), "when it can't accommodate demand and the audience shifts back to traditional media sources." Still, this line of criticism prefigures a somewhat narrow definition of what counts as online journalism. While conceding that serious problems existed with the coverage available from the major sites, Leander Kahney (2001a) nevertheless argued an opposing point of view: "under the radar, the Net responded magnificently; it was just a matter of knowing where to look."

## Tangled wires

Judging from some of the personal recollections published to date, few online journalists would dispute the claim that television led the way in covering the attacks during the early hours. "When the unexpected met the unimaginable," online journalist Wayne Robins maintained, the various newspaper websites available "were no match for the numbing live and taped pictures of the catastrophe broadcast on TV." This news story, he added, "was war, an unnatural disaster, with horrific developments overlapping before your eyes with such speed that the brain—never mind the computer keyboard—couldn't process the information" (Robins 2001a). Similarly, Nick Wrenn, an editor at CNN.com Europe, pointed out: "To be honest, it showed that the web is not quite up to the job yet. It couldn't meet the demand and millions of viewers would've gone from the web to TV for updates" (cited in the *Guardian*, September 17, 2001).

The dramatic footage of crashing jetliners was indeed such that individuals with access to television were much less likely to turn to the Internet than those who were deskbound, such as office workers. Even the homepage of the popular Google.com search engine posted an advisory message which made the point bluntly:

> If you are looking for news, you will find the most current information on TV or radio. Many online news services are not available, because of extremely high demand. Below are links to news sites, including cached copies as they appeared earlier today.
>
> (cited in Langfield 2001a)

A decision was taken at Google.com to transfer duplicates of news articles from the major news sites to a special news page, thereby making them available to those otherwise unable to access them. As the site's co-founder and president, Sergey Brin, stated when interviewed: "We took it upon ourselves to deliver the news, because the rest of the Internet wasn't able to cope as well" (cited in Walker 2001a).

Online news sites, painfully aware of their users' frustrations, struggled to make the best of a desperate situation. In the early hours of the crisis, efforts to cope with the huge upsurge in traffic were varied and met with limited success. Several news sites responded by removing from their web pages any image-intensive graphics, in some cases reducing advertising content, so as to facilitate access. CNN.com, for example, trimmed away all but the most essential graphics under its "America under Attack" title, allowing pages to be loaded much more efficiently. "Viewed another way," commented Bob Tedsechi (2001), "CNN.com's home page before the events held more than 255 kilobytes of information; the slimmed-down version was about 20 kilobytes." ABCnews.com adopted a similar approach, while the homepage for CBSnews.com consisted of a grey page featuring a single hyperlink to one story, accompanied by a photograph. Evidently efforts to access MSNBC.com occasionally met with the message: "You're seeing this page because MSNBC is experiencing high site traffic," and were unable to proceed beyond it (McWilliams 2001a).

Further strategies to improve the capacity of websites to respond included expanding the amount of bandwidth available, bringing additional computer servers online, suspending user registration processes and temporarily turning off traffic-tracking software (Outing 2001a; Robins 2001a). The New York Times site even dispensed with its famous masthead to streamline the loading process. Others, such as the New York Post's site, simply opted to point readers to an Associated Press story (Blair 2001). Still, for those restricted to their computers for information, the response time of some news sites—if and when they actually loaded—must have seemed painfully slow. It is significant to note in this context that advertising messages remained a constant feature on many news sites, despite the fact that their presence can slow the loading time of a webpage considerably. Amongst those sites which eliminated most of their advertising was USAToday.com, which apparently retained only one small advertisement on its homepage. Meanwhile WashingtonPost.com cleared its homepage of all advertisements but loaded them with individual stories (Langfield 2001b). In contrast, television stations did not interrupt their news coverage with advertising on September 11, nor for a good part of September 12.

In light of these and related difficulties associated with accessing the major news sites, many users were forced to look elsewhere on the Internet for information about breaking developments. Those turning to the websites associated with the wire services, such as Associated Press and Reuters.com, also encountered similar technical difficulties, however. News sites offering links to less well-known newspaper sources—such as the Drudge Report (www.drudgereport.com)—were typically less burdened with web traffic. Such was also the case with "specialty" news sites, such as those associated with business publications. The Wall Street Journal, its main office evacuated due to its proximity to the World Trade Center, made its website free of charge for the day. The stock markets having closed, Bloomberg.com, a financial news site, posted continuing updates while assessing the possible implications of the events for futures trading and interest rates.

Meanwhile news portals, namely sites which offer readers a range of links to newspaper and trade publications, also stepped into the breach. One such portal, Newshub (www.newshub.com), reportedly performed consistently throughout the day, offering information updates every 15 minutes (Wendland 2001).

Definitions of what counted as a "news" site were even more dramatically recast by the crisis. Several non-news sites stepped in to play a crucial role, their operators promptly recasting them so as to make information available as it emerged. In the case of a so-called "tech site" such as Slashdot.com ("News for Nerds. Stuff that matters"), for example, its editor posted this message 23 minutes after the first airliner struck the World Trade Center:

*World Trade Towers and Pentagon Attacked*

Posted by Cmdr Taco on Tuesday, September 11, @08:12AM [09:12 am EDT] from the you-can't-make-this-stuff-up dept.
   The World Trade Towers in New York were crashed into by 2 planes, one on each tower, 18 minutes apart. Nobody really knows who did it, but the planes were big ones. Normally I wouldn't consider posting this on Slashdot, but I'm making an exception this time because I can't get news through any of the conventional websites, and I assume I'm not alone.

*Update* We're having server problems. Sorry. Updated info, both towers have collapsed, pentagon hit by 3rd plane. Part of it has collapsed.

The site's founder, Rob "Cmdr Taco" Malda, decided not to offer links to mainstream news sites. "I couldn't get to CNN. MSNBC loaded but very slowly. Far too slowly to bother linking. I posted whatever facts we had" (cited in Miller 2001). Slashdot's staff of four people kept the site online throughout the day, according to Brad King (2001), even though at 60 page views a second it was experiencing nearly triple its average amount of traffic. Significantly, as online journalist Robin Miller (2001) later pointed out, "[w]hen media pundits talk about 'news on the Internet' Slashdot is almost never mentioned, even though it has more regular readers than all but a few newspapers." The secret of its success, he added, was that its contributors "don't use the Internet as a one-way, broadcast-style or newspaper-like information distribution medium, but as a collaborative, fully interactive network that has the power to bring many voices together and weave them into a single web."

On September 11, these kinds of alternative news sites, Jon Katz (2001) wrote at Slashdot.org, "were a source of clarity and accuracy for many millions of people, puzzled or frightened by alarmist reports on TV and elsewhere." Slashdot was joined by several other "techie" or community-news sites which similarly provided ad hoc portals for news, background information and discussion. Staff working at Scripting.com, a site ordinarily devoted to technical discussions of web programming, set to work redistributing news items otherwise inaccessible at their original news site (Glasner 2001). Also posted on the site were personal eyewitness accounts and photographs e-mailed to the site by users, thereby providing readers with fresh perspectives on the crisis. As one of the site's writers stated in a note posted on the opening page the following day:

> The Web has a lot more people to cover a story. We, collectively, got on it very quickly once it was clear that the news sites were choked with flow and didn't have very much info . . . There's power in the new communication and development medium we're mastering. Far from being dead, the Web is just getting started.
>
> (cited in Kahney 2001a)

Morpheus, a multimedia file-swapping service, was similarly transformed into an alternative news source. Posted on its start page was the notice: "Now you can do your part to make sure the news will always be available to members of the Morpheus Users Network. Imagine the power of a news organization with 20 million reporters around the world. BE THE MEDIA!" (cited in Hu 2001b).

## Personal journalism

This invitation to "be the media," and thus to challenge traditional definitions of what counted as "news" as well as who qualified as a "journalist," was very much consistent with the animating ethos of the Internet. Hundreds of refashioned websites began to appear over the course of September 11, making publicly available eyewitness accounts, personal photographs, and in some cases video footage of the unfolding disasters.

Taken together, these websites resembled something of a first-person news network, a collective form of collaborative newsgathering. Ordinary people were transforming into "amateur newsies," to use a term frequently heard, or instant reporters, photojournalists, and opinion columnists. Many of them were hardly amateurs in the strict sense of the word, however, as they were otherwise employed as professional writers, photographers, or designers. "Anyone who had access to a digital camera and a website suddenly was a guerrilla journalist posting these things," said one graphic designer turned photojournalist. "When you're viewing an experience through a viewfinder, you become bolder" (cited in Hu 2001b). The contributions to so-called "personal journalism" or what some described as "citizen-produced coverage" appeared from diverse locations, so diverse as to make judgments about their accuracy difficult if not impossible. These types of personal news items were forwarded via e-mail many times over by people who did not actually know the original writer or photographer. Presumably for those "personal journalists" giving sincere expression to their experiences, though, the sending of such messages had something of a cathartic effect. In any case, the contrast with mainstream reporting was stark. "[N]ot only

127

was so-called citizen-produced coverage sometimes more accessible," argued Leander Kahney (2001b), "it was often more compelling."

Certain comments about "personal journalism" posted by readers of different webpages suggested that these forms of reporting may have provided some members of the online community with a greater sense of connection to the crisis than that afforded by "official" news reports. To quote one posting to a website: "The news coverage thus far has been heavily skewed to talking heads, while the Internet has overflowed with (talkative) New Yorkers and DCites, telling the real story" (cited in Kahney 2001a). Such generalizations aside, of particular importance here was the crucial role played by weblogs (personal journals, generally thick with clickable hyperlinks to other items available elsewhere on the Web) in making these forms of journalism possible. "Most of the amateur content," Kahney (2001b) observed, "would be inaccessible, or at least hard to find, if not for many of the Web's outstanding weblogs, which function as 'portals' to personal content." Managers of these weblogs spent the day rapidly linking together any available amateur accounts and photographs onto their respective sites. "Some people cope by hearing and distributing information in a crisis," wrote the owner of one popular weblog. "I'm one of those people, I guess. Makes me feel like I'm doing something useful for those that can't do anything" (cited in Kahney 2001a). Another person stated: "I found that for me, posting videos and sharing these experiences was the best therapy. It's a modern way of a survivor of a disaster declaring, 'I'm still alive; look at this website. I got out'" (cited in Hu 2001b).

In stretching the boundaries of what counted as journalism, "amateur newsies" and their webloggers together threw into sharp relief the reportorial conventions of mainstream journalism. The webloggers, as Mindy McAdams pointed out, "illustrated how news sources are not restricted to what we think of as the traditional news media." Indeed, she added, the "man-on-the street interview is now authored by the man on the street and self-published, including his pictures" (cited in Raphael 2001). The significance of these interventions was not lost on full-time journalists, of course, as many of them turned to weblogs with interest. Commenting on this sudden recognition of weblogs as legitimate news sources, weblogger Edward Champion observed

> overworked journalists, laboring in twelve hour shifts, scrambling for a story amidst pressures, contending with demands from editors and the need to fill copy, did what any overworked journalist would do under the circumstances. They pilfered the leads found through the weblogs and followed up on the stories. In other words, it could be suggested that, while journalism has failed to live up to its initial investigative or objective roles, weblogs offered a polyglot of voices crying from the Babel Tower, demanding a media that actually mattered.
>
> (Champion 2001)

Just as television newscasts occasionally drew upon so-called "amateur" video footage to supplement their reports, the mainstream news sites instigated a similar type of practice. Several sites moved quickly to make space for eyewitness accounts and photographs produced by members of the public at one of the scenes. At the same time bulletin boards, such as one on the MSNBC site, enabled readers to post their experiences of what they had witnessed. WashingtonPost.com, which led with the Pentagon story, placed on its opening page: "Reporter's Query: How were you affected by today's events? E-mail your story and please include your name and phone number," followed by an e-mail address (cited in Langfield 2001a). Calm, level-headed descriptions were being set alongside deeply emotional outbursts. These first-hand accounts and survivor stories, in the words of one *New York Times* reporter, were "social history in its rawest, tear-stained form" (LiCalzi O'Connell 2001).

Further dimensions to online journalism's contribution to reporting the crisis became ever more apparent as the day unfolded. Several news sites extended their e-mail alert lists so as to notify registered users of breaking events. Some made available a timeline, enabling users to better grasp the sequence of occurrences. On other sites, a decision was taken not to impose narrative order on the available information, opting instead to lead with the latest details—in some cases presented in bullet-point form—as they emerged. Quite a few sites introduced "fact sheets" to help users to better distinguish between claims based in fact and those claims which could be more accurately classified as speculation. Sidebars to the main story, where they appeared, sometimes provided links to items from the wire services, as well as to more local information (the closing of airports, roads, schools, government offices, and so forth). Moreover, as photographs e-mailed in from users began to accumulate, some sites organized them into discrete collections. "At first I thought photo galleries on the Web might be superfluous, given the wall-to-wall television," stated Joe Russin, assistant managing editor at latimes.com. "But millions of page views can't be wrong. It appears people really wanted to look at these images in their own time, contemplating and absorbing the tragedy in ways that the rush of television could not accommodate" (cited in Robins 2001b).

Some journalists entered Internet chat rooms, requesting contact from people with eyewitness accounts or those willing to discuss efforts to reach relatives in New York City or at the Pentagon. Many such journalists worked for newspapers producing an extra edition that afternoon, and so they wanted to supplement news items with local takes or angles on the events (Runett 2001). In the first 48 hours after the attacks, according to the study by the Pew Internet and American Life Project discussed above, "13% of Internet users 'attended' virtual meetings or participated in virtual communities by reading or posting comments in chat rooms, online bulletin boards, or email listservs" (Pew Internet and American Life Project 2001: 3). This percentage represented a significant increase in these activities, as the authors maintained that only four percent of online Americans visit chat rooms on a typical day. Yahoo.com's New York room, according to Tim Blair (2001), "swelled to 1,600 (about 1,400 more than usual for early morning) as desperate web searchers sought updates." Meanwhile the Yahoo club Islam-Openforum, said to have 2,700 members, became caught-up in an anti-Muslim backlash. One posting after the next vented certain readers' fury as they sought to affix blame for the tragedy.

Particularly pertinent here were the online chats hosted by different news sites. Among the first to set up a chat area was ABCNews.com, where message titles reportedly included: "Pray for America," "Why? Oh Why?" and "Nuke the Middle East" (Wendland 2001). Users were also given the opportunity to discuss issues with invited experts on a diverse number of topics. Question and Answer discussions were held, as were "roundtable" online discussions. "Shaken, raw, and vulnerable, we all want—no, NEED—our opinions on the matter to be heard," wrote Winda Benedetti, a *Seattle Post-Intelligencer* reporter. "And with the Net," she added, "there is someone to listen, whether it's in some chat room, bulletin board, or at the receiving end of an endlessly forwarded e-mail." Describing her hunger for information in the days following the attacks as insatiable, she found the sheer volume of material on the Internet to be a comfort of sorts. "It's as though if I comb through enough Web pages, sift through the right chat rooms, click on the right e-mail, I might somehow find some semblance of an answer to this ugly mess" (Benedetti 2001).

## Alternative perspectives

By drawing upon the vast array of information resources available across the Web, online news sites can provide their readers with background details or context to an extent unmatched by any other news medium. However, few of the major news sites in the US made effective use of this capacity on September 11. For those users unable to access these sites or who wanted to draw upon news sources where different types of perspectives were being heard, international news sites became a necessary alternative.

Interestingly, just as people living around the world looked to US websites for breaking developments, far greater numbers of people in the US turned to foreign or international sites than was typical prior to the tragedy. The British Broadcasting Corporation's (BBC) news site (news.bbc.co.uk), widely regarded as the most popular news site in the world, received the greatest share of "hits" from US users looking abroad. The Corporation's new media editor-in-chief, Mike Smartt, stated:

> People appear to be increasingly turning to the web for their breaking news. It's the biggest story since the second world war. We decided to clear everything off the front page, which we've never done before and concentrate all our journalists on the story. We work hand in hand with the broadcast teams but don't wait for them to report the facts. It works both ways . . . Most important to us were the audio and video elements. It was among the most dramatic news footage anyone has ever seen.

The ability to put all that on the web for people to watch over again set
us apart.

(cited in the *Guardian*, September 17, 2001)

Nevertheless, the BBC site, likes its US counterparts (as well as those in countries elsewhere around the globe), was unable to cope with the traffic to its
servers at times. "Hits" numbered into the millions, a level of demand engender-
ing constant transmission problems. Streamlining the site's contents helped, but
it remained a struggle for staff to maintain a presence online. Also in London,
Philippa Edward, commercial director at Independent Television News (ITN)
New Media, stated: "More than 30% of our traffic comes from the US, and
people were sidestepping US sites to come to us, which was gratifying" (cited in
the *Guardian*, September 17, 2001).

For readers searching for news perspectives from further afield, most sites could
be categorized into one of two types. The first type referred to the so-called
"aggregate" sites, which operate to pull together links from an array of different
news sources. In addition to aggregate sites operated by the major wire services,
additional examples with extensive international content included Arab.net
(www.arab.net), China.org (www.china.org.cn/english), NewsNow (www.news-
now.co.uk/) or Northern Light (www.northernlight.com/). In the case of
Afghanistan specifically, where the Taliban had outlawed the Internet as being
anti-Islamic, compilations of news items could be found on sites hosted outside
the country. Examples included the Afghan News Network (www.myafghan.
com/) and Afgha (www.afgha.com/), amongst others. Here it is significant to
note, however, how few Western websites aggregated news from developing
world countries (see also Guest 2001a; Scheeres 2001b; Walker 2001c). Most of
those available required the payment of a subscriber's fee, although one important exception was Yahoo's world news section (dailynews.yahoo.com/h/wl
/nm/!u) which aggregated such items free of charge.

The second type of news sites included those operated by individual news
organizations. Among the sites attracting particular attention on September 11
was the BBC (news.bbc.co.uk), as noted above, while possibly less familiar sites
for many people included Middle Eastern Web portals such as Islam Online
(www.islamonline.net), as well as English language newspapers such as the *Dawn*
in Pakistan (www.dawn.com) or *The Hindu* (www.hinduonnet.com/) in India.
Most of the considerable traffic to the website of al-Jazeera (www.aljazeera.net),
the satellite news channel, was from the US, despite the fact that it was entirely
in Arabic. The Internet operation is operated from al-Jazeera's base in Doha,
Qatar, and plans are under way to develop an English language site (Hodgson
2001). Similarly available online were the transcripts of reports by Islamic and
Muslim television news organizations.

From one website to the next, an array of alternative voices and viewpoints
came to the fore, many systematically marginalized, even silenced, in the mainstream Western media. Still, for those users seeking to gain a sense of public

opinion about the crisis from elsewhere in the world, the information provided by some of these news sites had to be evaluated with care. The danger of extrapolating from opinions expressed on a news site in order to characterize the viewpoints of its readers always needs to be avoided, of course, but particularly so in those societies where state censorship is imposed as a matter of course. In the case of countries where public access to the Internet is minimal, if not non-existent, issues around source accuracy and accountability required due consideration. Nevertheless, while it was frequently difficult for readers to judge whether any given online source was reliable, the sheer diversity of the "market-place of ideas" available on the Internet enabled people to supplement their understanding of opposing views. "It's conceivable," argued Leslie Walker (2001c), "the medium could help folks bypass their governments and traditional media outlets to not only read alternative perspectives, but also directly ask questions of people who might be declared their 'enemy' if the conflict escalates." Thinking along similar lines, Tim Cavanaugh (2001b) observed: "For the first time in history we have a war where you can email the enemy."

Not surprisingly, many of those turning to the Internet looked beyond news sites for further background information to help them better understand the imperatives underpinning the day's events. In the first 24 hours following the attacks, the most popular search words at Lycos (www.lycos.com) included: "World Trade Center," "Nostradamus," "New York," "Osama Bin Laden," "Terrorism," "Pentagon," "Afghanistan," "Camp David," "FBI," "Palestinians," and "Taliban" (Mariano 2001). As this list of search terms suggested, at a time of national emergency people turned to government agencies. Such was clearly the case with regard to the Pentagon website (www.defenselink.mil), as well as that of the Federal Bureau of Investigation (FBI), which in any case offered little by way of news about the attacks. Several hours later, the FBI created an online form for people to use if they believed they had an important fact or tip to submit. "If anyone out there has information to relate," an FBI agent then announced at a news conference, "they can do so via the Web." Evidently, however, the webpage in question, with its "Report Terrorist Activity" link, was promptly overloaded and ceased to operate effectively (Langfield 2001b). More detailed news and information appeared on the Pentagon's site the next day, including the streaming of audio files of its briefings to reporters. One explanation for the delay was provided by an official: "Today there was more clarity as opposed to yesterday, when you literally didn't know what was going to go bang" (cited in Walker 2001a). Other government sites, such as the Federal Emergency Management Agency's FEMA.gov website at the federal level, as well as www.dc.gov and NYC.gov at the local level, did their best to remain accessible. In most cases, only brief news releases were made available at first, although the number and quality of news bulletins improved as the day unfolded.

The search for understanding took some online users into unexpected territory. "At a moment when the world's need for information has never been greater," wrote Amy Harmon (2001b) in the *New York Times*, "the Internet's role as the ultimate source of unmediated news has been matched only by its notorious ability to breed rumors, conspiracy theories and urban legends." Placing to one side this notion of "unmediated news," there was ample evidence as the hours wore on that an extraordinary amount of false information, frequently combined with apocalyptic speculation, was proliferating across the Web at rapid speed. Some rumors were hopeful, such as those revolving around claims that many people were being rescued from the ruins, or that one man had survived a fall from the 82nd floor by riding the falling debris. The rumor that an unburned Bible was found in the wreckage of the Pentagon may have been inspirational for some. More harmful rumors included the assertion that Britain had been attacked, or that more than four passenger jets had been hijacked. Further examples of rumors receiving wide public circulation via e-mail and websites included:

> The correlation of the date—9th month, 11th day—with the national telephone dialling code for emergencies in North America (911) was regarded by some to be non-coincidental.
>
> The alleged symbolic significance of the number 11. That is, the attack occurred on September 11 or 9/11, where 9 + 1 + 1 = 11, and also that "New York City," "The Pentagon" and "Afghanistan" each possess 11 letters. Still others pointed out that the twin towers had resembled the number 11 from a distance.
>
> Others alleged that a close examination of certain news photographs of the World Trade Center ruins revealed the "face of Satan" in the smoke billowing up from the wreckage.
>
> The allegation that the Israeli Mossad was behind the attacks. "In true developing-story fashion," journalist Tim Cavanaugh (2001b) writes, "this tale grew in the telling, with learned references to advanced intelligence and military precision, and the inevitable early-morning phone call to '3,000 Jews' warning them to stay home from work that day."
>
> The allegation that filmed footage shown on CNN of Palestinian children in Gaza ostensibly celebrating the attacks was actually shot in 1991 during the Gulf War. The Brazilian university student who posted the allegation to a social theory newsgroup subsequently apologized for this "uncertain information," while CNN released an official statement reaffirming the verity of the footage.
>
> Much was also made of the fact that typing NYC into a Microsoft Word document, highlighting it, and then changing the font to Wingdings creates: ♀✿☜. At the same time, the widely circulated claim that Q33NY—which becomes ✈▤▤♀✿ by the same process—was the flight number of one of the crashed planes was false.
>
> Finally, one of the most persistent hoaxes was the proclaimed foretelling of the tragedy by the sixteenth-century astrologer Nostradamus, namely his "prediction" of the attack on the World Trade Center: "the

third big war will begin when the big city is burning" after "two broth-ers" are "torn apart by Chaos" (cited in Harmon 2001b; see O'Leary 2001). Evidently there was an average of 140,000 daily unique visitors to Nostradamus-repository.org for the week ending September 16, while *Nostradamus: The Complete Prophesies* was the best-selling book on Amazon.com four days after the attacks.

In crisis situations, Stephen O'Leary (2001) argued, the "social functions of rumor" are virtually identical to those associated with "real news." In his view, "[p]eople spread rumors via the Net for the same reason that they read their papers or tune into CNN: they are trying to make sense of their world." Barbara Mikkel-son, who works to debunk urban legends for the popular www.snopes2.com website, argued that many people find such rumours strangely comforting. This type of practice, she maintained, "puts a sense of control back in an out-of-control world" (cited in Argetsinger 2001). These are somewhat benign interpretations of the phenomenon, although they clearly warrant further investigation.

## Testing the limits

"I think Internet news sites really came of age during this terrible crisis," argued Howard Kurtz, the *Washington Post*'s media reporter. "They blanketed the story with all kinds of reporting, analysis, and commentary, and provided readers with a chance to weigh in as well" (cited in Raphael 2001). A similar position was adopted by Jon Katz (2001), who contended that the Internet, as a news medium, was "the freest and most diverse," offering more accurate information and in-depth conversation than that typically provided by traditional media. "[F]or all the mainstream media phobias about the dangerous or irresponsible Net," he wrote, "it's seemed increasingly clear in the weeks since the attacks that the Net has become our most serious medium, the only one that offers informa-tion consumers breaking news and discussions, alternative points of view."

Research suggests that while the overall number of US Internet users dropped in the days immediately following September 11, significantly more users turned to online news sites than was typical in previous periods. Returning to the Pew Internet and American Life Project report mentioned above, it states:

> Overall, 36% of Internet users went online looking for news in the first two days after the attacks. On Tuesday alone, 29% of Internet users—or more than 30 million people—sought news online. That is one-third greater than the normal news-seeking population on a typical day online. (About 22% of Internet users get news online on a typical day.)
> (Pew Internet and American Life Project 2001: 3)

Between September 11 and 16, according to a study prepared by the Internet research company Jupiter MMXI, the online news category grew by almost 80 percent compared to the previous week in the US. Time.com reportedly saw the largest increase, up 653 percent, in unique visitor traffic compared to the average for the previous three weeks. Foxnews.com's traffic "spiked" at 437 percent above average for the week (Ross 2001). To help put these types of figures in context, some 17.2 million people reportedly visited CNN in the first four days after the attacks (McAuliffe 2001). Internet research conducted by Jupiter Media Metrix found more than 50 million US Internet users went to news websites during the month of September, more than half of everyone who went online in the country. CNN.com was the most frequently accessed news site (24.8 million people), followed by MSNBC.com. Of the newspaper sites, the *New York Times* received the most (10.6 million) visitors, with WashingtonPost.com coming next (see Hu 2001b). "The [online] coverage grew to the impact of the incident and the ongoing stories in Afghanistan," Neilsen/NetRatings analyst T. S. Kelly argued. "This is an indication that the Net is growing up a bit, going from infancy to adolescence and finding a proper role in the media" (cited in *USA Today*, October 16, 2001).

Not everyone is quite so enthusiastic about the state of online journalism, of course. Responding to those commentators who maintain that the Internet "came of age" during the crisis, Tim Cavanaugh (2001b), a journalist based in San Francisco, took an oppositional stance. "If anything," he wrote, "the World Trade Center assault is the story where the Internet showed its age, generating little more than sound and fury from a largely depleted bag of tricks." Angry about what he regarded as the failure of online news to live up to its potential, he criticized the way television was able to "re-assert its status as the world's foremost news source." Particularly vexing, in his view, was the amount of propaganda and disinformation in circulation across the Web and the apparent inability of some online journalists to correct for such biases accordingly. Still other commentators maintained that it was too early to say how online journalism would develop. "There's plenty of journalism *on* the Internet," argued Jay Rosen, but "[v]ery little of it is *of* the Internet." Precisely what "interactive journalism" actually entails, he said, is still unclear. "We don't know yet what the Net makes possible because we're still asking how the journalism we've known and loved translates to the new medium—or doesn't" (cited in Outing 2001c).

This process of translation, most commentators would seem to agree, is fraught with difficulties. "What the [news] sites are doing well is offering a diversity of features on all sorts of topics," argued Amy Langfield (2001c), but they "are failing to do that within the first few hours as news breaks." That is to say, one of the main advantages of online journalism—namely its capacity to provide news at speed—has not been fully realized. "As long as the major websites continue to rely on the same wire coverage for breaking news," she added, "viewers will stick with their TV when they need to know something fast about a developing story." In the early hours of September 11, this over-dependency on wire service coverage for breaking news was particularly problematic. Only as the day progressed were some news sites able to supplement wire copy with their own reporting and

135

crucially tap into news leads, information, and perspectives appearing elsewhere on the Web so as to enhance its investigative depth. Far more successful, in relative terms, were efforts to enhance interactive formats. From one news site to the next, it was clear that readers wanted to express their observations in the online forums being provided. Such ad hoc forums represented a far more inclusive space for diverse viewpoints than was typical for "letters to the editor" pages in mainstream newspapers, let alone the use of "vox pops" or "streeters" in television news. "As the story of the terrorist attacks evolved and the public demanded more information from more sources, the Internet became the perfect medium for this thing," argued Kourosh Karimkhany, senior producer for Yahoo News. "This medium will lead to a renaissance in the craft of journalism" (cited in Lasica 2001b).

It is this latter issue, namely the potential capacity of online news sites to provide readers with the means to hear voices beyond the broad parameters of establishment consensus, which has proved to be a central concern for the September 11 coverage. At a time of what he terms an "understandable patriotic frenzy," Katz (2001) contended that it was on the Internet that voices of dissent, including those of peace activists, first surfaced. The Internet, he wrote, has "become a bulwark against the one dimensional view of events and the world that characterize Big Media. All points of view appeared, and instantly." Basic to the Internet, he maintained, is a structure that is "architecturally and viscerally interactive," thereby ensuring that feedback and individual opinions are "an integral part of Net information dispersal, its core." Such a structure stands in sharp contrast with television news, he suggested, as in his view the latter "arguably transmits powerful images too often and for too long, creating an emotional, almost hysterical climate around big stories even when there's no news to report." Katz thus appeared to be one of an increasing number of commentators calling for reinvigorated types of online coverage, and with them new vocabularies for news narrative. Online journalism will have to be pushed even further, they are insisting, so as to make full use of the Internet as a communication resource (see Outing 2001b; Raphael 2001).

Of the obstacles in the path of this development, perhaps the most challenging revolve around the ownership of the major news sites themselves. Even a glance at the companies behind the major sites in the US—including AOL Time Warner, General Electric Co., Microsoft, Walt Disney Co. and Viacom—makes it obvious that what counts as "news" (or a "credible source") will be constrained within the limits of corporate culture. Even looking more widely across the Internet post-September 11, however, it is apparent that the diversity of available viewpoints has been steadily diminishing in the aftermath of the crisis. Internet service providers (ISPs) have brought pressures to bear, either directly or indirectly, to effectively silence voices of opposition and dissent. In the US, scores of websites have altered their content, and in some cases ceased to operate altogether for fear that they will be defined as pro-terrorist or anti-American. The government has yet to formally intervene, although some website owners maintain that people claiming to be representatives of the FBI have threatened to seize their assets if they do not comply with their demands. In many ways the chilling effect has been similar to that engendered by National Security Adviser Condoleezza Rice's request to television network executives that they "exercise judgment" (i.e., censorship) in broadcasting messages from Osama Bin Laden. Some site owners have resisted such pressures, insisting that they do so as to uphold their right to free speech. Others have reluctantly engaged in self-censorship, such as the owner of The Flagburning Page who closed down his site because of offensive e-mails, some containing death threats (Scheeres 2001c; Singer 2001).

Around the globe, governments are considering new forms of legislation to expand their capacity to monitor e-mail, telephone, and Internet traffic. Many administrations are removing from their country's official websites information which, they claim, could be used by terrorist groups. In the US, examples include the Nuclear Regulatory Commission's decision to delete details of the country's commercial nuclear power reactors, as well as the Environmental Protection Agency's removal of information about chemical risks and hazards at different sites. Critics pointed out that this was a highly questionable reversal of what had been a trend toward improving the public's access to information online. "[I]t seems like a lot of what is being alerted is not dangerous," observed one First Amendment attorney in Washington. "You haven't made life harder for the terrorist; you've just made it harder for taxpaying citizens" (cited in Newton 2001). Sharing this perspective are several journalism organizations, including the Society of Professional Journalists, the Poynter Institute, and the Radio-Television News Directors Association, who have united in protest against the government's actions. In a joint statement made on October 13, they argued that "these restrictions pose dangers to American democracy and prevent American citizens from obtaining the information they need" (cited in Kriz 2001).

Few would dispute that the tragic events of September 11 demonstrated several significant ways in which the Internet has become a vital communications resource. The "spikes" in traffic to Internet news sites have now subsided, but early indications are that daily usage levels remain higher for such sites than they were prior to September 11. It is somewhat ironic, then, that just as readership figures are improving, some news organizations now face renewed pressures to trim the financial expenditure on their sites. "At a time when Internet journalism was being pooh-poohed by a lot of people on the heels of the Internet crash," argued Sreenath Sreenivasan, "this has shown in many ways the necessity and importance of giving resources and attention to the Web and to Web journalism" (cited in Raphael 2001). The extent to which this happens remains to be seen. In the meantime, as J. D. Lasica (2001a) pointed out, "how we define our journalistic mission—how we perceive ourselves and our role in this new medium—will shape how we cover the still-unfolding drama of the biggest story of our lives." Indeed, as fellow online journalist Andy Reinhardt (2001) predicted: "Now, as shock gives way to uncertainty, the richness and diversity of views on the Web will play a vital role in our national conversation." In keeping with the potential of the Web, however, let us ensure that it becomes an international conversation.

## Note

1  I wish to acknowledge with gratitude the Arts and Humanities Research Board (AHRB), as well as my Faculty's Research Committee, for funding the sabbatical during which I researched and wrote this chapter (and co-edited the book). My thanks to Barbie Zelizer, Cynthia Carter, and Donald Matheson for helpful comments on an early draft, as well as to colleagues for invigorating discussions.

## References

Argetsinger, A. (2001) Terror rumors proliferate on Internet, Washtech.com, October 20.

Benedetti, W. (2001) Web becomes a network of support during crisis, *Seattle-Post Intelligencer*, September 17.

Benner, J. (2001) Onion's bitter tears of irony, *Wired News*, September 27.

Blair, T. (2001) Internet performs global role, supplementing TV, *Online Journalism Review*, September 11.

Borden, D. L. and Harvey, K. (eds) (1998) *The Electronic Grapevine*, Mahwah, NJ: Lawrence Erlbaum.

Brown, J. (2001) Purge our society, online bigots shout, Salon.com, September 11.

Cavanaugh, T. (2001a) The backlash that almost wasn't, *Online Journalism Review*, September 14.

Cavanaugh, T. (2001b) Another voice: net generates sound and fury, *Online Journalism Review*, September 21.

Champion, E. (2001) Weblogs: the misperceived consciousness, www.edrants.com, October 16.

Davis, R. (1999) *The Web of Politics*, New York: Oxford University Press.

Garreau, J. (2001) A shaken global village on the Internet, Washtech.com, September 12.

Glasner, J. (2001) Net slows in wake of attacks, *Wired News*, September 11.

Guest, T. (2001) Working the Web: views on Afghanistan, *Guardian*, October 18.

Hall, J. (2001) *Online Journalism*, London: Pluto Press.

Harmon, A. (2001a) Web offers both news and comfort, *New York Times*, September 12.

Harmon, A. (2001b) The search for intelligent life on the Internet, *New York Times*, September 23.

Hodgson, J. (2001) Hits soar for Arab news website, *Guardian*, October 26.

Hu, J. (2001a) Online chat ranges from hate to sympathy, CNET News.com, September 14.

Hu, J. (2001b) Home videos star in online attack coverage, CNET News.com, October 12.

Hua, V. (2001) Americans turn to web sites to post information, reactions, Sfgate.com, September 12.

Kahney, L. (2001a) Who said the web fell apart?, *Wired News*, September 12.

Kahney, L. (2001b) Amateur newsies top the pros, *Wired News*, September 15.

Katz, J. (2001) Net: our most serious news medium?, Slashdot.org, October 11.

Kelsey, D. (2001) Half of surfers visit news sites, Jupiter, ww.jup.com/home.jsp, October 15.

Kettmann, S. (2001) Venerable hackers urge restraint, *Wired News*, September 15.

King, B. (2001) Tech sites pick up the news, *Wired News*, September 11.

Konrad, R. and Hu, J. (2001) Spam, misinformation in wake of tragedy, CNet News.com, September 13.

Kriz, M. (2001) Agencies pull sensitive information from Web sites, GovExec.com, October 19.

Langfield, A. (2001a) When web sites caught up, then ran far, *Online Journalism Review*, September 11.

Langfield, A. (2001b) Commercial sites struggle to keep current, *Online Journalism Review*, September 12.

Langfield, A. (2001c) New news lethargy, *Online Journalism Review*, December 21.

Lasica, J. D. (2001a) A scorecard for net news ethics, *Online Journalism Review*, September 20.

Lasica, J. D. (2001b) Online news on a tightrope, *Online Journalism Review*, November 1.

LiCalzi O'Connell, P. (2001) Taking refuge on the Internet, a quilt of tales and solace, *New York Times*, September 20.

McAuliffe, W. (2001) Online news visitors double in week of US attacks, ZD Net UK, September 24.

McWilliams, B. (2001a) News sites trim down to handle traffic load, *Newsbytes*, September 11.

McWilliams, B. (2001b) A TV plea to patriot hackers, *Wired News*, September 26.

Manjoo, F. (2001) Good news for Arabs on MSNBC, *Wired News*, October 17.

Mariano, G. (2001) News, federal sites flooded during attacks, CNET News.com, September 17.

Miller, R. (2001) From niche site to news portal: how Slashdot survived the attack, *Online Journalism Review*, September 14.

Newton, C. (2001) Agencies remove info from web sites, *Editor and Publisher*, October 12.

O'Leary, S. (2001) Rumors of grace and terror, *Online Journalism Review*, October 5.

Olsen, S. (2001) Net offers lifeline amid tragedy, CNET News.com, September 11.

Outing, S. (2001a) How online journalists can recover lost ground, Poynter.org, September 11.

Outing, S. (2001b) Attack's lessons for news web sites, *Editor and Publisher*, September 19.

Outing, S. (2001c) The first shock of history, Poynter.org, November 5.

Pavlik, J. V. (2001) *Journalism and New Media*, New York: Columbia University Press.

Pew Internet and American Life Project (2001) How Americans used the internet after the terror attack, www.pewinternet.org/, September 15.

Raphael, J. (2001) Media critics see web role emerge, *Online Journalism Review*, September 18.

Reinhardt, A. (2001) On September 11, a multimedia search for info, *Business Week Online*, September 24.

Robins, W. (2001a) News web sites could not compete with TV, *Editor and Publisher*, September 11.

Robins, W. (2001b) Newspaper web sites bring tragedy home, *Editor and Publisher*, October 15.

Ross, S. (2001) News sites see enormous gains, *Editor and Publisher*, September 25.

Runett, R. (2001) Clicking from coast to coast during a crisis, American Press Institute.org, September 12.

Scheeres, J. (2001a) Blame game dominates chat rooms, *Wired News*, September 11.

Scheeres, J. (2001b) Afghanistan, on 50 websites a day, *Wired News*, October 8.

Scheeres, J. (2001c) Suppression stifles some sites, *Wired News*, October 25.

Schiesel, S. with Hansell, S. (2001) A flood of anxious phone calls clog lines, and TV channels go off the air, *New York Times*, September 12.

Singer, M. (2001) EFF lists post 9–11 censored sites, Siliconvalley.internet.com, October 18.

Tarlach, G. (2001) Onion saving new jokes for another day, *Journal Sentinel Online*, September 15.

Taylor, P. M. (2000) The world wide web goes to war, in D. Gauntlett (ed.) *Web Studies*, London: Arnold: 194–201.

Tedsechi, B. (2001) Internet surpasses its original goal, *New York Times*, September 17.

Walker, L. (2001a) The medium meets the emergency, WashingtonPost.com, September 13.

Walker, L. (2001b) Web-page collection preserves the online response to horror, WashingtonPost.com, September 27.

Walker, L. (2001c) Browsing during wartime, WashingtonPost.com, October 4.

Weil, N. (2001) Networks hit, but telecom stays operational, *The Industry Standard*, September 12.

Wendland, M. (2001) Overloaded Internet fails info-starved Americans, Poynter.org, September 11.

# 8

# TAKING IT PERSONALLY

## Supermarket tabloids after September 11

### S. Elizabeth Bird

The headline read: "Afghanistan: Violent world where women live in fear." The story described women's experiences in Afghanistan under the Taliban—the burquas, the ban on higher education, the careful supervision of daily activities—and quoted Eleanor Smeal, head of the Feminist Majority Foundation. Stories like these proliferated in the wake of the September 11 attacks and the subsequent "war on terrorism," as the news media scrambled to explain a once little-known land to their audiences.

The main thing that made this piece different was that it appeared in the *National Enquirer*, the American weekly "supermarket tabloid" best known for its juicy celebrity stories and medical miracles. Indeed, most of this issue from October 9 was devoted to post-September 11 stories, including a short piece on "what you need to know about the world's second largest religion," stressing that "99 percent of all Muslims will say that the Taliban is not correct." Perhaps most interestingly, the *Enquirer* sent reporter Alan Butterfield to the Pakistan/Afghanistan border, from where he reported for several weeks. One prominent story was his interview with Naseer, "a young Afghan who had just fled one of Osama Bin Laden's terrorist training camps." Butterfield used the 19-year-old Afghan to describe the camps in terms that are not especially implausible or "sensational":

> "The conditions in the camps are horrendous—there's no running water or electricity and sanitation is primitive," said Naseer. "While some camps have canvas tents, in our remote mountain camp we slept in mud houses or caves dug out of the mountain. On hot days there was the stench of human waste."
>
> (*National Enquirer*, October 9, 2001: 13)

In both the United States and Britain, it became a cliché to say that everything changed after the attacks, and journalists said it more often than most. September 11 became a moment of self-examination for journalists as stories such as the

Chandra Levy/Gary Condit scandal disappeared from the media.[1] As British journalist Susan Flockhart wrote, "on the day after thousands had been butchered by
suicide bombers, the trash mags' menu of showbiz glitz suddenly seemed trivial to
the point of imbecility" (2001). In the United States, "Our national preoccupation with . . . silliness was suddenly gutted on September 11" (Long 2001).

But even if the tabloid media briefly lost their central reason for existing, "the
beat of pop culture goes on" (ibid.), and for the American supermarket tabloids
the terrorist attacks were a fairly short-lived distraction, at least at first glance.
Nevertheless, the attacks did leave their mark on the tabloids. At one level, they
showed that the oft-lamented convergence between tabloid and mainstream
news values is very much a reality (Langer 1998). At another, they consolidated
the intrinsic conservatism of the tabloids, and perhaps blunted any role they
were developing as a critical or subversive voice.

## Supermarket tabloids: making it personal

Colin Sparks offers a typology of tabloid media, arguing that the American supermarket tabloid press "is only marginally, if at all, concerned with the same news
agenda as the serious press" (Sparks 2000: 15). This is certainly still true for the
more outlandish publications like the *Weekly World News* and the *Sun*, widely
understood to be largely fictional and cultivating loyal but relatively few readers
who love their bizarre stories about human monstrosities, space aliens, and the
ubiquitous "Batboy" (Bird 1992; Glynn 2000). It is less accurate when we look at
the larger circulation weeklies—the *National Enquirer*, *Star*, *Globe*, and *National
Examiner*. Popular perception (and journalistic criticism) still contends that all
feature the once typical tabloid fare of alien abductions and malicious celebrity
gossip, but the reality is somewhat different. Even though all six tabloids are now
owned by the same company, American Media Inc., each has striven to fill a particular niche, although with considerable overlap. These days, the *Enquirer*'s focus
is personality-driven investigative pieces, medical stories and celebrities. It prides
itself on accuracy, and delivery vans reportedly have one slogan on the side—"No
Elvis. No aliens. No Ufos"—and another on the back—"Get it first. Get it fast.
Get it right" (Lunsford 2001). Meanwhile, the *Star* focuses overwhelmingly on
celebrities, the *Globe* offers "edgier" (and more speculative) crime investigations,
and the *National Examiner* concentrates on eye-catching human interest stories,
rewritten from other media. The *Sun* and *Weekly World News* downplay celebrities
and any current news, the former focusing on psychics, human oddities, and miracles, while the latter has become essentially a parody of the stereotypical
supermarket tabloid, with virtually no expectation of being taken seriously.

All generally ignore foreign, political, and economic news, or indeed any news
that cannot be treated as a personal story. And at one time, "political" and "personal" news stories were so clearly distinguished from each other that it was
probably accurate to characterize the *Enquirer* and the *New York Times* as different
breeds, if not quite separate species. That distinction is not so clear today. As *Star*

editor Tony Frost said, "The tabloids have been arm wrestling with the mainstream press ever since the William Kennedy Smith case . . . today we're all fighting for the same slice of the pie."[2] Beginning with the *Enquirer*'s breaking of the 1987 Gary Hart scandal (Bird 1992), the tabloids realized that politicians can rival celebrities in providing juicy stories. Indeed, as *Globe* editor Candace Trunzo put it, "Washington has become like Hollywood. Everyone is extremely curious about politicians' lives . . . the quintessential bad boy of American politics is Bill Clinton, people *love* reading about Bill Clinton . . . and we have certainly taken advantage of that."

In fact, many commentators have pointed to the convergence of tabloid and mainstream news values, with the mainstream press often following the tabloids' lead on stories like the O. J. Simpson trial. "As the trial began, the biggest secret in the Los Angeles County Court-house wasn't OJ's guilt or innocence, but the fact that so many reporters were reading the *National Enquirer* religiously" (Sachs 1995). Recently the *Economist* (2001) remarked admiringly that "the weekly tabloids have this year been responsible for more hot political scoops than any of the mainstream media," citing, among others, Jesse Jackson's illegitimate child, the political pay-offs to Hillary Clinton's brother, Hugh Rodham, and the drinking problems of President George Bush's daughters, concluding that "The tabloids are arguably the papers of record of the Clinton years."

In the United States today, mainstream news is driven by market demand in a culture that has become more interested in personality-driven journalism, and less in serious economic and foreign news (Bird 2000). Clearly we can overstate the extent of convergence; the *National Enquirer* is still not the *New York Times* or any mainstream city newspaper. Those mainstream media have certainly moved toward the personal, and now give far more space to celebrity news, gossip, and human interest features. But this is only one dimension of what they do; for the tabloids, the political (and anything else) is *only* coverable in personal terms. For instance, the Enron debacle is covered as an exposé of how "free-spending executives used investors' funds for sex and booze" (*National Enquirer*, February 26, 2002: 15), with photos of extravagant parties and "insider" accounts of adultery, alcoholism, and uncontrolled excess.

Tabloid editors make no apologies for that—it is simply what they do. They do not claim to be informing the public as some kind of civic duty but are explicit that their goal is to give their readers what they want. Far more dependent on circulation than mainstream media, they must essentially sell their product anew each week. In Tony Frost's view, they reserve their scorn for "respectable" journalism: "Possibly if the mainstream press had concentrated on what they do well, and left us to do what we do well, the American public might have been more aware of the circumstances that led to September 11 . . . mainstream press coverage of foreign news has been very poor . . . people didn't know what was behind the attack on the USS *Cole*, they didn't know much about Osama Bin Laden, they didn't know much about the Taliban and al-Qaeda. Perhaps they should have concentrated on their mission statements instead of trying to cross into our territory."

## September 11: the immediate aftermath

So what was the distinct role of tabloids in the September 11 coverage? Sparks argues that while there are points of overlap, "dominant" and "tabloid" news values usually do diverge. Historically, the exceptions were 1915, 1940, and 1945. "In those years the news values of tabloids and serious newspapers were more or less identical" (Sparks 2000: 23). Of course, these years were crucial moments in the two World Wars, and it seems that we must now add late 2001 to that select list.

Like virtually everyone else in America, tabloid employees felt the impact of the attack as a personal trauma. Frost recalled: "I was at my gym when the first plane went into the North Tower . . . like many millions of others I watched the second plane plow into the South Tower in absolute horror and amazement." *Globe* editor Candace Trunzo agreed: "Everybody had their own personal moment of truth that something like that could happen here." In deciding how to cover the news, there was no question that the tabloids would put aside anything else they might be doing, and focus only on the tragedy. There was immediate soul-searching—"Will people ever want to read about the foibles and antics of celebrities again?" thought Trunzo. Each paper's staff looked to the distinctive "branding" of their title. Frost recalled: "There were all the horrific photos of those poor people jumping from the 90th floor to their deaths . . . we had to offer some hope. *Star* is probably the most upbeat of the tabloids, and pretty quickly I realized this was going to be a story about heroes." The special issue immediately following the attack featured the headlines "Our heroes—how everyday Americans joined cops and firefighters to battle terror," and "The fight for Flight 93—how doomed passengers attacked hijackers to save the capital." Frost's instincts paid off. "I felt we had to carry it forward in a positive way. It worked very well—we had a massive sale" (see Figure 8.1).

Tabloids have always known that the key to effective human interest writing is vivid language, concrete details, and a strong narrative, whether it is their intention to create heroes or demons. In the September 11 aftermath, all journalists turned to storytelling as the dominant mode of address. Particularly successful was the *New York Times'* "Portraits of Grief" series, in which the paper profiled victims in short narratives—a series that continued for some months after the event. The stories "typically focus on a single aspect of the subject's character or an especially endearing talent or trait. They often include a little life lesson—the extrovert who learned to seek out unhappy people at parties, the creator of family surprises, the friend who never lost touch" (Mitchell 2001). The series was reportedly "born of journalistic instinct in the middle of chaos," and struck a very responsive chord in readers (ibid.). As Lule (2002) commented about the series, "In times of crisis, journalism plays a largely mythological role . . . The myth turns death into sacrifice and victims into heroes."

The *Enquirer's* early coverage was not dissimilar, in such extended stories as "the home of the brave," offering capsule profiles of a firefighter, a priest, a rescue

*Figure 8.1* Cover of the *Star* (courtesy of American Media Inc.)

worker, a paramedic, and even a rescue dog (October 2, 2001). It added a typically harder edge with stories about the "terrorist plot" and a call to assassinate Bin Laden (see Figure 8.2 on next page).

Immediately after the attacks, the media responded by emphasizing patriotism and story-telling, rather than probing in depth into the geopolitical situation that might have fueled the terrorism. Journalism took on a therapeutic role, offering inspirational tales of heroism and tragic stories of bereavement. The tabloids printed pages of the same dramatic photos and first-person accounts that were seen across the media. For instance, all media covered the story of Todd Beamer, one of the passengers who attempted to overcome the hijackers of Flight 93, which crashed in Pennsylvania. His words, spoken on a cellular phone, have become one of the enduring symbols of September 11—"Let's roll." The difference between tabloid and mainstream stories is far from obvious; they use identical sources and quotes:

> "Are you guys ready? Let's roll!" That's how Todd Beamer lived.
>     And that's how he died, helping to lead a takeover by passengers on United Airlines Flight 93, which crashed Tuesday in Somerset County, Pa. It was the fourth plane to go down in last week's terrorist attacks.

145

*Figure 8.2* Cover of the *National Enquirer* (courtesy of American Media Inc.)

Beamer, an Oracle Inc. executive and Sunday school teacher from Hightstown, NJ, and others are being credited with foiling hijackers bent on crashing the Boeing 757 into what authorities say might have been a second target in Washington, DC, possibly the Capitol or the White House.

"That's Todd," his wife, Lisa, said Saturday of the "Let's roll!" command, which he made over the plane's in-flight telephone. A GTE supervisor talked with him for about 13 minutes before the plane crashed. "My boys even say that. When we're getting ready to go somewhere, we say, 'C'mon guys, let's roll.' My little one says, 'C'mon, Mom, let's roll.' That's something they picked up from Todd."

Beamer, 32, told the GTE supervisor, Lisa D. Jefferson, that he and others on the plane had decided they would not be pawns in the hijackers' suicidal plot.

Lisa said reports of her husband's heroic role had "made my life worth living again." Jefferson kept her promise and called Lisa Beamer at 8 pm Friday. "It was the best thing that I could've gotten (Friday). It totally changed the mood around here," Lisa said. "He was gentle by nature, he was also very competitive, and he wouldn't stand for anyone being hurt," said Lisa. "Knowing that he helped save lives by bringing that plane down . . . it brings joy to a situation where there isn't much to be found. Some people live their whole lives, long lives, without having left anything behind," Lisa said. "My sons will be told their whole lives that their father was a hero, that he saved lives. It's a great legacy for a father to leave."

(Chattanooga Times, September 17, 2001: A6, original byline,<br>Jim McKinnon Pittsburgh Post-Gazette)

"Let's roll!" Those were the last defiant words heard from Todd Beamer, 32, of Cranbury, NJ, an account manager for the software firm Oracle, as he prepared to fight the hijackers.

A Sunday school teacher and father of two boys, he was a high school basketball and baseball star who loved playing ball with his sons.

Beamer used an airphone to report the hijacking to GTE supervisor Lisa Jefferson. "I know we're not going to make it out of here," he told her . . . When asking Jefferson to call his wife to tell her that he loved her, Beamer recited the Lord's Prayer with her. Then she heard, "Let's roll"—and the connection went dead.

It's an expression Beamer used often . . . "he uses 'let's roll!' with our little boys all the time. As soon as I heard that, I knew it was Todd. He was gentle by nature, but he wouldn't stand for anyone being hurt. Some people live their whole lives without having left anything else behind. My sons will be told that their father was a hero, that he saved lives. It's a great legacy for a father to leave his children."

(National Enquirer, October 2, 2001: 4, byline Ellen Goodstein)

## Trying to make sense

After the initial coverage, journalism moved into a phase of explanation and analysis; for instance, many stories probed the mystery of how terrorists were apparently living among us. Again, apart from the tabloids' slightly more hyperbolic language, there was little to distinguish these stories in the tabloids from many in mainstream papers. For instance, we had the "Terrorists next door" in the *St Petersburg Times*:

The request was usual enough. Ziad Jarrahi, a flight student from Germany, wanted to learn the basics of self-defense, and that's what Bert Rodriguez taught him . . . How to escape choke holds and arm holds. How to fend off an attack. How to fight back effectively, even if outnumbered . . . On September 11, nearly two weeks after his last private lesson with Rodriguez at US 1 Fitness in Dania Beach, Jarrahi helped take command of . . . Flight 93 . . . "It hurts now to think I'm trying to teach someone something he used to harm others," said Rodriguez, a former New Yorker with a shaved head and his first name tattooed on his bulging right bicep. "When I found out I was involved this deeply, it took me until today for it just to sink in . . . We shared a lot. I feel violated. I feel betrayed."

(*St Petersburg Times*, October 2, 2001: 1D)

Meanwhile, the *Enquirer* offered, "I was a terrorist's lover":

A brilliant female med student lived intimately with one of the hijackers, but never knew she's given her heart to a monster until after the terror attacks on America . . . Turkish-born "Fatima," 26, was the sweetheart of Ziad Jarrahi . . . She says her "kind and gentle" lover changed for the worse over the months she knew him . . . "She said he liked to drink vodka, champagne, and wine," a friend told the *Enquirer* . . . "But then last August the man Fatima fell in love with changed from Dr Jekyll to Mr Hyde."

(*National Enquirer*, October 16, 2001: 6)

The specifics were different, but the question examined was the same: what motivated these apparently ordinary men, and how could we not have known that they were "monsters?"

As the weeks passed, the tabloids began to exhibit a gradual divergence from the mainstream. In all media, different news topics returned, although September 11 continued to loom large. Formerly huge stories like Gary Condit had temporarily disappeared, along with any coverage remotely critical of President George W. Bush and his administration, but the more routine mix gradually reasserted itself. Mainstream media coverage embraced the war in Afghanistan as well as the ongoing clean-up at "Ground Zero" and the continuing "war on terrorism." The tabloids looked for their particular take; the celebrity-driven *Star* showcased a special issue on "How stars' lives have changed":

The terrorist attacks that stunned the world have changed Hollywood forever too. Now home and family are where the heart is for Tinseltown's movie and TV stars . . . And patriotism is at an all-time high, with celebrities pledging millions in relief and showing their love of America by flying flags and wearing red, white, and blue.

(*Star*, October 26, 2001: 4)

We learned that the attacks made Tom Cruise and Nicole Kidman "realize what's really important and have convinced the pair to put an end to their bitter divorce bickering" (p. 37), while Lisa Marie Presley and Nicholas Cage "were brought so close together as they shared the horror . . . that they never want to be apart again " (p. 36). Arnold Schwarzenegger committed to spend more time with his family (p. 4), and estranged actors Meg Ryan and Dennis Quaid were considering reuniting (p. 5). Again, although the focus was on celebrities, the themes were very similar to stories that ran in all kinds of media. Mitchell pointed to surveys that documented attitude changes since September 11, leading to more news stories that probed human feelings and emotions. Various surveys reported that people were telling relatives that they were loved, were spending more time with their families, and "more than half say they're feeling a greater focus or purpose in life as a result of the attacks" (Mitchell 2001).

In the same issue, the *Star* moved away from celebrities to offer standard stories about people who barely survived the attack and more "behind-the-terrorists" reporting, developing a popular theme—the terrorists hated America but were drawn to its popular culture. In "The phony prophets of doom," reporters quoted a Las Vegas stripper who recalled giving lap dances to hijacker Mohamed Atta. "They professed to be devout Muslims, but they were hypocrites who defiled their respected faith with their debauchery and then discredited their cause by killing thousands of innocent people, leaders of Islam declare" (*Star*, October 26, 2001: 10).

It is quite striking that the tabloids scrupulously avoided any generalized anti-Islamic bigotry, while targeting Osama Bin Laden personally as a monster. The *Globe* led the way with a dramatic "Wanted" cover (October 2, 2001, see Figure 8.3). The *Enquirer* and *Globe* sustained the terrorism story for the longest period of time, and in many ways the patterns followed by the tabloids and the mainstream media were comparable, with blanket coverage followed by attempts to explain. But at this point we began to see a sharper divergence between the tabloid and mainstream news agenda, reflecting their different worldviews and philosophies of newsgathering. Both tabloid and mainstream journalists essentially use the same newsgathering techniques, which make it easy to move between the two worlds (Bird 1992). *Globe* editor Trunzo (a former *Time* magazine writer) said that although there were clear differences in language style and headlines, "I think a good journalist is a good journalist."

Being a good journalist means finding appropriate sources and creating stories around their quotes. In general, tabloid reporters use the same sources and draw on the same story models as all journalists (Bird and Dardenne 1988), and this certainly explains the similarity of the immediate coverage. As Trunzo put it, "We talked to a lot of people—ex-CIA people, ex-army people, current people . . . The same people who are the talking heads on many of the news shows." And while many of the issues raised by the tabloids were similar to those of the mainstream media, tabloid writers went where mainstream journalists would not. According to Trunzo, "We didn't speculate, but we certainly interviewed and quoted people who were in a position to speculate because they have knowledge that we do not." The encouragement of speculation produces stories such as two featured in the *Globe*'s November 6, 2001, issue: "I know where warlord lives" (p. 26) invited a geology professor to identify the location of the cave entrance

*Figure 8.3* Cover of the *Globe* (courtesy of American Media Inc.)

seen in a video released by Bin Laden. In another story, the *Globe* pointed to the Timex watch visible on Bin Laden's wrist in the video, set at 22:00 hours, with the alarm set at 45:00. "The settings . . . lead to passage 22:45 of the Koran, which sources say the terrorist warlord has interpreted to show his delight in the World Trade Center attack. It reads, 'How many cities teeming with sin, have we laid to waste!'"

One significant difference between mainstream and tabloid is that while many sources may be the same, tabloids also consult palmists, psychics, and others whose credibility would not pass muster in the mainstream (Bird 1992). Another distinction is the way tabloid writers may treat the quotes given by their sources. Larry Johnson, ex-CIA officer and former deputy director of terrorism at the US State Department, may well have said, "The watch is a fascinating connection." It is less apparent that he actually supported the significance of the connection, or that he genuinely "commends *Globe* for figuring out Bin Laden's secret Koran message" (p. 27). Similarly, tabloid reporters consistently use the time-honored technique of phrasing a question that produces a yes or no answer, producing the typically florid quotes that characterize many stories (Kovalic 1996).

As Trunzo put it, "we are echoing the pop culture." Tabloids "tackle the questions that higher-minded journalists steer clear of in their writing but then spend most of the week discussing at lunch" (*Economist* 2001). What is the Clintons' relationship all about? Who really killed Jon Benet Ramsey? Did sexual rejection lead Bin Laden to hate America? A "good" scandalous story is an evolving narrative that invites speculation from the audience—tabloids both respond to and feed those narratives in ways that are somewhat (but certainly not entirely) different from mainstream media (Bird 1997). In the weeks that followed the attacks, the tabloid sources speculated about everything from whether Bin Laden had developed a plot to kill Bush, through many possible ways he facilitated the international drug trade, to whether his anger at America was fueled by sexual inadequacy. On January 15, 2002, the *Globe* offered photos and reports suggesting that Bin Laden was dead (certainly the tabloids have not been alone in this), while on the same date the *Enquirer* attributed "American Taliban" John Walker's actions to the trauma of his father leaving his mother for another man. This latter story is a good example of a typical tabloid technique; it does seem apparent that Walker's father identifies as a gay man, but it takes particular reporting methods to tie that fact to Walker's decision to join the Taliban.

It is obvious that the more extreme tabloids are the least constrained and the least tied to conventional notions of news. But even they could not ignore September 11, and they treated it with the surrealistic parody that has made the *Weekly World News* a favorite among college students and other "ironic" readers (Bird 1992). The *News* published a cover on September 18 that caught Bin Laden's face in the sights of a rifle, with the single headline "Ed Anger takes on Osama Bin Laden: Need we say more?" "Ed Anger" writes hyperbolic columns that are much enjoyed by *News* readers and visitors to the popular website, as he produces stereotypically "redneck" fury about everything from women doctors to immigrants and now Bin Laden. The *News* followed up in October with an inspired piece featuring the popular "half-human, half-bat" Batboy. "In a bizarre turn of events, the . . . mutant has joined the US military—and is being trained to use his super-sensitive hearing [and] keen sense of smell to hunt down terrorists in the caves, holes, and hovels they hide in!" (*Weekly World News*, October 16, 2001: 6). Much later (February 8, 2002), the *News* revealed a "secret video" of Bin Laden and his henchmen enjoying a 1998 Las Vegas visit—an "orgy of high stakes, hookers, and hummus." The story featured the trademark *News* photographs—obviously-faked images superimposing Bin Laden's head on the body of a man cavorting with scantily-clad showgirls. Even though the *News* and the *Sun* are only marginally connected with other journalism, the fact that they also felt compelled to address the national trauma pointed to its overwhelming impact on the media and the national consciousness.

Finally, no discussion would be complete without mention of the tabloids' deeply personal experience of the anthrax terrorism that killed *Sun* photo editor Bob Stevens on October 5, 2001. Initially seen as an isolated case, the infection was later traced to the delivery of a letter to the American Media Inc. building in Boca Raton, Florida, on September 19. A second employee became seriously ill, and the AMI building was evacuated. Further anthrax attacks at national network news stations followed, and at the time of writing the case has yet to be solved. All the tabloids offered many possible scenarios and perpetrators, pointing to intriguing details of several of the hijackers' lives in the immediate vicinity of AMI in Florida, and with the *Enquirer* providing many details of a connection between the al-Qaeda terrorists and Iraq (November 6, 2001). The *Enquirer*'s early investigations of the attacks mention details that, at the time of writing, have taken on new significance in the mainstream media. For instance, the paper reported (October 30, 2001: 32) that a Delray Beach pharmacist recalls hijackers Mohamed Atta and Marwan al-Shehhi seeking treatment for a skin rash and flu-like symptoms respectively, a fact he reported to the FBI. The *New York Times* resurrected that information in late March 2002, when it broke the story that hijackers Ahmed Alhaznawi and Ziad Jarrahi, who lived and trained as pilots near American Media Inc. in Florida, had visited a hospital in Fort Lauderdale in June 2001 to receive treatment for Alhaznawi's leg lesion. A doctor who treated him now believes the lesion was caused by cutaneous (skin) anthrax (Broad and Johnston 2002).

In the six months after the attacks, authorities had focused on the probability of domestic terrorism, which may in part explain the lack of attention to the *Enquirer*'s reporting. Furthermore research suggests people tend to be much more skeptical of stories attributed to the *Enquirer*, compared to the same story appearing in the *New York Times* (Kaufman, Stasson, and Hart 1999). In any event, the public responded to the AMI anthrax attacks with fear, and AMI CEO David Pecker had to publicly affirm that the papers were being printed elsewhere to allay worries about anthrax contamination. The papers found that it was not profitable to dwell on the story for too long, and only after the targets became mainstream networks and legislators did the anthrax story become a truly national phenomenon. Pecker later expressed anger at the slow response of federal authorities and the lack of local support for AMI, whose business is sometimes seen as an embarrassment to upscale Boca Raton: "We've been a good corporate citizen, and then to be treated like this" (Pressley 2002). The company's business was drastically affected by the anthrax attack; it forced them out of an expensively-renovated building that may never be safely habitable.

## Six months later: the lasting impact

As I write this, six months have passed since the September 11 attacks. Mainstream media have returned to their regular news agenda, paying a great deal of attention to the war in Afghanistan, homeland security, and related topics. Many media are marking the six-month anniversary, returning to tried-and-true hero and survivor stories from both New York and Afghanistan. What about the March 12 tabloids? At the *Star*, the earlier questions about the continuing interest in celebrities have been answered, and we see a return to business as usual. The cover leads on gay talk-show host Rosie O'Donnell's fight to keep her foster child, reports on an expose of two actors' "sex romp," and promises a visit to the sumptuous homes of perennial favorites Joan Collins, Richard Chamberlain and Jane Seymour. Inside, terrorism and war are nowhere to be found. The *Enquirer* cover reserves most of the page for an unflattering photo of Hillary Clinton and her "secret divorce file." Meanwhile, the only story directly tied to post-September 11 events describes an investigation into how "Enron gave Taliban millions" as part of a deal for an energy pipeline in Afghanistan, suggesting that some of this money found its way to Osama Bin Laden and al-Qaeda (March 12, 2002: 10).

The *Globe* is back to its usual mix of celebrity coverage, high-profile crime, and personality-driven political stories. The cover launches a new attack on Gary Condit, and features three pages of stories and pictures about his "wild secret life" as both a womanizer and a bisexual "pervert." The earlier tabloid coverage of thoughtful, family-oriented celebrities has largely disappeared, as we learn about the "marriage from hell" endured by Maria Shriver and Arnold Schwarzenegger. Enron is covered in a palmreader's analysis of the hands of company executives that reveals that ex-CEO Kenneth Lay is an "evil schemer," while Jeffrey Skilling is a "frightened wimp." The *National Examiner* offers its usual rewrites of off-beat news stories, with nothing remotely connected to September 11. The *Sun* also ignores war news, although it does feature the prophecies of the late Padre Pio, who warned that "in a world gone mad, our only hope of salvation lies in heavenly intervention led by the Virgin Mary" (March 12, 2002: 22). The *Weekly World News*, amid the vampires, grossly obese people and girls found frozen alive since 1939, gives a typically tongue-in-cheek nod to the post-terrorism era with the "al-Qaeda work-out" guide, reportedly based on observation of the fighters imprisoned at Guantanamo Bay. Suggested exercises include the "Taliban tush tightener": "Kneel on all fours with your head bowed as if in prayer. Clench your butt cheeks together as hard as you can. Hold and release. Repeat 200 times. This tones your gluteal muscles for a scintillating rear view" (March 12, 2002: 42).

We might be forgiven for assuming that everything is back to normal at the tabloids. However, perhaps the most interesting legacy is one that may also have affected other media. It is not so much about what is being written, but about what is not. Suddenly, in a medium where almost anything goes, certain topics are off limits. Prior to September 11, politicians were all potential celebrities, vulnerable to both adulation and denigration. Gary Condit and the Clintons received the most negative coverage, but the Bush family had also received its share, focusing primarily on twin daughters Jenna and Barbara. The *Enquirer* prepared readers in December 2000 for the many stories that were to follow:

> Get ready, America! One of the toughest domestic issues Bush faces in the next few years is how to control his hard-drinking daughter. Jenna Bush, 19, has a reputation at the University of Texas at Austin as a wild party girl who flirts openly with fraternity hunks . . . Jenna is a chip off

153

the old block. George W. was a two-fisted drinker in his youth and Jenna is picking up where he left off.

(*Enquirer*, December 21, 2001)

Between then and mid-August 2001, the *Enquirer's* online site listed eight stories chronicling underage drinking charges and out-of-control behavior from both daughters, suggesting that their problems "have triggered an all-out First Family feud" (June 8, 2001). Laura Bush wished to discipline them, while "the girls have their father wrapped around their fingers." By August, "even as the President and First Lady have tried to divert attention from their daughters' behavior, Jenna continues to break the law, drinking alcohol in public while surrounded by the Secret Service!" (*Enquirer*, August 14, 2001). Other tabloids were equally relentless in their pursuit of the daughters and increasingly overt criticism of the Bush parenting style. The *Weekly World News* even got into the picture with a story about Batboy's reported crush on Jenna, as he stalked her at her Austin campus (May 28, 2001).

According to Trunzo, "The daughters were interesting for a while—the bad girls." However, she acknowledged a definite change: "I think September 11 changed any focus we would have on that . . . [Bush has] risen to the occasion, he's been an extraordinary President." In other words, it would be unseemly to draw negative attention to the Bush family now, whether it is the drinking problems of the daughters or the President himself: "Those stories have been done, and you leave them be after a while—why go back to them?" Yet going back to stories again and again is exactly what tabloids do best.

After September 11, the Bush family became untouchable. Trunzo commented, "People didn't know that President Bush had it in him to be as presidential as he has, rallying America, being the person we looked up to and the leader he became." The daughters were rehabilitated: "Gorgeous young Bush babes Jenna and Barbara got high—skydiving with pals . . . The girls landed safely and kept both feet on the ground—turning down flat the complimentary booze vouchers they were offered!" (*Enquirer*, October 2, 2001). By January 2002, the "wild daughters" had been tamed. A friend is quoted: "Since the terrorist attacks, Jenna has done a total turnaround, and many . . . are shocked at the person she's become at school." Laura Bush is credited with the successful transformation: "Even though she's had to keep a much higher public profile during America's war on terrorism, she is always a mother first. That will never change" (*Examiner*, January 29, 2002: 24–5).

It is not that the tabloids have stopped targeting political figures. The Clintons are still covered relentlessly, whether Hillary has decided to call off the divorce as they rekindle their love in the wake of September 11 (*Star*, November 13, 2001: 28–9) or has finally amassed enough evidence to pursue it (*Enquirer*, March 12, 2002: 36–7). The *Star* revisited the "lovegifts" from Monica Lewinsky to Bill Clinton (March 12, 2001: 24), while reporting on the same page that Lewinsky has "set her man-hungry sights on a yummy new guy." The *Enquirer's* "divorce file" story noted that Hillary Clinton garnered only eight percent of the vote in a poll of most-admired women—"well behind Laura Bush at 12 percent" (p. 36). And although Gary Condit disappeared for while, he had returned by November, when he was "caught in new DNA evidence shock" (*Star*, November 13, 2001: 16–17).

Similarly, the intermittent coverage of the Enron scandal has been careful never to raise questions about possible Bush administration connections, even when pointing to oil industry/Enron/Taliban links. In fact the only tabloid that referred to the Bushes in a less-than-reverent way was the *Weekly World News*, which pursued its own, wildly subversive agenda. The above-mentioned "Al-Quaeda work out" story featured a photo of Bush's head superimposed on a bulked-up body, suggesting he "may be using the exercise techniques himself" and perhaps subtly poking fun at his "superman" image. In the same issue, Ed Anger argued that the way to solve the Enron situation was to get the company going again: "We can start by having guys like Dick Cheney and Bush and all the politicians who accepted Enron campaign bucks return the money, for start-up cash." The company will then get back to work: "That's how this wonderful country was built. America wouldn't have any of the great oil companies or railroads . . . if it weren't for genius crooks like the Rockefellers, J. P. Morgan." Once stock prices rise again, all those people who lost money will be paid off, and "then we pull the plug and leave the big-wig sleaze-balls to start a new business—like drilling for oil in Alaska like the Lord intended" (*World Weekly News*, March 12, 2002: 17).

Of course the muted criticism of the Bush administration was not confined to the tabloids. As Hart and Ackerman (2001) wrote, the terrorist attacks "led to a wave of self-censorship as well as government pressure on the media . . . even mild criticism of the military, George W. Bush and US foreign policy is coming to seem taboo". They cite numerous incidences of journalists being fired and censored, as White House spokesman Ari Fleischer reminded Americans that "they need to watch what they say." Long-time CBS News anchor and managing editor Dan Rather declared on the David Letterman show (September 17, 2001): "George Bush is the President . . . he wants me to line up, just tell me where. And he'll make the call" (cited in Hart and Ackerman 2001). Other reporters made similar statements, while news mogul Rupert Murdoch said "We'll do whatever is our patriotic duty" (ibid.). For Murdoch's Fox News Channel, this involved perhaps the most unapologetic show of patriotic cheerleading ever seen on American TV news, with "its hostile, even insulting portrayal of their opponents—who have been described by Fox personnel as 'rats,' 'terror goons' and 'psycho Arabs'" (Hart and Naureckas 2002). Hart and Naureckas quote Fox's anchorman Brit Hume's rationale for the network's lack of coverage of civilian casualties: "The fact that some people are dying, is that really news? And is it news to be treated in a semi-straight-faced way? I think not." Fox completed the picture by hiring former tabloid TV personality Geraldo Rivera to cover the war in Afghanistan. "I'm feeling more patriotic than at any time in my life. Itching for justice—or maybe just revenge," Rivera declared (Hart and Naureckas 2002). The convergence between Fox style and tabloid style is most apparent in the person of Rivera, who made himself the focus of the story, much as the *Enquirer*'s Alan Butterfield had done in his Afghanistan reporting, which featured photos of him on the scene, as he "puts his life on the line" to get the story (*Enquirer*, October 9, 2001: 12).

Even casual attention to radio call-in programs and letters to the editor since September 11 shows that fervent, unquestioning patriotism was a significant element in public opinion, in which journalism was participating with varying degrees of comfort. In March 2002, letter writers were still attacking writers who expressed qualms about the lack of media criticism: "To question his [Bush's] decisions regarding issues of national security is not only foolish, but traitorous. 'Are you with us or against us?' applies even to reporters in their air-conditioned offices" (*St Petersburg Times*, March 31, 2002: 2D).

Once again the tabloids, with their adulation of Bush, their American flag logos, and their personal, subjective stances are not as far out of the mainstream as we might assume.

## Conclusion: the legacy of September 11

The terrorist attacks affected the US tabloids dramatically. They caused a certain degree of soul-searching, briefly bringing tabloid and mainstream news values into almost perfect convergence. But the effect was relatively short-lived and did not fundamentally change tabloid content or style. Tabloids continue to offer celebrity stories and dramatic human-interest tales, and particular titles still pursue national and political stories when these can be framed in personal terms. In the United States, there has been nothing as striking as the apparent transformation of the British *Daily Mirror* after September 11. After years on the same bandwagon as the celebrity-driven, sexually-titillating *Sun*, the *Mirror*'s editor, Piers Morgan, returned the paper to its roots as a populist purveyor of hard news and political comment, increasing sales by 2.5 million, and winning the 2001 Newspaper of the Year award. "The big lesson he had learnt was that serious news was not just stimulating, it also sold newspapers" (O'Driscoll 2001). While the *Sun*'s half-naked "page 3 girls" were back by September 20, the *Mirror* has become the voice of the left/liberal and anti-war position, while still maintaining its tabloid style and celebrity coverage. As Macdonald (2000) pointed out, personalization can be extremely effective in hard-hitting current events journalism.

In the United States, during a time when even mild dissent led to the censure of both journalists and academics, it would be suicidal for any popular newspaper to take such a position. Nevertheless, we should not forget that the tabloids have traditionally played a role in social and political critique, and here we may have seen a less obvious change in the tabloid worldview. As Sparks writes, "The fact that the tabloid media habitually concentrate on personalities and private issues does not mean that they do not address issues of social structure" (2000: 26). Indeed, the tabloids play a significant role in policing morality and defining symbolic values in our culture (Bird 1997; Langer 1998). Influential people from Bill Clinton to Jesse Jackson have learned about the power of the tabloids not only to monitor their activities but also to put those activities on the agenda of the mainstream media. "They instinctively realize that President Bush's tough stance on marijuana makes the question of whether his daughter has ever smoked that weed a compelling news story—Texas sends people caught with two ounces or less of marijuana to jail for 180 days" (*Economist* 2001).

American tabloids have long been socially conservative, overtly patriotic, and somewhat selective in their political targets, but they have functioned to draw attention to the foibles of the powerful. September 11 apparently cemented a position from which no critique of the Bush administration, personal or otherwise, was likely in the foreseeable future. As Candace Trunzo put it, "When the chips fell, you saw . . . who could make people believe it was going to be OK . . . and in our own very small way, that's what the tabloids could do—keep publishing and honoring the people who should be honored." Immediately after the attacks, the tabloids clearly stated their position. "We" are the American people, and "we" are behind whatever the administration wants. "We changed the logo—we used to have a globe, and now we have an American flag. We were a little subjective in terms of being an American publication and being proud of that. We never changed the logo back . . . and I like that."

Mainstream American media have been struggling with their desire to be "patriotic" yet objective, and their generally uncritical stance raises real concerns for the future. Perhaps it is less important to be concerned about tabloids, which by and large have returned to their diet of celebrity news. But it will be interesting to watch how the American tabloids continue to define "the people who should be honored," deciding who is still a legitimate political target for personal attack, and who will be spared their often devastating censure.

## Notes

1  Democratic congressman Gary Condit had been under a cloud of scandal for many months after a young congressional intern, Chandra Levy, disappeared. Condit admitted having an affair with her, but denied involvement in her disappearance. Condit failed to win re-election to Congress; the story regained momentum after Levy's remains were discovered in a Washington park on May 22, 2002. Other prominent scandals mentioned in this chapter include the trial of William Kennedy Smith, acquitted on rape charges in December 1991, and the affair between presidential candidate Gary Hart and model Donna Rice, which led to his withdrawal from the campaign in June 1987.
2  To avoid repeated, intrusive citations, I state here that all quotes from *Star* Editor Tony Frost and *Globe* Editor Candace Trunzo derive from telephone interviews, carried out March 6 and 7, 2002, respectively.

# References

Bird, S. E. (1992) *For Enquiring Minds: A Cultural Study of Supermarket Tabloids*, Knoxville, TN: University of Tennessee Press.

Bird, S. E. (1997) What a story! understanding the audience for scandal, in J. Lull and S. Hinerman (eds) *Media Scandals: Private Desire in the Popular Culture Marketplace*, Cambridge: Polity Press: 99–121.

Bird, S. E. (2000) Audience demands in a murderous market: tabloidization in US television news, in C. Sparks and J. Tulloch (eds) *Tabloid Tales*, New York: Rowman and Littlefield: 213–28.

Bird, S. E. and Dardenne, R. W. (1988) Myth, chronicle, and story: exploring the narrative qualities of news, in J. W. Carey (ed.) *Media, Myths and Narratives*, New York: Sage: 67–86.

Broad, W. J. and Johnston, D. (2002) A nation challenged: report linking anthrax and hijackers is investigated, *New York Times*, March 23: A9.

*Economist* (2001) The tabloid press: pass the Pulitzers, July 5. Available online at www.economist.com, accessed March 11, 2002.

Flockhart, S. (2001) Pap culture, *Sunday Herald*, Scotland, December 30. Available online at www.sundayherald.com/print21137, accessed February 22, 2002.

Glynn, K. (2000) *Tabloid Culture*, Durham, NC: Duke University Press.

Hart, P. and Ackerman, S. (2001) Patriotism and censorship, *Extra*, November/December. Available online at www.fair.org/extra/0111/patriotism-and-censorship.html, accessed March 31, 2002.

Hart, P. and J. Neurakas (2002). Fox at the front: will Geraldo set the tone for future war coverage? *Extra*, January/February 2002. Available online at www.fair.org/extra/0201/geraldo-fox.html, accessed March 31, 2002.

Kaufman, D. Q., Stasson, M. E., and Hart, J. W. (1999) Are the tabloids always wrong or is it just what we think? *Journal of Applied Psychology*, 29: 1984–97.

Kovalic, J. (1996) I was a teenage ghost of Elvis's UFO baby on a hot dog diet: enquiring minds want to know, *Madison Magazine*, Fall. Available online at detnews/AAEC/fall96/john/john.htm, accessed February 22, 2002.

Langer, J. (1998) *Tabloid Television: Popular Journalism and the "Other News,"* London and New York: Routledge.

Long, T. (2001) After September 11, pop-culture silliness toppled, *Lansing State Journal*, Gannett News Service, December 12. Available online at citguide.lansingstatejournal.com/fe/events/011228_popcult2001, accessed February 22, 2002.

Lule, J. (2002) Comments contributed to forum: "the democratization of death," *Chronicle of Higher Education*, XLVIII (21) February 1: B4.

Lunsford, D. (2000) Taming the tabloids, *American Journalism Review*, 22 (7): 52.

Macdonald, M. (2000) Rethinking personalization in current affairs journalism, in C. Sparks and J. Tulloch (eds) *Tabloid Tales*, New York: Rowman and Littlefield: 21–66.

Mitchell, B. (2001) Ordinary people, extraordinary stories, November 30. Available online at www.poynter.org/centerpiece/120301.htm, accessed March 1, 2002.

O'Driscoll, S. (2001) Where the press goes from here: Piers Morgan, *Belfast Telegraph*. Available online at www.ukeditors.com/articles/2001/October/Conference274.html, accessed February 22, 2002.

Pressley, S. A. (2002) Where anthrax is old news: Florida tabloids say their story has been forgotten, *Washington Post*, January 27: A1.

Sachs, A. (1995) Mud and mainstream: when the respectable press chases the *National Enquirer, Columbia Journalism Review*, May/June. Available online at www.cjr.org/year/95/3/mud.asp, accessed February 26, 2002.

Sparks, C. (2000) Introduction: the panic over tabloid news, in C. Sparks and J. Tulloch (eds) *Tabloid Tales: Global Debates over Media Standards*, New York: Rowman and Littlefield, 1–40.

# 9

# MEDIA FUNDAMENTALISM

The immediate response of the UK national
press to September 11

*Michael Bromley and Stephen Cushion*

The media of the United Kingdom are subject to levels of centralization and concentration which are rarely found in the media in other geo-social environments
(for the press, see *Media Ownership* 1995: 38; McNair 1996: 137–8). Newspapers
published in London for distribution throughout the UK—the national press—
while numerically small have accounted for a majority of daily circulations since
the 1920s. Unlike in, say, Germany or the United States, neither the regional nor
the metropolitan press (with the possible partial exceptions of Scotland and,
until the 1980s, Northern Ireland) has offered any serious challenge to the secular "rise of Fleet Street" (Lee 1976: 73–6; Harris 1997). Although aggregate
circulations have declined since the 1950s, almost 60 percent of the UK population still reads a national daily newspaper (Bromley 2000: 1). About as many
people—a fifth of the total population—read the *Sun*, a national daily tabloid, as
all 74 regional (metropolitan) evening newspapers combined (National Readership Survey 2002). The national daily press has remained substantially important
even in "the video age" (Tunstall 1996: 1–3, 7–17).

The relative resilience of this specific form of print has been credited, broadly
speaking, to a distinctive competitive dynamic which, since the nineteenth
century, has allowed national daily newspapers periodically to reconstitute themselves in response to social and cultural changes interpreted primarily through
the prism of commercialism (Engel 1996; Stothard 1997; Chalaby 1998:
esp. 167–76). While, on the one hand, this has led to recurrent concerns for the
standards of journalism and to anxieties over processes of "dumbing-down" as the
press has been seen to become increasingly "market-driven" (McManus 1994;
Bromley 1998b; Stephenson 1998; Sparks 2000: 8), the UK also has among the
highest proportions of newspaper readerships in the world. In September 2001
very nearly 13 million people bought a national newspaper each day (compared
to peak television news viewerships of 16 million on September 11).[1] The
national press has sustained a role both as a major provider of "news" (however

that may be defined—see McLachlan and Golding 2000 and Rooney 2000) and of engagement with the public. Following September 11, on one day the *Mirror*, another tabloid, published a 136-page issue (48 pages more than usual), and the numbers of letters to the editor received by the *Guardian*, a broadsheet, almost doubled to a peak of more than 600 a day (Wells 2001: 3; www.guardian.co.uk). As one trade commentator observed, September 11 and its immediate consequences demonstrated that in the UK "there still exists an appetite for newspapers" (Quinn 2001)—in contrast to claims about experience in the US (Donovan and Scherer 1992: 292–307; Moses 2001).

The most noticeable of these effects occurred on September 12. Sales of the *Guardian* that day were the highest in its history. In total, the ten national daily titles (*The Times, Independent, Guardian, Daily Telegraph, Financial Times, Daily Mail, Daily Express, Daily Star, Mirror*, and *Sun*) added about 2.5 million copies to their usual print runs: even so, by mid-morning (20 hours after the first pictures from New York City appeared on British television), many were sold out (Hodgson 2001a; Preston 2001b).

In this study we analyze not what the ten national daily newspapers reported on September 12, but some of *how* they did so.[2] We examine some of the pictures and headlines used most prominently in all the national daily newspapers published that day, and then offer a more specific comparison of the ways in which the *Mirror* and the *Daily Express*—a "popular," mid-market newspaper which is tabloid-sized—presented the story. We pay particular attention to the primary modes of address the papers utilized to assist their imagined readerships to make sense of the events in New York City, and suggest extrapolations of the linkages between those modes of address and the market constructs within which this highly commercialized press operates (McLachlan and Golding 2000: 76–7). The study was designed and implemented not as an outcome of a conscious decision to undertake a systematic content analysis, but more spontaneously as we scanned the front pages of the relevant issues as collective newspaper texts and, we felt, certain affects became apparent. We readily acknowledge that this work is necessarily exploratory and incomplete.

In that attempts to measure changes and convergences in news values— including processes of tabloidization and "dumbing-down"—have so far produced inconclusive results (McLachlan and Golding 2000), in this study news values have been removed as an independent variable: for British national newspaper journalists September 11 was the "story of a lifetime" (Evans 2001), and was uniformly treated as news. Nevertheless, some important evidence can be located in this extraordinary journalistic moment to suggest answers to a range of persistent questions, such as whether, to what extent, and how the journalism of these newspapers may have been routinely inflected with a shared tabloidism; whether the same news events, when reported, bear different implications—that newspapers, with their readers, construct significantly different stories from the same basic "facts"; and how the market definitions of newspapers intersect with their journalisms.

161

## The UK national press in perspective

In academic, popular, and trade discourses the UK national daily press is divided into entities which articulate commerce and culture in historically specific ways. On September 12, 2001 five of the papers analyzed here (*The Times*, *Guardian*, *Independent*, *Financial Times*, and the *Daily Telegraph*) were broadsheet in size, the rest tabloid-sized. All of the former were also considered to be "quality" titles, reflecting their antecedents in what in the nineteenth and early twentieth centuries was commonly called the "intelligent," "class," or "serious" press (Fox Bourne 1887: 297–365; Schalk 1988: 73–4). Ideally, such papers imagined their typical reader to be a "critical politician, who watched events," and they published "solid and instructive matter" (Fox Bourne 1887: 380; Ensor 1936: 314).

By 1904 the prominent Victorian journalist W. T. Stead had inventoried "Daily Journalism" into four "classes" or "ranks." The first two contained newspapers "of influence," at the head of which was *The Times*. In the third category of newspapers which supposedly emphasized generating advertising revenue and circulation over influencing public opinion Stead located two of the new "popular" or "cheap" newspapers of the late nineteenth and early twentieth centuries, the *Daily Mail* (1896) and *Daily Express* (1900). Then broadsheet in size and part of a much larger group of "popular" titles, by 2001 both had adopted the tabloid format and had been re-classified into a "mid-market." In his final category of titles with no pretensions in the way of exercising political influence Stead included the then *Daily Mirror*, an illustrated paper which had begun publication in 1903 in tabloid format (Baylen 1997: 94–5). In the mid-1930s the *Daily Mirror* instituted a more comprehensive "tabloid revolution" drawing on US examples, particularly the *New York Daily News* (Conboy 2002: 126–8). It was joined only in 1969 by the *Sun*, and supplemented from the late 1970s by the *Daily Star*, to constitute a new category of "red-top" tabloids (so called after their distinctive white-on-red mastheads, and to distinguish them from the *Daily Mail* and *Daily Express* which adopted the tabloid format from the 1970s). By September 2001, the red-top *Sun*, *Mirror*, and *Star* accounted for 49.8 percent of all national newspaper circulations. The mid-market *Mail* and *Express* made up 27.4 percent and the five broadsheets 22.8 percent. The highest circulation paper, the *Sun* (3,565 million copies) had greater numbers of sales than either the two mid-market titles or all of the broadsheet papers combined.

Newspaper classifications have never proved to be straightforward, however, and even in the nineteenth century commentators often sub-divided press categories (Fox Bourne 1887: 367–90). The *Daily Telegraph* was a "cheap" newspaper at its introduction in 1855 and Stead included it in his third "rank" along with the *Daily Mail* and *Daily Express* (Baylen 1997: 94–5). Raymond Williams considered the *Daily Express* to be the most tabloid-like of the old "popular" press (Williams 1961: 208). One contemporary trade organization continues to classify the red-top tabloids as "popular" papers, a term largely discontinued elsewhere. Williams' own preference was for a broad distinction to be drawn between those newspapers which he believed owed something to the (broadsheet) "news-sheet" of the emerging public sphere of the eighteenth century and the "magazine miscellany" offered by the rest (ibid.). More recently, Chalaby (1998: 170–4) suggested that competitive marketization has led to the polarization of the British press as "quality" and tabloid titles. In these analyses there is little room for the so-called mid-market—the press of "low brow" sensibilities and "aspirations of middle-class values" (Conboy 2002: 112). In attempting to allow for more subtle gradations than "a simple binary opposition between the serious and the tabloid," Sparks (2000: 13–16) proposed that the UK national press was largely located in three categories—the semi-serious, the serious-popular and the news-stand tabloid.

## September 11 in pictures and headlines

The first impression made by the front pages of the September 12 issues of the national papers is one of an apparent similarity among red-top tabloid, mid-market and broadsheet titles alike. These are dominated in every instance by a single photographic image. It is equally striking that only broadsheet papers carried any significant amounts of text with these pictures—the Daily Telegraph five columns of ten lines, The Times somewhat more, and the Financial Times almost half a page. Both the Guardian and the Independent, like all the other, tabloid-size papers, eschewed text, however. While McLachlan and Golding (2000: 79–81) argue that a more liberal use of pictures may be a measure of tabloidization, this evidence is at odds with their more general findings that in its use of illustration, over time The Times had become more tabloid-like than the Guardian. Moreover, the selection of photographs for the front pages of the September 12 issues also suggests a less than uniform broadsheet–tabloid division.

Eight of the ten titles used pictures—an image described as "ubiquitous" by the Guardian (September 12, 2001)—which shows, from a fairly tight angle, smoke billowing and flames and debris issuing from the twin towers of the World Trade Center at the moment of, or just following, the impact of the second airplane. That the Financial Times chose to publish a photograph of a wider shot, taken from across the Hudson River, of the devastation of downtown Manhattan could be rationalized as being congruent with the specialist business paper's more distant and broader perspective of the implications of the attacks on a major metropolis and financial services location; but that does not explain why the mid-market, tabloid-sized Daily Mail, which shares some rhetorical strategies with the red-top tabloid press (see Conboy 2002), opted for a similar picture. Thus, even at first—or, perhaps second—glance, these front pages connoted separations and linkages between journalistic approaches which were not amenable to reductionist explanations shaped by the simplistic language of the newspaper "market."

The headlines which accompanied these photographs reinforce this view.

There was a remarkable consistency of presentation and rhetoric, refracting popular responses to the events of September 11, among the three red-top tabloids. Not only did they choose to publish similar images; they all sought to set what was geographically, and perhaps even culturally, distant within a standard conceit of inclusiveness, rhetorically extending the New York community to the UK by setting what had happened in Manhattan in a wider, but nevertheless simultaneously more intimate, context (Conboy 2002: 161–5, 180–1). September 11 was the "Day that changed the world" (*Sun*). "Is this the end of the world?" asked the *Daily Star*. "War on the world," declared the *Mirror*. By comparison, four broadsheet newspapers made no attempt to conflate a British "us" with a US "them" into one "world." Their headlines were: "War comes to America" (*Times*), "War on America" (*Daily Telegraph*), "Doomsday America" (*Independent*), and "Assault on America" (*Financial Times*).

The juxtapositioning of "America" and "the world" would appear to be significant and telling. Even here, however, the situation is not straightforward. A fifth broadsheet, the *Guardian*, used almost the identical headline ("A declaration of war") as the tabloid, mid-market *Daily Express* ("Declaration of war"). Moreover, the word "war" was used by five of the newspapers—one red-top tabloid, one middle-market tabloid and three broadsheets. (The *Daily Mail's* headline was "Apocalypse: New York, September 11, 2001," and while this may seem to be at odds with the other nine titles, nevertheless it chimes with the *Independent's* use of "Doomsday.")

In sum, these readings suggest that stronger and weaker differences and similarities crisscross the whole UK national daily press-scape. To be sure, there are greater apparent congruences between the themes contained in these headlines and the newspapers' socio-market positions among both the broadsheet and the red-top tabloid press (see Table 9.1). Lower levels of apparent congruence— where titles located in different so-called markets nevertheless shared lexical strategies—are more evident among broadsheet and mid-market newspapers (eight instances). Of the three red-top tabloids only the *Mirror* makes an appearance towards this end of the scale. This would seem to confirm Sparks' (2000: 14–16) theory of a newspaper "continuum" where at times of conspicuous crisis, all titles, but especially the "serious-popular" (mid-market), veer away from an underlying tabloidization and return to "serious" forms of journalism. This view lends credence to the notion that, relying on a shared strategy of "saturation coverage and outrage," at such moments the otherwise competitive national daily press speaks "with one voice," implicitly unifying an idealized "Britain" (Kennedy 2002) and suspending the variegated "ingrained frames of reference and collective structures" which ordinarily define "news" (Smith *et al.* 1975: 246). However, historically this has not been the case. A study of 30 years of the then *Daily Mirror* and the *Daily Express* concluded that the crisis of World War II exacerbated, rather than challenged, the papers' "personalities" and "persistent core assumptions" about their readerships (ibid.: 232).

*Table 9.1* National daily newspaper headlines, September 12, 2001, grouped by theme (b = broadsheet, m = mid-market, t = tabloid)

| *Congruence between themes and "markets"* | *Themes* | *Newspapers* |
|---|---|---|
| High levels of congruence | America | *The Times* (b)<br>*Daily Telegraph* (b)<br>*Independent* (b)<br>*Financial Times* (b) |
| | War and America | *The Times* (b)<br>*Daily Telegraph* (b) |
| | World | *Sun* (t)<br>*Mirror* (t)<br>*Star* (t) |
| | War and world | *Mirror* (t) |
| Lower levels of congruence | War | *The Times* (b)<br>*Daily Telegraph* (b)<br>*Guardian* (b)<br>*Daily Express* (m)<br>*Mirror* (t) |
| | Declaration of war | *Guardian* (b)<br>*Daily Express* (m) |
| | Doomsday/Apocalypse | *Independent* (b)<br>*Daily Mail* (m) |

## The "new seriousness"

Just as it became axiomatic in the latter half of the twentieth century that the nature of news had been fundamentally altered—a transformation embodied by concepts such as "dumbing-down," tabloidization, and hyper-commercialization—and that journalism no longer retained the prior authority to define what constituted "news," the idea that the events of September 11 effected some kind of reversal of this process seemed to gain credence in the closing months of 2001. What was considered to be "a new seriousness," it was argued, represented "not just a moment where the press had to be seen to be decorous, but a genuine, fully paid-up cultural shift" (Soames 2002). News—"real" news—sold newspapers: "Nobody in Fleet Street," the former editor of the *Guardian* wrote in early October, "can remember a surge of sales to match the one which followed the suicide attacks" (Preston 2001b). September 11 was seen as reconfirming the essential journalistic role of newspapers "to report, to inform, to analyse, to comment, to bring us the news," promising the return to pre-eminence of "the old-fashioned, down-and-dirty news reporter" (Greenslade 2001a; cited in Wells 2001: 3). The

Pauline-like conversion of the *Mirror* newspaper epitomized this supposed shift, encouraging a form of journalistic revivalism and even suggestions of the imminent disappearance of its distinctive white-on-red masthead (Hodgson 2001b; Casey 2002). Piers Morgan, the editor of the *Mirror*, told a meeting of the Society of Editors in Belfast on October 22:

> What is the future of newspapers? If you'd asked me five weeks ago, I might have answered "*Big Brother*." The *Mirror*, like other tabloids, saw significant circulation rises through July and August almost entirely on the back of possibly the most inane television ever made. It seemed like we had finally found our perfect news story . . . It summed up the whole tabloid celebrity media circus that's evolved in the last 20 years . . . Then something happened on September 11 that changed just about everything . . . What happened next may well have redefined tabloid newspapers in as dramatic a way as it will redefine American foreign policy. The *Mirror* has splashed on the war on terrorism every day since, carrying at least 13 pages of the latest news every day. And we have sold an extra 2.5 million papers . . . What does this tell us? Well, it tells me that perhaps for the first time in 30 years, people in this country are rejecting the *Big Brother*-style trivia they so adored five weeks ago and realizing there really are more important things in the world . . . There is a sudden and prolonged hunger for serious news and information. And despite the astonishing array of 24-hour TV and radio news channels, they are turning to newspapers to give them even more news and information rather than the light entertainment that seemed so important in August.[3]

Such was the euphoria that even the most experienced, astute, and cautious commentators found it difficult not to join in: "This could be the start of something profound. It could also, of course, be more propaganda . . . [But] what if the agenda has, in fact, become more thoughtful?" (Preston 2001d).

Visual imagery was seen to have given way to the written word; television, notwithstanding its dominance as the mass medium of news, and the World Wide Web, with its threatening, incipient power, lacked "the experienced practitioners trying their best to make sense of the senseless" and could offer only "superficial" news treatments (Greenslade 2001a). A return to journalistic fundamentals meant more "serious" reporting, more journalists in the field, more prominence for "foreign" stories, with the eventual consequence that a newspaper such as *The Times* contemplated a reversal of the tendencies of the past quarter century to "permanently rebalance . . . [its] editorial priorities" (Wells 2001: 3). Such "pure journalism" (Greenslade 2001a) was also more pluralistic, more resistant to state endeavors to "spin" an unquestioning consensus on the "war on terrorism," and even in mainstream places (notably, the *Mirror* but also the *Guardian* and the *Independent*) sometimes virulently hostile to the project of manufacturing a universal coalition for "the war on terrorism" (Hodgson 2001b; Preston 2001b).

This apparent revitalization of journalism suggested a renewal of the belief that reporting was "the best way of getting under the skin of a society if you wish to be radical" (Cohen 1999: 124). Critics on the left were prompted to enthuse over newspapers rediscovering "their journalistic souls." The chairperson of the Campaign for Press and Broadcasting Freedom argued:

> Much of the reporting in the British press of September 11 and its after-math did a good deal to restore faith in British journalism. Most papers reported the events, both in words and pictures, with a breadth and depth that, in recent years, have been all too often conspicuously lacking.
>
> (Petley 2001)

Linked to this, news appeared no longer to be merely a fast-moving consumer good, available in variant forms, on demand from an array of outlets, the majority of them streaming audio and video literally "to air." September 11 seemed to offer an antidote to the "liberal lament" over trivialization and dumbing-down (Langer 1998: 1–4), reaffirming the notion that at least in news production there was such a thing as "prime time"—a temporal space in which journalists, acting "professionally," claimed the responsibility to construct what Lippmann called the "trustworthy and relevant news" essential to the proper working of dem-ocracy. September 11 was not "only a story" (ibid.: 158–9).

Not surprisingly, television, transmitting "live" pictures from New York of the second airliner crashing into the World Trade Center, built large audiences rising to 16 million through the afternoon and evening of September 11. The two main terrestrial channels, BBC 1 and Independent Television (ITV), Channel 3, began rolling news programs just after 2 pm British time: at 2.06 pm 3.6 million viewers were watching. By 3.30 pm all the terrestrial channels were showing rolling news, and the combined audiences had grown to almost seven million: three-quarters of people watching TV were tuned in to this news. By 6 pm more than 16 million were watching news on BBC 1, ITV and two pay-TV rolling news channels, BBC News 24 and Sky News, and the audience had not dimin-ished three hours later when BBC 1, ITV and Channel 4 were showing news specials (Deans 2001). Yet, notwithstanding "a world dumbstruck before TV screens," only by reading the papers, it was argued, could the British public satisfy its need "to know more and to understand more," because print news journalism provided "thinking and writing time" (Greenslade 2001a; Preston 2001a). "If newspapers are only the first rough draft of history," Preston argued "this was a week to cut out and keep them."

## Tabloidization and the British press

This argument was tenable if the British press could be regarded as not being irrevocably divided between those titles committed to "serious" journalism and the tabloids, but rather as a continuous entity of differing "bundles" of both "serious" and tabloid journalism, the individual configurations of which change over time as responses to actual or perceived shifts in internal competitive market conditions and/or wider cultural contexts. For the most part, the journalism of both "serious" and tabloid newspapers overlaps in this way, it is contended, at "less intense" levels to comprise a "preferred average mix of content." Occasionally (for example, during the hyper-competition within Fleet Street between 1987 and 1993, and at the death of Princess Diana in 1997—see Bromley 1998a), the conditions become so acute that national newspaper journalism as a whole converges towards either the tabloid or the "serious" end of the spectrum as manifestations of, on the one hand, secular changing social patterns of (dis)engagement with news and, on the other hand, an enhanced popular "direct existential interest in the world of public life." In sum, *all* newspapers strive to find "the exact formula," made up of both kinds of journalism, which will make them popular (Stephenson 1998: 20; Sparks 2000: 13–16, 20–3, 32–4).

For most of the twentieth century intermittent crises are regarded as having given rise to temporary—and partial—remission from a long-term drift towards the pre-eminence of tabloid journalism to the point where some critics argue that what was being published could no longer be regarded as newspapers at all (Stephenson 1998: 21–3; Rooney 2000: 107). During World War II, George Orwell already believed that an apparent resurgence of "seriousness" in the press did not detract from his view that, as a whole, Britain was a "low-brow country" inclined to "philistinism," in which print journalism was held by the majority of the population to be of little importance. By and large, very few newspaper readers were interested in news (cited in Bromley 1999: 94, 99–100; see also 102). Six decades later a former editor of the *Daily Mirror* noted that "News doesn't matter to many people . . ." (Greenslade 2001c: 6). This lack of any sustained popular interest in "big" news stories made itself apparent in a number of post-war crises (for example, the Suez, Falklands, and Gulf conflicts): Greenslade (2001b: 6) who edited the *Daily Mirror* during Operation Desert Storm, observed two months after September 11, "It is heartbreaking to be a journalist at such times."

From the 1950s, the red-top tabloid press (daily and Sunday) accounted for the major part of total national newspaper circulations in the UK. Between 1965 and 1995, sales of these papers remained stable at around 50 million copies each week. At the same time, the circulations of the "popular" (mid-market) press, which had been introduced in the late nineteenth century and the early twentieth century, declined from more than half to about a quarter of all national newspaper sales (Tunstall 1996: 8–11, 36, 40; Sparks 2000: 22). This reflected the emergence of a working-class domination of national daily newspaper reading from the decade 1937–47, but not as a unitary phenomenon. The British national tabloid daily was the newspaper of choice for a younger, more affluent, economically and socially independent, consuming, working class, associated with "lighter" industrial employment and located disproportionately in and around London and the English Midlands. As such, tabloid papers like the *Mirror* and, later, the *Sun* appealed to those who gained most materially from the cyclical acceleration of (particularly household and personal leisure) consumption among the working class in the 1930s, 1960s and 1980s (Bromley 1999: 98, 102–3; Rooney 2000: 94–9). The journalism offered to this constituency was one of an altered focus, from an economy of information (however artfully constructed) which retained a measure of appeal to the rational formation of something akin to a public sphere ("All the news in sixty seconds") (Tulloch 2000: 132) to "fun" rooted in the rhetoric of modes of address (Bromley and Tumber 1997: 373; Conboy 2002: 138ff). In 2000 one journalist complained of the triumph of "therapy news":

> Instead of a news reporter's starting point being facts and analysis about the outside world, people's inner lives and emotional reactions to events including the reporter's own dominate how events are perceived. Emotional indulgence and sentimentalism are replacing informative, facts-based news reporting. The classic Who-What-Where-When-Why news reporting formula is more likely to include Feel . . . Facts are being side-lined, sometimes ignored, or redefined so that news stories are influenced by what somebody felt about an event . . . These days, arguing for more "hard" news seems cold, inhuman or even boring.
>
> (Mayes 2000)

In the mid-1990s, while 29 percent of British journalists were motivated to enter journalism because they were "good at writing," and 23 percent because they saw it as an "exciting career," only 14 percent said that being interested in news was a factor (Delano and Henningham 1995: 15–16).

At about the same time many concerns were expressed that the process of tabloidization was incorporating, even overwhelming, the "serious" press (English 1997: 7; Bromley 1998b: 32; McLachlan and Golding 2000: 75–6). This view has been challenged from a number of perspectives (Sparks 1992; Bromley 1998b; Conboy 2002), where it has been argued that, whether so-called news values—the "range" and "form" of news (McLachlan and Golding 2000)—coincide or not, vital differences remain between more "serious" and genuinely tabloid journalisms.

## Paper Voices revisited

If the suggestion that distinctions of significance exist between "serious" and tabloid journalisms is to be credible, then it ought to be evident even among newspapers which otherwise share many characteristics. For almost 30 years the tabloid *Daily Mirror* and the then broadsheet *Daily Express* seemed to embody the very idea of "popular" journalism (Smith *et al.* 1975). After 1945 their combined circulations variously reached 9–10 million (at least 70 percent of the total sales of all national daily titles in 2001). If, as has been suggested, their journalisms had been coalescing (at the tabloid end of the spectrum) for 40 years, and in response to September 11 the *Mirror* began to move its journalism in the opposite direction, we might expect considerable similarities in their journalistic approaches to be evident in their September 12 issues.

From the outset, the *Mirror*'s "calmer" response to the events of September 11 drew comment, whereas the *Daily Express* was seen to sustain a greater stridency (*Guardian*: September 12, 2001). Yet while the *Express*'s 88-page special edition carried the cautious running tag line "World on the brink," the *Mirror* was more emphatic in re-iterating its "War on the world" theme. The *Mirror*'s comparatively modest 25 pages of coverage were notable for the limited use of demotic appeal (the exception being "We are all f\*\*\*ing dying in here"), but it had no hesitation in declaring the onset of "Total war:" "Not only something awful, way beyond our control, is about to happen to the world," it informed its readers but it used the Foreign Secretary, Jack Straw, to underline that "This touches each one of us." Quoting a London psychiatrist, the paper asserted that "Millions [would be] hit by trauma"—not least as a consequence of watching the "Gripping TV nasty on a sick, dark, contorted monster of a day."

The modes of personalization used by the two papers seem particularly suggestive. Whereas the back page of the wrap-around cover of the *Express* carried a single photograph of a woman escaping the scene covered in ash with the headline "Hell on Earth," the *Mirror* gave over a quarter of its cover to a photograph of George W. Bush, and alongside it the quote "Freedom itself was attacked by a faithless coward—freedom will be defended." The simplified illustrations of the impotence and vulnerability of individuals and governments, the chaos and surprise, were thus represented in quite surprisingly different ways—the "popular" paper resorting to an established mixing of public and private discourses, but the red-top tabloid initially leaving unaddressed the deeper (personal) social dynamics that surround news events.

The *Express* adhered to a traditional "popular" press discourse, conflating the public with the private, and tempering the distance implicit in the threat of a generic "war" with the closeness of one "world," and even the pseudo-explanatory set within an artfully constructed knowingness—how "The marriage of religion and terror creates an invisible foe" and "How could such evil be unleashed?" The paper's cover rather quaintly proclaimed that the September 12 issue contained "The most complete and up to date coverage." The *Express*, it seems, subject to the pressures of "the story of a lifetime," had not moved far from its roots in the mid-twentieth century when it imagined an archetypal reader who could "take a fairly long view, who appreciates the arrival of events in an explicable linear order, and who thereby feels himself (*sic*) to have some degree of control over his (*sic*) response" (Smith *et al.* 1975: 233). When the events of

September 11 threatened to disrupt the "daily reassurance of fixed order," the paper relied on underscoring the sensational with the logical (after all, the "Full horror [of the attacks]," the paper promised, was "hidden in jets' black boxes") in a form of public address which offered some challenge to the idea that "power has been structurally suppressed and is too 'remote' and 'uncontrollable' to be accessed by the 'normal' citizen" (Smith et al. 1975: 239; Sparks 2000: 35–6). The *Express* at least held out the prospect that September 11 could be comprehended and ultimately was subject to rational, linear explanation albeit through its own paternalist perspective (Conboy 2002: 111).

The performance of the *Mirror* appears more problematic, subsequently rationalized as a conscious adoption of a more "serious" tone and a rejection of tabloidism, yet still in the cause of "the public mood" (Seymour 2002). It must be acknowledged, too, that on September 11 the two papers shared many common reportorial, lexical, and illustrative devices which connote "professionalism" in UK journalism. Unlike the popular press, which constituted itself as a voice to the people, the tabloid has long laid claim to be the "voice of the people" or "the people's paper," however (Smith et al. 1975: 142; Conboy 2002: 181). Integral to this project has been the restless journalistic pursuit of the quintessential mosaic of emotive stories—a definitive sensationalization of topics not considered "nice" by common consent among other newspapers (Smith et al. 1975: 232; Bromley 1999: 104–5, 122; Conboy 2002: 126–8). Thus, how the *Mirror* initially negotiated September 11, when confronted by events so "naturally" sensational they possibly resisted further tabloid sensationalization (and, incidentally, soon challenged the *Sun* to resort to a more typically tabloid story of the Queen's bath-tub rubber duck), has been seen by some as a matter of "luck" (Preston 2001d). The significance of the prominence given to George W. Bush, then, lies not in the *Mirror*'s privileging the voice of a geo-political leader, counteracting its tabloid inclination to everyday "human interest" narrativity, but rather in the ambiguous reproduction of the incoherence of the US President, hovering between the carnivalesque and commonsense. For the *Mirror* the key to September 11 lies in its incomprehensibility—even to a US President. As Smith et al. observed, "The *Mirror* reader is invited to see himself (*sic*) as, in his (*sic*) private life and thought, more exposed to unforeseen events both good and bad, less able to understand their origin and implications, less able to control them . . ." (1975: 233).

## Conclusion

In the months following September 11, the divergence in approaches to news exhibited by an "heretical" *Mirror* and the unreformed *Sun* attracted much attention, based on the belief that the papers were competitors in the same tabloid "market" and that one of them was attempting to serve that market in a radically different way (Hodgson 2001b; Greenslade 2002). Rarely, and only incidentally, was the *Mirror* compared directly to the so-called mid-market *Daily Express* (Doward 2001) and not at all to any of the broadsheet titles. This was "a war

171

within a war" presaged on a direct correlation between journalism and commer-cialism, embedded in western liberal ideologies of the press, and which has become a journalistic commonplace (Kennedy 2002), overlaid on a longer run debate about tabloidization and "anxieties that a slippage of [bourgeois] control . . . is occurring" as a result of "the confusion of 'broadsheet subjects and tabloid subjects'" but not readerships (Bromley 1998b: 35; McLachlan and Golding 2000: 76; Conboy 2002: 181). It was assumed that the *Mirror*'s "seriousness" rep-resented an attempt to change the audience rather than to change its audiences.

Given the incompleteness of our research, any conclusions to be drawn must be highly tentative. Nevertheless, it suggests that it may be helpful to think of broadsheet newspapers and tabloids as two distinct cultural expressions, address-ing largely different social groupings rather than versions of a single artifact ranged along a continuum (see Bromley and Tumber 1997). This would posit the "serious popular" (tabloid-sized) press not as a hybrid, squeezed more or less uncomfortably between two extremes, but as the occupant of a discreet cultural and social space. Over the longer term, this "mid-market" has declined in politi-cal economy terms, which has led to inductive conclusions that "middle brow" journalism has been largely displaced, too, by either "quality" or tabloid forms (Tulloch 2000: 134–5).

Strangely, it is this journalism which was seen as representing the emergent "classlessness" of the affluent later twentieth century (Orwell 1940: 98, 122), and which, it is argued, is now served by "bundled" journalism, configuring other ("serious" and tabloid) forms in negotiation of the extremes of dumbing-down and dumbing-up. The marginally genteel lower middle class was in demographic and cultural decline in the 1940s, and with it the journalism which served it (Orwell 1946). The "mid-market" has survived, though in truncated form: on September 17, 2001 the *Daily Mail* had the second largest circulation after the *Sun* of any national daily newspaper in the UK. In many respects, the *Mail* is regarded as *the* success story of British newspapers over the past 30 years. Implicit in the tabloidization debate has been the belief that this "market" exists without a distinctive journalism of its own. The *Mail*'s achievement is generally seen as having been built not on an appeal to social class but to gender (Sparks 2000: 34).

Facing a "what-a-story," however, the *Daily Express* reacted, as Berkowitz pre-dicted, in tune with its social-market situation, and its journalists produced "stories" of September 11 which met those requirements (1997: 363–5, 374–5). Similarly, the *Sun* (as noted above) and, even more clearly, the third red-top tabloid, the *Daily Star*, stuck doggedly to a news agenda which largely skirted around the geopolitics of September 11. The *Daily Star* in particular opted instead for an unreconstructed tabloid news diet of *Big Brother* and *Pop Idol* gossip—and appeared to gain readers (Greenslade 2002). In the intensity of the moment, the journalism of the *Express* was neither parody nor imitation of either "quality" or tabloid journalism but a separate journalism of the "middle brow" and distanced from that of the *Sun* and the *Daily Star*.

At the time of writing, the editor of the *Mirror* was adhering to his newspaper's "conversion," although this may have been driven more by the paper's corporate owners' desire to reposition it, for whatever reasons, in the mid-market (Doward 2001; Greenslade 2002). Notwithstanding winning two major journalism awards, the *Mirror*'s circulation three months after September 11 was lower than it had been in August 2001 (Preston 2002). The "new seriousness," it appeared, was a failure. More than that, it was something of a charade. The paper's journalism—and that of all the other national daily press—on September 12 reflected the marketized competitiveness which has been a critical part of the reflexivity of Fleet Street for more than a century, and which is founded in the pragmatic understanding that newspaper "markets" are largely culturally and socially discrete and demand their own journalisms. Much of the case for a blurring of these distinctions—in the long term, in favour of dumbing-down, but occasionally as dumbing-up—has been based on evidence of a wider consensus on news values. When what constitutes "news" is removed from the calculation (as on September 11), then notions that "quality" newspapers can transmute, however incrementally and partially, into "broadloids" (a term originated by the editor of the *Guardian*), that "popular" mid-market titles like the *Daily Mail* and *Daily Express* become tabloids merely by changing size (in contrast to the deliberate supplanting of the *Daily Herald* by the *Sun* and its subsequent sale to Rupert Murdoch, or that a tabloid can transcend the genre by adopting a "new seriousness" all seem less tenable. Class may no longer be as useful a tool as it once was, and Orwellian hierarchies of culture may carry unacceptably pejorative connotations, but national daily newspaper journalism in the UK has three clear, if not uniform, variants which address different constituencies. The political economy interests of the press may dictate that changing constellations of titles address these publics, but notwithstanding the on-going play of these interests, the "what-a-story" of September 11 provoked the UK national daily press to revert to its pre-existing fundamentalist tripartite mode.

## Notes

1  Figures from the Audit Bureau of Circulations (ABC). The (Scottish) *Daily Record*, the *Daily Star* edition circulating in the Republic of Ireland, and the *Scotsman*, have been omitted.
2  Either all or some of these pages can be found on a number of websites, including www.mediaguardian.co.uk, www.newsday.com, www.september11news.com, www.bcr. org, www.tocsin.net, www.inma.org, www.poynter.org and www.newseum.org, all sites accessed March 11, 2002. Those of the *Guardian* and the *Independent* are included in *September 11: A Collection of Newspaper Front Pages Selected by the Poynter Institute* (2002). Many newspapers produced wraps for their September 12 issues, and so effectively had two "front pages."
3  Reproduced in the *Guardian* (October 23, 2001) posted at media.guardian. co.uk/Print/0,3858,4283387,00.html, accessed March 1, 2002.

# References

Baylen, J. O. (1997) A contemporary estimate of the London daily press in the early twentieth century, in M. Bromley and T. O'Malley (eds) *A Journalism Reader*, London: Routledge: 91–101.

Berkowitz, D. (1997) Non-routine news and newswork: exploring what-a-story, in D. Berkowitz (ed.) *Social Meanings of News*, London: Sage: 362–75.

Bromley, M. (1998a) Introduction, in H. Stephenson and M. Bromley (eds) *Sex, Lies and Democracy: The Press and the Public*, Harlow, Longman: 1–10.

Bromley, M. (1998b) The "tabloiding" of Britain: "quality" newspapers in the 1990s, in H. Stephenson and M. Bromley (eds) *Sex, Lies and Democracy: The Press and the Public*, Harlow, Longman: 25–38.

Bromley, M. (1999) Was it the *Mirror* wot won it? The development of the tabloid press during the Second World War, in N. Hayes and J. Hill (eds) *"Millions Like Us"? British Culture in the Second World War*, Liverpool: Liverpool University Press: 93–124.

Bromley, M. (2000) The British media landscape, in *European Media Landscape*, Maastricht: European Journalism Centre: 1–4.

Bromley, M. and H. Tumber (1997) From Fleet Street to cyberspace: the British "popular" press in the late twentieth century, *European Journal of Communication Research*, 22 (3): 365–78.

Casey, J. (2002) Black and white but is red all over at *Mirror*?, *Guardian*, January 28. Available online at www.media.guardian.co.uk/news/story/0,7541,640477,00.html, accessed February 25, 2002.

Chalaby, J. (1998) *The Invention of Journalism*, Basingstoke, Macmillan.

Cohen, N. (1999) The news is what we say it is, *Jewish Quarterly*, Autumn 1997, reproduced in *Cruel Britannia*, London: Verso: 123–71.

Conboy, M. (2002) *The Press and Popular Culture*, London: Sage.

Day, J. (2001) September 11 changed *Mirror* forever, says Morgan, *Media Guardian*, October 23. Available online at www.media.guardian.co.uk/Print/0,3858,4283393,00.html, accessed March 1, 2002.

Deans, J. (2001) 16m glued to news as tragedy unfolds, *Guardian*, September 12. Available online at www.media.guardian.co.uk/Print/0,3858,4255305,00.html, accessed March 1, 2002.

Delano, A. and Henningham, J. (1995) *The News Breed: British Journalists in the 1990s*, London: The London Institute.

Donovan, R. J. and Scherer, R. (1992) *Unsilent Revolution: Television News and American Public Life*, Cambridge: Cambridge University Press.

Doward, J. (2001) *Mirror* looks back to the future, *Observer*, November 4. Available online at www.media.guardian.co.uk/Print/0,3858,4291479,00.html, accessed January 22, 2002.

Engel, M. (1996) *Tickle the Public: One Hundred Years of the Popular Press*, London: Gollancz.

English, D. (1997) It's the people wot did it, *Media Guardian*, September 8: 6–7, 11.

Ensor, R. K. (1936) *England 1870–1914*, London: Oxford University Press.

Evans, S. (2001) The biggest story of my life, *British Journalism Review*, 12 (4): 7–11.

Fox Bourne, H. R. (1887) *English Newspapers: Chapters in the History of Journalism*, vol. 2, reprinted as *Chapters in the History of British Journalism*, vol. 7 (1998), London: Routledge.

Gibson, O. (2001) News websites struggle to cope, *Guardian*, September 12. Available online at www.media.guardian.co.uk/Print/0,3858,4254983,00.html, accessed March 1, 2002.

*Global Journalism Review* (n.d.) Record email reactions. Available online at www.-globaljreview.btinternet.co.uk/index_g.htm, accessed March 8, 2002.

Goodman, G. (2000) Pimps or pimpernels? *British Journalism Review*, 11 (4): 3–6.

Greenslade, R. (2001a) Pure journalism, *Media Guardian*, September 17: 4–5.

Greenslade, R. (2001b) The war isn't working, *Media Guardian*, November 12: 6–7.

Greenslade, R. (2001c) An annus horribilis, *Media Guardian*, December 17: 6–7.

Greenslade (2002) Starry, starry night, *Media Guardian*, March 11: 8–9.

Gripsrud, J. (2000) Tabloidization, popular journalism and democracy, in C. Sparks and J. Tulloch (eds) *Tabloid Tales: Global Debates over Media Standards*, Oxford: Rowman and Littlefield: 285–300.

*Guardian* (2001) How the tabloids reported events, September 12. Available online at www.mediaguardian.co.uk/Print/0,3858,4255057,00.html, accessed 1 March 2002.

Harris, M. (1997) Farewell to Fleet Street, in M. Bromley and T. O'Malley (eds) *A Journalism Reader*, London: Routledge: 283–95.

Hodgson, J. (2001a) US atrocity swells print runs, *Guardian*, September 12. Available online at www.media.guardian.co.uk/Print/0,3858,4255477,00.html, accessed March 1, 2002.

Hodgson, J. (2001b) Rusbridger scoops top award, *Guardian*, December 21. Available online at www.media.guardian.co.uk/Print/0,3858,4324623,00.html, accessed February 25, 2002.

Kennedy, G. (2002) Perspectives on war: the British see things differently, *Columbia Journalism Review*, March/April. Available online at www.cjr.org/year/02/2/kennedy.asp, accessed March 8, 2002.

Langer, J. (1998) *Tabloid Television: Popular Journalism and the "Other News,"* London: Routledge.

Lee, A. J. (1976) *The Origins of the Popular Press in England, 1855–1914*, London: Croom Helm.

McLachlan, S. and Golding, P. (2000) Tabloidization in the British press: a quantitative investigation into changes in British newspapers, 1952–1997, in C. Sparks and J. Tulloch (eds) *Tabloid Tales: Global Debates over Media Standards*, Oxford: Rowman and Littlefield: 75–90.

McManus, J. H. (1994) *Market-Driven Journalism: Let the Citizen Beware?*, London: Sage.

McNair, B. (1996) *News and Journalism in the UK*, 2nd edition, London: Routledge.

Mayes, T. (2000) Submerging in "therapy news," *British Journalism Review*, 11 (4): 30–6. Available online at www.bjr.org.uk/Data/Vol11_2000/No4/Mayes.html, accessed March 8, 2002.

*Media Ownership* (1995) The Government's Proposals presented to Parliament by the Secretary of State for National Heritage, Cm 2872, London: HMSO.

Moses, M. (2001) Ms Future and the Caveman: a civilized debate on the design of Wednesday's front pages. Available online at www.poynter.org/Terrorism/caveman.htm, accessed March 11, 2002.

National Readership Survey (2002) data. Available at www.nrs.co.uk/reports/newspapers.htm, accessed 21 March 2002.

Orwell, G. (1940) The lion and the unicorn: socialism and the English genius, reproduced in S. Orwell and I. Angus (eds) *The Collected Essays, Journalism and Letters of George*

*Orwell*, vol. 2: *My Country Right or Left, 1940–1943*, Harmondsworth: Penguin (1970): 59–109.

Orwell, G. (1946) The decline of the English murder, *Tribune*, February 15, reproduced in S. Orwell and I. Angus (eds) *The Collected Essays, Journalism and Letters of George Orwell*, vol. 4: *In Front of Your Nose, 1945–1950*, Harmondsworth: Penguin: 98–101.

Petley, J. (2001) The papers' war, *Free Press*, December 6. Available online at www.cpbf.org.uk/freepress/, accessed March 8, 2002.

Preston, P. (2001a) Papers went for it and won, *Observer*, September 16. Available online at www.media.guardian.co.uk/Print/0,3858,4257939,00.html, accessed January 22, 2002.

Preston, P. (2001b) War, what is it good for?, *Observer*, October 7. Available online at www.media.guardian.co.uk/Print/0,3858,4271774,00.html, accessed January 22, 2002.

Preston, P. (2001c) Too much jaw-jaw on war-war, *Observer*, October 21. Available online at www.media.guardian.co.uk/Print/0,3858,4281571,00.html, accessed January 22, 2002.

Preston, P. (2001d) Seeing the light is one way to eclipse the *Sun*, *Observer*, October 28. Available online at www.media.guardian.co.uk/Print/0,3858,4286559,00.html, accessed January 22, 2002.

Preston, P. (2002) Papers feel pain, but hope for gain, *Observer*, January 20. Available online at www.media.guardian.co.uk/Print/0,3858,4338978,00.html, accessed January 22, 2002.

Quinn, I. (2001) Broadsheets win sales war, *MediaWeek*, October 19: 7.

Rooney, D. (2000) Thirty years of competition in the British tabloid press: the *Mirror* and the *Sun*, 1968–1998, in C. Sparks and J. Tulloch (eds) *Tabloid Tales: Global Debates over Media Standards*, Oxford: Rowman and Littlefield: 91–109.

Schalk, H. (1988) Fleet Street in the 1880s: the new journalism, in J. Wiener (ed.) *Papers for the Millions: The New Journalism in Britain, 1850s–1914*, London: Greenwood: 73–87.

Seymour, D. (2002) Tabloid wars and the Queen's rubber duck, talk in the *Reporters and Reported* series, Wales: Cardiff University, January 4.

Smith, A. C. H. with Immirzi, E. and Blackwell, T. (1975) *Paper Voices: The Popular Press and Social Change, 1935–1965*, London: Chatto and Windus.

Soames, E. (2002) Welcome to the brave new world of seriousness, *Daily Telegraph*, February 25. Available online at www.dailytelegraph.co.uk/opinion/main.jhtml?xml, accessed February 25, 2002.

Sparks, C. (1992) Popular journalism: theories and practice, in P. Dahlgren and C. Sparks (eds) *Journalism and Popular Culture*, London: Sage: 24–44.

Sparks, C. (2000) Introduction: the panic over tabloid news, in C. Sparks and J. Tulloch (eds) *Tabloid Tales: Global Debates over Media Standards*, Oxford: Rowman and Littlefield: 1–40.

Stephenson, H. (1998) Tickle the public: consumerism rules, in H. Stephenson and M. Bromley (eds) *Sex, Lies and Democracy: The Press and the Public*, Harlow: Longman: 13–24.

Stothard, P. (1997) And looking up from the coalface, *British Journalism Review*, 8 (2): 25–31.

Tulloch, J. (2000) The eternal recurrence of new journalism, in C. Sparks and J. Tulloch (eds) *Tabloid Tales: Global Debates over Media Standards*, Oxford: Rowman and Littlefield: 131–46.

Tunstall, J. (1996) *Newspaper Power: The New National Press in Britain*, Oxford: Clarendon Press.

Wells, M. (2001) Caught short, *Media Guardian*, October 1: 2–3.

Williams, R. (1961) *The Long Revolution*, London: Chatto and Windus.

# 10

# TELEVISION AGORA AND AGORAPHOBIA POST-SEPTEMBER 11

*Simon Cottle*

". . . many of our traditional ways of thinking about social and political matters are shaped by a certain model of public life which stems from the ancient world, from the *agora* of classical Greece, and which envisions the possibility of individuals coming together in a shared space to discuss issues of common concern . . . Today we must reinvent the idea of publicness in a way that reflects the complex interdependencies of the modern world, and in a way that recognizes the growing importance of forms of communication and interaction which are not face-to-face in character."

John Thompson, *The Media and Modernity*, 1995: 6

"Agoraphobia—the morbid dread of wide open spaces"

*Oxford Dictionary*

The televisual images of the events of September 11, 2001 seared into the consciousness and historical memory of all those who witnessed them. Such was their iconic power to capture the enormity of this crime against humanity and symbolism of US dominance visibly under assault. Television "mediated" the events of September 11 for vast majorities around the globe—for many of us in real time—and it was by these images that we first came to know of them. In the West such scenes undoubtedly played a huge role in initial feelings of shock and disbelief, but soon these reactions needed to give way to a time of considered reflection and analysis if public deliberation was not to be short-circuited into a blind endorsement of military retaliation involving indiscriminate killing, casualties, and inflicted humanitarian crises (see Glover 1999). Independent estimates confirm that by December 2001 the civilian death toll by US bombing in Afghanistan was in excess of 3,500 people—more than were killed in the collapse of the two

World Trade Towers on September 11 (Herold 2001)—and the US bombing and civilian deaths continued thereafter. Images of these scenes, however, are conspicuous only by their absence from our television screens. Of course, as a medium, television is capable of providing more than searing images. Its different program forms and subject treatments can variously prompt and sustain (or displace and trivialize) public reflection, questioning, analysis, and debate. What forms did these programs take and how well did they live up to their democratic promise?

The "public" is not a pre-existent and unitary social mass; nor does it simply reside behind national borders or transcend them in international solidarity. Rather, the "public" remains for the most part a dormant or at best nascent collectivity, loosely affiliated by different social groupings, political allegiances and cultural dispositions that can temporarily coalesce into "publics" when addressed through public spaces and in response to shared concerns and projects. Television has the capacity to provide such a public space. It assembles audiences and gives vent to the clash of different political interests and cultural viewpoints that are the building blocks for wider public understanding and opinion formation. In so doing, it can powerfully constitute "publics," whether as hegemonic and relatively united or minority-based and embattled.

Such is the nature of today's differentiated societies. Uniform "public opinion" rarely exists, except within rhetorical appeals to an "imagined community." Today the most momentous events—warfare (Morrison 1994; Taylor 1998), potentially catastrophic risks (Beck 1992; Cottle 1998; Allan, Adam, and Carter 2000) or the extreme threats posed by terrorists aimed at Western governments and civil societies—are as likely to unleash a profusion of differing interpretative and prescriptive responses as to prompt a sense of "national unity." This is all the more so when the geopolitical resonance of the events in question extends beyond national boundaries. In times of crisis, then, the "public" becomes constituted in the exchange and contestation of different points of view as well as rhetorical appeals and emotion-laden symbols. Courses of political and military action—or inaction—invariably must be defended and publicly legitimated if power-holders are to maintain their grip on the levers of state. Invariably they do this by invoking "the public." Television is a potent medium in this play of power.

Of all TV genres, current affairs programming has traditionally been charged with going behind the imagery and event-orientation of TV news. Because of its longer production gestation, it can provide a temporally longer view and deeper contextualization of the events in question as well as a more expansive forum for engaged public debate and deliberation. Current affairs programming, however, can assume a diversity of forms, adapting and evolving in response to the changing commercial pressures of the marketplace and cultural demands of audiences. Indeed, in the UK as elsewhere, it has recently been subject to enormous pressures to change—more populist magazine formats and "infotainment" series, schedules offering relatively marginal schedule slots outside of weekdays and prime-time, and new forms of "reality TV" (Cottle 1993; Bromley 2001). Even so, the genre enjoys flagship status, especially within the public service sector of broadcasting: its key presenters can become respected national figures and even honored with "knighthoods"; and the form is often promoted as fulfilling corporate and statutory obligations in respect of processes of democratic representation.

In Britain, for example, broadcasters produced and transmitted a number of current affairs and documentary programs dealing with September 11 and its aftermath. Predictably most confined their sights to the threats posed by Osama Bin Laden and other terrorist organizations to Western governments and civilian populations (for example, BBC 1 *Panorama, The World's Most Wanted*, September 16, 2001; Channel 4, *Dispatches, Bin Laden's Plan of Terror*, November 1, 2001) as well as Western government responses to these (BBC 1, *Panorama, Britain on the Brink*, September 30, 2001; *Circumstances Unknown*, December 2, 2001); the (scant) biographical details known about Osama Bin Laden himself (for example, Channel 5, Most Evil Men in History Series, *The World's Most Wanted Man*, November 29, 2001); or other human interest dimensions (for example, Channel 4, *Islam and America Through the Eyes of Imran Khan*, November 2, 2001; Channel 4, *Heroes of Ground Zero*, November 30, 2001).

Exceptionally, however, three programs deliberately sought to provide a wider public forum for contending arguments and perspectives on the events and aftermath of September 11, and it is these programs that form the basis of this discussion. Two were produced as "specials" within existing BBC program series—*Panorama* (*Clash of Cultures*, BBC 1, October 21, 2001) and *Question Time* (*Question Time Special*, BBC 1, September 13, 2001)—reflecting the ability of TV institutions to accommodate important developments within extant scheduling and established program formats. *Panorama* is the BBC's flagship current affairs program. Broadcast for nearly 50 years, it has become the longest-running public affairs TV program in the world. *Question Time* was first broadcast in 1979 and has also become something of a national institution in the UK. According to its own publicity, it offers "British voters a unique opportunity to quiz top decision-makers on the events of the day." The third program was especially commissioned by Channel 4 (*War on Trial*, October, 27, 2001) in a rapidly convened series of programs under its "War Without End Season." Before examining these three particular programs it is first necessary to address their possible democratic value, given the marginalization of current affairs as an object of interest within contemporary positions of media theory.[1]

## On mediated publicness, dialogic exchange and deliberative democracy

There has been a surprising paucity of studies within the field of media communication about current affairs programming. This can be traced in part to the influence of theoretical approaches that have tended to orient research towards "popular culture" rather than "public knowledge" (Corner 1991), "ritual" as opposed to "transmission" models of communication (Carey 1975), and the valorization of communication as "dissemination" over "dialogue" (Peters 1999). While these rightly point to the importance of the expressive, affective, and symbolic dimensions of communication, each risks underestimating the continuing importance of appeals to reason, rationality, and deliberation, conducted in the public sphere and expressed within particular media genres. Notions of reasoned public debate and rational intercourse are embedded in journalistic traditions, its professional practices and informing epistemology.[2] And some forms of journalism aim to stage public debate and the exchange of opposing interests and viewpoints. While these contain no guarantee of "reason," much less consensual outcome, they nonetheless remain a direct means of giving expression to, and wider deliberation of, opposing arguments. Different arguments can be made, opposing claims and counter claims can be voiced, and the rhetorical appeals and performances involved witnessed and visualized. This is so whether one is physically present as a direct interlocutor or whether one is an interested witness only, viewing and hearing such dialogic intercourse through temporary "symbolic locales" (Thompson 1995) created by television. It is useful to remember that even within the ancient agora of classical Greece not all of those citizens assembled would be able to speak and participate directly. Dialogic debate is invariably conducted for an over-hearing, over-seeing, and hopefully "deliberating" audience—whether situated within a shared physical place or mediated symbolic locale.

While deliberative democracy cannot involve us all in direct forms of face-to-face dialogic exchange, it must entail being able to over-hear and preferably over-see the dialogic exchanges of others. We need to listen to and preferably see those who may "represent" our views and to deliberate on the validity of arguments and exchanges if we are to formulate our own point of view and arrive at judgments about the credibility of the participants and performances in play. Importantly, some program forms are better suited to this task than others, and we need to examine them if we are to better understand their democratic promise and possible contribution to processes of deliberative democracy. Abstract theorization of "mediated publicness" (Thompson 1995) now needs to be empirically grounded in respect of the complexity of different program forms on offer as well as their adaptation and future democratic potential.[3]

In other words, there is no reason to presume that *dialogic* formats cannot serve wider processes of mediated deliberative democracy. Indeed, as we shall see, they are particularly well suited to this task. If this is so, then current affairs programs that publicly display and engage differing political views and arguments deserve careful analysis, especially in respect of the principal ways in which each stages public debate, orchestrates access and enables (or disables) engaged dialogue and wider public deliberation. This is not to suggest that the democratic promise of all such programs is always realized in practice, but there is a complexity here that has direct bearing on contemporary questions of democratic deepening or the *democratizing of democracy* within the sphere of the liberal democratic polity (Giddens 1994), ideas of deliberative democracy (Thompson 1995; Held 2000), as well as the contemporary mediation of "subpolitics" also (Beck 1997). How such programs mediated the politics of September 11 is, of course, an important case in point. It is time to take such formats seriously.

## TV current affairs: democratic agorai

The three principal UK current affairs programs that addressed September 11 did so through the vehicle of very different program formats. These provided different public spaces, or "agorai," variously facilitating and containing the engaged display of contending perspectives and political prescriptions. Each is also characterized by its own internal complexity.[4] The first, BBC 1's *Question Time Special* broadcast two days after September 11, provides a program agora that is closely modeled on the ideas and institutional practices of representative parliamentary democracy. The program chair (parliamentary "speaker") officiates from his commanding position center stage and delegates who is permitted to speak from the studio audience ("represented public") and who is permitted to pose (mainly preselected) questions to a panel of "representatives" (MPs from the main political parties and public opinionated figures) who are assembled either side of the program chair. These assembled "senior figures" then hold forth on the various topics put to them. The opening words of the chair, David Dimbleby, as well as the first delegated questioner (and pre-selected question) and delegated panel member to answer perfectly illustrates *Question Time*'s hierarchical and deferential stance to a model of parliamentary representative democracy as well as its general *modus operandi*.

*David Dimbleby:* Good evening. The full horror of Tuesday's terrorist attack is still sinking in as more and more gruesome details are being reported. Several hundred Britons are now feared dead and the question on many people's minds is how the United States should respond and what role the United Kingdom and the NATO allies should play in that response. Arguments range from mounting all-out war against terrorists and those who harbor them on the one hand, and on the other, examining the whole American strategy in the Middle East. So with us here tonight to discuss these issues, Lord Ashdown the former Leader of the Liberal Democrats, Philip Lader was the American Ambassador here until February of this year, he served four years. Tam Dalyell, Father of the House, the longest serving Member and a critic of Western policy towards the Middle East, and Yasmin Alibhai-Brown, columnist for the *Independent*. And of course our *Question Time* audience who are going to be putting the questions tonight, and the first one comes from Wally Bacari who is an Administrator. Mr Bacari.

182

*Mr Bacari:* Thank you, good evening. My question is to the former Ambassador Lader. In the midst of this carnage won't a harder response provoke more action, which will affect innocent lives?

*David Dimbleby:* So, a hard response will provoke more violence? I come to Mr Lader in a moment, Paddy Ashdown what is your answer to that?

*Paddy Ashdown:* Yes it could, and I think that is a matter we have to bear very carefully in mind. I mean one thing is clear: after Tuesday nothing is ever going to be the same again. The view of the superpower, alone, invincible and inviolate is gone. We are now into the year of global-ized power, globalized terror to match it and the extent to which we are able to combat this will be measured by the extent to which we are able to act internationally and multilaterally, not unilaterally. The second point is the one you identified precisely Mr Bacari. If we mis-handle this, I fear that this could be the first event of a chain of events that leads to war between nations—maybe not ourselves, but cer-tainly in the regions that are affected. And we need to bear in mind one fact when deciding what to do. And that fact is this. What was the aim of the terrorists? The aim of the terrorists was to provoke us into over-reaction, in exactly the same way as Israel has been pro-voked into over-reaction by suicide bombers in their cities. (Audience applause) To provoke us into deepening the instability in those areas that they want to see war and conflict. And the extent to which our actions result in that outcome will be the extent to which they continue to win and we continue to lose.

*Question Time Special*, BBC 1, September 13, 2001

As we can see from this opening sequence, notwithstanding *Question Time's* claims already quoted that it enables British citizens to quiz top decision-makers on the events of the day, the program in fact enacts a tightly controlled and hier-archical agora. Who is delegated to speak, in what sequence, about what topic, and how, all remain firmly under the control of the program chair as does the dif-ferential opportunity to put questions, elaborate views, and engage directly with the expressed views of other program participants. This agora, in other words, is not premised on free and unrestricted discourse, guaranteed by *isegora*, or "the equal right to speak in the sovereign assembly" (Held 2000: 18). Diagrammati-cally this deferential "parliamentary" agora can be represented as in Figure 10.1 (page 186; key page 187).

A different forum or program agora was enacted by the *Panorama Special* broadcast under the title of *Clash of Cultures* (BBC 1, October 21, 2001). Impor-tantly, this deliberately set out to incorporate a wider range of international opinions and cultural viewpoints than the predominantly national based opinion of *Question Time*, and then forward some of these to senior politicians in studio interviews. To facilitate this, the program deployed satellite technology to bring into being a simultaneous "electronic agora" with participants based in London,

183

New York, and Islamabad—three parts of the world directly affected by the events and aftermath of September 11. Again hosted by the BBC's ubiquitous David Dimbleby, the introductory sequence illustrates how this program form sought to incorporate differing views and frame these in terms of a deep cultural opposition—a clash of cultures.

*David Dimbleby:* A straight fight against terrorism or a war between two cultures? Tonight on television and radio worldwide *Panorama* hears from live audiences in New York and Islamabad about what they hope for and what they fear from what's being called the first war of the 21st century. With American troops now fighting on the ground against the Taliban, President Bush is sticking to the bold war aims he set out at the start.

*President Bush (film clip):* This conflict is a fight to save the civilized world and values common to the West to Asia, to Islam.

*David Dimbleby:* George Bush isn't alone in asking the world to take sides. Osama Bin Laden, in the video messages to al-Jazeera Television says this is a war against Islam.

*Courtesy of al-Jazeera TV (film clip/voice of translator):* Now every Muslim has to stand up and support Islam and support Muslim brothers in order to wipe out this act of aggression.

*David Dimbleby:* Good evening. *Panorama* tonight joins Radio 5 Live, the BBC World Service and on television BBC World. After two weeks of military action in Afghanistan to destroy the Taliban and find Bin Laden, the dilemma for the West is whether its actions are winning acceptance in the Muslim world or are increasingly seen as an attack on Islam. Is there a conflict of cultures and if so how can it be resolved? We're going to be hearing tonight from audiences in Islamabad with Nisha Pillai, we're going to be hearing from New York with Nicky Campbell, and I'll be putting the arguments to a member of the British War Cabinet, the former Foreign Secretary Robin Cook, and to Richard Perle, Chairman of the Pentagon Advisory Board, and also to a prominent politician, former Pakistani Ambassador to the United States, Abida Hussain. Now we begin by going to New York and joining Nicky Campbell.

*Nicky Campbell:* Good evening David, welcome a cross section of New Yorkers and Americans here. We are indeed in Times Square just to tell listeners to World Service and Radio 5 Live of the backdrop, conspicuous consumerism, I can see a hoarding with half undressed women advertising lingerie, we've got champagne bottles, every sort of globalized brand you can think of is advertised here. Niki Hayden, what we can see out the window there, is that one of the reasons why there is this rage against America?

*Niki Hayden, estate agent:* Perhaps. Perhaps it is our freedoms that we enjoy here and our many choices, a misconception on the other side of really what we're all about.

*Nicky Campbell:* And do you see any contradictions about that lack of understanding and comprehension of what America means, what American ideals are? Lisa.

*Lisa Pinto, housewife:* Nicky, they think our women are too liberated, our press is too free and our free market is not a system they ascribe to. So absolutely, they have it in for the Western way of life.

*Panorama Special: Clash of Cultures*, BBC 1, October 21, 2001

Potentially this program agora begins to serve the processes of cultural recognition or "cultural citizenship" (Murdock 1999; Cottle 2001), in that it aims to give voice to different cultural outlooks and views and encourage intercultural recognition and understanding, if not agreement. In a context informed by deep-seated geopolitical divisions and cultural antipathies such representation is vital. To what extent, however, the producers' meta-frame organizing their program treatment—"clash of cultures"—actually encourages or hinders this deeper cultural recognition requires more detailed analysis. But we can at least acknowledge the program's unique attempt to constitute an "electronic agora" populated by very different "publics" as well as senior decision-makers and politicians. Like *Question Time*, however, the format remains heavily dependent upon the program presenters which, in this instance, also involved an internal presenter hierarchy orchestrating and relaying the various voices and perspectives in play. Questions of program access and delegation—of who is given the right to speak, when and how—and editorial mediation are also no less pertinent to this program agora. Again this can be expressed diagrammatically as shown in Figure 10.2 (page 186).

Here we can see how in fact the program format both facilitates and contains the intercultural exchange between the respective audiences positioned in studios in Islamabad and New York. The presenters in each are delegated by the program chair in London to invite comment and questions from their respective studio-based audiences but these are then interpreted, summarized, and selectively fed-back to the chair in London for further possible mediation either via the other studio-based presenter to the other audience, or via the program chair in London to selected senior politicians and spokespersons in interview.

The third program treatment of September 11, *War on Trial*, provides yet a further form of program agora replete with differing discursive opportunities and forms of containment. This program agora mirrors the format of a legally conducted trial or debate.

*Jon Snow:* Following the worst terrorist atrocity the world has ever seen Britain and America are allies in war.

*George Bush: (film clip)* On my orders the United States military has begun strikes against al-Qaeda terrorist training camps, the military installations of the Taliban regime in Afghanistan.

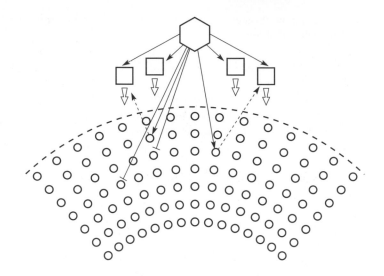

*Figure 10.1* BBC 1 *Question Time Special*: deferential "parliamentary" agora

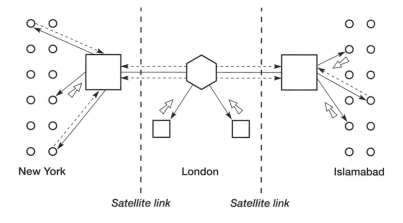

*Figure 10.2* BBC 1 *Panorama Special, Clash of Cultures*: cultural citizenship agora

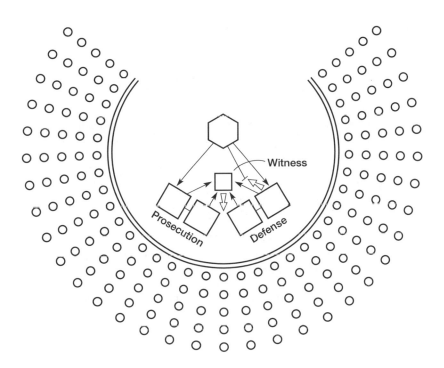

*Figure 10.3* Channel 4, *War on Trial*: legalistic (debate) agora

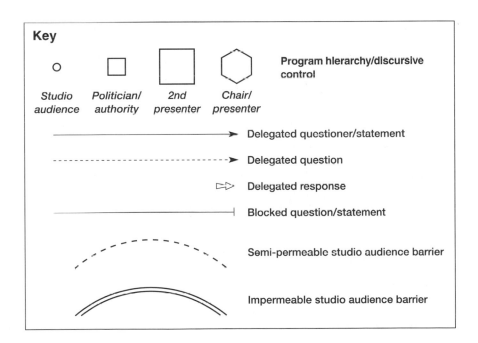

*Tony Blair:* *(film clip)* The military action we have taken is targeted against those known to be involved in the al-Qaeda network of terror or against the military apparatus of the Taliban.

*George Bush:* *(film clip)* We will win this conflict by the patient accumulation of successes. By meeting a series of challenges with determination and the will to succeed.

*Jon Snow:* As Britain's Chief of Defence Staff warns of the most difficult military operation since the end of the Cold War, we ask is this the sort of legitimate response to a terrorist outrage or a misguided attack that will only make matters worse? Tonight we put the war on trial.

Music, Logo: *War on Trial*, applause.

*Jon Snow:* Good evening. It is a war like no other. The target, Osama Bin Laden's al-Qaeda terrorist network and its protectors, the Taliban. An enemy prepared to attack at the heart of America, first with the appalling events of September 11 and more recently perhaps with a spate of anthrax attacks across the United States. But is the British and American response of air strikes and military raids misguided and dangerous? Tonight to launch Channel 4's *War Without End* season, a studio jury of 250 drawn from around the country, representative of the nation as a whole, will make its judgment. Our charge is that: "The war is misguided with no clear strategy or end; it exacerbates tensions between the west and the Muslim world, compounds the humanitarian crisis and plays into the hands of the terrorists."

*Words on screen and read by Jon Snow:* Now, as with any trial the prosecution will have to prove guilt beyond reasonable doubt, otherwise our studio jury must acquit. The team for the prosecution are Peter Osborne, Political Editor of the *Spectator* magazine who has questioned the military strategy from a conservative viewpoint and the feminist author, academic and cultural critic, Germaine Greer, who is an active supporter of the Stop The War Movement. Germaine Greer, what is your case against the war?

*Germaine Greer:* War is no antidote to terrorism. The terrible events of September 11 were intended to traumatize the Americans and to disrupt an already shaky world order. Terrorism exists to induce terror which can make societies jettison the rule of law, curtail their own civil liberties and lose their quality of life. America is like a man smashed in the face with a glass who instead of seeking medical attention is trying to blow up the pub. We are being locked into a cycle of atrocity. We must jump the trap that the terrorists have laid for us. We have to come up with a better idea.

*Jon Snow:* Thank you Germaine Greer

Channel 4, *War on Trial*, October 27, 2001

Structured according to the logic and sequencing of a trial, this debate format also permits and contains discursive contributions and elaborations by different speakers. Though the presenter remains in overall program control the actual conduct of the debate is delegated for the most part to the "prosecution" and "defense" counsel. Once begun, the trial/debate moves relentlessly towards closure: in this instance a final vote by the studio audience in response to the program's opening contention. The audience, we are told, while "representative of the nation as a whole," only bears witness to the preceding debate and is not allowed to cross the impermeable boundary excluding it from active participation. Unlike the agora of the two previous programs, this format works towards narrative and discursive closure by forcing the issues at stake into a contest dependent on the final judgment of the studio audience—and, by invitation, the wider audience watching at home. The structure of this legalistic (debate) agora serves, then, to polarize arguments, heighten combative styles of public engagement and throw into sharp relief the differences of perspective at play and the issues at stake (as well as differences of personality and public performance). Diagrammatically, this agora can be represented as in Figure 10.3 (page 187).

This third dialogic program form, then, provides yet a further agora for the exchange of views and engagement of contending program participants—all vital resources for wider deliberative processes.

As this cursory introduction to these three different program agorai has illustrated, each is characterized by internal complexities of form that have direct bearing for wider processes of public deliberation. Each provides qualitatively different opportunities for the public elaboration and dialogic engagement of differing political and cultural perspectives on, and arguments about, the events and aftermath of September 11. Though such programs only punctuate television schedules occasionally in comparison to mainstream daily news provision, their value in providing meaningful public spaces ("symbolic locales") supportive of wider deliberation should not be underestimated or overlooked. This is so despite the structural constraints of form, presentational hierarchies, and processes of delegation already identified. Oppositional voices and viewpoints to the US- and British-led coalition and its military action in Afghanistan, as we have already heard, did find a way to argue their case. If the media, to borrow Oliver Boyd-Barrett's telling phrase, generally sought to "foreclose doubt" in respect of the legitimacy, efficacy, and morality of military intervention (Boyd-Barrett 2002), here at least were program spaces that permitted wider deliberation. Consider, for example, the following sequence of delegated speech and exchange between the *Question Time Special* chair, audience members, and panel speakers.

*David Dimbleby:* Yes, the woman in pink there. Sorry I can't hear you, start again, sorry.
*Woman in pink:* The panel briefly talked about America wanting to establish blame before they actually take action, but how long do the panel think Americans will wait before blame is established?
*David Dimbleby:* Tam Dalyell please.

*Tam Dalyell:* In the case of Lockerbie, blame takes a very long time, but you know if innocent people are killed just because of a feeling that we must do something, that will make the situation worse and not better. (Applause) If innocent people are killed there is one group who will be delighted, Bin Laden and his like. And why? Because Arab sympathy, genuine Arab sympathy with the United States will simply evaporate when there is innocent, gratuitous loss of life, collateral damage, or call it what you will.

*David Dimbleby:* All right, I'll take a point from the woman in the third row from the back and then I'm going to move on.

*Woman in the third row:* What scares me about the use of the word "war" at the moment is the grim task of counting the dead. It's still not finished in America. How can we as a democratic nation justify killing other mothers, fathers, children of another nation?

*David Dimbleby:* Let me ask quite simply, if anybody in the audience disagrees with that point of view and believes that America should act and act swiftly. You Sir, on the left here (pointing).

*Man on the left:* The Americans that have been innocently killed, Tam Dalyell, you always come in on the side of the terrorists and have done for years.

*Tam Dalyell:* That I refute. I simply point out that when President Bush says that this is the first war of the 21st century, it is not so. A war has been going on for ten years of the daily bombing of Iraq. (Applause) Maybe it's the brothers and sisters of these people who are killed that evil men like Bin Laden like to exploit. These are very unpalatable facts; they had better be addressed.

Even within the hierarchical structure of the *Question Time* agora, where members of the audience are often symbolically reduced to the colour of their shirt or where they happen to be sitting, such studio exchanges arguably contribute resources for deliberative democracy. Here, opposing perspectives and arguments, claims and counter-claims as well as reference to the credentials of the speakers involved all become publicly expressed in the cut and thrust of debate, a debate requiring the listener/viewer to make up his or her own mind on the contending perspectives and performances. Lest there should be any presumption that this exercise in deliberative democracy is pretty much a consensual affair, one need only witness how this can also lead to robust accusations and even attempted defamations of character, calling into doubt the political credibility of the speakers concerned. This is not genteel democracy or democracy for the faint-hearted but it is part of deliberative democracy nonetheless. Consider, for example, the following exchange between David Aaronovitch defending the military intervention in Afghanistan and George Galloway MP opposed to the war in Channel 4's *War on Trial*.

*David Aaronovitch:* So you think the Taliban were right not to extradite Bin Laden after the bombings of September 1998 in which over 200 black African people as well as people from the American Embassies were killed?

*George Galloway:* Don't try and hang Bin Laden on me, he is a British and American invention, not mine. Nothing to do with the left.

*David Aaronovitch:* That's perfectly true George Galloway, your friends are elsewhere. In the *Guardian*, in April 2001, you said of the things that you had done during the first Labour party administration, "I am proudest to have stood firmly against a new imperialism, an Anglo-American aggression around the world." Why aren't you proud to stand up against other aggression?

*George Galloway:* Your friends are elsewhere for you of course, you were a hard line communist before you shaved your beard off for tickling Tories' backsides.

*David Aaronovitch:* I am not going to bother to refute that, largely because I have never been "hard line" in my entire life.

*George Galloway:* You were a hard line communist last . . .

*David Aaronovitch:* No, no.

*George Galloway:* You were a communist party member for years.

*David Aaronovitch:* Well let's talk about what you are, George Galloway.

*George Galloway:* You were a communist party member for years.

*David Aaronovitch:* The Associated Press, and I read from November 1999, Aziz, the Deputy Foreign Minister, Prime Minister Tariq Aziz with whom you spent Christmas 1999, made the remarks that "our senior Iraqi leaders give a hero's welcome to British Labour Party member George Galloway who arrived in Baghdad to highlight the plight to the Iraqis of UN sanctions. Young girls sang the praises of Saddam as they showered Aziz and Galloway with roses and offered dates and yoghurt and symbols of war." How must the Kurds have been choking on the yoghurt and roses that you were showered with!

*George Galloway:* Hear me out, hear me out. They may have sung hymns of praise to the leaders—I don't but you do.

*David Aaronovitch:* No, you most certainly do. I have never spent Christmas with a mass murderer and somebody who could have . . .

*George Galloway:* But you're in bed with, you're in bed with George W. Bush.

*Jon Snow:* There I think we must leave it, George Galloway. George Galloway thank you very much. Now Rosemary Reiter for the defense. Would you please call your first witness.

Programs, as we have already seen, tend to be informed by an editorial presumption about who the key players and what the key views are, and how far the range of "legitimate" opinion extends. Even so, "difficult" views that fell outside mainstream opinion found an outlet as the following contributions by studio audience members in Islamabad to the *Panorama Special: Clash of Cultures* illustrate.

*Nisha Pillai:* Why is it that the people of Pakistan are so hostile towards the US? This is something that has been going on for years, isn't it?

*Qazi Zulqader Sidiqui, Internet consultant:* Nisha, I think the issue is not that the people of Pakistan are hostile towards the United States. That is not really the case. I think it's totally misunderstood. The issue really is that just as much as the lives of people in the World Trade Center were valuable, that those people who died there, died wrongly. They should not have died. Nobody had the right to take their lives. Likewise, I don't believe that anybody has a right to take the lives of the innocent people of Afghanistan. It is the civilians of Afghanistan that are being bombed that are being killed, and nobody seems to think that has any value. That's collateral damage which I think is a horrendous word that has been coined by the government of the United States. It is so bad that it is saying that life has no value whatsoever. How can anybody say that life has no value? If it's a Muslim life, it has no value. If it is somebody else's life that has value?

*Nishai Pillai:* Well you're nodding your head there Amina. How should a superpower like the US behave under these circumstances? We can't expect them to do nothing when 6,000 people were killed?

*Amina Sajjad, teacher:* Exactly, exactly. A superpower like America would be expected to show maybe more justice than they are showing. We would expect them to be international benefactors and supporters of international humanitarian causes. But they have proven themselves to be international bullies. They want that terrorism be uprooted. I find it very interesting that they have planted the seeds of terrorism all over the world. Hiroshima, Nagasaki, Cuba, Palestine, Kashmir, you name it. They have supported their interests, and it's really not about the Taliban. It's never been about Iraq invading Kuwait; it's really all about their interests in oil and now their interest in gas.

*Nisha Pillai:* At this point I'm sorry to say we're going to return to New York to see what their response is to what our Pakistani audience is saying. Nicky.

In the responses by program participants above, the informing premise of the studio-based presenter ("people of Pakistan are hostile to the US") is effectively challenged as is the "common-sense" reaction ("we can't expect the US to do nothing") embedded in the following question. These and many other encounters illustrate something of the porosity of such program agora. Political views and challenges to informing program premises can often leak out into the wider public domain. This can happen through studio-based audience members or the relatively more generous conditions granted to prominent politicians (who may well have strategic reasons of their own for challenging simplistic oppositions and frames put in place by program-makers). Again, *Clash of Cultures*:

*David Dimbleby:* Robin Cook, you said three years ago that we'd let misunderstanding and distrust develop between us and Islam. Could this have
been avoided? Was there something that we should have been doing
over the past three years that we've failed to do and that the chick-
ens are coming home to roost now as you hear from Islamabad?

*Robin Cook, MP, Leader of the House of Commons:* What I stressed then is it is
very important that we do have a dialogue between our civilizations
and that we reject the theory that there has to be a clash of these civilizations. Can I just try and put in the context of this discussion? I do
find it unfortunate that we're getting into a confrontation between
the two studio audiences. After all, both these audiences are living
with governments who are working together to carry forward this
project, and the reason for that is this is not the West versus Islam, it
is the West and Islam together against terrorism.

## The paradox of democratic TV agorai: producer agoraphobia

As we have seen, the agorai of current affairs programs are for the most part subject to tight editorial controls enacted principally through processes of program
access and presenter delegation. As the three diagrams clearly indicate, these dif-
ferentially enable and disable program participants to ask questions, advance
comments, elaborate on points of view, or engage with and contest the viewpoints of others. Herein lies the paradox at the heart of participatory current
affairs programs of the kind described. On the one hand, they publicly proclaim
themselves to be spaces for democratic representation and debate; on the other,
they strive for control of program access, agendas, and the flow of "free speech" at
all costs. Program-makers for the most part act with the best of professional
intentions. They seek to ensure that their programs will engage audiences and
address relevant/interesting subject matter and are packaged and delivered
within strict time frames. They are also concerned that their programs should not
cause offence or infringe other legal obligations and professional guidelines.
Taken together, these norms of professional practice result in programs being
structured according to tight editorial controls, even when they promise democratic debate and an "open" forum for public discussion.

The inherent tension between enacted program controls including processes
of speaker and speech delegation, on the one hand, and the tendency for mediated debate and discussion to develop "a life of its own" and break through such
editorial conventions, on the other, is therefore ever-present. Such "outbreaks,"
for the reasons outlined, are likely to be experienced with professional dread by
producers of serious current affairs programs.[5] Engaged debate, deeply held convictions, and the play of conflicting interests are not easily contained within the

staged "symbolic locales" of television. When participants seek to circumvent program mediation and engage directly with their interlocutors, as they often do, this poses a direct threat to the sought control and program authority of the presenter—no matter that such outbreaks can be both illuminating and insightful in a deliberative sense. Interestingly, even the tight controls and evident paternalism of *Question Time* can sometimes fail to hold back the pent-up tide of unexpressed sentiments embodied within studio audience members. On such occasions, views that have not been selected or sanctioned through formal processes of delegation break out as a direct threat to the credibility and authority of the presenter concerned, requiring the immediate restoration of program order:

*David Dimbleby:* The woman in the fourth row.

*Woman in fourth row:* You mentioned that when President Bush talks about the terrorists and those that harbor them, does he and the American Government consider the fact that one of the reasons why the world despises America, is because it sees Israel as a terrorist and America as one who harbors Israel and the terrorists? That should be considered, I am talking about foreign policy again. (Applause)

*David Dimbleby:* All right, Phil Lader how do you answer that point?

*Philip Lader:* I have to share with you that it is hurtful that one can suggest that a majority of the world despise the United States. My parents were immigrants to the United States, and I have to tell you that we have fought as a people and as a nation as Paddy suggests for the rule of law. And I simply want to say that it saddens me how it is possible on this night, within 48 hours, that one, because of the intensity of feeling on policy issues can frankly distract ourselves from the senseless human victimization and suffering that has occurred before us.

*Woman in fourth row:* I just want to point out, that it is not true that we don't feel anything, I think everyone will admit that within hours of this catastrophe, it is the American Government that started talking about war, talking about culprits. I am sorry, if the American Government was so concerned about casualties, I am sorry the Government made me think about these things because they brought it up on public TV.

*David Dimbleby:* The woman on your left.

*Woman on left:* I am sorry but there are twenty thousand, thirty thousand, forty thousand casualties of war . . .

*Woman in fourth row:* Five hundred children die every month in Iraq . . .

*David Dimbleby:* Let her answer your question.

*Woman on left:* . . . buried under the rubble who didn't realize this was going to happen, they were going to work. They were normal people, they didn't understand. It's a life for a life. An eye for an eye.

*Woman in fourth row:* Why did the Americans, it makes them no better. You're always talking about war, like he said . . . .

*David Dimbleby:* Will you take the microphone away please, there is no way you can argue with each other with one microphone, we can't hear what you are saying.

*Woman in fourth row:* Are American lives worth more than Iraqi lives?

*David Dimbleby:* The people at home can't hear what you are saying. So there will be an end to it. And I come to the gentleman here in a blue shirt.

In the example above, program order is restored in no uncertain terms following this "unlicensed" (but deliberatively revealing) exchange. The professional agoraphobia that threatens to overwhelm producers and presenters with the next outbreak of open speech and exchange results in formats designed according to tight editorial controls. The latter, as far as possible, aim to direct the course of dialogic discussion and contain this within the known walls of particular formats. In the event of participants breaking through these, perhaps in a bid to reach the open spaces of engaged public discussion outside, repair work is likely to follow. In the case above, for example, no less a person than the Director-General of the BBC, Greg Dyke, felt obliged to publicly apologize for this and other animated exchanges in this *Question Time Special.* Two days after the attacks in the US, people in the UK and elsewhere were beginning to ponder the possible causes and legitimacy of different political and military responses. Revealingly, the *Question Time Special* audience at 5.6 million was bigger that night than it had been for any previous program. Engagement in such processes of deliberation was absolutely necessary for the formation of both opinions and "publics" on this issue—especially given the UK government's momentum to line up behind US military action. Mr. Dyke, according to the BBC's own news release (September 14, 2001), said he "would like to apologize to the viewers who were offended by it," that it was an inappropriate program to broadcast live just two days after the attacks, and that the program should have been recorded and edited, by presumably cutting the "offensive" commentary and forthright exchange of views. He also personally apologized to the then US ambassador to Britain, Philip Lader, for any distress caused.

This should prompt careful consideration. The democratic promise of TV current affairs agorai and their contribution to processes of deliberative democracy should not be underestimated by media academics. But neither should we permit them to succumb to the debilitating malaise of professional agoraphobia of media producers. Too much is at stake.

## Conclusion

Current affairs programs of the kind described provided different agorai for the public display and engagement of contending perspectives surrounding September 11. As a sub-genre of current affairs programming they constituted an invaluable and vital resource for deliberative democracy. Mediated dialogic exchange conducted within these agorai cannot be viewed as, or indeed criticized for, departing from the ideal of direct or participatory democracy. As John Thompson has cogently argued, the nature of broadcasting by definition institutes a break between producer and recipient with the latter having little if any opportunity to originate messages or actively participate in communication exchange (Thompson 1995). Unlike the classical agora of ancient Greece, the forms of "mediated publicness" constituted by broadcasting are neither localized in time and space nor for the most part dialogical. He therefore concludes that, "a deliberative conception of democracy is not necessarily a dialogical conception" and "The formation of reasoned judgments does not require individuals to participate in dialogue with others" (Thompson 1995: 256). While abstractly this may be so, these findings demonstrate that some program forms, exhibiting their own internal complexities, are better able than others to sustain and promote deliberation for an over-seeing, over-hearing audience. The three current affairs programs discussed represented a drop in the ocean of dominant news agendas washing around the UK public shores, but they signaled nonetheless that "public opinion" could be taken as neither homogenous nor as simplistically lined-up behind the UK government's support of US war aims. There was a complexity "out there" composed of emergent, conflicting, and plural "publics" and these differences of perspective demanded wider public expression, engagement, and deliberation. The tight editorial controls delegating the who, what, how, and when of mediated public speech, based in part on institutionalized professional agoraphobia, sought to channel and control the flow of "free" speech within these different agorai. But even so their democratic promise was not entirely curtailed. Oppositional views, robust engagement, and critical challenges did find some means for expression. In a time of "mediated publicness" the democratic promise as well as complexities of these and other programs' forms have yet to be fully acknowledged and adequately theorized. The mediated events of September 11 underline that they must also be politically developed and deliberately deepened in the future.

## Notes

1   It is notable that major social and political theorists appear to continue the tradition of political science with its conspicuous silences towards mediated processes of political communication—notwithstanding the media's central involvement in processes of reflexive modernization, democratic deepening and the conduct of subpolitics (see Beck 1992, 1997; Giddens 1994; Held 2000). In this respect the work of John Thompson represents a major advance.
2   Which is not to say, however, that TV news journalism does not also assume a diversity of forms some of which are informed by competing objectivist and subjectivist epistemologies (Cottle 1993, 2000a, 2000b, 2001).
3   The author, with the assistance of Mugdha Rai, is currently undertaking a major comparative, historical, and production-based study of Australian, UK, US, Indian, and Singaporean news and current affairs television and "deliberative democracy" supported by the University of Melbourne.
4   What follows cannot be an exhaustive and detailed analysis of the complexities of

current affairs programs ranging across ethnomethodological analyses of the micro-politics of turn-taking, agenda-setting and agenda-shifting techniques institutional-ized within media interviews (Heritage and Greatbatch 1993) to historical consideration of their institutionalization within everyday life, processes of communicative entitlement, and democratic deepening (Scannell 1989, 1992). Rather, the analysis offered here simply begins to map something of the different forms—"agorai"—of these programs and how these impact on processes of dialogic speech and wider deliberative processes.

5   This is not to suggest however that different genres of participation TV, for example certain day-time TV shows, do not deliberately court such manifestations of audience "break outs" if the conflict effect can produce high ratings. That said, such staged conflict invariably remains within the control and orchestration of the program-makers.

# References

Allan, S., Adam, B., and Carter, C. (eds) (2000) *Environmental Risks and the Media*, London and New York: Routledge.

Beck, U. (1992) *Risk Society: Towards a New Modernity*, London: Sage.

Beck, U. (1997) *The Reinvention of Politics: Rethinking Modernity in the Global Social Order*, Cambridge: Polity Press.

Boyd-Barrett. O. (2002) Doubt foreclosed: US corporate media and the attacks of September 11, 2001, forthcoming.

Bromley, M. (ed.) (2001) *No News is Bad News: Radio, Television and the Public*, Harlow: Longman.

Carey, J. (1975) A cultural approach to communication, *Communication*, 2: 1–22.

Corner, J. (1991) Meaning, genre and context: the problematics of public knowledge in the news audience studies, in J. Curran and M. Gurevitch (eds) *Mass Media and Society*, London: Edward Arnold: 141–60.

Cottle, S. (1993) *TV News, Urban Conflict and the Inner City*, Leicester: Leicester University Press.

Cottle, S. (1998) Ulrich Beck, "risk society" and the media: a catastrophic view?, *European Journal of Communication*, 13 (1): 5–32.

Cottle, S. (2000a) TV news, lay voices and the visualisation of environmental risks, in S. Allan, B. Adam and C. Carter (eds) *Environmental Risks and the Media*, London and New York: Routledge: 29–44.

Cottle, S. (2000b) New(s) times: towards a "second wave" of news ethnography, *Communications—The European Journal of Communication Research*, 25 (1): 19–42.

Cottle, S. (2001) Television news and citizenship: packaging the public sphere, in M. Bromley (ed.) *No News is Bad News: Radio, Television and the Public*, London: Long-man: 61–79.

Giddens, A. (1994) *Beyond Left and Right—The Future of Radical Politics*, Cambridge: Polity Press.

Glover, J. (1999) *Humanity: A Moral History of the Twentieth Century*, London: Jonathan Cape.

Held, D. (2000) *Models of Democracy*, 2nd edition. Cambridge: Polity Press.

Heritage, J., and. Greatbatch, D. (1993) On the institutional character of institutional talk: the case of news interviews, in D. Boden and D. Zimmerman (eds) *Talk and Social*

*Structure: Studies in Ethnomethodology and Conversation Analysis*, Cambridge: Polity Press: 93–137.

Herold, D. (2001) *A Dossier on Civilian Victims of United States' Aerial Bombing of Afghanistan: A Comprehensive Accounting*, research report, December 2001. Durham, NH: University of New Hampshire, available online at www.zmag.org/herold.htm.

Morrison, D. E. (1994) *Television and the Gulf War*, London: John Libby.

Murdock, G. (1999) Rights and representations: public discourse and cultural citizenship, in J. Gripsrud (ed.) *Television and Common Knowledge*, London: Routledge: 7–17.

Peters, J. (1999) *Speaking into the Air: A History of the Idea of Communication*, Chicago, IL: University of Chicago Press.

Scannell, P. (1989) Public service broadcasting and modern public life, *Media, Culture and Society*, 11: 135–66.

Scannell, P. (1992) *Radio and Television and Modern Life*, Cambridge: Blackwell.

Taylor, P. (1998) *War and the Media: Propaganda and Persuasion in the Gulf War*, Manchester: Manchester University Press.

Thompson. J. (1995) *The Media and Modernity: A Social Theory of the Media*, Cambridge: Polity Press.

Part 4

# REPORTING TRAUMA
# TOMORROW

# 11

# JOURNALISM, RISK, AND PATRIOTISM

*Silvio Waisbord*

"Two dangers threaten the world—order and disorder."

Paul Valéry

Much has been said about the emergence of a "new journalism" since September 11. Amid a phenomenal surge in ratings and news-stand sales in the weeks after the attacks, analysts talked about a new sense of purpose sweeping newspapers and newscasts (Auletta 2001). Mention was made of a "colossal shift" from frivolous to serious journalism (Jensen 2001). Pundits assessed that the media sobered up after a decade-long binge on sensationalism, and they assuredly decreed "the end of soft news." Observers also applauded the fact that, after having slashed budgets and coverage in the post-Cold War era, news organizations rediscovered foreign news in the wake of September 11 (Parks 2002).

We do not know yet whether these changes are long-term or only temporary adaptations to a time of crisis. Without undermining their merits, such proclamations are versions of the media's well-known appetite for instant-trend reporting more than judicious evaluations of the depth and extent of change. Time will tell whether such rushed assertions perceptively assessed the situation or these changes were short-lived alterations, introduced in the aftermath of the tragic events before journalism returned to the news from before September 11.

What appears evident is that, despite much-praised changes, journalism resorted to standard formulas and stock-in-trade themes to cover risk after September 11.[1] Comforting and warning became two of journalism's most obvious functions during the crisis triggered by terrorist strikes in New York and Washington. To provide comfort to a grieving, shocked country and alert it to possible future attacks, the media relied on a well-known nationalistic trope: a shared, national culture provides solace and unity to a community that has suffered foreign incursion. Risk was framed from this perspective. Any threat existed as a potential danger to "the nation." Hawkish patriotism provided the script to make September 11 and subsequent risk intelligible. Journalism

201

uncritically propagated patriotism as both a cultural comfort and an analytical framework in which to understand risk. This chapter accounts for why patriotic journalism emerged after September 11 and discusses its limitations and problems at a time of "anxiety in a risk society" (Wilkinson 2001).

## A nation at risk

September 11 crashed the idea of "Fortress America," the conviction that two oceans and a vast military network protect the continental US from any foreign threat. The 1812 war was the last time that foreign invaders had struck in US territory. Since World War II, the sentiment of geographical invulnerability has been central to US identity. Pearl Harbor prominently stood in the collective memory as the last moment of vulnerability. The absence of military incursions on US soil cemented the idea of invulnerability as a defining element of American nationhood. Neither attacks on US properties nor the defacing of symbols of American nationhood abroad (e.g. the bombing of embassies, the burning of flags, the egging and hooting of Presidents on tour) could rattle the American consciousness of invulnerability. Those events were too far from the perception of national territories to chisel away at the feeling of a secure home. The conviction of "safety at home" has been the flip side of the image of a world out of control that the media constantly propagated. In a "runaway world" (Giddens 2000) of war and instability, the United States stood as the bastion of invincibility. A world in chaos was intelligible from a perspective in which insecurity was seen as foreign. Insecurity was "othered," believed to be characteristic of other societies and excluded from the national sense of self. Supported by the constant news of suffering and unpredictability worldwide (Moeller 1999), US borders meant safety in a dangerous world.

The "culture of fear" (Glassner 1999) that the media helped to perpetuate is populated by a vast array of threats. Media-friendly fears typically made it into the news. Having alerted the population about all possible imaginable fears, the media failed to anticipate the possibility that attacks could happen on US soil. In retrospect, the warnings of *New York Times* columnist Thomas Friedman about terrorist dangers stood out precisely because they were exceptional. Before September 11, risks other than terrorism captured media attention. No wonder, then, that the tragic events in New York, Washington, and Pennsylvania came as a full surprise to a vast majority of the US public. Before September 11, *Time*'s covers in 2001 featured 11 stories on health/biology/medicine, six on family topics, five on politics, four on fear, two on sports, two on celebrities, two on finance, one on history, and one on AIDS in Africa (the newsweekly's only international cover story).

The lack of media reports on possible terrorist attacks showed that we live in a "world risk society" (Beck 2000), but risk as a structural condition is different from the perception of risk. Ulrich Beck has eloquently argued that risk underlies contemporary societies. Late modernity represents the massive diffusion of a host of risks (e.g. nuclear war, global warming, chemical warfare) that threaten the complete destruction of life on planet Earth. These are all-encompassing risks from which, as Anthony Giddens (1991) affirms, no one escapes. Beck's and Giddens' argument that our civilization has created risks with potentially terrible consequences provides, however, few insights to understand which risks are perceived. Although their conception of risk straddles realist and constructivist views, they do not place risk perception at the center of their analysis. More interested in understanding why risk sets apart contemporary societies in the history of human civilization rather than how risk is known and experienced, Beck even states that the perception of risk and risks themselves are identical (1992: 55).[2]

To comprehend the relation between media and risk consciousness before and after September 11, Mary Douglas and Aaron Wildavsky's (1982) cultural perspective serves us better. While Beck and Giddens primarily view risk as a product of late capitalism, Douglas and Wildavsky understand risk to be a product of knowledge. What societies defined as risk is an expression of what their cultures fear. A perspective that emphasizes "the social construction of risk" (see Vail, Wheelock, and Hill 1999) allows us to understand why, for example, people overestimate their vulnerability to specific risks and underestimate other risks, an issue extensively discussed in the literature on risk and health communication (Stephenson and Witte 2001). Understanding risk means to understand how societies construct perceptions about the social distribution of risk (Who is vulnerable? Why?) and the responsibility for risk (Who is responsible?). This construction, however, is no mere reflection of cultural fears in contemporary societies, but rather the result of the process of the governmentality of risk. What people come to understand as fearful is the consequence of what is socially constructed to be risky. Risk assessment is a form of imposing order and discipline, as Foucaultian analysts would have it (see Burchell, Gordon, and Miller 1991). Risk is the product of conflicts among ideologies of risk. Different interests struggle to identify risk, for example, through the use of information media to shape public consciousness and policy about risk.

Although there is no consensus on the dynamics of the interrelationship between media and risk, the media do play an important role in bringing societies in contact with risk. We do know that media reports on risk have a different impact on the social perception of risk and anxiety. This does not invalidate, however, the argument that in large-scale societies, the media is a "contact zone" between the public and risk, the linchpin between objective and subjective risk. Media representations provide crucial information used to estimate the social distribution of risk and the identity of who is responsible for risk.

From a perspective that prioritizes the social construction of risk, media representation of risk is of fundamental importance to understanding risk post-September 11 in the United States. September 11 not only painfully attested to the failure of US intelligence to alert the public and prevent the attacks, but also to the failure of the media. The risk of terrorism only gained wide media attention after hijacked planes slammed into the World Trade Center and the Pentagon. Critics pointed out that news organizations missed terrorism because they had substantially cut down coverage of international news. The possibility of terrorism in the continental US or the hatred towards the United States in Arab countries went unreported because, like US intelligence, journalism was also asleep at the wheel. In failing to cover foreign news and terrorism, the media provided a false sense of security.[3]

No doubt, the meager attention to international news notably reduced the chances that threats of anything like September 11 could be reported, let alone such an attack predicted. The absence of media attention cannot be attributed solely to the remarkable shrinkage of space to international news in the 1990s (or even, as some critics have suggested, to the fact that the media were distracted chasing celebrity scandals and other "soft" news). Like news about risk in general, news about terrorism as a potential threat largely depended on whether what are deemed to be legitimate sources effectively convey the sense that, indeed, there is a risk. Journalists rely on scientific and professional expertise to define risk. The definition of risk is typically initiated by sources rather than by the media (Singer and Endreny 1993). As a number of studies have demonstrated, sources in government, industry, and science are generally those who identify risk that is reported in the press (Sandman 1986, 1993; Dunwoody 1992; Eldridge 1999). In this sense, the failure of US intelligence was not only that it did not take precautions to prevent the attacks, as some journalists have concluded (Miller, Van Natta, and Gerth 2001), but also that it failed to warn the public through the media. No alleged risk according to authoritative sources meant no media stories about risk. There is the possibility, however, that intelligence warnings leaked to the media met only slight interest from media organizations preoccupied with other news. Even the limited availability of news pegs (such as a string of attacks on US properties in the 1990s, from the bombing of the World Trade Center in 1993 to the bombing of the USS Cole in Aden in 2000) did not prod the media to pay serious attention to examining the chance of terrorism on US soil. It is also possible that even if the media had exhaustively covered the topic, news might have gone unnoticed by an apathetic public, obsessed with private pursuits.

## Risk and identity politics

September 11 turned objective risk into subjective, experienced risk. Once risk materialized, US journalism had no choice but to report on its dramatic effects and the possibility that terrorism might strike again. Terrorism as risk could not be denied. While risk became front-cover news as the world was watching, the media were thrown into the midst of a nation recovering from a traumatic situation.

September 11 has been defined as a traumatic event in the news media (Cowley 2001; Farley 2001). Post-traumatic disorders were widely reported in the weeks after the attacks (Begley 2001; Goode 2002). In the psychoanalytical literature, trauma refers to an experience that shatters the cognitive-perceptual apparatus of the ego (Leys 2000). It refers to an event outside the individual's usual experience that results in a sense of dislocation and loss. Applied to collective identity, one could think of September 11 as a moment of rupture, a "break-in" through the protective shield of post-war American national identity. It is the catalyst of a shift from a moment of security to a moment of vulnerability, splitting time in the collective sense of self between then and now, between a time of protection and a time of danger. Similar to what the ego experiences in post-traumatic situations, a sensation of loss and dissociation followed the terrorist attacks.

What is important to emphasize is that traumatic events damage self perception. The traumatic force of any given event lies in its capacity to unbind the sense of self. Trauma affects how individual and collective actors come to terms with their identities. By ripping a sense of existing boundaries, trauma destabilizes a sense of self. In their aftermath, individuals and societies experience the need to reinstate a sense of order. It is too early to tell how September 11 will become etched and remembered in the collective memory. Events that ostensibly carry traumatic consequences may not necessarily have similar impact in the long term. Selective remembering or integration into individual or collective consciousness suggest that the life of an event in memory and identity are not predicated from its immediate impact. The possibility of "a structural disjuncture between an experience and its integration into narrative memory," as Ulrich Baer (2000) notes, suggests that traumatic experiences are assimilated in multiple ways.

Trauma is inseparable from the narratives through which events are perceived to affect individual and collective identities (Antze 1996). The narrative of "the nation at risk" has set the parameters to interpret September 11 in the United States. The idea that September 11 meant an attack on the nation was visible in the patriotic fervor that saturated the country immediately after the strikes. The surge in patriotism brought together a highly divided country that, emerging from one of the most contentious and divisive elections in its contemporary history, was suddenly confronted with terrorism. Patriotism paved over the dissent that had surfaced during the 2000 electoral contest that concluded with a much-debated Supreme Court decision.

Patriotic reaction in the wake of the attacks should not be surprising. One could argue, paraphrasing Hannah Arendt's observation about responding like a Jew to anti-Semitic acts, that Americans reacted as such because they had been attacked as Americans. The attackers identified by the Bush administration carried a furious anti-American message. Patriotic enthusiasm, however, was more than just a mere response to the fact that the attacks clearly had an anti-American intention. It emerged as the only possible way to provide reassurance to a community facing insecurity and anxiety in a global era. September 11 offered an opportunity to position patriotic identity by articulating the Other, as, most notably, theorized by Stuart Hall and Edward Said; that is, identity as a

205

discursive process through which the Other ("the perpetrators") is defined as different and excluded from the national community. It was a moment to reinvigorate American nationalism in a post-Cold War era, a time of fragmented and fractured identities.

News organizations became saturated with patriotic spirit after September 11. More than just an unwilling prisoner or passive supporter, journalism was a mobilizer of national identity that actively contributed to such atmosphere. Rather than convey the horror and document the tragedy without taking sides, journalism became an "American" journalism that constructed and reinforced national identity vis-à-vis the attacks. It seemed as if journalistic rules cherished during "normal" times had to be suspended for journalism to do its job. Typical rules seemed to put a straitjacket on journalism. The "journalism of crisis" was a journalism that snubbed the professional requirements of detachment and objectivity and willingly embraced patriotic partisanship.[4]

Patriotic journalism was particularly pronounced in the weeks after the attacks. Fox News Channel anchors and local television reporters wore red, white, and blue ribbons on their lapels. Led by CNN, the networks displayed logos covered in the US flag. Local and regional newspapers featured star-and-stripes colors and ribbons in their covers. Time magazine's name was in the colors of the flag the week after the attacks. In David Letterman's show, CBS News anchor Dan Rather declared himself to be ready to receive orders from President Bush. Journalism made numerous gestures that showed cultural membership of the national community.

Aside from personal and institutional expressions, journalism fostered uncritical patriotism through endless coverage of "banal nationalism" (Billig 1995), that is, everyday reminders of the nation. Logos such as "America under attack" that the networks used soon after the attacks, or Time's September 24 cover headline "One nation indivisible" over a photo of the flag and display of a lighted "God bless America" banner to illustrate the article "We gather together" (on the country's mood before Thanksgiving) were just a few examples of a news media that ostensibly articulated nationalistic sentiments by culling examples from society.

Why did journalism unwaveringly become wrapped in the flag? As Herbert Gans has argued, Americanism is a bedrock value of US journalism. Gans writes, "when the news is tragic or traumatic, it becomes the nation-cum-individual whose character and moral strength is tested" (1980: 20). While muted during "normal circumstances" under the observance to professional rules, sheer patriotism fully emerges in situations in which the "national community" is considered to be at risk. Although one could argue that patriotism was the result of journalists' personal reaction to the attacks, it is necessary to understand it as journalism's response as a cultural and political institution. True, members of the media had plenty of reasons to feel that they were in terrorism's bull's-eye. Islamic fundamentalists showed nothing but contempt for the principles of democratic journalism. Mullah Omar's offer of money for the murder of Western journalists and the brutal murder of *Wall Street Journal* journalist Daniel Pearl patently attested to the visceral opposition of fundamentalist Islam to the US media. It was even speculated that al-Qaeda wanted to attack the media because it "embod[ied] both freedom and excess" (Lemonick 2001a). The reaction to these attacks (even to the anthrax-laced letters that targeted reporters and newsrooms) was framed in professional terms; that is, they reflected an ideology that contradicted fundamental ideals of journalism in democratic societies (rather than "American" journalism). Journalists interpreted the threats and the murder as attacks on the freedom of the press more than a blow to the American nation. Even though both could be articulated as part of the same discourse ("freedom of the press is essential to the American nation"), it was remarkable, given how much American patriotism impregnated coverage of the war in Afghanistan, that journalists and pundits could maintain that the assassins showed a despicable attitude towards basic press rights.

More than a personal revenge against an enemy that abhorred the Western media, open demonstrations of patriotic reporting expressed journalism's search for a safe place in the "national" community. Uninterested in questioning the jingoistic drum-banging that took US society by storm after September 11, journalism readily adopted "patriotism as nationalism." Were other versions of patriotism possible? Could American patriotism mean solidarity, empathy, and concern for others devoid of flag-waving sentiments? Was it possible to understand American patriotism as dissent and freedom of speech, values enshrined in the mythology of US journalism? Could patriotism mean stating that press freedom was at risk after the Bush administration requested the networks to filter images of Osama Bin Laden or announced it would disseminate lies to confound "the enemy"?

Both versions of patriotism were certainly available in the American imagination. Numerous manifestations of compassion with the victims of September 11 expressed a mood of generosity, tolerance, and muted politics that was not confounded with strident jingoism. Likewise, civil rights advocates and progressive journalism stressed the importance of upholding democratic values such as criticism and freedom as the best safeguard of democracy against the perpetrators.

In a social climate in which patriotism rapidly suffused the public sphere, mainstream journalism opted to ignore dissent and avoided questioning the dangers of exuberant patriotism. Journalism was complicit in cementing such a climate. It was uninterested in pushing the boundaries of the responses to September 11, in stepping outside the "groupthink" mentality that rapidly dominated the public sphere, or in remaining cool amid heated emotions. It would have seemed quixotic, almost a quaint academic or leftist preoccupation, to ponder whether patriotic journalism is a "conflict of interest" (see Borden and Pritchard 2001) in a profession arguably concerned about whether the judgment and performance of journalists are unduly influenced by the same interests they cover. When journalism believes itself to be a member of a nation just like any other one, it implicitly assumes that it has no conflicts of interest with the same community it covers. Journalism quickly recoiled from running against the patriotic flow that engulfed the country. Was there any alternative? Could journalism genuinely step aside from a community mentality and run against the flow? Truly, the conditions were difficult for journalism to remain a voice of impartiality or propose a patriotism that did not lead to war-mongering. It would have taken courage to question swirling cries of revenge that suffocated dissent after September 11. Even commendable efforts to produce even-handed coverage, such as giving voice to Arab sources, or mild criticisms of the decisions of the Bush administration in the aftermath of the attacks, met a vocal reaction from the audience. Journalism seemed more comfortable following polled public opinion and flag-waving sentiments than warning about the dangers of hawkish patriotism to sacrosanct values of the democratic press.

Mainstream journalism was not willing to raise doubts about the merits of blatantly biased reporting such as Fox News' brand of journalism. The proudly defended position of Fox—"be accurate, be fair, be American"—was factually reported rather than questioned. It remained undiscussed whether it is suitable for democratic discourse in a society in crisis (see Rutenberg 2001). Regardless of whether patriotism truly represented the sentiment of the majority of journalists, it was tolerated and accepted as unproblematic. Whereas journalists who participate in anti-abortion or environmental demonstrations are roundly criticized, hardly anyone in the mainstream media raised questions about a journalism tightly wrapped in the flag. Patriotism stifled any possibility of raising doubts about the merits of a journalism that opted for flag-waving reporting over facticity.

Post-September 11 patriotic journalism confirmed the adage that the media want to be loved more than believed. CNN's Walter Isaacson was reported as having said "If you get on the wrong side of public opinion, you are going to get into trouble." After decades of ranking low in public opinion polls and being lambasted by critics, the media seemed to enjoy a newfound legitimacy. A survey conducted by the Pew Research Center in November 2001 suggested that the polled public had a more favorable view of the media. While 43 percent thought that journalists "stand up for America" before the attacks, 69 percent thought so afterwards; the percentage of those who believed that the media "protect democracy" grew from 46 percent to 60 percent (Jurkowitz 2002). The jump in the ratings of Fox News seemed to confirm not only that biased and jingoistic reporting excluding any dissent was acceptable, but that it also resonated with the public. Op-ed pieces and editorials in conservative magazines applauded journalism for having chosen patriotism over objectivity.

Since September 11, leftist critics have blamed economic factors for journalism's patriotism: caving in to audiences full of patriotic fervor, to advertisers ready to exploit patriotism for commercial purposes, and to parent corporations interested in pleasing policy-makers in exchange for future communications legislation. Journalism also propagated patriotism because it solidified its professional credentials as a loyal, integral member of the national community. While the display of political sympathies is unbefitting to truth-seeking journalism, patriotism was accepted at a time defined as "a nation challenged," to paraphrase the *New York Times* series devoted to September 11-related news. Journalists who eschewed professional rules and acted like any other citizen, full of patriotism and emotion, showed allegiance to the values of the community at large. Patriotism became a measure of professional legitimacy that trumped quintessential values. The discourse of "the nation in danger" displaced values of democratic journalism such as dissent and fairness. The risk of patriotism eliminating dissent was ignored; instead, the risk of "terrorism" endangering the nation was prioritized.

Patriotism excluded the possibility of criticizing the Bush administration or pondering critical questions about September 11 and its aftermath.[5] The notorious absence of investigative reporting on "why September 11 happened" or on who should bear the brunt of responsibility for the attacks was a symptom of the limited boundaries of public debate. Blinded by patriotism, it was easier to make "them" solely responsible (as in *Time*'s cover story "Why they hate us"?) than introspectively ponder why violence hit US territory or why the US state failed to protect citizens from violence. Patriotism as chauvinism dangerously bordered on a culture of absolute integration which, as Theodore Adorno somberly observed, facilitates a politics of murder and destruction.

## Patriotism and the anthrax attacks

The shortcomings of patriotic journalism became obvious in the coverage of anthrax, a story that absorbed the media between October and November 2001 after letters contaminated with anthrax were mailed to legislators and media companies. "The nation at risk" narrative that emerged after September 11 was superimposed onto the coverage of bio-terrorist risk. Journalism offered a vision of a country in panic, reeling from the September 11 attacks and now confronting a new risk that also threatened the nation. Like the risk of terrorism, the threat of bio-terrorism became a risk worth media coverage only after it materialized and resulted in billions of dollars in losses.

The coverage of the anthrax attacks showed that the media have trouble reporting risk in a cautious and watchful manner. The "press panic" at the height of the anthrax scare in late 2001 confirmed that the media are better at scaring than reassuring. Too late to identify risk, the media suddenly encountered risk after it exploded and opted to fuel anxiety without transmitting a comforting message. Repeating the message that "life is full of risks," it failed to provide reassuring information that would reduce public anxiety. This deficiency was accentuated by the fact that, in the case of anthrax, government and experts lacked solid responses that the media could have relayed to reassure the population. If the "Anthrax war has gone well," as a *Newsweek* article affirmed (apparently given the small number of cases and deaths), that was hardly the result of media coverage.

According to Centers for Disease Control Communications Director Vicki

Freimuth (2002), 12,454 print stories were published between October 1, 2001 and January 19, 2002. A Lexis-Nexis search for the word "anthrax" in major news organizations shows that the story had a seesaw pattern between early October and late December 2001. The bulk of the coverage was concentrated in the six weeks between October 4 and November 22, the period when anthrax killed five people. Coverage peaked with the discovery of anthrax in the Senate offices, remained at the front of the news every time there was an anthrax-related death, and substantially declined towards the end of November.

The first wave of anthrax stories hit the news in late September when it was reported that media personnel at the *New York Post* and NBC News had symptoms of anthrax infection. The issues gained wider attention in early October after American Media Inc. photo editor Robert Stevens contracted the illness (he died on October 5). The number of stories substantially increased, and anthrax leapt to the front pages a week later in the second wave of illness. On October 12, it was reported that an assistant to NBC Nightly News anchor Tom Brokaw had a form of cutaneous anthrax after a letter addressed to Brokaw had been opened. On October 15, another letter was opened in the office of Senate Majority Leader Tom Daschle. It was then that the story gained impressive momentum. The highest number of anthrax-related stories was scored between October 17 and 19. The fact that anthrax had hit the political center of the country drove the media frenzy. Not even the deaths of two postal workers in Washington DC on October 21 and 22 had a similar effect on the number of stories. On October 31, the death of Kathy Nguyen in New York City kept the media focused on anthrax, particularly because it challenged standard explanations about how anthrax could be contracted. After this death, the story began to lose steam and the number of stories dropped.

In a country still reeling from the September 11 attacks, the letters and the death of a photo editor renewed a sense of panic. The media themselves had been the target of the attacks. Anthrax-laced letters had been mailed to NBC Nightly News, the *New York Post* and the *National Enquirer*. New York Times science reporter Judith Miller, H. Troxler at the *St Petersburg Times*, CBS News in Washington, DC, and Fox News received hoax letters. Days after the first cases, a scare-mongering journalism pumped fear and anxiety. In its eyes, the "nation" was terrified; if citizens remained calm and went on their business as usual, one could not tell from media coverage. *Newsweek* featured articles headlined "Anthrax anxiety" and "Anxious about anthrax." *US News and World Report*'s October 29 cover title read "High anxiety: Are anthrax scares just the beginning?" against an image of a police officer standing in front of the Capitol. Its November 5 cover title continued fanning the flames of anxiety: "Death by mail: The terrifying anthrax maelstrom has America on edge." *Time*'s cover "The fear factor" portrayed a "nation on edge" after the anthrax letters.

The media panic differed from the tone of testimonies by high-powered politicians. Newly appointed Domestic Security Chief Tom Ridge tried to calm fears in his first public appearance (Purdum and Becker 2001). Senator Ben Nelson

(Democrat, Nebraska) was quoted as saying anthrax "is not a weapon of mass destruction, it is a weapon of mass confusion." Senator John McCain (Republican, Arizona) stated, "More people have been struck by lightning in the last 10 days, I'll bet, than have contracted anthrax. The country badly needs to settle down" (*New York Times* 2001).

Coverage of the anthrax attacks showed two themes that are central to media representation of risk: the social distribution of risk and the responsibility of risk. The first one alluded to anthrax as a matter of public health; the second one referred to its political dimensions. The former dealt with issues such as how anthrax spreads and what the population should do; the latter reported on who was responsible for the anthrax attacks.

Amid one of the most high-profile public health emergencies in recent times, the coverage attempted to provide plenty of information on how victims contracted anthrax, the precautions to take, and medicines. These reports conveyed a sense of uncertainty that reflected the absence of unanimous explanations on several questions among expert sources. Neither the government nor bio-terrorism experts offered a convincing theory about how anthrax spreads. Nor was there consensus about what to do in case someone contracted anthrax, nor on the risks of vaccines. It became clear that not only people directly exposed could become infected, as the cases of victims infected by letter cross-contamination suggested. Also, the cases proved wrong previous understanding about the quantity of anthrax spores needed for someone to become ill. Anthrax was a story about science gone awry but also about the lack of solid scientific knowledge about what to do once anthrax hits. Uncertainty about the medical aspects of anthrax paralleled the uncertainty among government officials about the possibility of new attacks that the media also transmitted. The fact that the United States was unprepared to respond to biological attacks became obvious (Miller, Engelberg, and Broad 2000).

The media sounded alarm bells and conveyed despair. Notwithstanding the efforts of news organizations to provide relevant information, contradictions in the scientific community about anthrax were patently reflected in coverage. While science is typically portrayed as an institution with infallible knowledge and unanimous explanations, anthrax coverage laid bare a different picture. Journalism's picture of "science in agreement" was impossible in the middle of a public health crisis combined with a heightened sensitivity to terrorism. The existence of different theories among a number of anthrax-related matters became so patently obvious that the media could not ignore them. Journalism's penchant for reporting scientific findings as revealed truth (Hornig Priest 2001) was not viable when testimonies revealed glaring contradictions and divergences among experts. It was a complex subject between science and policy that journalism found difficult to cover. It was hard to dichotomize a subject packed with untested and controversial claims.

If September 11 showed the tragic failure of US intelligence, the anthrax panic demonstrated the failure and pitfalls of science. Anthrax coverage revealed the lethal consequences of scientific endeavors allied with military and political interests, as well as that science lacked solid information to protect the public. On November 12, *Newsweek*'s article "How little we know" captured the predominant feeling among quoted experts after four deaths and a dozen illnesses. A *Washington Post* story on November 19, describing how experts were at a loss in identifying how postal workers had contracted anthrax, added more evidence that scientists could not provide unanimous conclusions and recommendations (Twomey and Blum 2001).[6]

The media reflected an unsettling fact: experts were learning as the events unfolded. Many lessons were learned during those weeks: among others, the number of spores needed to be inhaled in order to contract anthrax, the difficulty in aerosolizing the spores, who needs to get treatment, the effects of vaccination, and whether the country had a sufficient supply of ciprofloxacin. No wonder, then, that uncertainty dominated media information about "what to do."

While coverage of anthrax as a public health matter reflected disagreement and confusion among experts, coverage of anthrax as a political issue reflected hawkish patriotism at work. In the first weeks it seemed almost certain that the attacks were connected to al-Qaeda and Iraq's bio-terrorism projects, but gradually it became more apparent that a domestic source was responsible.

Anthrax coverage confirms two well-known findings in the literature on risk and media: risk management lies in official hands, and journalism strongly depends on official sources to report risk. The reporting of terrorist risks after September 11 confirmed this pattern. The Bush administration remained in full control of assessing the chances of new terrorist attacks. We still do not know whether such assessments were based on credible information that effectively suggested the possibility of imminent attacks or expressed the sentiment of an administration which, unwilling to be caught again "sleeping at the wheel," exaggerated the chances of another terrorist assault. No matter the veracity of the information or the intention of the White House, the media plainly transmitted the administration's estimation of risk, without independently questioning the solidity of the information. To the White House's alarming communiqués and statements, staple images of worried and distressed faces were added, such as the "Altered States of America" cover of *US News and World Report* on November 12.

Although reporting showed that sources did not agree on the origins of the attacks, those that suspected or charged foreign parties with the attacks were prominently quoted. President George W. Bush's thunderous declaration that anthrax was "the second wave of terrorism" set the tone for coverage. During October 2001, sources seemed convinced that al-Qaeda and/or Iraq were behind the anthrax letters even though they did not offer evidence, as a *Washington Post* reporter indicated (Vedantam 2001). A *New York Times* story on October 16 reported that government officials were considering that the September 11 attackers were also connected to the anthrax cases (Johnston 2001). A day later, the newspaper quoted scientists who cited involvement of a "state" and directed their suspicions to the former Soviet Union and Iraq. On October 19, another article stated that investigators suspected that the anthrax-laced letters were related to the September 11 attacks. The newsweeklies presented a similar view. *Time* featured an investigation entitled "What does Saddam have?" which, based on testimonies from government officials, presupposed an Iraqi connection in the anthrax attacks. *US News and World Report*'s front cover story stated that "the finger of blame pointed most readily at Osama Bin Laden's al-Qaeda terrorist network," while admitting that investigators did not rule out a domestic source (Pasternak *et al.* 2001). Most sources talked about involvement of "another nation's biological weapons program," the fact that the Soviet Union had trained thousands of scientists "to produce deadly germs," Iraq's purchase of strains of anthrax, and a meeting between hijacker Mohamed Atta and Iraqi intelligence agents. Not having to bow to journalistic objectivity, New York City tabloids directly charged Iraq. On October 22, the *New York Post*'s cover screamed "Dr Germ: Saddam's scientist behind anthrax outbreak." The lead story accused "notorious" scientist Rihab Taha for participating in the planning of the attacks. Similarly, health and bio-terrorism experts on television shows went beyond speculations, and affirmed that Iraq was involved in the attacks (James 2001).

Aside from the merits of available evidence, the probability that foreigners were threatening the nation again seemed plausible at a time when hawkish patriotism was the dominant prism to understanding September 11 and its consequences. Patriotism establishes that only external forces pose threats to the nation. It excludes the possibility of internal actors interested in disrupting a seemingly unified community. If risk was a way of "ordering reality" (Dean 1999), reporting on anthrax patently shows that the idea of "the nation at risk" became the dominant discourse to make sense of risk post-September 11 in the United States.

While the media hammered at the idea that the anthrax attacks were connected to September 11, it was hardly surprising that opinion polls showed an overwhelming majority believed that to be true. According to a *Time/CNN* poll, 63 percent believed that Osama Bin Laden was responsible for the attacks, 40 percent blamed Saddam Hussein, and 16 percent said that US citizens with foreign terrorists were the culprits (Lemonick 2001b).

Towards late October, the media reported that the Bush administration privately was steering representatives away from the Iraq–anthrax connection, and that the Federal Bureau of Investigation and the Central Intelligence Agency suspected the participation of US extremists. In a series of presentations and a widely-quoted paper, biological arms control expert Barbara Hatch Rosenberg (2002) argues that the FBI had known that the perpetrator was American but was reluctant to make an arrest for political reasons, namely, that the suspect had ties to secret US military biological weapons programs. On November 9, the FBI reported that the main suspect was a domestic source, an "opportunist" who took advantage of the post-September 11 fear and anxiety. Once the FBI admitted that possibility, news articles leaned toward the hypothesis that the culprit was not foreign, and the attacks were unrelated to September 11. However, despite growing evidence pointing at a domestic source, the White House remained convinced "that anyone that evil could not be American," as President Bush put it (Simon 2001: 17). According to a government official quoted in the story, prime suspects were Arab-Americans with a background in biotech, medicine, and pharmacology and associates of the hijackers and other extremists.

In early December, the *New York Times* reported that research concluded that the anthrax spores mailed to the Hart Senate building matched bacteria that the US Army had had since 1980 (Broad 2001). Towards mid-December, the Bush administration publicly admitted the possibility that the anthrax attacks had been instigated domestically, as White House spokesman Ari Fleisher stated on December 17.

Once legitimate sources started to shift their view about the presumed identity of attackers, the anthrax story started to fade. Its gradual disappearance from front-page news confirmed, as Beck and others have argued, that risk underlies contemporary life but it only becomes news under certain conditions. The coverage followed patterns already identified in risk reporting and journalism, in general. Risk becomes a "hell of a story" when journalism has news pegs, offering ways to personalize the story and portray the image of "a disease out of control." The discovery of the anthrax-laced letters and related deaths sustained coverage for weeks, but after the last anthrax-related death in November 21, journalism did not find events that could anchor stories about anthrax or angles to personalize the disease and anthrax gradually receded from the front pages. Journalism's obsession with immediate events rather than interest in long-term considerations meant that once there were no more events, even about a disease that hit the US Senate and the country's postal system weeks earlier, anthrax became abstract.

Additionally, the story became more difficult to cover once official sources were quoted as leaning towards the hypothesis that domestic perpetrators were behind the attacks. Such conviction contradicted the trope of "the nation at risk" and made the production of mediated risk more complex. The media could no longer render an account that fitted, in Michel Foucault's sense, the "regime of truth" in place since September 11. At a time when patriotism was still pervasive, indications that fellow members of the nation apparently sent anthrax-laced letters flew in the face of the "united we stand" patriotism that the media helped to perpetuate.

## Journalism and its choices of patriotism

To a press that closely followed the Bush administration's conception of risk after September 11, terrorism emerged as the major risk to "the nation." Patriotism had a twofold role: to make risk intelligible and to offer protection against risk. It functioned as the prism to define a world in turmoil and to put order in a disordered world.

The vitality of post-September 11 patriotism seems to challenge the postmodernist idea that we live in times in which coherent narratives have broken down. Nationalism, a quintessential modernist narrative, continues to mediate "our being in the world," to use Heidegger's phrase. In a messy, uncertain, and violent world, patriotism provides a ready-made discourse of safety. When risk and insecurity are pervasive, the nation allegedly offers a safe haven and warmth in a cold, menacing world. Global risk is made intelligible in terms of its threats to the nation. When identities are seemingly multiple, patriotism provides the dream of a unified identity, of an "imagined" community (Anderson 1991) coming together despite differences. When globalization unsettles pre-existent connections, patriotism comes in full force to offer a sense of connectedness.

September 11 is a watershed moment that brutally rattled, at least temporarily, the American consciousness of stability and protection. It offers evidence that post national prognosticators, whether of a globalization business bent or progressive cosmopolitan persuasion, rush to conclusion when they pronounce patriotism passé. It also suggests that journalism is central to the continuous vitality of patriotism. In patriotism, journalism finds a cultural anchor to legitimize its social function as a full card-carrying member of the national community; in journalism, patriotism has a loyal ally, a loud defender and propagandist.

Whether such an alliance should be celebrated or criticized depends on how patriotism is understood. Nationalism comes in many forms, as Craig Calhoun (1997) suggests. Patriotism and chauvinism are not identical. In one interpretation, patriotism as "benign nationalism" (Ignatieff 1999) embodies human solidarity, tolerant integration, an ethos of compassion and service, and the respect of democratic values. This is the form of patriotism endorsed by Benjamin Barber (1996) and Richard Rorty's "achieving our country" argument (Rorty 1998). Both authors find this interpretation of American patriotism democratic and progressive, different from the "blood and soil," "my-country-right-or-wrong" version that fuels hatred and military conflict.[1] For them, civic patriotism is possible and desirable and should not be collapsed with atavistic forms of nationalism. An alternative interpretation sees patriotism irremediably linked to xenophobia, jingoism, violence, conquest, intolerance, and other ills, painfully demonstrated in many bloody conflicts in the contemporary world. Intolerant patriotism is the target of universal cosmopolitans and multicultural critics of the nation-state. It is the thorn in the side of those who believe that nationalism is nothing but an obstacle towards achieving a more egalitarian and humane world.

If we cannot do without patriotism in the contemporary world, as Charles Taylor (1996) suggests, it is worth considering a number of questions. Which version of patriotism does journalism choose in specific circumstances? Does it opt to vindicate civic or belligerent patriotism? When? How do we account for those selections? More specifically, why did US journalism overwhelmingly march behind and sustain hawkish patriotism after September 11? Why did it not forcefully promote a constitutional patriotism that prioritizes other good old American values, such as holding government accountable and freedom of speech? Can constitutional patriotism be defended only outside war times? Is

215

hawkish patriotism the only answer to violence upon fellow citizens, and inva-sion of territory? Why cannot civic patriotism be upheld in traumatic situations when citizens brace for sympathy and community, compassion, and protection? When violence rips the sense of geographic invulnerability, why did journalism not make speech and civic rights the defining elements of "a nation at risk"? Why did the media find conservative patriotism seemingly more appealing than liberal patriotism?

It is difficult not to think that there is a strong affinity between journalism and conservative patriotism. Liberal patriotism is often sacrificed on the altar of the nation, particularly when external aggression is seen as a justification for "blood-and-soil" counteraction. Constitutional patriotism and the truth suffer when governments and the public fan the flames of a patriotism of war and intolerance. Even in a globalized world, journalism continues to be governed by national demands, audiences, public opinion, advertisers, economies, laws, and govern-ments. As long as this remains true, then, journalism is likely to be patriotism's perennial partner, a reliable associate that cosmopolitan citizenship and global consciousness continue to lack despite the ascent and consolidation of global media. The media's choice of patriotism has terribly important consequences for democratic life. When they opt for "a love of country" that quickly transmogrifies into chauvinism, they prepare the cultural ground for violence and do a disser-vice to national and global democracy. Journalism needs to resist the temptation to dance to the tune of deafening nationalism often found in public opinion. Instead, it could courageously show patriotic spirit by keeping criticism alive rather than becoming compliant with "home essentialism." It could provide reas-surance by lowering the fear volume and offer community by defending diversity and tolerance rather than foundational, ethnocentric patriotism. A choice for the latter not only excludes democratic dissent from patriotism, but it also mini-mizes the possibility that citizens of the nation imagine that they also belong to a world community of equals. What conception of patriotism is chosen is of crucial importance in risk assessment at a time of disorder and violence in a global world. What is defined as risk ultimately depends on whether patriotism is associ-ated with a "blood-and-soil" superiority, "us-versus-them" mentality, or the idea of community, civic rights, and sympathy for fellow human beings against any form of intolerance and violence.

## Notes

1  Risk is a contested notion (see Lupton 1999). According to Ulrich Beck (1992: 21), one of the foremost analysts of the subject, "risk is a systematic way of dealing with hazards and insecurity." For the purpose of this study, risk alludes to discursive forms in which risk is defined. There are no risks per se, but *ways* in which events, people, and issues are defined as risks. The definition of risk is an attempt to impose order, that is, to manage and to regulate, society. Risk management is an exercise in power to out-line and maintain boundaries between security and threat.

2  For a different assessment on Beck's discussion of risk perception and media, see Cottle (1998).
3  However, according to a report published in *The Quill*, Reuters disseminated a story headlined "Bin Laden fighters plan anti-US attack" on June 23. It stated that "Followers of exiled Saudi dissident Osama Bin Laden are planning a major attack on US and Israeli interests." On June 25, United Press International spread similar news when it informed that "Saudi dissident Osama Bin Laden is planning a terrorist attack against the United States." The following day, another UPI report ("Bin Laden forms new Jihadi group") described the formalization of ties between Bin Laden's al-Qaeda and the Egyptian branch of Islamic Jihad. Yet, the article states, barely any of the major US newspaper and broadcast network Web sites "considered the stories worthy of publication" (www.spj.org/quill_issue.asp?ref=233).
4  Even emotional reporting not wrapped in nationalism was legitimate, such as the countless television reporters who could not hide their emotions while interviewing people minutes after the attacks, or when NBC newscaster Tom Brokaw departed from his usual cool delivery and, visibly emotional, announced that one of his producers had contracted anthrax after having opened a letter mailed to him (see Kurtz 2001).
5  *Sacramento Bee* publisher Janis Besler Heaphy received an angry response from a crowd at California State University in Sacramento when she questioned decisions by the Bush administration in the "war against terrorism" on the grounds that they threatened civil liberties.
6  Infighting over turf among agencies certainly did not help to reduce the anxiety that the media transmitted. The fact that the FBI controlled the investigation and impeded access by scientists for the Centers for Disease Control prevented the latter from receiving first-hand knowledge and possibly better information about postal workers who had contracted anthrax (Siegel 2002).
7  Their version of patriotism has generated numerous responses (see, among others, Nussbaum and Cohen 1996, Brennan 1997, and Robbins 1999).

# References

Anderson, B. (1991) *Imagined Communities*, London: Verso.
Antze, P. (1996) Telling stories, making selves: memory and identity in multiple personality disorder, in P. Antze and M. Lambe (eds) *Tense Past: Cultural Essays in Trauma and Memory*, New York: Routledge: 3–24.
Auletta, K. (2001) Battle stations, *New Yorker*, December 10: 60–7.
Barber, B. (1996) Constitutional faith, in M. C. Nussbaum and J. Cohen (eds) *For Love of Country: Debating the Limits of Patriotism*, Boston, MA: Beacon Press, 30–7.
Baer, U. (2000) *Remnants of Song: Trauma and the Experience of Modernity in Charles Baudelaire and Paul Celan*, Stanford, CA: Stanford University Press.
Beck, U. (1992) *Risk Society: Towards a New Modernity*, London: Sage.
Beck, U. (2000) *World Risk Society*, Cambridge: Polity Press.
Begley, S. (2001) Will we ever be safe again?, *Newsweek*, September 24: 58–61.
Billig, M. (1995) *Banal Nationalism*, London: Sage.
Borden, S. L. and Pritchard, M. S. (2001) Conflict of interest in journalism, in M. David and A. Stark (eds) *Conflict of Interest in the Professions*, New York: Oxford University Press: 73–91.
Brennan, T. (1997) *At Home in the World: Cosmopolitanism Now*, Cambridge, MA: Harvard University Press.

Broad, W. (2001) Terror anthrax resembles type made by US, *New York Times*, December 3: A1.

Burchell, G., Gordon, C., and Miller, P. (eds) (1991) *The Foucault Effect: Studies in Governmentality*, Hemel Hempstead: Harvester Wheatsheaf.

Calhoun, C. (1997) *Nationalism*, Minneapolis, MN: University of Minnesota Press.

Cottle, S. (1998) Ulrich Beck, "risk society" and the media: a catastrophic view? *European Journal of Communication*, 13 (1): 5–32.

Cowley, G. (2001) After the trauma, *Newsweek*, October 1: 32–6.

Dean, M. (1999) Risk, calculable and incalculable, in Deborah Lupton (ed.) *Risk and Sociocultural Theory: New Directions and Perspectives*, Cambridge: Cambridge University Press: 131–59.

Douglas, M. and Wildavsky, A. (1982) *Risk and Culture: An Essay on the Selections of Technological and Environmental Dangers*, Berkeley, CA: University of California Press.

Dunwoody, S. (1992) The media and public perceptions of risk: how journalists frame risk, in D. W. Browley and K. Segerson (eds) *The Social Response to Environmental Risk*, Boston, MA: Kluwer.

Eldridge, J. (1999) Risk, society and the media: now you see it, now you don't, in G. Philo (ed.) *Message Received*, London: Longman: 106–11.

Farley, M. (2001). Hoaxes, rumors, and wishful thinking spawned by trauma, *Los Angeles Times*, September 28: A1, 16.

Freimuth, V. (2002) Presentation at Rutgers University, New Jersey, March 7.

Gans, H. (1980) *Deciding What's News*, New York: Vintage.

Giddens, A. (1991) *Modernity and Self Identity*, Stanford, CA: Stanford University Press.

Giddens, A. (2000) *Runaway World*, London: Routledge.

Glassner, B. (1999) *The Culture of Fear*, New York: Basic Books.

Goode, E. (2002) Thousands in Manhattan needed therapy after attack, study finds, *New York Times*, March 28: A15.

Hatch Rosenberg, B. (2002). Analysis of the anthrax attacks, Federation of American Scientists, www.fas.org/bwc/news/anthraxreport.htm, February 5.

Hornig Priest, S. (2001) *A Grain of Truth: The Media, Public, and Biotechnology*, Lanham, MD: Rowman and Littlefield.

Ignatieff, M. (1999) Benign nationalism? the possibilities of the civic ideal, in E. Mortimer with R. Fine (eds) *People, Nation, and State: The Meaning of Ethnicity and Nationalism*, London: Tauris: 141–8.

James, C. (2001) Television, like the country, loses its footing, *New York Times*, November 4: A1.

Jensen, E. (2001) Study shows "colossal shift" in news, *Los Angeles Times*, November 19: F11.

Johnston D. (2001) In shift, officials look into possibility anthrax cases have Bin Laden ties, *New York Times*, October 16: A5.

Jurkowitz, M. (2002) The media: pro-US tendency is seen in survey, *Boston Globe*, January 28: A9.

Kurtz, H. (2001). Tom Brokaw, Putting a familiar face on the anthrax story, *Washington Post*, October 18, C1, C7.

Lemonick, M. D. (2001a) Deadly delivery, *Time*, October 22: 32–8.

Lemonick, M. D. (2001b) Profile of a killer, *Time*, November 19: 60–3.

Leys, R. (2000) *Trauma: A Genealogy*, Chicago, IL: University of Chicago Press.

Lupton, D. (1999) *Risk*, London: Routledge.

Milbank, D. (2001) Fear is here to stay, so let's make the most of it, *Washington Post*, October 21: B2.

Miller, J., Van Natta Jr, D., and Gerth, J. (2001) Planning for terror but failing to act, *New York Times*, December 30: A1.

Miller, J., Engelberg, S., and Broad, W. (2000) *Germs: Biological Weapons and America's Secret War*, New York: Simon and Schuster.

Moeller, S. (1999) *Compassion Fatigue*, New York: Routledge.

*New York Times* (2001) Quote of the day, October 18: A2.

Nussbaum, M. C. and Cohen, J. (1996) *For Love of Country: Debating the Limits of Patriotism*, Boston: Beacon Press.

Parks, M. (2002) Beyond Afghanistan, *Columbia Journalism Review*, available online at www.cjr.org/year/02/1/parks.asp, January.

Pasternak, D., Boyce, N., and Samuel, T. (2001) Tools of mass distraction, *US News and World Report*: 13–16.

Purdum, T. S. and Becker, E. (2001) Bush officials step out in force to calm anthrax fears, *New York Times*, October 19: A1.

Robbins, B. (1999) *Feeling Global: Internationalism in Distress*, New York: New York University Press.

Rorty, R. (1998) *Achieving our Country: Leftist Thought in Twentieth-century America*, Cambridge, MA: Harvard University Press.

Rutenberg, J. (2001) Fox shows a war of good and evil, and many are tuning in, *New York Times*, December 3: C5.

Sandman, P. M. (1986). *Explaining Environmental Risk*, Washington, DC: US Environmental Protection Agency.

Sandman, P. M. (1993) *Mass Media and Environmental Risk: Seven Principles*, Center for Environmental Communication, New Brunswick, NJ: Rutgers University.

Siegel, M. (2002) The anthrax fumble, *The Nation*, March 18: 14–17.

Simon, R. (2001) Anthrax nation, *US News and World Report*, November 5: 16–18.

Singer, E. and Endreny, P. M. (1993) *Reporting on Risk*, New York: Russell Sage Foundation.

Stephenson, M. T. and Witte, K. (2001) Creating fears in a risky world: generating effective health risk messages, in R. Rice and C. Atkin (eds) *Public Communication Campaigns*, Thousand Oaks, CA: Sage, 88–104.

Taylor, C. (1996) Why democracy needs patriotism, in M. C. Nussbaum and J. Cohen (eds) *For Love of Country: Debating the Limits of Patriotism*, Boston: Beacon Press, 119–21.

Twomey, S. and Blum, J. (2001) How the experts missed anthrax, *Washington Post*, November 19: A1, A6.

Vail, J., Wheelock, J., and Hill, M. (1999) *Insecure Times: Living with Insecurity in Contemporary Society*, London: Routledge.

Vedantam, S. (2001) Bioterrorism's relentless, stealthy march, *Washington Post*, October 18: A16.

Wilkinson, I. (2001) *Anxiety in a Risk Society*, London: Routledge.

# 12

# TRAUMA TALK

## Reconfiguring the inside and outside[1]

*Annabelle Sreberny*

Globalization's metaphoric emblem was once the butterfly, whose gently flutter-ing wings above the Amazon caused not quite a tsunami but were felt on the other side of the earth, as far away as Japan. The gentle image of small move-ments in one place producing large effects in others delicately evoked the complex and multilayered system that is globalization.

The violent and crudely terrifying events of September 11, with their global real-time images of horrific destruction, have superseded the butterfly as the face of globalization. The initial construction of the event presaged an emerging new order, in which new kinds of actors and politics were unfolding. But temporal and physical distance allow for a rethinking of that claim.

### September 11

September 11 was a colossal unplanned media event (Dayan and Katz 1992). A global television audience of millions watched horrified yet transfixed, together in real time, as the second plane flew into the World Trade Center and the twin towers collapsed. Much pathos derived from the fact that viewers thousands of miles from the scene knew more than did many of the people inside either build-ing and yet were impotent to act.

New York's media-saturated environment fed the hungry global audience with photographs, video, and audio recordings. They saw people trying to escape, including throwing themselves from upper stories. They heard poignant expres-sions of love on mobile phones, last messages on answering-machines, and the repetitive replay of the collapse of the twin towers. The Internet was clogged as millions worldwide logged on, desperate for more news, more information, and more interpretation. While the media in ordinary times help to structure and order the everyday (Silverstone 1994), in times of crisis their role in allaying anxiety is even more crucial. In catastrophic times, information plays "a thera-peutic service, a ritual akin to prayer or chanting. Cloaked as an episteme, a desire to know, it soothes our anxiety, becomes story, therapy, and collective ritual" (Mellencamp 1990: 248). Later, she adds, "it will be known as myth."

## Journalism after September 11: emotion and attachment?

For a moment, the event was represented as a massive global trauma implicating everyone. Journalists were severely challenged in their ability to impose sense on the event, resorting often to simple narrative formats. The manner in which the event took over the airwaves and dominated the papers in itself signified massive crisis and a new hierarchy of significance that downplayed ongoing conflicts.

The event's sheer scale and surprise prompted a breakdown of the usual journalistic frameworks and a scramble for interpretation. How could journalists help interpret the event if the experts could not agree? How could we, the audience, think about this event? Some of the best material appeared on the Internet, in that rapid-response mode that net-work does so well. Many of the best sites were constructed from the US, perhaps in response to a politically-constricted media environment.

The event seemed to demand, and quickly spawned, new or renewed genres of writing. There was the eyewitness account, sometimes written or told by the people who were in the twin towers and escaped and other times by people nearby who could describe the scene. There were the final messages and the tearful stories of those left behind, sometimes desperate to find out if a loved one was still alive. There were instant expert opinions, many now possibly cause for regret in the over-rapid rush to judgment. There were instant cod histories.

The everyday, taken-for-granted norms of journalism were shaken, in rushed opinion and emotion, and an affective public sphere evolved. The balance seemed to shift between the ordinary work of journalism and a kind of extraordinary writing that people seemed to need to write and others to read—writing as catharsis, writing trauma out of ourselves, trauma talk.

One response to trauma is alexythemia, or psychic numbing, "a cutting of feelings, which if allowed into existence, would be overwhelming" (Prince 1999: xi). This process has been identified in work with Hiroshima victims by Lifton (1967) and with Holocaust survivors (Prince 1999) and their second generation (Wardi 1992). An opposite response is talking it out, a supposedly therapeutic process of sharing, thinking about, and processing the material. Yet in an excessively mediated culture this may simply encourage a kind of simulacrum of emotion and a form of affective manipulation by the culture industries. The debate about the increasing emotionalism and pseudo-therapeutic dynamics of media has focused on television talk-shows, although Rapping (2000) critiques the talk show exemplar for adopting a depoliticized, over-individualized approach to social problems. Miller (2002) has already written scathingly about the over-emotionalization of US current affairs television post-September 11 that substituted analysis of politics and economics with feelings, "feelings of firefighters, viewers, media mavens,

R-Word and D-Word politicos, and brain-dead Beltway state-of-the nation pundits . . . in the name of raw, apolitical truth."

In Britain, a range of voices was invited onto television and radio discussion
programs and into the pages of the press. It felt as though there was an awareness,
at least in parts of the liberal media, about the problem of Islamophobia, and
many programs worked hard to find speakers from Muslim communities and to
solicit the opinions of Muslims including, in March 2002, a wide-ranging series
of television programs *Muslim and British* produced for Channel 4.

The newspaper the *Guardian*, together with its Sunday sister the *Observer*, are
the liberal papers of choice among the middle-class chatterati. The titles are
operated by the Scott Trust of ten trustees—two members of the original Scott
family, six members from the *Guardian*'s own staff, and two external members,
making it unique within a press landscape of growing conglomeratization by press
barons. It has a long history of publishing think-pieces by writers who are not
part of its regular staff, who contribute to a lively public debate about controversial matters. Starting immediately after September 11, it published articles by a
range of well-known and respected writers and commentators, some filed from
New York or taken from US newspapers and others from further afield. The list of
authors included Martin Wollacott, Saskia Sassen, Ian McEwan, Simon Schama,
Rana Kabbani, Ian Buruma, Arundhati Roy, Christopher Hitchins, Anne Karpf,
Caryl Philips, Salman Rushdie, Blake Morrison, Ahdaf Souief, Ziauddin Sardar,
Polly Toynbee, Gary Younge, Yusuf Islam, Edward Said, Pete Hamill, Katie
Roiphe, Larry Elliot, Darryl Pinkney, and others. Constructed not as experts on
Islam, terrorism, or military ordinance, they were regarded as independent writ-
ers and thinkers voicing personal, often emotional, responses.

A collection of some of their pieces was issued as a magazine, entitled simply
*September 11* (October 2001), with all of the writers waiving their fees to support
the Afghan Crisis Appeal organized by the Red Cross/Red Crescent. Editor Alan
Rusbridger wrote on the inside front cover about the collection: "Some of it is
raw, some controversial, some prescient, some overtaken by subsequent information or events."

What I examine here is not populist talk-show fare. This is print journalism
and the material was written rather than performed, albeit produced hurriedly in
the urgency of the event. It was published in Britain, a culture less inclined to
overt expressions of emotion than the US (although the emotional public reactions to the death of Princess Diana triggered interesting public debate; see
Blackman and Walkerdine 2001). These pieces of commentary were published
within a serious broadsheet newspaper, albeit one that over the years has shifted
into softer culturalist content in its daily tabloid section that, from considerable
informal comment, seems better read than the worthy hard news and commentary of the larger section. This was not regular column material, nor written by
regular columnists, though many have written occasional pieces before.[2]

This writing deserves serious consideration for a number of reasons. The dominant US political discourse kicked in immediately after the event with President

Bush's speech and continues in spring 2002 with the construction of the "axis of evil." While these authors do not represent the voices of hegemony, they do reveal how the process of hegemony is internalized. In their rapidly written and emotional expressive form, these voices reflect something of the collective unconscious, of the anxieties and mistrust as well as the shared understandings and attachments that trauma summons up. They thus reveal something of "ourselves," but just which selves I will pursue.

Another element that makes this writing worthy of attention is that the collective outpouring of grief and fear reversed the usual response to international news, which is to keep the other at a distance (Boltanski 1999) or to produce "not existential anger and horror . . . but a mixture of entertainment and listless ennui" (Tester 2001: 28). Most academic analysis and public debate about the impact of international news coverage on audiences focuses on a lack of affect and compassion fatigue; while they disagree about the effects of television news, both Silverstone and Robins stress the importance of the medium, as "distancing and denying" (Silverstone 1994) or "defusing . . . painful reality" (Robins 1994: 459). Thus, often the biggest problem about news audiences is their indifference. Tester (1997: 30–1) writes of the news audience in the developed Western world that "we are indifferent in so far as we tend to have no sustained interest in what we see and hear; for us what we see and hear of horror in other places lacks importance or deep meaning." But two implications need comment. One is that amongst this "we" of audience there are no others who *do* deeply identify with the matter in hand. For example, Britain's Asian populations are agonized about and deeply divided over the religious violence in India. American-Arabs watch CNN's coverage of the Middle East with different eyes than others, as well as utilize other sources of information. The second point is through the narrow definition of "we" the viewer, the news violence never happens to "us." Part of the deep shock of September 11 was that "we" had become the object of violence, not its perpetrator.

In this case, instead of indifference, there was over-identification. So many international writers and commentators were somehow merged with Americans in a cultural geography of attachment. This was partly an effect of America as the global universal, an indication of the internalization of a steady drip-feed of hegemonic values. In Britain, there was also a deep sense of cultural proximity, "our" familiar and much loved New York of the movies, television, tourism, Americans as people very like "us." Then there was the sheer unexpectedness of the event, the attendant difficulty in understanding it, and a generalized anxiety by big city-dwellers that they could be next. All of this fostered an unusually emotive response to this event in many places, which was clearly expressed through these articles.

What intrigued me after reading much of this material were some repetitive thematics and turns of phrase that seemed to speak more of certain collective fantasies and concerns than the event at hand. The texts abounded with notions of collective identity alongside a confusion about the collectivity, its nature, and whom it encompasses. There seemed to be also a confusion about the audience, for whom one was writing, and why one was writing—in short, a confusion about who "we" are. At issue, then, in these writings was the almost visceral, un-thought, unquestioned location of some of these authors, the semi-conscious groupishness that lurked in their minds and thus perhaps in "ours."

## September 11 and the "inside–outside"

The rich conceptual tool of the "inside–outside" relationship is helpful here (Sre-berny 2002). It is utilized in psychotherapy, framed by Freud (1915) as one of the three great polarities that dominate mental life and as the inner and outer psy-chological worlds by Melanie Klein (1988), in social theory, as individual–group and We–I balances by Norbert Elias (1987, 1991) and in international relations, as state-systemcentric notions of actors and attachments by Walker (1993), this pairing runs from the most micro and primary of interpersonal relations—(m)other and child—through the level of national social structures to the most macro of global system processes. These are not to be seen as differing spatial "levels" of analysis, but rather as structuring imaginaries that simultaneously compete for our identification. While their focus moves outward from the indi-vidual's inner psychological world to the actual dynamics of the global state system, I do not imply a hierarchy of significance in either direction. Rather, I use them to explore the discursive structures of some journalistic responses post-September 11. This foundational pair helps to problematize overly binary structures and allows an analysis of shifting boundaries—discursive, political, imaginary—through which the inside and outside are configured at particular his-torical conjunctures.

A powerful strand of psychotherapeutic thinking and post-Kleinian object relations takes the self as foundationally constituted through imaginative encounters with the other. Intersubjective understanding is built in the baby's experiential, affective encounters with the (m)other, generating powerful feel-ings of love and hate managed only by splitting them off from the self and reducing them to good or bad objects—the bad mother, bad breast, paranoid–schizoid position. With good enough (m)othering, a more mature posi-tion, that of the depressive, develops in which bad parts of the self are reintegrated, clearer boundaries are established between self and other, and a richer more ambivalent understanding is reached.

But trauma can produce a regression to the earlier psychological position. To paraphrase Winnicott (1971: 114), trauma implies a break in life's continuity, so that primitive defenses organize to defend against a repetition of "unthinkable anxiety" or a return of the acute confusion that might disintegrate the nascent ego structure. Thus, one response to trauma might be regression to an earlier less integrated psychological stage. The paranoid–schizoid defenses include excessive splitting, omnipotent thinking, and denial. All hostility/badness is offloaded on to the other. Bush's early political rhetoric readily invites such a reading as can the US government and media's refusal to have any sense of the anger and hurt that led to September 11 and the difficulty of even entertaining the question "Why do they hate us?" Hence, one of the central outcomes of September 11 was to draw a line, not this time in the sand but in our minds—between us and them, we and they. Additionally, the sense of global terror was induced partly with the sense that the world's only superpower, the biggest and strongest, was suddenly seen as vulnerable, creating high anxiety for all.

Many writers noted the crude binaries that were rapidly (re-)established. Some focused particularly on the constructions of collectivities. For example, Edward Said wrote about post-September 11 journalism and its wish to project American "unity":

> There really is a feeling being manufactured by their media and the government that a collective "we" exists and that "we" all act and feel together, as witnesssed by such perhaps unimportant surface phenom-ena as flag-flying and the use of the collective "we" by journalists in describing events all over the world in which the US is involved. We bombed, we said, we decided, we acted, we feel, we believe, etc., etc. Of course, this has only marginally to do with the reality, which is far more complicated and far less reassuring.
>
> (Said 2001)

Elias (1991) moved from the family environment into the wider social field, while echoing the impossibility of conceiving of an individual separate from the social environment. Two elements of his theory are relevant here. One is that the balance between we-identities and I-identities alters over social-historical time. The preoccupation with the experience of the single isolated adult individual emerges out of the European civilizing process from the Renaissance and I-identities gain in strength and significance in the processes of individualization (1991). Elias himself suggested (1991: 197–9) that one way of tracking down these changes was through language use, "especially the way in which pronoun functions are symbolically represented as different stages of language develop-ment"; thus the use of "we" and "I" are indications of the shifting balance toward greater detachment, which then tips over, in Elias' terms, to "the *homo clausus* of the 'we-less I'."

But he also recognized that the content and definition—the figurations—of the "we" may change over an individual lifetime in the life-process:

> One's sense of personal identity is closely connected with the "we" and "they" relationships of one's group, and with one's position within those units of which one speaks as "we" and "they." Yet the pronouns do not always refer to the same people. The figurations to which they currently refer can change in the course of a lifetime, just as any person does him-self. This is true not only of all people considered separately, but of all

groups and even of all societies. Their members universally say "we" of themselves and "they" of other people, but they may say "we" and "they" of different people as time goes by.

(quoted in Mennell 1992: 265)

Identity is conscious awareness by members of belonging to a group and implies some degree of reflection, articulation, emotional connection, sharing commonalities and difference from others. This might change over time as long-term increases in the scale and complexity of social interdependence produce more complex layers of we-image in people's habitus. Significantly, "habitus and identification, being related to group membership, are always—and in the modern world where people belong to groups within groups within groups—multilayered" (Mennell 1994: 177).

Elias offered an account of processes of identification which links micro- and macro-level processes. He argued that the long-term trend in the development of human society has been toward larger and larger networks of interdependent people organized in more and more interlocking layers, the essence of the civilizing process. In a globalized environment this is clearly seen in the emergence of a growing global consciousness, cross-border networks of affiliation, new social movements, and multiple transnational communities. Globalization processes challenge a society-bound sociology and increase the spatial imaginary of our encounters with others. But the anxiety and risk involved in all encounters with others are also potentially increased. More encounters are face-to-face through increased tourism, travel, migration, but much also remains highly mediated. The communication circuit of postmodern culture

> restructures the local/global intersection, and hence our experience of otherness . . . interpersonal communication is projected into larger national and global spaces. Postmodern culture creates new possibilities as regards the extensional links between self and other: immersion in the other, and particularly fantasized aspects of the other, is continually invoked and negotiated through the key role of media stimulation.
>
> (Elliott 1996: 28–9)

Walker (1993) also utilized the spatial metaphor of the "inside–outside" in relation to the nation-state system. This level can be seen at work in at least two ways in relation to September 11. One is the peculiar nature of the actors, the "terrorists," who cannot be readily configured within the nation-state system and whose use of violence and implied politics pose a challenge to the very nature of that system. This of course produced the confusion about how to name the response to the event, given that "war" can only be declared against a state. The second way was in the instant synechdochic collapse of the entire world, or the global system, into America as its heart. Thus, an attack on the US was also an attack on "us" in Britain, as suggested in a speech by Prime Minister Tony Blair.

## Issues of pronounciation: who do "we" think "we" are?

Keeping these varied constructions of the "inside–outside" in mind, what follows is a detailed commentary on three texts. The first two are by well-known British writers, white and middle-class. The third is by the *Observer*'s editorial staff. The *Guardian* included a wide range of voices, to which I cannot do justice here. I am being deliberately, even crudely, heuristically selective. Further analysis might excavate how "typical" these positions were and how much they were counter-pointed by other writers, for example, Faisal Bodhi and Ziauddin Sardar, who offered perspectives from within British Islam. These writers are not regular columnists but pen one-off think pieces that are published on a page headed "Commentary."

Martin Amis is the author of many novels including *The Information* and *London Fields*, a recent autobiography *Experience*, and a collection of writing, *The War against Cliché*. He published an article on September 18 (Amis 2001) en-titled "Letter from London," that played with Alistair Cooke's "Letter from America," the long-running BBC radio weekly talk. The article immediately invoked some far-off unnamed recipient, presumably the US itself. Amis started with the change brought about by the second plane. Before that, it was simply "the worst aviation disaster in history." But the second plane, "galvanized with malice, and wholly alien . . . meant the end of everything." And he continued: "for us, its glint was the worldflash of a coming future." Who are this "us"? City-dwellers? Britons? Westerners, thus eliding the invitation of the title? Amis then recounted in detail the events of the morning, overstating the perpetrators' intentionality as did so many of the early commentators by underscoring that the global real-time media audience was planned and the perpetrators knew the twin towers would implode. Since he was not there, he appropriated the experience of "my wife's sister" who stood on Fifth Avenue and Eleventh Street at 8:58 am under the flight path of one of the planes and cut back to another "we," a pre-sumed modern city-dweller or airplane-spotting nerd: "We have all watched aeroplanes approach, or seem to approach a large building. We tense ourselves as the supposed impact nears, even though we are sure that this is a parallax illu-sion, and that the plane will cruise grandly on."

The twin towers "flail and kick" as they come down and Amis talked of the "demented sophistication" of the suicide killers who belonged in a different psychic category: "Clearly, they have contempt for life. Equally clearly they have contempt for death." "We should know our enemy." Here the division was not complicated, a simple binary echoing that of Bush. These people are quite unlike "us," who implicitly both love life and revere death. The stereotype of the callous Oriental who devalues life lurks dangerously close, and the bodycounts against the West are too easily forgotten in both the political rhetoric and Amis' commentary.

Then Amis slipped back to a British "we": American parents will feel their inability to protect their children, "but we will also feel it." So while the event was over there, in America, its impact shattered British parental illusions about our abilities to protect our children. We share your fate. He then allowed himself imaginings of even worse scenarios, involving biological, chemical, and nuclear weapons. The slip back into binary processing summoned up our own paranoid tendencies.

He talked of how difficult it would be for Americans to realize that they are hated, since "being right and being good support the American self to an almost tautologous degree" and an adaptation of national character was needed. This sounded like the criticism of a close friend, as perhaps only a Brit can say to a Yank, the patronizing hierarchy of colonialism.

However, "on the other side," reflexively acknowledged in the phrase "the world suddenly feels bipolar," even more fundamental change was required: "We would have to sit through a renaissance and a reformation, and then await an enlightenment. And we're not going to do that." This proclaimed a crude and obvious Eurocentrism, with the assumption that "they" represent the entire Muslim world that needs to replicate the Western historical process. The Briton was safely camped back in "the US-led side," which did not have the patience to wait for change over there. So his rhetorical "what are we to do?" was given a clear answer: "violence must come; America must have catharsis," thus appearing both empathetic and justificatory. But "we would hope that the response will be, above all, non-escalatory." Here, the "we" is really "he," his own opinion which appears for the first time in the first person, a kind of Eliasian reversal. Did speaking as "I" simply feel too lonely? Was the "we" a retreat into some kind of collective security? Amis actually offered a novel idea, that the Afghanis not be bombarded with missiles but with consignments of food, a practice that was indeed followed during the Afghan war, even if the contents were ready meals for GIs and not the rice that Afghanis eat.

In the final paragraph, Amis then suggested that "our best destiny, as planetary cohabitants," was the development of "species consciousness—something over and above nationalisms, blocs, religions, ethnicities." Amis tried to apply this: "Thinking of the victims, the perpetrators, and the near future, I felt species grief, then species shame, then species fear." Thus, in a literary but convoluted manner, Amis finally addressed the very nature of collectivities and what "we" all share in common, and he did so in a voice that sounded much like Elias' civilizational reach extending over old boundaries. To do this, Amis detoured through at least eleven, ambiguous usages of "we," that in itself made his piece interesting.

Deborah Moggach is also a prolific novelist whose titles include *To Have and To Hold*, *Tulip Fever* and *Final Demand*. Her piece (Moggach 2001) was entitled "Cares of the world: how should individuals respond at a time of crisis?"

Already in her first sentence, instead of the individuals of the title, an uncertain groupishness was invoked: "In these strange times, we've all become hypochondriacs, charting our symptoms day by day." Overly dramatic, instead of drawing her reader in, this triggers the response of "no, we have not." In a three-page article she used "we" no less than 26 times (let alone "our" and other derivatives) in often vague invocations of audience segments to be inferred from the sentence or line of argument. For example, "We're all caught up in the same narrative and we're learning together—both about our own psyches and about things of which a few weeks ago we were entirely ignorant." If this was supposed to invoke the nation, it presumed that "we" knew little before about Islam, or Middle East politics, thus constructing the national audience as essentially Christian and white. There was little sense of a multicultural nation.

A similar tone was struck in the next paragraph: "We're stupefied by the bizarre nature of it all—for instance, that somebody who can't spell penicillin can send the whole of America into panic; that even with our sophisticated media and a thousand TV channels, the one thing we can't see is what we're doing in Afghanistan." Here the Other, the culprit whose name was not spoken, was an illiterate, quite opposite to his construction by Amis as a highly prescient structural engineer. But the commonality was a recourse to the simple personification that helped politically drive the adventure into Afghanistan: al-Qaeda is Osama Bin Laden (as Iraq is Saddam, as Iran was Khomeini). Synecdoche and personalization are common tropes of journalistic practice (see, for example, Zelizer's 1992 detailed exposition in relationship to the Kennedy assassination); that they run so powerfully through these individual columns shows how hard it is even for the most imaginative of writers to think "outside the frame." That individualized pieces of writing should echo the dominant political frames of the day is perhaps not a surprise; but "we" (academics?) don't often get a chance to see this happening so clearly.

Moggach's theme was about "our own helplessness," exacerbated because "we cannot identify the enemy." This seemed to echo Walker's (1993) arguments about state-centric politics: if this was not a nation acting, then what was the political animal with which we had to deal? But the helplessness was not really political; it was writers unable to write, with Moggach admitting that she too would be paralyzed if she were in the middle of a writing project. Part of her problem was the ever-shifting story:

> And the process of bereavement we've all been going through has its rhythms too: already we are different people from the stunned TV audience watching the towers explode, from the people a day later who flinched when a plane passed overhead, from the people a week later in a state of shock and sadness. We can hardly recognize those early selves, let alone the selves that preceded them and went about their daily business before September 11.

This evoked a dramatic over-identification with the events in New York, an ironic reversal of the usual tendency to dis-identify with international news events. For, as Fatma Alloo (2002: 95) writes, "How come no-one mourned the killings of thousands of people in Rwanda and Sierra Leone? We need to mourn collectively at every step of atrocities and not just when it happens to America."

What was interesting in Moggach was that the ties that bind "us" were not articulated but presumed, a simplistic elision into Westerners, English-speakers, metropolitan city-dwellers, middle-class, white. And again, if "we" was multicultural Britain, then how sustainable was the presumption that "we" were more moved by this event than by the numerous other violent episodes happening around the world during this period?

The risk of contemporary life particularly upset Moggach, and so the piece shifted gear to the personal: "we went to a cinema in Piccadilly only to find that it was full. So we changed our plans and went to another." There had been rumors of an attack on London, and the chance and randomness of modern life was suddenly acutely felt but almost immediately denied: "fanatics need hold no terror for us because it's always been like this. Ultimately they are as helpless as we are. Chance can conspire against us, but it can also save our lives." No political rationale for the events of September 11 was entertained, and now its nature as a motivated act was also erased. Acts of nature, acts of fanatics, were all incoherently random. "And in these peculiar and most interesting days, perhaps there's a comfort in that." An odd kind of fatalism settled in, one more in tune with fundamentalist teleology than modernist sentiment, a reduction to the helplessness described in the text.

The third and last text was an editorial comment from the *Observer*, the *Guardian's* Sunday embodiment, which produced a special supplement "9/11 six months on" (*Observer* 2002).

Again, "we" was used 12 times in a short column. The article began: "The moment the first plane hit the first tower we wanted to know: Why had this happened? What would the future bring? Who was safe?" But exactly who experienced this epistemophilic drive? All Westerners? All Britons? All *Observer* readers? The *Observer* staff? Clearly the invitation was that the readers of this issue read themselves into this position.

But the column recognized the passing of time and the fading urgency of the questions. "Because the center held. Things did not fall apart. Chaos was not unleashed upon the world" (with obvious waves toward Yeats, Achebe, the Bible).

The powerful fear that gripped "us" in mid-September subsided. And "our" world was not altered so radically:

> We are not at war. Bombs are not exploding on the streets of British cities. There is no blackout. There are no no-go zones. We go to work, we go out, we go home, we take holidays, we sleep and we eat. And when we look out of the window we can see, with our own eyes, what appears to be a simple truth. Life as we know it did not end on September 11.

This was a fascinating paragraph for a number of reasons. At the time of its writing, some 200 Royal Marines were based in Afghanistan, a fact noted lower down on the very same page. And while perhaps not formally at war, the Western military machine was still very much involved in violent incidents inside

Afghanistan. Because we Britons were safe in our cities, that did not make the Afghans safe in theirs; not declaring this a war, politically or discursively, allowed for weasel maneuvers. There was also accumulating evidence that British Muslims felt less at ease than before September 11, yet their experience did not seem to be factored into this account. From a different tack, the economic downturn, rising unemployment, and negative impact on aviation and travel since September 11 raised doubt as to whether or not all middle-class *Observer* readers were in work or taking holidays. And yet there emerged an important distinction between the early rhetoric surrounding the event and a more tempered perspective now, six months later, underscored in a critical recognition of "the dramatic extension of American military might across the globe."

The over easy elision of all Britons into the social and economic mores of *Observer* readers was harder to swallow. Indeed, further down the column, recognition was made of "subtle . . . changes to our culture, our politics, our lifestyles" yet what these changes are was not clarified or explored. The column ended by suggesting that "the questions we were asking [Britons? *Observer* journalists? Middle-class *Observer* readers?] six months ago—about Islam [are no readers Muslim?], security, the law, globalization, poverty, business, America, international finance—are as important now as they were then. And the answers are more important than ever." To that one might add many other important questions, about ethical foreign policy, new strategies for the Middle East, the global arms race, or Britain's role in Europe *vis-à-vis* the United States.

## To conclude

The importance of the Amis and Moggach pieces is the sense they gave of ordinary responses to events. Oddly, if each had been written in the first person, there would have been less to say about them; it is precisely the claims to shared experience made through their shifting use of "we" that was problematic. Their very rawness and immediacy provided a powerful indication of the way discourses about the self and feelings are imbricated with hegemony and of how political discourses are taken up in private imaginings, here made public. If regular fact-based journalism helps configure and confirm our views of the world, the Comments pages filled by writers showed the extent to which these views were taken up. In this sense, Rorty (1989) is correct to point us to a wider range of voices, including the fictional, that all partake of a conversation about the nature of politics; it is also rather ironic that two novelists, who in their fictional work summon up the contingency of social life, seem to inhabit a far more rigidified socioscape in their personal voices.

There is a contradiction between the demand for a more affective public sphere, or one that better balances head and heart in human affairs, and a quick dismissal of its content. It was positive for the *Guardian* to solicit and publish such writing, and indeed its Comments pages remain relatively open and discursive. The authors too took risks in publishing such raw material. Being critical about such texts was a way of taking them seriously and accepting their role in a more open universe of journalistic forms. It seems important to accept the validity of affect but also challenge its origins.

In all cases, the act of splitting off refused a relational politics. For Amis and Moggach, the "other" was fanatical, mad, "evil" but nothing to do with "us." Elias, by contrast, increasingly privileged the "I" over the "we." It seems that in times of trauma, there is a powerful need to invoke the "we," to reclaim trust and build attachment. In a somewhat similar vein Sennett (1998: 136–8) has called it "the dangerous pronoun" and describes how the "we" of attachment to community can also become the defensive weapon for self-protection. Additionally, Elias recognized the shifting "others" that a culture and individuals experience over the course of time, even simultaneously. Both writers moved back and forth through a register of "we" constructions, multiple yet inexplicitly articulated connections to others.

The particular nature of September 11 summoned up the ambivalences of the nation-state system and its difficulties in fully addressing non-state actors. Over time, the over-identification with America/New York also gave way to a more detached and critical discussion, with different national interests and political cultures recovering their voice. Indeed, in Britain, the political environment in the early spring of 2002 was one of growing anti-American sentiment, a long way from the universalization of American grief of only six months before. The *Observer*'s position reclaimed the British audience, albeit in a problematic construction of its own.

The discursive structuring of affect and attachment implied an ethics about what was allowed to happen to others and to us. This suggests that Bauman's challenge remains

> a post-modern ethics would be one that readmits the Other as a neighbour, as the close-to-hand-*and*-mind, into the hard core of the moral self . . . an ethics that restores the autonomous moral significance of proximity; an ethics that recasts the Other as the crucial character in the process through which the moral self comes into its own.
>
> (Bauman 1993: 84)

The challenge is one of better discrimination. These articles suggest not only the difficulty of beginning to think of "the terrorist" in this way but, more urgently perhaps, the on-going difficulty of recognizing our own neighbours, some "others" who live next door, as people with whom some things are shared but who may also have different yet equally valid constructions of the world.

The voices of Amis and Moggach might be taken to represent "our" common sense, one deeply impregnated with cultural categorizations that repeat the deep divides that Western audiences have been invited to inhabit for a very long time. The doxic, toxic truth is that "we" do think of "ourselves" as different from "them" and the content of that we/they divide remains quite fixed, and post-

September 11 even reinforced. A more ambivalent position, holding love and hate in tension rather than trying to deny one or the other, might, as Samuels (2001: 199) suggests, allow for a return of passion to politics without the fear that it would overwhelm the process.

At a different moment, in October of 1966, the brilliant Peter Brook devised a performance piece in relation to a different trauma, the Vietnam War. Performed at the Aldwych Theatre in London under the playful title US, the play was later made into a film called Tell Me Lies.[3] Fascinating and controversial, it received a huge range of responses, including one by Sulik, who wrote:

> Tell Me Lies is not really about Vietnam . . . [it] is in fact an investigation of British political attitudes, mainly middle-class ones . . . the most disturbing feature of this film, intentional or not, is that it shows orthodox pacifist feelings, the finest public expression of middle-class decency, as impotent in the face of an issue like Vietnam . . . perhaps he doesn't believe in solutions.

> (Sulik 1968: 207)

The pieces I have interrogated are not primarily about September 11 or terrorism. They are about "us" and who "we" think "we" are. This is not about resolution.

## Notes

1  I'd like to thank Gill Allard, Frank Morgan, David Paletz, Paula Saukko and Gillian Youngs for their critical engagement with drafts of this chapter. Thanks also to Barbie Zelizer and Stuart Allan for proving that the techniques and purpose of editing are not yet dead. I wish I could blame all of them for its final shape.
2  Alan Rusbridger, Editor of the Guardian, suggests that "writers—whether they be novelists, poets, or academics—can offer different perspectives. They may see larger truths, they may have more time in which to reflect or think, they may have a wealth of historical or political research to draw on . . . All this is no substitute for conventional reporting and analysis, but it did give a different texture to our coverage, which seems to have been widely appreciated" (personal correspondence, April 12, 2002).
3  So called because of one of its crescendoing refrains (which I can still hear in my mind's ear): "so coat my eyes with butter, / Fill my ears with silver, / Stick my legs in plaster, / Tell me lies about Vietnam."

## References

Alloo, F. (2002) The events of 11 September 2001 and Beyond, in Forum, International Journal of Feminist Politics, 4 (1): 95–6.

Amis, Martin (2002) Letter from London, Guardian, www.guardian.co.uk/Archive/Article/0,4273,4259170,00.html, September 18.

Bauman, Z. (1993) Postmodern Ethics, Oxford: Blackwell.

Blackman, L. and Walkerdine, V. (2001) Mass Hysteria, London: Palgrave.

Boltanski, L. (1999) Distant Suffering, Cambridge: Cambridge University Press.

Brook, P., Canna, D., Hunt, A., Jacobs, S., Kustow, M., Mitchell, A., and Peaslee, R. (1968) *The Book of US*, Playscript 9, London: Calder and Boyars.

Dayan, D. and Katz, E. (1992) *Media Events: The Live Broadcasting of History*, Cambridge, MA: Harvard University Press.

Elias, N. (1987) *Involvement and Detachment*, Oxford: Basil Blackwell.

Elias, N. (1991) *The Society of the Individuals*, Oxford: Basil Blackwell.

Elliot, A. (1996) *Subject to Ourselves*, Cambridge: Polity Press.

Freud, S. (1915) Instincts and their vicissitudes, in *On Metapsychology*, Penguin Freud Library, Penguin Books, 1984, 11: 105–38.

*Guardian* (2001) September 11, A *Guardian Special*, October.

Klein, M. (1988) *Envy and Gratitude*, Virago Press.

Lifton, R. J. (1967) *Death in Life: Survivors of Hiroshima*, New York: Random House.

Mellencamp, P. (1990) TV time and catastrophe: or beyond the pleasure principle of television, in P. Mellencamp (ed.) *Logics of Television*, Bloomington, IN: Indiana University Press: 240–66.

Mennell, S. (1992) *Norbert Elias*, Dublin: University College Dublin Press.

Mennell, S. (1994) The formation of we-images: a process theory, in C. Calhoun (ed.) *Social Theory and the Politics of Identity*, Oxford: Blackwell: 175–97.

Miller, T. (2002) September 2001, *New Media and Society*, 3 (1) February: 4.

Moggach, D. (2001) Cares of the world: how should individuals respond at a time of crisis? *Guardian*, www.guardian.co.uk/Archive/Article/0,4273,4286332,00.html, October 27.

*Observer* (2002) Out of the ashes, 9/11 six months on, eight-page special, www.guardian.co.uk/Archive/Article/0,4273,4286332,00.html, March 10.

Prince, R. (1999) *The Legacy of the Holocaust*, New York: Other Press.

Rapping, E. (2000) US talk shows, feminism and the discourse of addiction, in A. Sreberny and L. Van Zoonen (eds) *Gender, Politics and Communication*, New Jersey: Hampton Press: 223–50.

Robins, K. (1994) Forces of consumption: from the symbolic to the psychotic, *Media, Culture and Society*, 16: 449–68.

Rorty, R. (1989) *Contingency, Irony, Solidarity*, Cambridge: Cambridge University Press.

Said, E. (1997) *Covering Islam*, New York: Vintage Books.

Said, E. (2001) Suicidal ignorance, *Al-Ahram Weekly Online*, November 15–21, issue 560, www.ahram.org.eg/weekly/2001/560/op2.htm.

Samuels, A. (2001) *Politics on the Couch*, London: Profile Books.

Sennett, Richard (2001) *The Corrosion of Character*, New York: W. W. Norton and Co.

Silverstone, R. (1994) *Television and Everyday Life*, London: Routledge.

Sreberny, A. (2002) Globalization and me, in J. M. Chan and B. I. Mcintyre (eds) *In Search of Boundaries*, Connecticut: Ablex Publishing.

Sulik, B. (1968) Search for commitment, in P. Brook *et al.*, *The Book of US*, London: Calder and Boyars: 206–7.

Tester, K. (1997) *Moral Culture*, London: Sage.

Tester, K. (2001) *Compassion, Morality and the Media*, Buckingham: Open University Press.

Walker, R. B. J. (1993) *Inside/Outside: International Relations as Political Theory*, Cambridge: Cambridge University Press.

Wardi, D. (1992) *Memorial Candles*, London: Routledge.

Winnicott, D. W. (1971) *Playing and Reality*, London: Pelican Books.

Zelizer, B. (1992) *Covering the Body: The Kennedy Assassination, the Media, and the Shaping of Collective Memory*, Chicago, IL: University of Chicago.

# 13

# JOURNALISM AND POLITICAL CRISES IN THE GLOBAL NETWORK SOCIETY

## Ingrid Volkmer

It is widely recognized that the events of September 11 created new international political alliances. At the same time, given the media coverage of the attacks and the subsequent war in Afghanistan, questions are being raised about whether a new "world news order" is similarly emerging in the context of a changed *Weltanschauung*, a philosophy of life, of modernity.

It can be argued that the attacks created the first worldwide political crisis of the twenty-first century. Their impact on the established worldwide political balance of the twentieth century has been astonishing, as has been the traumatic destabilization of the sense of security previously felt by Western nations. There is now a heightened awareness of the transnational political conflicts raging across the global arena, each with its own configuration of center and periphery. All of these and related factors have challenged the dominant worldview of the West, in part by bringing previously unknown vulnerabilities to the surface. All of a sudden, it seems, the world has become a "common place," a "single community" (Robertson 1992: 81). Terrorism has entered the global age, and thus it is no longer tied to "crisis regions" or to a particular national "space." Further attacks may happen anywhere and anytime, indeed the particularism of ostensibly isolated events may be transforming into terrorism on a global scale. Alongside the economic, political, and cultural structures at stake, however, a new layer of reality is being re-consolidated *vis-à-vis* differentiated, heterogeneous, and decentralized processes of globalization (Robertson 1992) and "risk" (Beck 1992).

The implications of the September 11 attacks continue to resonate far beyond the national borders of the United States. Few would dispute that the atrocity was an event of global proportions. It seems that from now on, terrorist attacks will occupy center stage in media coverage, their significance re-articulating otherwise familiar distinctions between particular and universal contexts. Central to this process has been the role of the news media. Political journalism has not only had to redefine conventional formats of domestic and foreign reporting, but also—given the rise of a global information society—to reassess new responsibilities for establishing a more globally oriented political discourse.

When examining the changing dynamics of journalism in global terms, it becomes apparent that three political themes have been particularly salient over recent years: ecology, human rights, and democracy. These grand themes of global political discourse were each aligned, in turn, with seemingly universal values, beliefs, and ideals that were held to be self-evidently pertinent to all regions of the globe. Precisely how their meaning was negotiated in different national contexts, however, was a question of how the global was transformed into the local. Tensions between the global and the local frequently revolved around issues of authenticity, and who had the right to define it. Allegations of human rights violations in China, or ecological catastrophes in South America, had the potential to affect government policy and political activism worldwide, but there was no guarantee that this would be the case. The promise of a truly global citizenship to be engendered through an increasingly globalized media infrastructure has yet to be realized.

The events of September 11, some commentators have argued, possessed the potential not only to create the basis for a new sense of global space, but also to help bring about an enhanced network of communication. Journalism, in this equation, was charged with the responsibility of contributing to the establishment of a worldwide discourse that would be sensitive to the different perspectives arising from local situations across the "network society" (Castells 1996). These same commentators, not surprisingly, have claimed that the failure to bring about this transformation was attributable in part to forms of news coverage which reaffirmed first world dualisms. Arguably chief amongst these dualisms was the distinction between foreign and domestic news, a distinction conventionalized against the backdrop of the nation-state.

War and crisis journalism have historically played a major role in the process of nation building (Hoehne 1977; Allen and Seaton 1999). Whereas the war in Vietnam, for example, introduced new dimensions to international reporting—courtesy of television news, it became known as the "living room war"—it was the war in the Persian Gulf in 1991 that has arguably had an even greater impact. The dawning age of globalization had brought with it new broadcast technologies (such as the famous "flyaway" satellite dish, used by CNN journalist Peter Arnett) and re-invented the familiar forms and practices of war reporting. Moreover, associated with the conflict was a tremendous expansion of news space, such as through the advent of so-called "rolling" coverage that provided constant updates in breaking news formats. The daily news flow also included "direct coverage from the enemy camp" (Halliday 1999: 129). It was restricted, clean, pool-based reporting that was being "simulcast" via CNN (that is, images were simultaneously aired in the US and internationally, though with a clear focus on the US audience; see also Kaplan 2002).

236

This phenomenon of transborder "simulcasting" of crisis journalism inaugurated a new era of war journalism. Whereas war reporting had previously been defined largely within the terms of the nation-state, the international reach of the program strategies operationalized through CNN-I's unique global satellite platforms promptly established the network as a global news leader in world crises. Through its use of international outlets—even on the territory of Iraq at the time—CNN recast the principles of war coverage (Nieman Reports 2001; see also Zelizer 1992). So-called "foreign" and "national" news flows were no longer easily distinguishable. However, since the time of the Gulf War, the international news infrastructure has changed even more dramatically. Today, around 400 satellites, with C- and K-band broadcast capacity, are lined up across the equator, carrying signals no longer "in thirty minutes" around the world (as a CNN promotional slogan stated during the Gulf War) but via the Internet instantaneously. Moreover, signals are increasingly diversified, providing transnational "point-to-point" and "point-to-multipoint" live news transmission.

Not only do the lines between domestic and foreign journalism diminish in such a global news infrastructure, but the media's role as "actors" or influential factors in "media diplomacy" (Gilboa 2000) changes as well. In essence the media become "reflectors," that is, they act as reflectors of a global reality which is otherwise inaccessible and yet which increasingly shapes the context for the identity of political communities within a new global public sphere. In this new global public sphere, the "zones of relevance, as key factors of the perception of conflict," are divided into close and remote zones and are increasingly separated from geographical locations, where proximity as a key factor in news coverage seems to disappear (Cohen, Adoni, and Bantz 1990: 36). As reflectors, the media become the independent variable even in crisis situations, re-formatting political crises and shaping the rationale for subsequent political action.

This proximity disappeared on a global scale on September 11. The crash of the second airplane, watched by a worldwide audience via the "worldstage" of CNN with its real-time images of the burning towers, created a global community. In my view, the intensity of images formed a network of human beings, linked by immediate shock in reaction to the image of tragedy but also by the painful helplessness of being forced into the observer role. Breaking news, otherwise an attractive program format with a guarantee of high ratings, was degraded into a real-time landscape of horror and destruction, in which journalists themselves were somehow trapped, eye-witnessing the inexplicable and attempting to grasp rational explanations for a surrealistic scenario. Indeed, it was the role of the media, of CNN international, and not of politicians and the government, which had the burden of not only telling the story to the world as it happened, but also of providing crucial information on public safety, particularly in light of fears about further attacks elsewhere in the world. Based on the media coverage, other world capitals declared a state of emergency, reacting to the media's reflecting role. It appeared as if the world stood still for hours.

However, as the French philosopher Paul Virilio (2001) remarked, the role of the media in providing a breaking news worldstage for the September 11 events was highly critical. Through the extensive coverage of breaking news, and the framing of terrorism into an "event," Virilio argued, the media became collaborators with terrorism. That is to say, they became complicit by providing this worldstage which magnified, in turn, the political impact of the attacks. Indeed, in future this very process of reflection might even become a calculated factor in worldwide—sarcastically phrased—"prime time" terrorism. Whereas more traditional notions of breaking news, such as the student protests in Beijing, or the first attacks on Baghdad, can be viewed within a conventional international political framework, live broadcasting of terrorist attacks fundamentally alters the strategic calculus of terrorists.

In the immediate aftermath of September 11, an almost McLuhanian "global village"-type "implosion" (McLuhan 1964) shifted the global "zone of relevance" (Cohen, Adoni, and Bantz 1999). Notions of a "horizontal" global public sphere were rapidly giving way to the pull of "vertical" (and thus hierarchical) public spheres aligned with nation-states. In the US, the national public sphere centered on a new polarization, which even called into question its own ideal of the multinational society. "Why do they hate us so much?" became the dominant question in subsequent days, not only in the Boston Globe (September 16, 2001), but also in other newspapers across the US. Although the question seemed to focus on the perception of the US in Arab nations, it also illuminated obvious gaps across different religious and cultural worldviews. Instead of reflecting the question in a global discourse, in alliance with other media worldwide, which would have provided a widened spectrum of perspectives, it instead appeared that the question was one of a particular religious worldview. For some days, the clash between the "West" and the "East" appeared to be deeper than ever.

Samuel Huntington's (1996) controversial thesis regarding "The clash of civilizations" routinely served in the media in both the US and Europe as a justification of sorts for the otherwise inexplicable—"us," being the enlightened, modern, Christianized West, "they" being the anti-modern, anti-democratic Islam. It soon appeared that this new polarization, discerned along the lines of violent fundamentalism in otherwise peaceful religions, immediately triggered a spiral of further violence and intimidation across the country. The distinction of "us" and "them" as the major media theme contributed, in my opinion, to numerous assaults of Muslims (despite the fact many had sought to publicly reaffirm their identity as US citizens). Similar occurrences took place in other countries. It is in this context that it is important to recall the "chilling discovery," as it was often characterized in the news coverage, that the people behind the September 11 attacks were in many respects more indicative of an "us" than they were of a "them."

One media profile after another suggested that several of these individuals had been enjoying the comforts of a middle-class suburban life, that they were to some degree multilingual cosmopolitans, frequently commuting between continents, even shopping for Western goods in duty-free shops. It has been reported that they orchestrated the attacks by communicating via e-mail from Internet-cafés in the US and worldwide. They tended to be educated, some having studied at well-known Western universities, had visa status in the US, and evidently appreciated much of what Western lifestyles have to offer. What lies implicit in several of these media profiles of the suspects is arguably a new side effect of globalization, that is, a new cultural dialectical space between "Jihad" and "McWorld" (Barber 1996). From this space, new political identities are emerging. As Barber (ibid.: 5) argued, "Jihad not only revolts against but abets McWorld, while McWorld not only imperils but re-creates and reinforces Jihad. They produce their contraries and need one another." The almost cartoon-like unidimensional polarization scheme of "us" and "them" reiterated by some journalists was thus deeply misleading. It helped to mystify the otherwise brutally clear calculation made by the terrorists.

From a global perspective, the theme of the subsequent weeks can be described as a further regionalization of the events, mainly limited to the World Trade Center attacks. The attack on the Pentagon and the forced airplane crash in Pennsylvania slowly began to disappear from public discourse, which today remains the case internationally. This was both because the World Trade Center events were signified through strong visual images and because New York was a substantial element of the "lifeworld" of new global communities. I would describe the latter as "transnational cosmopolitan classes," that is, opinion leaders who belong to a new global public.

Whereas in the first weeks, the US media served as a co-orientation source for international coverage on further details of the investigation, European media were becoming energized by a new solidarity with the US. Many European journalists picked up the "us" and "them" theme and slowly began to reconstruct what had happened using now familiar local or regional coordinates. German newspapers, for example, expressed political and emotional solidarity proclaiming on September 12, "Wir sind alle New Yorker" ("We are all New Yorkers"), referring to President Kennedy's famous phrase "Ich bin ein Berliner," as a message of unshaken solidarity for the then divided city of Berlin. However, in the following days, the polarization of "us" and "them" slowly resurfaced in national public spheres, now often being reframed by the metatext "war on terrorism," in which the frontline was defined as "us," the allied nations in the fight against terrorism, and "them" being, in President Bush's phrase, "those nations that harbor terrorists."

Furthermore, familiar local, domestic contexts were being used to integrate the global events in more and more local discourses. In Spain, for example, the events of September 11 were brought into the context of local ETA terrorism. In Britain, "regionalization" consisted of interpreting the events in light of the strength of the US–UK political alliance, the so-called "special relationship." In France, "we" and "they" were rephrased in light of a long history of terrorism from Islamic fundamentalism from northern Africa. In India, the constant conflict with

Pakistan was now viewed in a new international context, that of the new solidarity between Pakistan and the US. It seemed that the conventional filters of local and global, of foreign and national, not only narrowed the global scope but also created new political tensions worldwide.

In the US, a Project for Excellence in Journalism (2002) study based on a survey of four newspapers, nightly TV news broadcasts and three morning TV shows revealed that the first weeks after September 11 were dominated by factual journalism developing the themes of the "potential war on terrorism," "attacks and rescue efforts," "personal connections" stories, and responses by "citizen, community, and state." By November, the coverage had shifted to more analysis but also speculation and opinion, based on the fact that access to sources had became increasingly difficult as the war newsgathering process gained momentum. Forms of so-called "patriotic" journalism developed in these niches of speculation and opinion. It is argued that this journalistic approach was caused, to some degree, by the information policy of the US government, which restricted access to information sources in relation to the unfolding war in Afghanistan. However, viewed from a perspective of a global news infrastructure, where not only simulcasting strategies but also domestic newscasts distribute potentially sensitive information worldwide, this information policy may be seen as a reaction to the increased globalization processes of news flow in times of political crisis.

In the critical media debate on "patriotic" journalism, it is claimed that these restrictions in a new era of information flow caused the media to turn inwards and to create an emotionally loaded news vacuum around evolving issues. As Robert J. Samuelson, a journalist himself, claims: "Our new obsession with terrorism will make us its unwitting accomplices . . . we will become (and have already become) merchants of fear" (*Washington Post*, quoted in Nieman Reports 2001: 21). Others claim that journalists "have engaged in self-censorship or pressure on peers" (McMasters 2002). Others argued that this journalistic climate was shaped by the steady decline in international reporting across the news media spectrum, while some singled out for criticism "the growing xenophobia within the television news business" (Bamford 2001: 21). As Bamford stated

> foreign bureaus provided only a third as many minutes of coverage for the evening newscasts on ABC, CBS and NBC in 2000 (1,382) than they did in 1989 (4,032), which was a high point. At the same time, foreign news bureaus are closing down at an alarming rate. ABC went from seventeen 15 years ago to seven in 2001.
>
> (Bamford 2001: 21)

Besides these types of cutbacks, it seems that in many cases freelancers and local journalists were "playing a crucial role in Central Asia in ensuring the world understands these events" (Thayer 2001: 28).

However, whereas in the Gulf War CNN remained the only information source on the scene, a variety of new transnational news channels have been launched in the last decade, all of which are changing what counts as foreign journalism.

## New global (micro-) spheres

In crises situations, when live and on-location coverage is required despite the international cutbacks of US media, authentic angles are in particularly high demand. These new media outlets quickly gain a fresh status in the global news flow. It can be argued that in future they will increasingly create counter-flows to mainstream news coverage—internationally and domestically—and create "micro-spheres" in an extra-societal, global public space. These micro-spheres establish a new dimension in the global news flow, which not only refines domestic and foreign news in national journalism during times of crisis but also the news angle of transnational channels, such as CNN. In the context of September 11, the Arab language news channel al-Jazeera provided such a counter-flow internationally with great success. Whereas CNN gained tremendous popularity during the Gulf War, al-Jazeera became the media winner of the War in Afghanistan.

Al-Jazeera, founded in 1996 as one of the transational news channels targeting Arab nations, provides such a counter-flow not only in presenting opposing views to Western societies but also even within the Arab world. Until the war in Afghanistan began, however, it was largely ignored by the Western media. Airing from the smallest, though most modernized Arab Emirate, Qatar, the channel provides critical news in the context of Arab politics in the Arab world and the Arab view of the world to Western nations. Whereas MBC (Middle East Broadcast Center), founded in 1991, another transnational Arab language channel based in London, provides a rather conservative view, al-Jazeera targets the emerging politically critical middle class in politically divided Arab countries. It employs CNN-type discursive formats, such as call-in segments that are otherwise quite uncommon in the state-controlled television of Arab nations. "In Algier's Casbah, in Cairo's slums, in the suburbs of Damascus, even in the desert tents of Bedouins with satellite dishes, the channel has become a way of life" (*New York Times*, July 4, 1999).

In the current crisis, al-Jazeera has risen almost from nowhere—in a Western viewpoint—to be a major player in the global news arena. It gained this prominence worldwide because of a news monopoly (at least in the first weeks of the war in Afghanistan) ensured by the Taliban regime. As Zednick argued:

Suddenly, al-Jazeera was not only delivering the news to its 35 million viewers, including 150,000 in the US, it was telling the world's top story to billions of people around the planet via international media that had little choice but to use al-Jazeera's pictures. It was not simply covering

241

the war, it became an important player in the global battle for public opinion.

(Zednick 2002)

Al-Jazeera is now expanding internationally through cooperation agreements (with ABC, BBC, and German public broadcaster ZDF), as well as via satellite distribution, such as in the UK, Indonesia, and Malaysia (translated into Malay) (ibid.). In response, CNN has launched an Arabic language website— cnn.arabic.com—in order to counter al-Jazeera's political influence in the Arab world. In so doing, it has added another layer of news flow within this global micro-sphere.

In recent years, a variety of other new transnational channels have been launched, such as Thai Global Network, operated by Royal Thai Army Television and distributed by satellite to 144 countries worldwide. The channel reaches around 350 million viewers worldwide and includes entertainment, information, and news. In the US this channel reaches large ex-patriot Thai audiences, especially in California and New York. Besides these extra-societal channels, however, new exile national broadcasters have attempted to focus on particular audiences in their home countries in order to influence opinion leaders. One example is National Iranian Television (NITV), founded in 2000 and located in Los Angeles. NITV's goal is to influence politics in Iran by an in-flow of critical information delivered by satellite. "Just after September 22 (the editor-in-chief, I. V.) asked Iranian youth to show solidarity with the United States by carrying a candle into the streets. Thousands in Tehran complied, and hundreds were thrown in prison" (Lewis 2002: 33).

Within this new transnational news infrastructure, it becomes obvious that the terms "foreign" and "domestic" journalism are rapidly becoming obsolete. The examples of al-Jazeera and NITV reveal a new dualism of supra- and subnational journalism, creating political communities within nations. Other players in global micro-spheres are national broadcasters, who expand their audience by transnational satellite distribution of primarily domestic programs, such as TRT International, which some years ago encouraged the political activism of right-wing Turkish communities in Germany.

Significantly, however, these new indigenous or—from a global view—nation-based news outlets are being widely ignored in the everyday news flow. This is despite the fact that they provide unique news angles. Still, it appears likely that they will be duly activated in future world crises, thereby creating dispersed micro-spheres of discourse worldwide. In this sense, national and transnational news media are converging into a new context, one which relocates the vertical national viewpoint within national borders into a somewhat horizontal global angle. Several far-reaching ramifications for the role of journalism are just starting to become apparent, and it is to them that I now turn.

## Global journalism in the sphere of mediation

In light of this converging infrastructure, it is vitally important to understand journalism as an integral element of the emergent global public sphere. As I have argued elsewhere (Volkmer 1999), from a strictly theoretical viewpoint, the (national) public and its opinion—in philosophical terminology, its reasoning and rational consensus—are no longer a substantial element of a political system of *one* society. Instead the system has been widened into a more or less autonomous global public sphere, which is complex and does not appear to have a particular order. Given the increasing development of micro-spheres, it also has neither a center nor a periphery. A message posted on a website can kick off an international news event almost in the same way as a carefully researched investigative report.

This global public sphere increasingly integrates national public spheres, thereby undermining the dualism separating domestic from foreign journalism. It may be viewed as a new political space, reaching from the sub- to the supra-national extra-societal, global community. This global public sphere can also enforce political pressure on national politics and provide a communication realm, which would otherwise not be possible on the national level (in terms of September 11, al-Jazeera's interview with Osama Bin Laden; during the Gulf War, CNN's interview with Saddam Hussein). Another example is the new type of reciprocal journalism, which uses global platforms, such as CNN's "World Report," to distribute political news from "outside" to a domestic audience. This is news that would otherwise be censored, if aired by a national broadcaster. Other examples are the numerous websites and online publications, such as those launched by Chinese ex-patriots on servers located in the US. In this way they are free to criticize Chinese politics because they have circumvented Chinese censorship. This re-mapping of discursive space from a national to an extra-societal, global context is, in my view, the key factor of global communication.

In fact, when considering the global public sphere as an enlarged political communication space, journalists may be seen to be operating within a "sphere of mediation." That is to say, they are mediating not between the state and society, as Hegel (1820/1967) used this term in conjunction with the formation of nations in Europe and the increasing political participation of an emerging citizen class, but between the nation and an extra-societal global political space. Whereas the global public sphere is strongly tied to the civil societal process in Europe (see Habermas 1991, 2000), in which the public/private dialectic is one of its key constitutive elements, the "sphere of mediation" defines a new space of political communication. In this space the public/private dialectic transforms into the dialectic of the societal/extra-societal. Moreover, under this new structuring of global and international extra-societal media, the public sphere, originally defined as a sphere of societal reasoning within one nation, is increasingly influenced by this sphere of mediation. The dialectic of the societal and extra-societal, or national and global, requires new, distinct roles for journalists as reflectors.

One could argue that the media have always operated within this "sphere of mediation." International journalism is hardly new, of course, and it has consistently played an important role in creating national identity in previous centuries. Following this argument, it is possible to suggest that, in a modern view, journalists were indeed mediators in this process of public communication. In fact, international journalism or, to be more precise, the reporting of events beyond the borders of one's own kingdom, offered the main content of the first newspapers founded in the sixteenth century in Europe. During this time, newspapers "were restricted almost exclusively to foreign news" (Stephens: 165). It was in the late seventeenth and early eighteenth centuries that newspapers in France and England, for example, began to cover "a broader range of news, cover that news with more authority, and distribute it more frequently" (ibid.: 166). The invention of new technologies in the nineteenth century, such as the telegraph, telephone, and cable (trans-Atlantic and trans-Pacific), inaugurated a new phase of foreign journalism, where the media, already to a certain degree commercialized and focused on consumer interests, were able to cover events occurring at remote locations. The emerging class of citizens, who began to participate politically, had an increased interest in political and economical news. The enhanced interest in foreign affairs was not only served by reporters based abroad but also by news agencies, such as Reuters or Agence France Presse, which operated along the lines of colonial internationalism. In this sense, international news journalism covered events in strong relation to the political entity of a nation.

Foreign journalism may be therefore viewed in this modern approach as extending the imperatives of the national public sphere internationally. This genre of journalism focused exclusively on those international regions located on the political periphery of their home countries. Communication technologies helped to support the political and commercial spheres of influence abroad; in fact, this was the major purpose of employing new technological advancements. The world wire and cable systems, for example, improved military communication as well as communication with governments of colonized countries. This modern approach to internationalization continued in a moderated form even through the first satellite decade, simply because the satellite technology did not allow other means of communication between countries. It was also as expensive as it was exclusive. News alliances were formed, such as the European Broadcasting Union (and the newspool "Eurovision"). However, foreign journalism still "mediated" international foreign events from a strictly national viewpoint.

Globalization as a paradigm of international communication became obvious in terms of political journalism in the early 1990s. Parallel to the more advanced satellite age, where individual channels could be constantly carried around the world, a new notion of this "sphere of mediation" appeared in close relation with CNN. All of a sudden, the concept of foreign journalism seemed to be challenged. Ted Turner's famous memo to CNN's news staff, in which he requested to replace the term "foreign" with "international" in news reports, seemed from today's standpoint a first sign that the conventional dualism of domestic/foreign journalism was about to be reframed. CNN invented a new form of international reporting, which extended the narrow, "national" journalistic concept by including new political contexts and enlarging the political horizon beyond a single nation-state.

CNN offered a fresh news agenda, one based on the coverage of a great variety of issues typically neglected by other channels. The launching of the program *World Report*—in which international journalists aired their angle of a story, even if it was controversial for US viewers—was unique (see Volkmer 1999). CNN's journalism thus played throughout the 1990s an important role in the global public sphere by reconfiguring journalistic styles and formats. Still, although CNN can be viewed as the leading network in the age of globalization, even the paradigm of the global "network" society (Castells 1996), its authority is increasingly open to challenge. How best to establish a global discourse, to make events from different "micro-spheres" comprehensible to everyone—these are the issues which will determine the future of crisis journalism in the global public sphere of the twenty-first century.

# References

Allen, T. and Seaton, J. (eds) (1999) *The Media of Conflict: War Reporting and Representations of Ethnic Violence*, London and New York: Zed Books, 127–46.

Bamford, J. (2001) Is the press up to the task of reporting these stories? in Nieman Reports, Nieman Foundation, 55 (4) Winter: 19–22.

Barber, B. (1996) *Jihad vs. McWorld*, New York: Ballantine Books.

Beck, U. (1992) From industrial society to risk society: questions of survival, social structure and ecological enlightenment, *Theory, Culture and Society*, 9 (1), 97–123.

Castells, M. (1996) *The Information Age: Economy, Society and Culture*, 3 volumes, Oxford: Blackwell.

Castells, M. (1998) Information technology, globalization and social development, paper prepared for the UNRISD Conference on *Information Technologies and Social Development*, Geneva, June 1998.

Cohen, A. and Adoni, H., Bantz, C. (1990) *Social Conflict and Television News*, London: Sage.

Dayan, D. and Katz, E. (1992) *Media Events: The Live Broadcasting of History*, Cambridge, MA: Harvard University Press.

Galtung, J. and Ruge, M. H. (1965) The structure of foreign news, *Journal of Peace Research*, 2: 64–91.

Gilboa, E. (2000) Mass communication and diplomacy: a theoretical framework, *Communication Theory*, 10 (3) August: 275–309.

Habermas, J. (1991, 2000) *The Structural Transformation of the Public Sphere: an Inquiry into a Category of Bourgeois Society*, Cambridge, MA: MIT Press.

Halliday, F. (1999) Manipulation and limits: media coverage of the Gulf War (1990–1), in

T. Allen and J. Seaton (eds) *The Media of Conflict: War Reporting and Representations of Ethnic Violence*, London and New York: Zed Books, 127–46.

Hegel, Georg F. (1820, 1967) *Philosophy of Right*, Oxford: Oxford University Press.

Hoehne, H. (1977) *Die Geschichte der Nachricht und ihrer Verbreiter*, Baden-Baden, Germany: Nomos.

Howard, M. (2002) What's in a name?: how to fight terrorism, *Foreign Affairs*, 81: 8–13.

Huntington, S. (1996) *The Clash of Civilizations and the Remaking of World Order*, New York: Simon and Schuster.

Kaplan, R. (2002) Notes from conversation with Rick Kaplan, President of CNN-US 1997–2000.

Lewis, M. (2002) The satellite subversives, *New York Times Magazine*, February 24: 30–5.

McLuhan, M. (1964) *Understanding Media: The Extensions of Man*, New York: McGraw-Hill.

McMasters, P. (2002) The war on journalism, www.newhumanist.com/journalism.html.

*New York Times* (1999) Arab TV gets a slant: newscasts without censorship, September, 4: 1.

Nieman Reports (2001) Coverage of journalism, Nieman Foundation for Journalism at Harvard University, 55 (4), Winter.

Project for Excellence in Journalism (2002) *Return to Normalcy? How the Media Have Covered the War on Terrorism*, New York, www.journalism.org.

Robertson, R. (1992) *Globalization: Social Theory and Global Culture*, London: Sage.

Seaton, J. (1999) The new "ethnic" wars and the media, in T. Allen and J. Seaton, *The Media of Conflict: War Reporting and Representations of Ethnic Violence*, London and New York: Zed Books: 43–63.

Stephens, M. (1988) *A History of News: From the Drum to the Satellite*, New York: Viking.

Thayer (2001) Nate freelancers' vital role in international reporting, in Nieman Reports Coverage of Journalism, The Nieman Foundation for Journalism at Harvard University, 55 (4): 28–31.

Virilio, P. (200) Phantom des Terrors, Die Gewalt im Zeitalter ihrer medialen Potenzierbarkeit, *Frankfurter Allgemeine Zeitung*, September 18.

Volkmer, I. (1999) *News in the Global Sphere: A Study of CNN and Its Impact on Global Communication*, Luton: University of Luton Press.

*Boston Globe* (2001) Why do they hate us so much?, September 16.

Zednick, R. (2002) Perspectives on war: inside Al Jazeera, *Columbia Journalism Review*, www. cjr.org/year/02/2/zednick.asp.

Zelizer, B. (1992) CNN, the gulf war and journalistic practice, *Journal of Communication*, 42 (1): 66–81.

# 14

# REPORTING UNDER FIRE

## The physical safety and
## emotional welfare of journalists

*Howard Tumber*

The September 11 attack on the twin towers and the subsequent anthrax incidents have created a growing debate and subsequent concern with what is now
termed urban war corresponding. A realization is emerging that those correspondents who covered September 11 (who may not be war correspondents) may also
need help and training in order to deal with possible post-traumatic stress disorder (PTSD).

At the same time the horrific visual representation of the death of Daniel
Pearl, the *Wall Street Journal* reporter kidnapped and then murdered in Pakistan
in March 2002, encapsulates the extreme danger for reporters working in conflict zones. It also tragically illustrates how journalists themselves have become
news.

## Background

According to the International Federation of Journalists (IFJ) 100 journalists and
media personnel were killed during 2001, the highest total for six years. The
deaths took place not only in war zones but also through targeted assassinations
and by simply being "in the wrong place at the wrong time." Seven of these
media workers were among the victims in New York on September 11, 2001, and
up to the end of December 2001, eight journalists had been killed after September 11 in Afghanistan. Furthermore, several employees of US media companies
were exposed to anthrax, including a photo editor at the *Sun* in Boca Raton,
Florida, who died from inhaling the bacterium (CPJ 2001a and b).

The 2001 IFJ report shows that the number of deaths of media personnel is
increasing. In 2000, 62 journalists were killed, while the 87 deaths recorded in
1999 were the combined outcome of conflicts in the Balkans, Sierra Leone and
Colombia. The 1999 total was second only to the 1994 toll, when wars in
Bosnia and genocide in Rwanda were primarily responsible for a sudden surge in

journalists' deaths (IFJ 2001). The majority of journalists killed are local ones targeted because of their reporting of organized crime, drugs, and arms deals. The numbers indicate that the physical safety of media workers is under increasing threat and consequently the pressure on media organizations to create a safety framework that will safeguard the lives of their employees is intensifying.

The International Code of Practice for the safe conduct of journalists, formally introduced at the News World conference in Barcelona in 2000, requires media organizations to provide risk-awareness training, social protection (i.e. life insurance), free medical treatment, and protection for freelance or part-time employees, coupled with the public authorities' respect for the rights and physical integrity of journalists and media staff (IFJ 2000). Yet it is viewed as only a start. Although this Code of Practice was accepted by some leading media organizations (such as CNN, the BBC, Reuters, and Associated Press), an industry-wide response that would enable all media workers to benefit from risk-awareness training has not yet been established. The broadcasters and agencies have kept to their pledge to extend training to all of their local stringers and "fixers," but the newspapers have not made a similar commitment so far. Furthermore, the deaths of journalists in Afghanistan are leading to more urgent demands for a better understanding of the reasons behind those deaths (Owen 2001a).

It is, however, imperative to realize that the issue of journalistic safety is a complex one. The difficulties and problems of reporting embrace a number of issues, including possible captivity, torture, death from road traffic accidents, enteric diseases, and other injuries. The prevention of some of these categories (i.e. road accidents) is more difficult than others (i.e. enteric diseases which are prevented with water purification) (Kain 2001). But the diversity of dangers in war reporting is not the only issue that complicates the issue of safety. One would expect that these dangers would occur mainly under hostile regimes and in war zones, but the problems are not confined solely to these places. Compare the September 11 attack and the war zone in Afghanistan. The conditions under which the news crews reported the war in Afghanistan were far from easy. They worked by torchlight and their vehicles came under fire as they drove towards the front line (Tomlin 2001). For some, reporting of the September 11 attack in New York was equally dangerous: *New York Daily News* photographer D. Handschuh was injured as the South Tower collapsed and had to be rescued by firefighters (CPJ 2001a).

In the cases of captivity during the Afghan war, according to reports, crowds stoned French and Pakistani journalists arrested for spying by the Taliban regime, after they were paraded in the streets of Jalalabad. Back in the US media personnel came under different attack, with media companies warning their employees that they were targets (IFJ 2001). Further fatalities occurred not only in the Afghanistan war zone but also at "home." Before the bodies of four international journalists were discovered and identified after their convoy was ambushed on a road to Kabul, the body of freelance photojournalist William Biggart was found on September 15 at Ground Zero, where he had rushed with his camera shortly after hearing about the attacks (CPJ 2001a).

The casualties are not confined to one or two areas in the world. The IFJ report identifies killings in 38 countries, including that of Martin O'Hagan, an investigative reporter who was shot by terrorists in Northern Ireland, and Mario Coelho, a campaigning editor in Brazil shot dead by a contract killer the day before he was due to testify in a criminal defamation suit (IFJ 2001).

## The changing character of international conflicts

To understand the issues surrounding the safety of journalists, definitions of the conflicts in which correspondents report need to be clarified. Although war is not a new phenomenon, it was only in the twentieth century that war became a truly mass phenomenon, covered by the media in a "serial fashion" (Carruthers 2000: 1; Owen 2001b: 1). From the end of World War II, a series of "minor wars" according to Western terminology (wars classified under a variety of labels such as revolutions, uprisings, little wars, imperfect wars) came into being (Gray 1997: 156). Conflicts such as the Gulf War, Bosnia, Rwanda, and Kosovo pose new challenges for the categorization of these conflicts.

The first category that proves problematic within the contemporary mapping of war is the distinction between "conventional/limited" war and "total war." Traditionally, the former was thought to involve only the "selected army and the uniformed few" while civilians experienced it as media audiences (Taylor 1997: 130; Carruthers 2000: 2). The concept of "total wars," on the other hand, involved the entire population and eroded the distinction between civilians and military. The emergence of "total wars" can be traced back to the 1939–45 war or even, to a lesser extent, the 1914–18 war. The mobilization of the entire population was achieved through professional armies of volunteers, mass male conscription into the armed forces, and replacing the workforce of the war industry with female workers (Taylor 1997: 130; Carruthers 2000: 1).

Progressively, however, the modern character of conflicts has created a number of paradoxes. Firstly, while the mobilization of the resources and population of an entire nation since World War II may be a rare phenomenon at least for the Western world (e.g. the Gulf War, The Falklands), the technological progress related to the mass media has transformed twentieth- and twenty-first-century civilians into "witnesses of war" (Taylor 1992: 33; Carruthers 2000: 2). In this respect, contemporary wars have a "total" impact on society: they redefine gender relationships, they affect the structure of economy, and they become part of the political campaign discourse (Gray 1997: 22). The actual battles between major powers, however, remain limited and even when they involve major powers they are thought of within the framework of "minor" wars (ibid.: 22–3, 156). For the non-industrial societies, they are total wars, since their whole culture and population are distracted. From the point of view of the West, however, they remain only "limited wars" (ibid.: 156).

249

So although in terms of actual participation, contemporary wars are limited at least for the Western powers involved, in terms of the emotional engagement of the Western media audiences, they are "total wars." While the actual military combat is limited, the effects on many cultures are "total."

This paradox creates a further confusion. The distinction between "our wars" and "other people's wars" is blurred. The media coverage of "our wars" ("our troops" fighting alongside "our allies" against the enemy) and "other people's wars" (wars that do not involve our armies or we are not involved as allies of one side of the conflict) is fundamentally different in relation to the degree of engagement (Taylor 1997: 130). In the first case, the media coverage supports "our" side and the audiences' emotional involvement is much greater. In the second case, the coverage and the media involvement is more detached. Although the distinction between "ours" and "theirs" is not totally irrelevant, the dividing line between "theirs" and "ours" in many cases is blurred (see also Carruthers 2000: 198). The war in former Yugoslavia, for example, did not start as a war between Yugoslavia and NATO. NATO's intervention, justified on humanitarian grounds, was the intervention of a "neutral" power mediating between the opposing sides. Nevertheless, the Western reporting during the wars in Yugoslavia was predominantly anti-Serb (Taylor 1997: 130). It was clear by the time of the NATO intervention in Kosovo that the Serbian side was perceived as the enemy of the NATO forces and the conflict had become "our war." Similarly, the Taliban/Northern Alliance was "their" conflict, a conflict distant and irrelevant for US and Western society. After September 11, however, it became the US war on terrorism; only then did information about the Taliban/Northern Alliance conflict become a major subject for the Western media.

One reason for the increasing attempts to place any military action within the political discourse of one's nation is the increasing realization that political preparation and political justification at home play an important role in winning over public opinion. The important decisions that define the outcome of any war action are not taken only at the field of battle but increasingly in the political arena (Gray 1997: 169–70). The reporting of "other people's wars" may be less engaged until the dominant political discourse for whatever reason is transformed and "their war" becomes "ours."

Another feature of the modern-day conflict is the technological sophistication of war. Although this has been a feature of war for the last 50 years, it is only recently that the incorporation of new technologies created a different picture of the war, such as "cyber war." The implications of this new type of war are many: battles are three dimensional (including air and space), time is compressed so postmodern battles are a matter of hours instead of days and months, and machines replace humans in spreading destruction (Gray 1997: 40–3). The war, then, is transformed into a spectacle, more bearable, glamorous, and capable of bringing audiences awe, pleasure, and horror (ibid.: 44). The Gulf War became the landmark of this highly sophisticated spectacle. "Smart" weaponry's ability to kill from a distance, offering the best form of infotainment without morally implicating the soldiers of the allies, created a video-game perception of the war (ibid.: 42–4; Carruthers 2000: 3).

It was not until the September 11 attack on the twin towers that the war gained back its worrying and lethal dimension. While the Gulf War and to some extent Kosovo extinguished at least momentarily the images of brutality, casualties, and consequences of the war, portraying the war in its most clinical form, and showing pictures only after the war was over (Taylor 1992: 4, 48), the attack on the twin towers turned war back into a worrying "reality."

A further characteristic of modern-day war is the blurring between terrorism and war, with terrorism becoming an increasingly dominant form of international conflict. The paradox is that despite the "smart" weapons and the "distant" targets, terrorism is bringing war back into one's own home. While in classical war theory, war was conducted between uniformed enemies and endeavored to limit civilian casualties and "keep the use of force proportionate to the ends in question," today "war is coming home." Terrorism, on the other hand, refuses the civilian immunity and the agreed warfare conventions (Carruthers 2000: 163). Although the difficulties with this definition become apparent when one thinks of the mass bombing of civilians from both sides during World War II or the atomic explosions at Nagasaki and Hiroshima (ibid.: 164), terrorism gives another dimension to war: it targets the heart of a nation geographically and emotionally—geographically because it attacks a nation within its own territory, emotionally because it targets civilians.

The September 11 attack was characterized as terrorist, not only because it was engineered by a non-legitimate army but also because of its random selection of innocent civilians as targets. Both the aim and proximity of the targets created an atmosphere characterized by "coercion through fear" and "the absence of popular mandate" (ibid.: 164). The September 11 attack did not lack the popular support of at least some Muslim fundamentalists, but it managed to create an environment of fear that will far outlast the period of actual conflict. The attack made clear that while the US sees innocent victims and civilian territory outside of the war zone, the terrorists view the US as a legitimate target. Both the victims and the material targets of the twin towers represented the mind and body of American capitalism.

While terrorist attacks become part of modern international conflicts, the concept of "total war" gains even greater significance (ibid.: 166). From the side of those attacked, September 11 engaged and mobilized the entire American nation. From the opposite side, one can argue that it engaged a large part of the Muslim populations.

## The media coverage of international conflicts

The coverage of international conflicts has a specific status in newsgathering and reporting, where media personnel report under physical and psychological danger. Wars are events that involve at least some degree of controversy. Under these parameters the issue of objectivity becomes complex. Objective reporting is more difficult when controversial events are reported or when the reporter is part of the events (Bovee 1999: 120, 128).

Can the war correspondent be a disinterested, objective, or impartial observer? The first assumption is that the war correspondent, despite physical and psychological hardships, can and should "give the facts." That does not imply that the reporter should give "the whole truth." It rather claims that journalists should strive to gather and communicate knowledge about events, people, and circumstances that will enable their audience to decide themselves about the events, people, and circumstances (ibid.: 114–15). Another theoretical trend, however, emphasizes the limitations of human knowledge and the impossibility of a perfect knowledge of events. Taking into account the specific circumstances under which war reporting takes place, journalistic objectivity is almost impossible (Morrison and Tumber 1988: xi; also Taylor 1992: 12). Constraints and pressures such as deadlines, problems of access and speed of events, all undermine objectivity (Taylor 1997: 100). Even if one could piece together a picture, the picture would still be open to various interpretations (Hudson and Stanier 1997: 150).

A second problem related to objectivity is the possibility and desirability of dispassionate, detached reporting. The journalist should not take sides nor let his/her subjective feelings become part of the report (Frost 2000: 36). It is acknowledged, however, that a truly human individual can never be free of emotions (Bovee (following Aristotle) 1999: 126). The reporting of emotionally charged events often makes it difficult and even emotionally impossible for the journalist to control indications of his feeling, as in the case of John F. Kennedy's assassination (ibid.: 127; see also Zelizer 1992). Similarly, war is an emotionally charged event for any human being, but it is even more so for media people. In the words of one journalist:

> It's one thing to walk into a room full of dead bodies and then walk out again. It's quite another thing to walk into a room full of dead bodies and spend 20 minutes trying to find the best way to get a picture. You are more likely to see things that remain with you.
>
> (Freedom Forum 2001: 2)

Speaking at a recent conference the BBC World Service journalist, Mark Brayne, who is also a trained psychotherapist, argued that burnt-out journalists who have seen and experienced too much conflict may be incapable of reporting impartially on wars and disturbances. He contended that they are tortured souls who need to restore their sense of balance internally in order to distance themselves more effectively when they write and broadcast their stories (Brayne 2002).

Journalists, then, could be thought of more as "active witnesses of happenings," happenings whose meaning is not fully transparent even to journalists themselves (Taylor 1997: 101). The standards (objectivity, detachment) of professional journalism are always tested, especially during the reporting of conflicts such as the Falklands or Vietnam. For the journalist in the Falklands conflict, "faced by events that threatened their [journalists'] own lives and the deaths of soldiers they had become fond of, the basis of their own activities was opened for self-inspection to an unusual degree" (Morrison and Tumber 1988: xii). In other cases, the journalists become the voice of the victims. The hardships of the latter are mediated and put in words by the journalists (Carruthers 2000: 236; see also Tumber 1997). This is more often the case with humanitarian interventions in which the journalist becomes part of the aiding forces. The form of these humanitarian interventions is changing, however. Previously they took the form of medical or food aid, while now the tendency is for military intervention. See, for example, the role of the NATO alliance as a humanitarian agent in the Kosovo conflict (Carruthers 2000: 236).

A further issue is the assumption that the same journalistic standards apply to all areas of reporting. The danger here is to oversimplify a very diverse practice. The diversity of the different media (press, television) and the diversity of the audiences that different outlets try to address play a significant role in the way information is presented (Taylor 1997: 101). The physical and psychological hardships of war correspondents can affect the way in which the coverage is constructed and represented.

Vietnam, as the first truly televised war, opened up a series of issues on the relationship between government and media (Hallin 1986: 9, 105). The conditions of coverage, including the absence of military censorship and routine accreditation of journalists accompanying the military forces, at least in theory permitted the reporting of both sides (ibid.: 126, 147) and played a significant role in shaping the standards under which journalists operated. As the morale among the American troops declined in the second half of the war, the reporting of the Vietnam war after 1967 became increasingly more ambivalent (ibid.: 163).

How did this environment affect the physical and psychological conditions that the Vietnam reporters faced? The reporters were young, without long experience as Asia correspondents, taking up a dangerous assignment. The limited duration of the assignment (six months to one year) prevented their professional maturity as Vietnam correspondents (ibid.: 135). As one may have expected, identification with the young American soldiers was inevitable. Both groups were facing death in an unknown and culturally very different environment, without any useful knowledge (such as Vietnamese language or familiarity with the conflict) to draw upon (ibid.: 205). The brutality of the war and the discrepancy between the official reports and their experiences in the field were shocking (ibid.: 213). All of these resulted in an increasing number of pessimistic reports related to the frustration of the war (ibid.: 131–3).

The coverage of the Falklands War, in contrast, was hindered by the special arrangements set by the British government. The welfare of the 29 British representatives of the media was compromised firstly by their lack of experience as war correspondents (only three of the 29 were defense correspondents or had experience with military matters). This, however, was viewed as part of "a long tradition of being thrown in the deep end and learning on the job" (Morrison and Tumber 1988: 6–8). Secondly, it was compromised by the lack of any adequate briefing or preparation by the news organizations and the Ministry (ibid.: 16). Surprisingly, there was only one case of a journalist's imprisonment by the Argentinians—Simon Winchester of the *Sunday Times*, arrested while reporting from Ushuaia in the Argentine mainland (Hudson and Stanier 1997: 170).

Apart from the physical dangers, the psychological implications of such an operation should not be overlooked. The first reason for psychological turmoil was the unfamiliar experience of symbiosis on the ships of the task force. The journalists' lack of cohesion and their competitiveness, according to the psychiatrist of the task force, would cause some degree of suffering (Morrison and Tumber 1988: 73). The psychological welfare of the journalists was also undermined by the close relationships and identification that developed between them and the military.

Similarly, the conditions of coverage during the Gulf War defined the role of the journalists during the conflict. The "hyper war," the video-game-like images of the war in the international media, was an effort to deal with the Vietnam syndrome, to present the enemy as a multifaceted and immediate threat to democracy without allowing war's brutality to affect the public support at home. This became possible through the creation of a controlled information environment, a "two-tier system of news pools attached to military units and a headquarters catering for the remainder" (Taylor 1992: 11, 36). The close interaction between journalists and military led to close identification and mutual understanding (ibid.: 55). The sense of risk that was felt by the journalists (for their lives as well as those of the troops') was exploited by the military when they warned that the satellite telephones used by journalists could "radiate signals to the Iraqis" (ibid.: 58).

Those journalists that rejected the pool system (unilaterals) faced even more outrageous conditions. Their safety was seriously compromised as a result of their refusal to comply. "Sneaking through military roadblocks, living off their wits and disguising themselves as soldiers," they faced the possibility of capture by the enemy and subsequent prosecution for spying (ibid.: 59, 61). During the mass departure of Western journalists from al-Rashid, Reuters photographer Patrick de Noirmont and two more European colleagues were accused of spying, and "were beaten up with rifle butts" as they tried to leave for Jordan (ibid.: 99). Another group of reporters was arrested and accused of helping the allies to target the bombing (ibid.: 99).

The working conditions for reporters in Baghdad also deteriorated due to the allies' bombing. Selected journalists, permitted by the Iraqis to remain in Baghdad, described scenes of chaos and panic. The explosions buffeted their hotel. The lights went off and in an atmosphere of chaos everybody rushed to the hotel bomb shelter in the basement. Another group of journalists (the BBC's John Simpson and his crew) had to return to the hotel despite their desire to watch the action (ibid.: 92).

## Why do they do it?

One question that emerges from the reporting of international conflicts in the last century is why journalists are willing to subject themselves to psychological and physical dangers, sometimes going even further than the minimum necessary risks, in order to get a story. What are the journalistic practices and the motivation that lie behind the desire to report and the dangers that follow?

The issue of journalists' motivation became a major story during the Afghan War, when *Sunday Express* reporter Yvonne Ridley was captured in Taliban-ruled Afghanistan. Ridley, who fuelled a heated discussion between newspaper personnel after her return home, said her illegal entrance to Afghanistan was a "calculated risk" that she had been prepared to take in order to get the truth (Morgan 2001). It was reported that her decision to enter Afghanistan divided the editors and news editors of her newspaper. Those in favor saw the operation as "plausible," and after her captivity and her release they praised her courage and professionalism. Those against the escapade viewed her enterprise as "sheer folly." After her return, reporters of other newspapers criticized her not only because of the "foolishness" of her decision but also because she endangered her still imprisoned guides who could face execution (ibid.). According to Ridley, her decision was based on a desire to find and report the "truth." Janine di Giovanni of *The Times* made a similar point, when she argued that the motivation might spring from the fact that one is a witness in the middle of history (Giovanni 2001: 8). Many journalists are also accused of adding to their role as witnesses specific commitments toward a cause, espousing a journalism of attachment. Instead of complying with the norms of neutrality, objectivity, and detachment, they have committed themselves to the "something must be done" brigade (Carruthers 2000: 240; see also Tumber 1997).[1] Nevertheless, the reasons behind similar decisions may be less honorable.

The motivation behind journalists' actions can also be interpreted within a psychological framework. According to Antony Feinstein, who recently conducted a study of the psychological effects on media personnel of reporting in conflicts, war journalists belong to a personality group exhibiting what is called a borderline personality. The feeling of emptiness and the sudden mood changes experienced by the group may be among the reasons that drives them to the specific work (Feinstein 2001: 6). Another psychological explanation offered is that they do it "because they enjoy it" and because they "love that little sprint along the edge of death" (Knightley 2001: 18).

Heroism or psychology, however, are not the only possible explanations. Cases of cynicism[2] in reporting violence, if they do not reveal a self-protective mechanism, may emanate from the competitive and individualistic culture of the journalistic profession. The pressure and temptation to "get the story first" is a theme in all modern warfare. To take only one example from the Falklands War, despite the limited sources of new material and the need for cooperation which sometimes prevailed, the symbiosis of the journalists was hued by the desire "not to fail," to do better than one's so-called colleagues by getting the news first (Morrison and Tumber 1988: 60). The relationship between journalists, despite the exceptions, was characterized by an absence of cooperation and continual mistrust ("cutting each other's throat"), as well as occupational possessiveness (ibid.: 64–5, 69, 73). The Ridley episode during the Afghan war is another example of the high risks news organizations are prepared to take within the "cut-throat and competitive news markets" (Owen 2001a). Many journalists may be pressed into covering hostile environment news by big news organizations. If one wants to be seen as one of "the boys," one cannot refuse (unidentified participant, Freedom Forum 2001: 16).

It would appear, then, that there are three different clusters of issues related to the decision to risk one's life while reporting a war: psychological; commitment to "truth"; and occupational pressures.

## The changing culture of journalism

As the journalist's role as an active interpreter becomes more pronounced and recognized, the psychological dimension of war reporting is opening up a new debate. Since September 11 there has been a change in journalistic culture. This progressive change is illustrated through:

- a debate on journalistic norms with the possibility of accepting a more "human face" in war reporting;
- a discourse that prioritizes safety and downplays competitive demands;
- an admission by journalists, editors, and news organizations that there is a need for measures to safeguard the physical and psychological welfare of war correspondents.

The more "human face" was illustrated most vividly by Chris Cramer, CNN's president of international networks, who recently attacked the old culture of newsgathering, the "old fart" as he characteristically called it. Within this outdated framework, any display of emotion or psychological anguish was a potential threat to one's career. In defense of a CNN health correspondent, Liz Cohen, who broke down while reporting from Ground Zero, Cramer argued that employers should allow the display of emotion. Especially when back from a war zone, "people should be allowed to do their laundry . . . and their head laundry too" (Hodgson 2001b).

Cramer had been traumatized himself when, in 1980, he was taken hostage during the siege of the Iranian embassy in London. After his release he criticized the reaction of his BBC employers and stressed the need for support in dealing with trauma. Similarly, CBS News producer Susan Zaritsky argued that emotional responses to disasters such as that following September 11 make better journalists (Hodgson 2001b).

This changing attitude toward the norms of reporting, however, is not embraced by all. Tony Burman, executive director at the Canadian public broadcaster CBC, objected to emotional displays by newscasters and journalists, especially Dan Rather of CBS who shed tears on the Letterman show, believing them to be "over the top" (Hodgson 2001b). The old journalistic culture maintains a strong hold when post-traumatic stress disorder (PTSD) is discussed in relation to journalism. In a conference on PTSD, organized by the Freedom Forum, some participants admitted that within the old tradition, the only way to avoid stigmatization when encountering the syndrome was to avoid any discussion about it with one's editor, drink to tranquilize it and maybe talk about it with a colleague (Ochberg 2001: 12). Some participants, still using the "old culture" conceptual framework, argued that the best way to deal with psychological traumas resulting from war reporting was by oneself. The solution is simple: you face that your life is not normal and then you "educate yourself about your own head" (Little 2001: 19). Other journalists saw PTSD as a character flaw. As one participant suggested, "I'm not sure whether the people that have it may not have it because they come from very unstable backgrounds and don't have a strong sense of self" (Di Giovanni 2001: 8).[3]

With regard to safety, there seems to be wide consensus in the industry on the need to prioritize it. Sky News chiefs, for example, reportedly relayed to their staff the rather shopworn saying that "no news story is worth getting killed for" (O'Carroll 2001). Many British editors refused to allow their correspondents to enter Afghanistan to obtain exclusive reports as Ridley or the BBC war correspondent John Simpson had done. The difference between Simpson and Ridley, however, was that the latter apparently lacked equipment and training and followed a rushed and irresponsible decision on the part of her editors. Simpson's assignment in contrast was the outcome of a long debate in which both reservations and his expertise in reporting countless wars were considered (Owen 2001).

## Training organizations

Two of the leading safety training companies are AKE and Centurion. Former SAS soldier Andrew Kain formed AKE in 1991, to design and deliver courses specifically for journalists working in hostile environments. According to Kain, the dangers related to particular regions or environments can be placed in a pyramid form (Kain 2001). Although injuries are high on the risk pyramid, disease and illness are also major aspects that compromise safety and should not be neglected. The courses (normally lasting one to five days) cover a wide variety of subjects: weapons and effects, weapons employment, casualty assessment, control of bleeding, military media relations, hostage survival. The aim is to increase the level of awareness, anticipation, and avoidance in order to minimize risk (AKE 2002).

Centurion was formed in 1995 by Paul Rees, a former British Royal Marine Commando. The aim of the week-long training program is "to raise awareness of the hidden danger of a given environment," so people can better assess the risks (Centurion Risk Assessment Services Ltd 2002). Its topics range from map reading to risk assessment, biological warfare to mines and body traps. Both organizations offer training in dealing with PTSD.

Most journalists who take part in the training programs are international journalists of major media organizations, such as BBC, ITV, Reuters, CNN, and the *New York Times*. They cover a wide spectrum of nationalities including British, American, Scandinavian (the first that embraced the idea of training), South Korean, and African. Despite the provisions and the growing awareness in matters of safety, the training does not occur in a social vacuum. Part of the wider cultural framework that shapes journalistic practice also shapes the training itself, which may be subjected to the same norms and limitations.

For example, it is often argued that the culture of journalism is a macho one. War journalists as a group are overwhelmingly male. As Feinstein pointed out in his report on PTSD, his research group was dominated by men (80 percent) since the list of names from the news organizations was dominated by men (Feinstein 2001: 5, 13). It comes as no surprise, therefore, that female participants in the training programs amount to one third.

Gender differences often shape the form of competitiveness among war journalists. One female war correspondent in Afghanistan, for example, was accused of using her physical charms in order to access Northern Alliance leaders. ITN's Julian Manyon made a comparison with Mata Hari (Hodgson 2001a). Her presence at the front was justified (if justification was needed) as the result of her interpersonal skills that helped her build up good contacts. For women reporters nowadays, these instances reveal the battles they still face from male colleagues, "some of whom may feel threatened by the star status accorded to several women reporters, others of whom resent what they see as special privileges granted them; a few merely patronize their female colleagues" (Sebba 1994: 9). This is in contrast to the attitude of editors who recognize the advantages in using female correspondents to report on conflict situations (ibid.: 9). Training programs, then, should take into account gender differences, since they may provide insight into the motivation and pressures of journalists in war zones. Similarly, differentiation within the profession should be considered. One issue that came out of the News World 2001 conference in Barcelona was that, although in many cases both international and local journalists are trained to face the demands of war reporting, the training is applicable only to those local journalists affiliated to international organizations. The responsibility of news organizations toward the local fixers and journalists is just as important. The Ridley incident is only one example that opens up the demand for accountability in the field.

Another distinction within the profession is the difference between freelance and media employees. After September 11, it became increasingly difficult for freelancers to obtain insurance. The Rory Peck Trust, set up to deal primarily with issues affecting freelancers, reported that according to Feinstein's research, freelancers do not display PTSD symptoms more frequently. Nevertheless, the same research shows that depression, social dysfunction, and cannabis consumption are more prominent among freelance journalists. One possible reason may be that freelance journalists are less experienced in war zones and slightly younger than other war correspondents (Rory Peck Trust 2001). In addition, freelancers do not have the security of an organization backing them. They return to their isolated lives and face new anxieties about their next assignments. They do not have a built-in community in a bureau or office.

Similarly, a distinction between print and broadcast journalists exists. Current US studies with the National Press Photographers Association suggest that there are no differences in PTSD between print reporters and photographers. Nevertheless, these studies are not yet conclusive (Ochberg 2001: 14). The difference is that "with photographers, it's here and now" (Feinstein 2001: 13). According to Turnbull, PTSD is related to memory processes that imprint the traumatic event onto the non-dominant hemisphere of the brain. The narrative sense however is related to the dominant hemisphere. That suggests that the reporting of a traumatic event is a narrative account of the images which helps one make sense of the event. If this is correct, it may point to a difference between photojournalism and narrative reporting (Turnbull 2001: 14).

## From macho culture to "touchy-feely"

The realization among journalists that they are a serious target post-September 11 was encapsulated in an email from Leroy Sievers and the ABC *Nightline* staff to list members following the murder of Daniel Pearl and the shooting at journalists by Israeli forces in the West Bank:

> Covering wars has always been dangerous, but it used to be different. In Vietnam . . . reporters were pretty free to travel with American units. When I was covering the wars in Latin America in the late '80s, we all put "TV" in big letters on our cars. That was supposed to provide safe passage. It did, until the death squads started putting "TV" on their cars too. But I think no one but us actually believed that we were the neutral observers that we thought we were. Now I know some will want to take this in a political direction, and the old accusation of political bias. But that is not what I mean by neutral. In a war setting, neutral means the ability to cover both sides, if possible, and to cover the war as objectively as possible. But at best we were seen as agents of our government. John Donvan . . . remembers that in his days in the Middle East, anyone who was obviously American was always assumed to be CIA. In those same years, in Latin America you were assumed to be DEA. But the result was the same. But journalists will still flock to wars for their own reasons. It just seems that in recent years, our ability to cover these conflicts has been steadily eroded. And the Pearl case shows that terrorists see journalists as simply American targets, and handy ones at that. All

of this adds up to less reporting, and less information for all of you. And some journalists face even more dangers in their own countries. All over the world, repressive regimes are arresting, jailing, and killing journalists for trying to shine a light on what is happening. I think that the bottom line, and it's all fairly simple, is that in all these cases, people do not want the rest of the world to see what is happening. And the easiest way to stop that is to go after the journalists.

(Sievers 2002)

This reasoning may be correct up to a point. However, it fails to address the steady erosion of foreign news over the last decade made by the owners of news organizations who are anxious to remain competitive.

Although recent wars have led to the traditional conflict between the media and the state over the control of information, debate has also moved into the profession itself, where the nature of the journalist's role as participant or observer has been questioned. The problems for participant journalists (or as recently described, the journalism of attachment), wedded to the events around them, are how to respond when events force a choice between professional commitment and participatory loyalties (Morrison and Tumber 1988). Displaying views that may be sympathetic to the "other" side risks the admonishment or flak of governments and politicians while displaying support for "our" side may be acceptable to government but risks accusations of unprofessionalism.

The concern over physical safety is largely uncontested. Everyone agrees on its importance. The problem remains for freelancers and the journalists working for small outfits who are unable to enjoy the training and security provisions provided for those in the big organizations. In contrast, emotional welfare is problematic. Showing emotion on camera or even in print is rarely acceptable within the profession. There is a perceptible change of culture allowing for the acknowledgement of PTSD and the need for treatment, but a large degree of skepticism remains. Foreign correspondents remain a specialist group within journalism, which traditionally enjoys a trenchcoat culture. It is the specialism which provides fodder for Hollywood. To forsake a macho image involves the destruction of a myth. Journalism is not at the forefront of the touchy-feely culture. Journalists may report it but rarely embrace it.

## Notes

I would like to thank Marina Prentoulis and John Owen for their help in writing this chapter.

1 See the case of the BBC reporter Martin Bell during his coverage of the Balkan wars, and Maggie O'Kane of the *Guardian* who took a pro-Bosnian interventionist stance (Tumber 1997: 4–5; Carruthers 2000: 240).
2 Mort Rosenblum writes of cameramen, keen to film emaciated children in the UN International Children's Emergency Fund compound in Mogadishu, asking aid-

workers where they might find some "stick action" (Carruthers, 2000: 240). Freelance journalist Richard Dowden also describes television crews, restless with filming merely terminal sickness, requesting relief workers' assistance in capturing Somalis actually dying in front of the camera (ibid.).

3   For a full explanation of what constitutes PTSD, its symptoms and the research findings see Feinstein 2001: 4–7.

# References

AKE (2002) www.akegroup.com.

Bovee, W. G. (1999) *Discovering Journalism*, Westport, CN, and London: Greenwood Press.

Brayne, Mark (2002) Emotions, trauma and good journalism conference, London 2002.

Carruthers, S. L. (2000) *The Media at War*, Basingstoke: Macmillan Press.

Centurion Risk Assessment Services Ltd (2002) www.centurion-riskservices.co.uk.

CPJ (The Committe to Protect Journalists) (2001a) US photojournalist among World Trade Center dead, www.cpj.org/news/2001/US20sep01na.html.

CPJ (The Committe to Protect Journalists) (2001b) CPJ concerned about threatening incidents in the US, www.cpj.org/news/2001/US13oct01na.html.

Di Giovanni, J. (2001) Risking more than their lives: the effects of post-traumatic stress disorder on journalists, in *Freedom Forum*, www.freedomforum.org, April 12.

Feinstein, A. (2001) Risking more than their lives: the effects of post-traumatic stress disorder on journalists, in *Freedom Forum*, www.freedomforum.org, April 12.

Freedom Forum (2001) Risking more than their lives: the effects of post-traumatic stress disorder on journalists, unidentified participant, www.freedomforum.org, April 12.

Frost, C. (2000) *Media Ethics*, Harlow: Longman.

Gray, H. C. (1997) *Postmodern War*, London: Guilford Press.

Hallin, D. C. (1986) *The "Uncensored" War: The Media and Vietnam*, Oxford: Oxford University Press.

Hodgson, J. (2001a) GMTV's Logan counters "Mata Hari" jibe, November 5, *Media Guardian*, www.media.guardian.co.uk/broadcast/story/0,7493,588087,00.html, accessed January 21, 2002.

Hodgson, J. (2001b) Let reporters show emotion, November 19, *Media Guardian*, www.media.guardian.co.uk/attack/story/0,1301,596093,00.html, accessed January 21, 2002.

Hudson, M. and J. Stanier (1997) *War and the Media*, Stroud: Sutton Publishing.

IFJ (International Federation of Journalists) (2000) International Code of practice for the safe conduct of journalists in IFJ *Report on media casualties in the field of journalism and newsgathering*, www.ifj.org.

IFJ (International Federation of Journalists) (2001) www.ifj.org/hrights/killlist/kill11.html.

Kain, A. (2001) contribution to News World Conference, Barcelona, November.

Knightley, P. (2001) contribution to Risking more than their lives: the effects of post-traumatic stress disorder on journalists, in *Freedom Forum*, www.freedomforum.org, April 12.

Little, A. (2001) contribution to Risking more than their lives: the effects of post-traumatic stress disorder on journalists, in *Freedom Forum*, www.freedomforum.org, April 12.

Morgan, J. (2001) Rivals backlash against "foolhardy" Ridley, *Press Gazette*, October 11, www.pressgazette.co.uk, accessed January 21, 2001.

Morrison, D. E. and Tumber, H. (1988) *Journalists at War*, London: Sage Publications.

O'Carroll, L. (2001) No news story is worth getting killed for, *Media Guardian*, November 19, www.media.guardian.co.uk/attack/story/0,1301,602085,00.html, accessed January 21, 2002.

Ochberg, F. (2001) contribution to Risking more than their lives: the effects of post-traumatic stress disorder on journalists, in *Freedom Forum*, www.freedomforum.org, April 12.

Owen, J. (2001a) Training journalists to report safely in hostile environments, Nieman Reports, 55 (4) Winter: 25–7.

Owen, J. (2001b) contribution to Risking more than their lives: the effects of post-traumatic stress disorder on journalists, in *Freedom Forum*, www.freedomforum.org, April 12.

Rory Peck Trust (2001) The free lens, www.oneworld.org/rorypeck/freelens/lens9/ptsd.htm), accessed January 22, 2002.

Sebba, A. (1994) *Battling for News: The Rise of the Woman Reporter*, London: Hodder and Stoughton.

Sievers, L. (2002) *Nightline*: dangerous business, online posting. Available email: nightline mailing list (l@alist0.starwave.com), accessed March 12, 2000.

Taylor, P. M. (1992) *War and The Media*, Manchester: Manchester University Press.

Taylor, P. M. (1997) *Global Communications, International Affairs and the Media since 1945*, London: Routledge.

Tomlin, J. (2001) War zone news crews resort to torchlight TV, Pressgazette online, www.pressgazette.co.uk, October 11.

Tumber, H. (1997) Bystander journalism, or the journalism of attachment, *Intermedia*, 25 (1): 4–7.

Turnbull, G. (2001) Risking more than their lives: The effects of post-traumatic stress disorder on journalists, *Freedom Forum*, www.freedomforum.org, April 12.

Zelizer, B. (1992) *Covering the Body: The Kennedy Assassination, The Media, and the Shaping of Collective Memory*, Chicago: University of Chicago Press.

# INDEX